Our American Sisters:
Women in American Life and Thought

edited by

Jean E. Friedman
Old Dominion University

William G. Shade
Lehigh University

Allyn and Bacon, Inc.   Boston

FOR *A.F.* AND *E.J.S.*

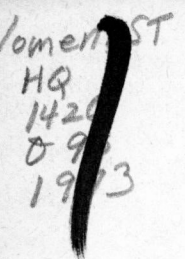

Contents

Preface   **v**

Introduction: Women in American History   1

PART I   Women in Colonial America

1. The Puritans and Sex   16
   Edmund S. Morgan

2. Husbands and Wives   30
   John Demos

3. Participation in Public Affairs   45
   Julia Cherry Spruill

4. The Dynamics of Interracial Sex in Colonial America   60
   Winthrop D. Jordan

PART II   The Victorian Image

1. The Lady and the Mill Girl: Changes in the Status of
   Women in the Age of Jackson   82
   Gerda Lerner

2. The Cult of True Womanhood: 1820–1860   96
   Barbara Welter

iii

3. Reality and the Southern Lady   124
   Anne Firor Scott

4. Hagar and Her Children   137
   E. Franklin Frazier

5. The Grimké Sisters: Women and the Abolition Movement   152
   Gerda Lerner

PART III   The Progressive Impulse

1. Woman as Alien   168
   Christopher Lasch

2. The "New Woman" in the New South   187
   Anne Firor Scott

3. Charlotte Perkins Gilman on the Theory and Practice of
   Feminism   197
   Carl N. Degler

4. Woman Suffrage in Perspective   219
   Aileen S. Kraditor

PART IV   The Illusion of Equality

1. The American Woman's Pre-World War I Freedom in
   Manners and Morals   237
   James R. McGovern

2. The Campaign for Women's Rights in the 1920's   260
   Clarke A. Chambers

3. The Decline and Fall of the Double Standard   284
   Erwin O. Smigel and Rita Seiden

4. Feminism as a Radical Ideology   301
   William L. O'Neill

5. The Liberation of Black Women   326
   Pauli Murray

6. Women's Liberation: Theory and Practice   340
   Jean E. Friedman

Preface

The emergence of the Women's Liberation movement has focused a new interest upon the place of women in American life. The purpose of this volume is to bring together for the student a wide variety of scholarly essays on women in American history in a form available for use as supplementary reading for American history survey courses or courses on women's history. The articles were chosen both for their historical merit and their general readability. They are, in the main, reprinted in full, and footnotes are included to help guide readers to further writings and sources on the subject.

Our general view that the history of women in America must be seen in a broad perspective is presented in the introduction which sets forth the organizational schema of the book. The text is divided into four parts which are ordered chronologically and which correspond roughly to shifts in societal perception of women's roles. In general each part includes essays on American attitudes towards women and sex, on female roles and the position of women within the society, and organized responses to the women's situation and other social questions of their day.

We are grateful for the help given us by Betty Potash, Beverly Beeton, Mary Jo Hill, Joe Dowling, Jim Saeger, Leon Tipton, Neil Neamand, Terry Racosky, Virginia Frey, and the staffs of Muhlenberg College and Lehigh University libraries.

J.E.F.
W.G.S.

Introduction

Women in American History

I know this—that as free I can die but once; but as a slave I shall not be worthy of life. I have the pleasure to assure you that these are the sentiments of all my sister Americans. A Philadelphia Lady, 1775[1]

In curious ways women have been at the same time a part of and outside of American civilization. At the time of the American Revolution many women like the Philadelphia lady quoted above supported the revolutionary cause, but the ringing phrases of the Declaration of Independence applied "to men only." Such paradox has characterized the history of women in American life and thought.

In his classic analysis of politics and society in the United States, *Democracy in America,* Alexis de Tocqueville, who deeply respected American women, missed a number of important nuances but caught the basic anomaly of their existence.[2] On the one hand he observed that "nowhere are young women surrendered so early or so completely to their own guidance." The young American women impressed the Frenchman as self-reliant, confident, intelligent, and governed, for the most part, by reason: "she indulges in all permitted pleasures without yielding herself up to any of them, and her reason never allows the reins of self-guidance to drop, though it often seems to hold them loosely."

However, Tocqueville also noted that "In America the independence of woman is irrecoverably lost in the bonds of matrimony. If an unmarried woman is less constrained there than elsewhere, a wife is subjected to stricter obligations. The former makes her father's house an abode of freedom and of pleasure; the latter lives in the home of her husband as if it were a cloister." As part of the division of labor so representative of their economic system, and in response to the moral necessities of a democratic society, Americans traced "two clearly distinct lines of action for the two sexes." Business and politics remained exclusively the domain of men; while women, the custodians of morality and culture, dominated the home and the family. In law and practice this division of spheres led to a condition in which the social inferiority of women was allowed to continue, while morally and intellectually they were raised to the level of men. In defining the quality of the sexes in terms of men's and women's spheres, Tocqueville believed that Americans showed a clear understanding of "the true principle of democratic improvement."

More recent writers have seen in the problem of spheres and the search for the meaning of equality between the sexes an essential dualism. In his analysis of twentieth century politics and society, *America as a Civilization,* Max Lerner addresses what he calls "The Ordeal of the American Woman."[3] In his view American women have been plagued by the problem of identity. Although women have benefited from a variety of social and technological changes in the twentieth century and seem free in law and theory, they remain bound by culture and custom to a society dominated by the masculine image. The American woman has been "bedeviled by a dilemma that reflects the split both within herself and her culture. She is torn between trying to vie with men in jobs, careers, business, and government, and at the same time find her identity as wife, mother, and woman."

Historian David Potter showed how this dualism has led to intellectual confusion among both female and male commentators upon women.[4] On the one hand most major historical generalizations totally ignore women. On the other the generalizations about women made by historians and social scientists are wildly inconsistent. He suggests that the best strategy for understanding the influence of women on the development of America is to "focus carefully upon what we really know with some degree of assurance" particularly the contrasting ways that historical trends in America have influenced men and women.

However, the energetic student wishing to follow Potter's advice will find there is precious little that we really know about women in America. As Gerda Lerner has written, "The striking fact about the historiography of women is the general neglect of the subject by historians."[5] Few aspects of the history of women in America have been studied in detail and today the situation is little better than in 1922 when Arthur Schlesinger noted that: "An examination of the standard histories of the United States and of the history text-books in use in our schools raises the pertinent question whether women have ever made any contributions to American national progress that are worthy of record."[6] The number of monographs and scholarly essays on women has grown, but their publication has had little effect on more general perceptions of the American past. One can choose at random any of the most popular textbooks and investigate the current situation. Even those volumes which pride themselves on an emphasis on social history are woefully deficient in their treatment of women.

Women's history has aroused more interest in some periods than others. Since 1920 cycles of interest have coincided with general attitudes toward women in the society, the place of women within the historical profession, and the status of social history among historians.

The passage of the Nineteenth Amendment sparked a good deal of professional interest in women's history and a number of the major books on the subject were produced during the inter-war period. Feminism was probably in better repute then than at any time in American history, and the revolution in manners and morals which had begun before World War I altered women's dress and liberated their sexual behavior during the Roaring Twenties. What many observers viewed as the disintegration of traditional values was accompanied by a revision of traditional definitions of women's roles. During this decade the birthrate fell precipitously, while increasing numbers of women entered the graduate schools. The proportion of women earning M.A.s and Ph.D.s rose dramatically to a high point in 1930 and then declined slightly in the following depression decade. The number of women college teachers increased and women played a more important role within the history profession than they do today.[7] At the same time that this generation of women entered the historical profession, several of the period's most influential male historians evidenced heightened interest in the role of women in American history, as part of their attempt to introduce into history new conceptions and fresh points of view. The Progressive historians, who had gained ascendancy in the historical profession in the 1920s, rebelled against the legalistic and narrowly political history of their predecessors. "The desire to widen the scope of

3

history, to relate it to the present, and to link it with the social sciences were conscious objectives [of this group] at a very early date."[8]

The interest the Progressive historians showed in social and economic history, and their tendency to view American history in terms of the conflict between conservatives and reformers led at least two of the most important and widely read of this group to study the role of women in American history. In 1922 Arthur Schlesinger published *New Viewpoints in American History,* a brilliant series of interpretive essays reflecting Progressive scholarship. One of the most original essays in this volume was that on women protesting "the pall of silence" cast over the subject and urging further investigation. Later in the decade Charles Beard's widely read and extremely influential *The Rise of American Civilization,* co-authored with his wife Mary Beard, devoted a large amount of space to women, emphasizing their economic importance.[9] During the interwar years men and women influenced by Schlesinger, Beard, and other Progressives integrated discussions of women's roles into studies of social history and produced a number of the basic monographs on women in America.[10]

However, by 1940, although historians trained in the 1920s and 1930s maintained their concern for women's history, a reversal of earlier trends had become apparent. The feminists whose story Schlesinger thought "one of the noblest chapters in the history of American democracy" fell into increasing public disrepute. The birthrate rose dramatically as a generation of women following World War II seemed dominated by what sociologist Jesse Bernard has called the "Motherhood Mania."[11] The percentage of women completing M.A. and Ph.D. degrees declined as the birthrate climbed. Not only did the attitude of women toward competition in the male world change, but the attitudes of academic men toward women changed for the worse. As reported by the American Historical Association Committee on the Status of Women: "Lawrence Simpson's [study done in the late 1960s] ... has shown that those who practice discrimination against women in academic employment also hold general views concerning female inferiority. Prejudiced attitudes are strongest among men who have been in teaching and/or administration for a period of from five to twenty years."[12] During this strange interlude not only did interest in women's history wane, but even the spheres of American life in which women have played important roles went unstudied. At the very time that families in America were once again growing and the role of the homemaker was exalted in the media, the historical study of the family languished.

Beginning in the late 1950s the fortunes of women's history slowly revived. In addition to the work sampled in this volume, four general histories of American women have appeared in the past decade.[13] This shift in interest coincided not only with the rise of contemporary feminism in the form of the Women's Liberation movement and the revival of social history, but also a decline in the birthrate and an increase in the number of women entering graduate schools.

Too often those historians who have written women's history have focused narrowly upon the history of the feminist movement and what Schlesinger called women's "contributions to American national progress." This approach characterized the writings of the feminist chroniclers which served as a major form of feminist propaganda. As Aileen Kraditor put it: "Propaganda along these lines had a double function: first, it was a plea for wider range of opportunities; second, it exploited every bit of evidence it could uncover to prove that women had already demonstrated the qualifications for fulfilling these roles, perhaps as much to instill self-confidence in women as to show that women's talents were as varied as men's."[14] It was only natural that the Progressive historians who were both sympathetic to the feminist cause and concerned with reform might carry these views over into professional history.

Today the study of women in America continues to bear the marks of its origins in the feminist movement. The literature generally falls into two categories: biographies of feminists and reformers; and general studies of the woman movement which focus particularly on efforts to attain the vote. A more comprehensive approach emphasizing the many aspects of women's history is obviously necessary.

Primarily an aspect of the general field of social history,[15] women's history is also related to political history. From the Seneca Falls Convention to the struggle for the proposed Equal Rights Amendment, women have acted energetically and often effectively in the political arena. The most widely studied area of women's history has been the political activities of women in relation to the abolition movement, the temperance crusade, and the struggle for the vote.[16]

Other, less obvious ways in which women have affected American political development remain to be studied.

Further women's history relates to intellectual history in several ways.[17] Just as an understanding of the black experience requires a knowledge of the development of attitudes toward race, women s history must begin from an understanding of how past generations dealt with the question of the "nature of women." What were the attitudes of both men and women towards feminine sexuality at any given time in the past? How did these attitudes relate to the definition of feminine roles? Similarly feminism as an ideology deserves more extensive analysis so that it might be related to other trends in American intellectual development as well as to the success or failure of the movement at any given time. For example one might ask to what degree the middle class feminists of the nineteenth century were constrained from more radical efforts by their adherence to the liberal individualism which limited other humanitarian reformers? Finally, Potter has reminded us that when historians speak about American attitudes they mean *male* attitudes. Thus historians must attempt to find clues to those attitudes which characterized women as a group or which differentiated men from women within a single social group at any time in the past.

The prerequisite of any intellectual or political analysis in women's history is, of course, a more detailed and sophisticated study of women's roles and status within the society and the way in which these were altered by social and economic change. The history of American family life is of primary importance. The new demographic historians have altered radically beliefs about the nature of the colonial family;[18] and it is clear that the family performed decidedly different functions in the socially atomized nineteenth century than the more socially stable eighteenth. An integral part of the corporate society of colonial America, the family filled a wide variety of religious, educational, and economic functions. By the mid-nineteenth century many of these functions were taken over by other institutions. "The duties of the 'home,' which once had reached outward into the local community and its economy in various ways had become circumscribed within the four walls of the household."[19] How did such basic changes alter the roles of women within the family?

Equally important questions may be raised concerning the economic and social roles of women in the larger society.[20] Since access to positions of high status has often been limited by inferior education, the nature of women's education must be studied in much greater detail. The economic functions of women have been the subject of several books, but such subjects as women servants in colonial America, the lives of working women in the nineteenth century, and the development of discriminatory practices in trade unions and the professions are examples of areas which need examination. It would be useful to determine the social and economic forces that led to the feminization of elementary school teaching and the near total exclusion of women from medicine and law.

Women's history thus encompasses at least three related areas of study: the society's definition of the nature and roles of women; the actual conditions of women and the roles in which they did function; and the feminist response to the intellectual, social, and political problems of women. Further distinctions within these areas are also necessary to accommodate the sub-groups within the general population group called women. In dealing with any one of these three major areas the historian must take into account the effects of at least class, race, religion, and section. Although contemporary sociological studies have shown the important effects of these variables on attitudes and behavior, practically no systematic research has been done on their importance in the history of women in America.

Recently historians have shown increasing interest in the subject of women's history, publishing articles in a wide variety of journals. We have drawn together the best of these articles and supplemented them with several fine older pieces from the inter-war period in order to reconstruct the general history of women in America. The work is subdivided into four chronological sections each preceeded by an introduction which attempts briefly to lay out the major themes of the period covered and relate the essays to these themes. Within each section the essays are arranged to coincide with the organizational scheme for women's history sketched above. Despite the differences in outlook and purpose of the authors, these essays, taken together, demonstrate a degree of internal cohesion and highlight the ambiguous position which women have occupied in the American past. We hope that our general approach to women's history will help the student synthesize the following selections, suggest new areas of interest, and perhaps even stimulate further interest in a field which remains largely ignored.

NOTES

1. Quoted in Arthur Schlesinger, *New Viewpoints in American History* (New York: Macmillan, 1922), 131.

2. Alexis de Tocqueville, *Democracy in America,* rev. by Phillips Bradley (New York: Alfred A. Knopf, 1945), II, 202-25, relate to the roles of women.

3. Max Lerner, *America as a Civilization: Life and Thought in the United States Today* (New York: Simon and Schuster, 1957), 599-611. Lerner touches on the subject of women in America at numerous points throughout the book.

4. David Potter, "American Women and the American Character," in ed. John A. Hague, *American Character and Culture: Some Twentieth Century Perspectives* (DeLand, Fl.: Everett Edwards Press, 1964), 65-84.

5. Gerda Lerner, "New Approaches to the Study of Women in American History," *Journal of Social History,* III (Fall, 1969), 53. This article along with Professor Lerner's, "Women's Rights and American Feminism," *The American Scholar,* XL (Spring, 1971), 235-248, provide recent critical assessments of the state of women's history by one of its leading practitioners.

6. Schlesinger, *New Viewpoints . . .,* 126.

7. Willie Lee Rose *et al.,* "Report of the Committee on the Status of Women of the American Historical Association, November 9, 1970" (Washington, D.C.: American Historical Association, 1970), and Jessie Bernard, "The Status of Women in Modern Patterns of Culture," *The Annals of the American Academy of Political and Social Science,* CCCLXXV (January, 1968), 3-14, review a broad body of literature on the subject.

8. John Higham *et al., History: The Development of Historical Studies in the United States* (Englewood Cliffs, N.J.: Prentice-Hall, 1965), 171. Cf. Robert Allen Skotheim, *American Intellectual Histories and Historians* (Princeton, N.J.: Princeton University Press, 1966); and Richard Hofstadter, *The Progressive Historians: Turner, Beard, Parrington* (New York: Alfred A. Knopf, 1969).

9. Charles A. and Mary R. Beard, *The Rise of American Civilization* (New York: Macmillan, 1930).

10. Elizabeth Anthony Dexter, *Colonial Women of Affairs* (Boston and New York: Houghton Mifflin, 1924); Alma Lutz, *Emma Willard* (Boston: Houghton Mifflin, 1929); Richard B. Morris, "Women's Rights in Early American Law," in *Studies in the History of American Law* (New York: Columbia University Press, 1930); Mary Sumner Benson, *Women in Eighteenth-Century America* (New York: Columbia University Press, 1935); Julia C. Spruill, *Woman's Life and Work in the Southern Colo-*

nies (Chapel Hill: University of North Carolina Press, 1938); and Alma Lutz, *Created Equal: A Biography of Elizabeth Cady Stanton* (New York: John Day, 1940), are the best such monographs. The work of Mary Beard deserves a special place although she ranges far beyond American history: *On Understanding Women* (New York: Longmans, Green, 1931), *America Through Women's Eyes* (New York: Macmillan, 1934), and *Woman as a Force in History* (New York: Macmillan, 1946). Typifying attempts to integrate the history of women into general studies are: Arthur Meier Schlesinger, *The Rise of the City, 1878-1898* (New York: Macmillan, 1933), Harold Underwood Faulkner, *The Quest For Social Justice, 1898-1914* (New York: Macmillan, 1931), and, to a lesser extent, their companion volumes in "The History of American Life" series edited by Schlesinger and Dixon Ryan Fox; Merle Curti, *The Growth of American Thought* (New York: Harper and Brothers, 1943); and Alice Felt Tyler, *Freedom's Ferment* (Minneapolis: University of Minnesota Press, 1944).

11. Bernard, "The Status of Women . . .," 8.
12. Rose *et al.,* "Report of the Committee on the Status of Women . . .," 12.
13. Andrew Sinclair, *The Better Half* (New York: Harper and Row, 1965); Robert E. Riegel, *American Women: A Story of Social Change* (Teaneck, N.J.: Fairleigh Dickinson University Press, 1970); Page Smith, *Daughters of the Promised Land* (Boston: Little, Brown, 1970); and Gerda Lerner, *The Women in American History,* (Menlo Park, Calif.: Addison Wesley 1971). Riegel has a useful bibliography which has a fairly exhaustive list of biographies of leading women.
14. Aileen S. Kraditor, ed., *Up from the Pedestal: Selected Writings in the History of American Feminism* (Chicago: Quadrangle Books, 1968), 17. This is a well chosen set of documents with a useful introduction.
15. Rowland Berthoff, *An Unsettled People: Social Order and Disorder in American History* (New York: Harper and Row, 1971), xi-xii, defines social history as the study of the functional interplay of institutions and population groups constituting society.
16. Alma Lutz, *Crusade for Freedom: Women in the Anti-slavery Movement* (Boston: Beacon Press, 1968); Alma Lutz, *Susan B. Anthony* (Boston: Beacon Press, 1959); Elinor P. Hays, *Morning Star: A Biography of Lucy Stone* (New York: Harcourt, Brace and World, 1961); Gerda Lerner, *The Grimké Sisters of South Carolina* (Boston: Houghton Mifflin, 1967); Robert E. Riegel, *American Feminists* (Lawrence: University of Kansas Press, 1963); Andrew Sinclair, *Prohibition: The Era of Excess* (Boston: Little, Brown, 1962); James H. Timberlake, *Prohibition and the Progressive Movement* (Cambridge, Mass.: Harvard University

Press, 1966); David M. Kennedy, *Birth Control in America: The Career of Margaret Sanger* (New Haven: Yale University Press, 1970); Elinor Flexner, *Century of Struggle: The Woman's Rights Movement in the United States* (Cambridge, Mass.: Harvard University Press, 1959); Aileen S. Kraditor, *The Ideas of the Woman Suffrage Movement, 1890–1920* (New York: Columbia University Press, 1965); Alan P. Grimes, *The Puritan Ethic and Woman Suffrage* (New York: Oxford University Press, 1967); and William L. O'Neill, ed., *The Woman Movement: Feminism in the United States and England* (London: George Allen and Unwin, 1969).

17. Two books by William L. O'Neill illustrate this: *Divorce in the Progressive Era* (New Haven: Yale University Press, 1967) and *Everyone Was Brave: The Rise and Fall of Feminism in America* (Chicago: Quadrangle Books, 1969).

18. John Demos, *A Little Commonwealth: Family Life in Plymouth Colony* (New York: Oxford University Press, 1970); Philip J. Greven, Jr., *Four Generations: Population, Lord and Family in Colonial Andover, Massachusetts* (Ithaca: Cornell University Press, 1970). Cf. Bernard Bailyn, *Education in the Forming of American Society* (Chapel Hill: University of North Carolina Press, 1960); Edmund S. Morgan, *The Puritan Family: Essays on Religion and Domestic Relations in Seventeenth Century New England* (New York: Harper and Row, 1966 ed.); Edmund S. Morgan, *Virginians at Home: Family Life in the Eighteenth Century* (Chapel Hill: University of North Carolina Press, 1952).

19. Berthoff, *An Unsettled People* . . ., 212. This general volume contains three perceptive chapters on the family. Arthur W. Calhoun's three-volume work, *A Social History of the American Family* (New York: Barnes and Noble, 1960 ed.), remains the basic source on the subject, but is seriously dated. A new history of the family profiting from the work by colonial historians and the insights in Philippe Ariés' brilliant study, *Centuries of Childhood: A Social History of Family Life* (New York: Alfred A. Knopf, 1962), is badly needed.

20. Mabel Newcomer, *A Century of Higher Education for American Women* (New York: Harper and Brothers, 1959); and Elizabeth A. Dexter, *Career Women of America, 1776–1840* (Francestown, N.J.: Marshall Jones, 1950), suggest useful beginnings.

Part One

Women in Colonial America

From the settlement of Jamestown until the outbreak of the American Revolution, the colonists struggled to establish a stable society based upon the English model. In each new settlement they rebuilt familiar social, political, and economic institutions and endeavored to reaffirm those ideals and values that made up English civilization. Sometimes immediately, but more often gradually, the new environment and the absence of central authority altered institutions and attitudes. Colonial society slowly evolved into one quite different from the mother country; the transplanted Englishman became by the mid-eighteenth century a new man, an American. The effects of this process upon the status of women highlight their anomolous position in American history.

The first mainland colonies were founded as business ventures; it was not until the decision was made to establish societies in the New World that any significant number of women emigrated. Throughout the colonial period men outnumbered women. This basic demographic fact accounted for the earlier age at which colonial women married and the greater "liberties and privileges" which they enjoyed in relation to European women. Isolation and a limited labor supply enhanced the woman's value to the family. "The wife and mother in the rude settlement on or near the frontier was more than a housekeeper; she was an indispensable part of the apparatus of survival."[1] Elsewhere in an economy dominated by farms and small shops, women worked side by side with men; and often ran large plantations or carried on the family business following the death of a husband or father. Necessity determined that few jobs were deemed inappropriate for colonial women; they could be found as blacksmiths and barbers, tanners and tavern keepers.

The first three selections below dealing with the day-to-day lives of colonial women reveal why foreign observers generally believed women occupied higher status than their European counterparts. The community placed strong emphasis on the social role of the family and close surveillance on moral life; but as Edmund Morgan shows in "The Puritan and Sex," the colonists were neither so unrealistic nor "puritanical" about sexual matters as has often been charged. They were well aware that "sexual intercourse was a human necessity" and believed that "marriage was the proper place for it." Although they were unable to contain all sexual impulses wholly within the bounds of marriage—Morgan reminds us that "illicit sexual intercourse was common"—the Puritan magistrates encouraged early marriage and took every means to insure "peaceful cohabitation." Adultery was severely punished, but divorces and annulments were *relatively* easy to obtain. Perhaps the most interesting aspect of the Puritan attitude toward sexual intercourse was the degree to which the magistrates acknowledged and respected sexual needs of women as well as men. John Demos extends Morgan's analysis in his study of Plymouth Colony, *A Little Commonwealth,* showing that the court records of Plymouth reveal only minor traces of a double standard. Furthermore this study of decision-making in the family also reveals that in their day-to-day lives women stood more nearly equal to their husbands than has generally been supposed.

Clearly the family was an essential element of the community in which women shared joint responsibility for a variety of religious, social, and economic functions, and in which the roles of husband and wife were less neatly compartmentalized than they would become in the nineteenth century. This cooperation and intimacy between husbands and wives which characterized colonial marriages sometimes led women outside the home into business and political affairs. As Julia Cherry Spruill shows in the selection from her book *Women's Life and Work in the Southern Colonies,* colonial women often shared their husbands' lives, mending political fences or fomenting revolution. She also discusses the remarkable exploits of Margaret Brent, executrix of the estate of Governor Leonard Calvert and one of the "most prominent personages" in Maryland "whose business and public activities fill many pages of court records and suggest a career which the most ambitious modern feminists might envy."

By the eighteenth century common social practice, specific legislation, and the development of equity law freed married women from complete domination by their husbands and gave them a certain amount of legal autonomy unknown to the common law. However, it should not be forgotten that colonial society was basically masculine in orientation. Attitudes toward women during the period remained traditional, differing little from those of contemporary Europeans. The belief in the inferiority of women was universal. While American women were far better off than their English sisters and in some areas their legal position improved during the colonial period, women, particularly married women, suffered under numerous legal and social restrictions. If some women participated in public affairs, the roles of most women were generally circumscribed within the family where wives were expected to be subservient to their husbands.

Political rights were almost completely restricted to men as heads of families; and access to the professions was closed to women on the grounds that they should "refrain from such things as proper for men whose minds are stronger."[2] Although colonial Americans considered piety a major feminine grace, only a few denominations allowed women to preach. The formal education of women mirrored the society's attitudes. In the lower grades boys and girls attended school together, but beyond that point the colleges which trained men for the professions and the grammar schools which prepared men for the colleges were closed to women as a matter of course. Even when co-education became more popular at the end of the eighteenth century, its advocates emphasized the need for educated mothers to raise children in a republican society rather than the intellectual equality of women.

In the long run the situation of women may have been deteriorating at the end of the colonial period. While the close relationship between husband and wife described by Demos continued on the frontier and in rural areas—where men and women of necessity shared the responsibilities of home and family—among the upper classes the roles of men and women were becoming more clearly differentiated and the first signs of the so-called Victorian morality appeared.

During the Revolution women had acted in a variety of ways to aid the patriot cause. Women organized to oppose the Stamp Act, the tea tax, and the coercive acts. There were Daughters of Liberty as well as Sons of Liberty; during the war Ester De Berdt Reed and Sara Bache, Benjamin Franklin's daughter, headed an association to supply troops with badly needed clothing. Yet the Revolution brought little change in women's status or men's attitudes toward them. Abigail Adams chided her husband, "I cannot say, that I think you are very generous to the ladies; for whilst you are proclaiming peace and goodwill to men, emancipating all nations, you insist upon retaining an absolute power over all wives."[3]

The increasing differentiation of sex roles and the acceptance of English ideals concerning the relations of the sexes were related to the appearance of sharper class distinctions and growing economic specialization which separated the functions of men and women both physically and psychologically. "In the creation of a middle class, essentially urban style of life, women who early had shared in the direction of farms and the rigors of pioneer existence, were expected to preside gracefully over drawing rooms."[4] In the South the idealization of white womanhood was intertwined with miscegenation and the growth of slavery. The selection from Winthrop Jordan's *White Over Black* reveals the interrelationship between racial attitudes and sexual myths in early America and hints at the deep effect this had on southern women of both races. Like Morgan and Demos, he portrays a much freer climate of discussion of sex and a much more open acceptance of sexuality in the early part of the period. Yet with the development of slavery, sexual relations became warped and a double standard emerged in a form that irreparably scarred southern women.[5] Spruill notes that "In the Southern colonies the eighteenth century saw a decline in the vigor and self-reliance of women in wealthier families and a lessening of their influence in public matters." Jordan relates this change to slavery and the effect which the degradation of black women had on white women.

Little is known about the lives of the large number of Afro-American women brought into the colonies as slaves, but certain things may be inferred from the work of writers such as Jordan. Early in the eighteenth century the status of slavery was codified and conditions became more severe. Nearly everywhere miscegenation was outlawed, but widely practiced; and as the century wore on manumission grew increasingly difficult. For slave women the harshness of their lives was compounded by physical and sexual abuse.

The Revolution led to the abolition of slavery in the northern states, but had little positive effect on the status of the vast majority of blacks enslaved below the Mason-Dixon line.

NOTES

1. Carl Degler, *Out of Our Past: The Forces That Shaped Modern America* (New York: Harper and Row, 1970), 55-56.
2. John Winthrop, *Journal*, reprinted in *Up from the Pedestal: Selected Writings in the History of American Feminism*, ed. Aileen S. Kraditor, (Chicago: Quadrangle Books, 1968), 30.
3. Quoted in Arthur Schlesinger, *New Viewpoints in American History* (New York: Macmillan, 1922), 131.
4. Page Smith, *Daughters of the Promised Land* (Boston: Little, Brown, 1970), 68. Smith refers to this shift of attitudes as "The Great Repression."
5. For a modern white southern woman's poignant discussion of this subject see: Lillian Smith, *Killers of the Dream* (New York: W. W. Norton, 1949). The long-term effects on black women of the sexual mythology connected with slavery and the subsequent caste system can be seen in Allison Davis and John Dolland, *Children of Bondage* (New York: Harper and Row, 1964) and William H. Green and Price M. Cobbs, *Black Rage* (New York: Basic Books, 1968).

Article 1

The Puritans and Sex

Edmund S. Morgan

Henry Adams once observed that Americans have "ostentatiously ignored" sex. He could think of only two American writers who touched upon the subject with any degree of boldness—Walt Whitman and Bret Harte. Since the time when Adams made this penetrating observation, American writers have been making up for lost time in a way that would make Bret Harte, if not Whitman, blush. And yet there is still more truth than falsehood in Adams's statement. Americans, by comparison with Europeans or Asiatics, are squeamish when confronted with the facts of life. My purpose is not to account for this squeamishness, but simply to point out that the Puritans, those bogeymen of the modern intellectual, are not responsible for it.

At the outset, consider the Puritans' attitude toward marriage and the role of sex in marriage. The popular assumption might be that the Puritans frowned on marriage and tried to hush up the physical aspect of it as much as possible, but listen to what they themselves had to say. Samuel Willard, minister of the Old South Church in the latter part of the seventeenth century and author of the most complete textbook of Puritan divinity, more than once expressed his horror at "that Popish conceit of the Excellency of Virginity."[1] Another minister, John Cotton, wrote that

> Women are Creatures without which there is no comfortable Living for man: it is true of them what is wont to be said of Governments, *That bad ones are better than none:* They are a sort of Blasphemers then who dispise and decry them, and call them *a necessary Evil, for they are a necessary Good.*[2]

These sentiments did not arise from an interpretation of marriage as

From *The New England Quarterly*, XV (December, 1942), 591-607. Reprinted by permission of the author and *The New England Quarterly*.

a spiritual partnership, in which sexual intercourse was a minor or incidental matter. Cotton gave his opinion of "Platonic love" when he recalled the case of

> one who immediately upon marriage, without ever approaching the *Nuptial Bed,* indented with the *Bride,* that by mutual consent they might both live such a life, and according did sequestring themselves according to the custom of those times, from the rest of mankind, and afterwards from one another too, in their retired Cells, giving themselves up to a Contemplative life; and this is recorded as an instance of no little or ordinary Vertue; but I must be pardoned in it, if I can account it no other than an effort of blind zeal, for they are the dictates of a blind mind they follow therein, and not of that Holy Spirit, which saith *It is not good that man should be alone.*[3]

Here is as healthy an attitude as one could hope to find anywhere. Cotton certainly cannot be accused of ignoring human nature. Nor was he an isolated example among the Puritans. Another minister stated plainly that "the Use of the Marriage Bed" is "founded in mans Nature," and that consequently any withdrawal from sexual intercourse upon the part of husband or wife "Denies all reliefe in Wedlock vnto Human necessity: and sends it for supply vnto Beastiality when God gives not the gift of Continency."[4] In other words, sexual intercourse was a human necessity and marriage the only proper supply for it. These were the views of the New England clergy, the acknowledged leaders of the community, the most Puritanical of the Puritans. As proof that their congregations concurred with them, one may cite the case in which the members of the First Church of Boston expelled James Mattock because, among other offenses, "he denied Coniugall fellowship vnto his wife for the space of 2 years together vpon pretense of taking Revenge upon himself for his abusing of her before marryage."[5] So strongly did the Puritans insist upon the sexual character of marriage that one New Englander considered himself slandered when it was reported, "that he Brock his deceased wife's hart with Greife, that he would be absent from her 3 weeks together when he was at home, and wold never come nere her, and such Like."[6] There was just one limitation which the Puritans placed upon sexual relations in marriage: sex must not interfere with religion. Man's chief end was to glorify God, and all earthly delights must

17

promote that end, not hinder it. Love for a wife was carried too far when it led a man to neglect his God:

> ... sometimes a man hath a good affection to Religion, but the love of his wife carries him away, a man may bee so transported to his wife, that hee dare not bee forward in Religion, lest hee displease his wife, and so the wife, lest shee displease her husband, and this is an inordinate love, when it exceeds measure.[7]

Sexual pleasures, in this respect, were treated like other kinds of pleasure. On a day of fast, when all comforts were supposed to be foregone in behalf of religious contemplation, not only were tasty food and drink to be abandoned but sexual intercourse, too. On other occasions, when food, drink, and recreation were allowable, sexual intercourse was allowable too, though of course only between persons who were married to each other. The Puritans were not ascetics; they never wished to prevent the enjoyment of earthly delights. They merely demanded that the pleasures of the flesh be subordinated to the greater glory of God: husband and wife must not become "so transported with affection, that they look at no higher end than marriage it self." "Let such as have wives," said the ministers, "look at them not for their own ends, but to be fitted for Gods service, and bring them nearer to God."[8]

Toward sexual intercourse outside marriage the Puritans were as frankly hostile as they were favorable to it in marriage. They passed laws to punish adultery with death, and fornication with whipping. Yet they had no misconceptions as to the capacity of human beings to obey such laws. Although the laws were commands of God, it was only natural—since the fall of Adam—for human beings to break them. Breaches must be punished lest the community suffer the wrath of God, but no offense, sexual or otherwise, could be occasion for surprise or for hushed tones of voice. How calmly the inhabitants of seventeenth-century New England could contemplate rape or attempted rape is evident in the following testimony offered before the Middlesex County Court of Massachusetts:

> The examination of Edward Wire taken the 7th of october and alsoe Zachery Johnson. who sayeth that Edward Wires mayd being sent into the towne about busenes meeting with a man that dogd hir from about Joseph Kettles house to goody marches. She came into William Johnsones

and desired Zachery Johnson to goe home with her for that the man dogd hir. accordingly he went with her and being then as far as Samuell Phips his house the man over tooke them. which man caled himselfe by the name of peter grant would have led the mayd but she oposed itt three times: and coming to Edward Wires house the said grant would have kist hir but she refused itt: wire being at prayer grant dragd the mayd between the said wiers and Nathanill frothinghams house. hee then flung the mayd downe in the streete and got atop hir; Johnson seeing it hee caled vppon the fellow to be sivill and not abuse the mayd then Edward wire came forth and ran to the said grant and took hold of him asking him what he did to his mayd, the said grant asked whether she was his wife for he did nothing to his wife: the said grant swearing he would be the death of the said wire. when he came of the mayd; he swore he would bring ten men to pul down his house and soe ran away and they followed him as far as good[y] phipses house where they mett with John Terry and George Chin with clubs in there hands and soe they went away together. Zachy Johnson going to Constable Heamans, and wire going home. there came John Terry to his house to ask for beer and grant was in the streete but afterward departed into the towne, both Johnson and Wire both aferme that when grant was vppon the mayd she cryed out severall times.

Deborah hadlocke being examined sayth that she mett with the man that cals himselfe peter grant about good prichards that he dogd hir and followed hir to hir masters and there threw hir downe and lay vppon hir but had not the use of hir body but swore several othes that he would ly with hir and gett hir with child before she got home.

Grant being present denys all saying he was drunk and did not know what he did.[9]

The Puritans became inured to sexual offenses, because there were so many. The impression which one gets from reading the records of seventeenth-century New England courts is that illicit sexual intercourse was fairly common. The testimony given in cases of fornication and adultery—by far the most numerous class of criminal cases in the records—suggests that many of the early New Englanders possessed a high degree of virility and very few inhibitions. Besides the case of Peter Grant, take the testimony of Elizabeth Knight about the manner of Richard Nevars's advances toward her:

The last publique day of Thanksgiving (in the year 1674) in the evening as I was milking Richard Nevars came to me, and offered me abuse in putting his hand, under my coates, but I turning aside with much adoe, saved my self, and when I was settled to milking he agen took me by the

19

shoulder and pulled me backward almost, but I clapped one hand on the Ground and held fast the Cows teatt with the other hand, and cryed out, and then came to mee Jonathan Abbot one of my Masters Servants, whome the said Never asked wherefore he came, the said Abbot said to look after you, what you doe unto the Maid, but the said Never bid Abbot goe about his businesse but I bade the lad to stay.[10]

One reason for the abundance of sexual offenses was the number of men in the colonies who were unable to gratify their sexual desires in marriage.[11] Many of the first settlers had wives in England. They had come to the new world to make a fortune, expecting either to bring their families after them or to return to England with some of the riches of America. Although these men left their wives behind, they brought their sexual appetites with them; and in spite of laws which required them to return to their families, they continued to stay, and more continued to arrive, as indictments against them throughout the seventeenth century clearly indicate.

Servants formed another group of men, and of women too, who could not ordinarily find supply for human necessity within the bounds of marriage. Most servants lived in the homes of their masters and could not marry without their consent, a consent which was not likely to be given unless the prospective husband or wife also belonged to the master's household. This situation will be better understood if it is recalled that most servants at this time were engaged by contract for a stated period. They were, in the language of the time, "covenant servants," who had agreed to stay with their masters for a number of years in return for a specified recompense, such as transportation to New England or education in some trade (the latter, of course, were known more specifically as apprentices). Even hired servants who worked for wages were usually single, for as soon as a man had enough money to buy or build a house of his own and to get married, he would set up in farming or trade for himself. It must be emphasized, however, that anyone who was not in business for himself was necessarily a servant. The economic organization of seventeenth-century New England had no place for the independent proletarian workman with a family of his own. All production was carried on in the household by the master of the family and his servants, so that most men were either servants or masters of servants; and the former, of course, were more numerous than the latter. Probably most of the inhabitants of Puritan New England could remember a time when they had been servants.

Theoretically no servant had a right to a private life. His time, day or night, belonged to his master, and both religion and law required that he obey his master scrupulously.[12] But neither religion nor law could restrain the sexual impulses of youth, and if those impulses could not be expressed in marriage, they had to be given vent outside marriage. Servants had little difficulty in finding the occasions. Though they might be kept at work all day, it was easy enough to slip away at night. Once out of the house, there were several ways of meeting with a maid. The simplest way was to go to her bedchamber, if she was so fortunate as to have a private one of her own. Thus Jock, Mr. Solomon Phipps's Negro man, confessed in court

> that on the sixteenth day of May 1682, in the morning, betweene 12 and one of the clock, he did force open the back doores of the House of Laurence Hammond in Charlestowne, and came in to the House, and went up into the garret to Marie the Negro.
> He doth likewise acknowledge that one night the last week he forced into the House the same way, and went up to the Negro Woman Marie and that the like he hath done at severall other times before.[13]

Joshua Fletcher took a more romantic way of visiting his lady:

> Joshua Fletcher . . . doth confesse and acknowledge that three severall nights, after bedtime, he went into Mr Fiskes Dwelling house at Chelmsford, at an open window by a ladder that he brought with him. the said windo opening into a chamber, whose was the lodging place of Gresill Juell servant to mr. Fiske. and there he kept company with the said mayd. she sometimes having her cloathes on, and one time he found her in her bed.[14]

Sometimes a maidservant might entertain callers in the parlor while the family were sleeping upstairs. John Knight described what was perhaps a common experience for masters. The crying of his child awakened him in the middle of the night, and he called to his maid, one Sarah Crouch, who was supposed to be sleeping with the child. Receiving no answer, he arose and

> went downe the stayres, and at the stair foot, the latch of doore was pulled in. I called severall times and at the last said if shee would not open the dore, I would breake it open, and when she opened the doore shee was all undressed and Sarah Largin with her undressed, also the said

Sarah went out of doores and Dropped some of her clothes as shee went out. I enquired of Sarah Crouch what men they were, which was with them. Shee made mee no answer for some space of time, but at last shee told me Peeter Brigs was with them, I asked her whether Thomas Jones was not there, but shee would give mee no answer.[15]

In the temperate climate of New England it was not always necessary to seek out a maid at her home. Rachel Smith was seduced in an open field "about nine of the clock at night, being darke, neither moone nor starrs shineing." She was walking through the field when she met a man who

asked her where shee lived, and what her name was and she told him. and then shee asked his name, and he told her Saijing that he was old Goodman Shepards man. Also shee saith he gave her strong liquors, and told her that it was not the first time he had been with maydes after his master was in bed.[16]

Sometimes, of course, it was not necessary for a servant to go outside his master's house in order to satisfy his sexual urges. Many cases of fornication are on record between servants living in the same house. Even where servants had no private bedroom, even where the whole family slept in a single room, it was not impossible to make love. In fact many love affairs must have had their consummation upon a bed in which other people were sleeping. Take for example the case of Sarah Lepingwell. When Sarah was brought into court for having an illegitimate child, she related that one night when her master's brother, Thomas Hawes, was visiting the family, she went to bed early. Later, after Hawes had gone to bed, he called to her to get him a pipe of tobacco. After refusing for some time,

at the last I arose and did lite his pipe and cam and lay doune one my one bead and smoaked about half the pip and siting vp in my bead to giue him his pip my bead being a trundell bead at the sid of his bead he reached beyond the pip and Cauth me by the wrist and pulled me on the side of his bead but I biding him let me goe he bid me hold my peas the folks wold here me and if it be replyed come why did you not call out I Ansar I was posesed with fear of my mastar least my master shold think I did it only to bring a scandall on his brothar and thinking thay wold all beare witnes agaynst me but the thing is true that he did then begete me with child at that tim and the Child is Thomas Hauses and noe mans but his.

In his defense Hawes offered the testimony of another man who was sleeping "on the same side of the bed," but the jury nevertheless accepted Sarah's story.[17]

The fact that Sarah was intimidated by her master's brother suggests that maidservants may have been subject to sexual abuse by their masters. The records show that sometimes masters did take advantage of their position to force unwanted attentions upon their female servants. The case of Elizabeth Dickerman is a good example. She complained to the Middlesex County Court,

> against her master John Harris senior for profiring abus to her by way of forsing her to be naught with him: . . . he has tould her that if she tould her dame: what cariag he did show to her shee had as good be hanged and shee replyed then shee would run away and he sayd run the way is befor you: . . . she says if she should liwe ther shee shall be in fear of her lif.[18]

The court accepted Elizabeth's complaint and ordered her master to be whipped twenty stripes.

So numerous did cases of fornication and adultery become in seventeenth-century New England that the problem of caring for the children of extra-marital unions was a serious one. The Puritans solved it, but in such a way as to increase rather than decrease the temptation to sin. In 1668 the General Court of Massachusetts ordered:

> that where any man is legally convicted to be the Father of a Bastard childe, he shall be at the care and charge to maintain and bring up the same, by such assistance of the Mother as nature requireth, and as the Court from time to time (according to circumstances) shall see meet to Order: and in case the Father of a Bastard, by confession or other manifest proof, upon trial of the case, do not appear to the Courts satisfaction, then the Man charged by the Woman to be the Father, shee holding constant in it, (especially being put upon the real discovery of the truth of it in the time of her Travail) shall be the reputed Father, and accordingly be liable to the charge of maintenance as aforesaid (though not to other punishment) notwithstanding his denial, unless the circumstances of the case and pleas be such, on the behalf of the man charged, as that the Court that have the cognizance thereon shall see reason to acquit him, and otherwise dispose of the Childe and education thereof.[19]

As a result of this law a girl could give way to temptation without the fear of having to care for an illegitimate child by herself. Furthermore, she could, by a little simple lying, spare her lover the expense of supporting the child. When Elizabeth Wells bore a child, less than a year after this statute was passed, she laid it to James Tufts, her master's son. Goodman Tufts affirmed that Andrew Robinson, servant to Goodman Dexter, was the real father, and he brought the following testimony as evidence:

> Wee Elizabeth Jefts aged 15 ears and Mary tufts aged 14 ears doe testyfie that their being one at our hous sumtime the last winter who sayed that thear was a new law made concerning bastards that If aney man wear aqused with a bastard and the woman which had aqused him did stand vnto it in her labor that he should bee the reputed father of it and should mayntaine it Elizabeth Wells hearing of the sayd law she sayed vnto vs that If shee should bee with Child shee would bee sure to lay it vn to won who was rich enough abell to mayntayne it wheather it wear his or no and shee farder sayed Elizabeth Jefts would not you doe so likewise If it weare your case and I sayed no by no means for right must tacke place: and the sayd Elizabeth wells sayed If it wear my Caus I think I should doe so.[20]

A tragic unsigned letter that somehow found its way into the files of the Middlesex County Court gives more direct evidence of the practice which Elizabeth Wells professed:

> der loue i remember my loue to you hoping your welfar and i hop to imbras the but now i rit to you to let you nowe that i am a child by you and i wil ether kil it or lay it to an other and you shal have no blame at al for I haue had many children and none have none of them. . . . [i.e., none of their fathers is supporting any of them.][21]

In face of the wholesale violation of the sexual codes to which all these cases give testimony, the Puritans could not maintain the severe penalties which their laws provided. Although cases of adultery occurred every year, the death penalty is not known to have been applied more than three times. The usual punishment was a whipping or a fine, or both, and perhaps a branding, combined with a symbolical execution in the form of standing on the gallows for an hour with a rope about the neck. Fornication met with a lighter whipping or a lighter fine, while rape was treated in the same way as adultery. Though the Puritans established a code of laws which demanded perfection—which demanded, in other words, strict obedience to the will of God, they nevertheless knew that frail human beings could never live up to the code. When fornication, adultery, rape, or even buggery and sodomy appeared, they were not surprised, nor were they so severe with the offenders as their codes of law would lead one to believe. Sodomy, to be sure, they usually punished with death; but rape, adultery, and fornication they regarded as pardonable human weaknesses, all the more likely to appear in a religious community, where the normal course of sin was stopped by wholesome laws. Governor Bradford, in recounting the details of an epidemic of sexual misdemeanors in Plymouth, wrote resignedly:

> it may be in this case as it is with waters when their streames are stopped or damned up, when they gett passage they flow with more violence, and make more noys and disturbance, then when they are suffered to rune quietly in their owne chanels. So wickednes being here more stopped by strict laws, and the same more nerly looked unto, so as it cannot rune in a comone road of liberty as it would, and is inclined, it searches every wher, and at last breaks out wher it getts vente.[22]

The estimate of human capacities here expressed led the Puritans not only to deal leniently with sexual offenses but also to take every precaution to prevent such offenses, rather than wait for the necessity of punishment. One precaution was to see that children got married as soon as possible. The wrong way to promote virtue, the Puritans thought, was to "ensnare" children in vows of virginity, as the Catholics did. As a result of such vows, children, "not being able to contain," would be guilty of "unnatural pollutions, and other filthy practices in secret: and too oft of horrid Murthers of the fruit of their bodies," said Thomas Cobbett.[23] The way to avoid fornication and perversion was for parents to provide suitable husbands and wives for their children:

> Lot was to blame that looked not out seasonably for some fit matches for his two daughters, which had formerly minded marriage (witness the contract between them and two men in *Sodom*, called therfore for his Sons in Law, which had married his daughters, Gen. 19. 14.) for they seeing no man like to come into them in a conjugall way . . . then they plotted that incestuous course, whereby their Father was so highly dishonoured. . . .[24]

As marriage was the way to prevent fornication, successful marriage was the way to prevent adultery. The Puritans did not wait for adultery to appear; instead, they took every means possible to make husbands and wives live together and respect each other. If a husband deserted his wife and remained within the jurisdiction of a Puritan government, he was promptly sent back to her. Where the wife had been left in England, the offense did not always come to light until the wayward husband had committed fornication or bigamy, and of course there must have been many offenses which never came to light. But where both husband and wife lived in New England, neither had much chance of leaving the other without being returned by order of the county court at its next sitting. When John Smith of Medfield left his wife and went to live with Patience Rawlins, he was sent home poorer by ten pounds and richer by thirty stripes. Similarly Mary Drury, who deserted her husband on the pretense that he was impotent, failed to convince the court that he actually was so, and had to return to him as well as to pay a fine of five pounds. The wife of Phillip Pointing received lighter treatment: when the court thought that she had overstayed her leave in Boston, they simply ordered her "to depart the Towne and goe to Tanton to her husband." The courts, moreover, were not satisfied with mere cohabitation; they insisted that it be peaceful cohabitation. Husbands and wives were forbidden by law to strike one another, and the law was enforced on numerous occasions. But the courts did not stop there. Henry Flood was required to give bond for good behavior because he had abused his wife simply by "ill words calling her whore and cursing of her." The wife of Christopher Collins was presented for railing at her husband and called him "Gurley gutted divill." Apparently in this case the court thought that Mistress Collins was right, for although the fact was proved by two witnesses, she was discharged. On another occasion the court favored the husband: Jacob Pudeator, fined for striking and kicking his wife, had the sentence moderated when the court was informed that she was a woman "of great provocation."[25]

Wherever there was strong suspicion that an illicit relation might arise between two persons, the authorities removed the temptation by forbidding the two to come together. As early as November, 1630, the Court of Assistants of Massachusetts prohibited a Mr. Clark from "cohabitacion and frequent keepeing company with Mrs. Freeman, vnder paine of such punishment as the Court shall thinke meete to inflict." Mr. Clark and Mrs. Freeman were both bound "in XX £ apeece that Mr. Clearke shall make his personall appearance att the nexte Court to be holden in March nexte, and in the meane tyme to carry himselfe in good behaviour towards all people and espetially towards Mrs. Freeman, concerneing whome there is stronge suspicion of incontinency." Forty-five years later the Suffolk County Court took the same kind of measure to protect the husbands of Dorchester from the temptations offered by the daughter of Robert Spurr. Spurr was presented by the grand jury

> for entertaining persons at his house at unseasonable times both by day and night to the greife of theire wives and Relations &c The Court having heard what was alleaged and testified against him do Sentence him to bee admonish't and to pay Fees of Court and charge him upon her perill not to entertain any married men to keepe company with his daughter especially James Minott and Joseph Belcher.

In like manner Walter Hickson was forbidden to keep company with Mary Bedwell, "And if at any time hereafter hee bee taken in company of the saide Mary Bedwell without other company to bee forthwith apprehended by the Constable and to be whip't with ten stripes." Elizabeth Wheeler and Joanna Peirce were admonished "for theire disorderly carriage in the house of Thomas Watts being married women and founde sitting in other mens Laps with theire Armes about theire Necks." How little confidence the Puritans had in human nature is even more clearly displayed by another case, in which Edmond Maddock and his wife were brought to court " to answere to all such matters as shalbe objected against them concerning Haarkwoody and Ezekiell Euerells being at their house at unseasonable tyme of the night and her being up with them after her husband was gone to bed." Haarkwoody and Everell had been found "by the Constable Henry Bridghame about tenn of the Clock at night sitting by the fyre at the house of Edmond Maddocks with his wyfe a suspicious weoman her husband being on sleepe [sic] on the bedd." A similar distrust of human ability to resist temptation is evident in the following order of the Connecticut Particular Court:

> James Hallett is to returne from the Correction house to his master Barclyt, who is to keepe him to hard labor, and course dyet during the pleasure of the Court provided that Barclet is first to remove his daughter from his family, before the sayd James enter therein.

These precautions, as we have already seen, did not eliminate fornication, adultery, or other sexual offenses, but they doubtless reduced the number from what it would otherwise have been.[26]

In sum, the Puritan attitude toward sex, though directed by a belief in absolute, God-given moral values, never neglected human nature. The rules of conduct which the Puritans regarded as divinely ordained had been formulated for men, not for angels and not for beasts. God had created mankind in two sexes; He had ordained marriage as desirable for all, and sexual intercourse as essential to marriage. On the other hand, He had forbidden sexual intercourse outside of marriage. These were the moral principles which the Puritans sought to enforce in New England. But in their enforcement they took cognizance of human nature. They knew well enough that human beings since the fall of Adam were incapable of obeying perfectly the laws of God. Consequently, in the endeavor to enforce those laws they treated offenders with patience and understanding, and concentrated their efforts on prevention more than on punishment. The result was not a society in which most of us would care to live, for the methods of prevention often caused serious interference with personal liberty. It must nevertheless be admitted that in matters of sex the Puritans showed none of the blind zeal or narrow-minded bigotry which is too often supposed to have been characteristic of them. The more one learns about these people, the less do they appear to have resembled the sad and sour portraits which their modern critics have drawn of them.

NOTES

1. Samuel Willard, *A Compleat Body of Divinity* (Boston, 1726), 125 and 608–613.
2. John Cotton, *A Meet Help* (Boston, 1699), 14–15.
3. *A Meet Help*, 16.
4. Edward Taylor, Commonplace Book (manuscript in the library of the Massachusetts Historical Society).
5. Records of the First Church in Boston (manuscript copy in the library of the Massachusetts Historical Society), 12.
6. Middlesex County Court Files, folder 42.
7. John Cotton, *A Practical Commentary ... upon the First Epistle Generall of John* (London, 1656), 126.
8. *A Practical Commentary*, 126.
9. Middlesex Files, folder 48.

10. Middlesex Files, folder 71.
11. Another reason was suggested by Charles Francis Adams in his scholarly article, "Some Phases of Sexual Morality and Church Discipline in Colonial New England," *Proceedings* of the Massachusetts Historical Society, XXVI, 477-516.
12. On the position of servants in early New England see *More Books,* XVII (September, 1942), 311-328.
13. Middlesex Files, folder 99.
14. Middlesex Files, folder 47.
15. Middlesex Files, folder 52.
16. Middlesex Files, folder 44.
17. Middlesex Files, folder 47.
18. Middlesex Files, folder 94.
19. William H. Whitmore, editor, *The Colonial Laws of Massachusetts. Reprinted from the Edition of 1660* (Boston, 1889), 257.
20. Middlesex Files, folder 52.
21. Middlesex Files, folder 30.
22. William Bradford, *History of Plymouth Plantation* (Boston, 1912), II, 309.
23. Thomas Cobbett, *A Fruitfull and Usefull Discourse touching the Honour due from Children to Parents and the Duty of Parents towards their Children* (London, 1656), 174.
24. Cobbett, 177.
25. Samuel E. Morison and Zechariah Chafee, editors, *Records of the Suffolk County Court, 1671-1680, Publications* of the Colonial Society of Massachusetts, XXIX and XXX, 121, 410, 524, 837-841, and 1158; George F. Dow, editor, *Records and Files of the Quarterly Courts of Essex County, Massachusetts* (Salem, 1911-1921), I, 274; and V, 377.
26. *Records of the Suffolk County Court,* 442-443 and 676; John Noble, editor, *Records of the Court of Assistants of the Colony of Massachusetts Bay* (Boston, 1901-1928), II, 8; *Records of the Particular Court of Connecticut, Collections* of the Connecticut Historical Society, XXII, 20; and a photostat in the library of the Massachusetts Historical Society, dated March 29, 1653.

Article 2

Husbands and Wives

John Demos

No aspect of the Puritan household was more vital than the relationship of husband and wife. But the study of this relationship raises at
once certain larger questions of sex differentiation: What were the
relative positions of men and women in Plymouth Colony? What
attributes, and what overall valuation, were thought appropriate to
each sex?

We know in a general way that male dominance was an accepted principle all over the Western World in the seventeenth
century. The fundamental Puritan sentiment on this matter was
expressed by Milton in a famous line in *Paradise Lost:* "he for God
only, she for God in him;" and there is no reason to suspect that the
people of Plymouth would have put it any differently. The world of
public affairs was nowhere open to women—in Plymouth only males
were eligible to become "freemen." Within the family the husband
was always regarded as the "head"—and the Old Colony provided
no exceptions to this pattern. Moreover, the culture at large maintained a deep and primitive kind of suspicion of women, solely on
account of their sex. Some basic taint of corruption was thought to
be inherent in the feminine constitution—a belief rationalized, of
course, by the story of Eve's initial treachery in the Garden of Eden.
It was no coincidence that in both the Old and the New World
witches were mostly women. Only two allegations of witchcraft turn
up in the official records of Plymouth,[1] but other bits of evidence
point in the same general direction. There are, for example, the
quoted words of a mother beginning an emotional plea to her son:
"if you would beleive a woman beleive mee. . . ."[2] And why *not*
believe a woman?

The views of the Pilgrim Pastor John Robinson are also interest-

From *A Little Commonwealth: Family Life in Plymouth Colony* (New York: Oxford
University Press, 1970), 82-99. Copyright © 1970 by Oxford University Press, Inc.
Reprinted by permission.

ing in this connection. He opposed, in the first place, any tendency to regard women as "necessary evils" and greatly regretted the currency of such opinions among "not only heathen poets . . . but also wanton Christians." The Lord has created both man and woman of an equal perfection, and "neither is she, since the creation more degenerated than he from the primitive goodness."[3] Still, in marriage some principles of authority were essential, since "differences will arise and be seen, and so the one must give way, and apply unto the other; this, God and nature layeth upon the woman, rather than upon the man." Hence the proper attitude of a wife towards her husband was "a reverend subjection."[4]

However, in a later discussion of the same matter Robinson developed a more complex line of argument which stressed certain attributes of inferiority assumed to be inherently feminine. Women, he wrote, were under two different kinds of subjection. The first was framed "in innocency" and implied no "grief" or "wrong" whatsoever. It reflected simply the woman's character as "the weaker vessel"—weaker, most obviously, with respect to intelligence or "understanding." For this was a gift "which God hath . . . afforded [the man], and means of obtaining it, above the woman, that he might guide and go before her."[5] Robinson also recognized that some men abused their position of authority and oppressed their wives most unfairly. But *even so*—and this was his central point—resistance was not admissible. Here he affirmed the second kind of subjection laid upon woman, a subjection undeniably "grievous" but justified by her "being first in transgression." In this way—by invoking the specter of Eve corrupting Adam in paradise—Robinson arrived in the end at a position which closely approximated the popular assumption of woman's basic moral weakness.

Yet within this general framework of masculine superiority there were a number of rather contrary indications. They seem especially evident in certain areas of the law. Richard B. Morris has written a most interesting essay on this matter, arguing the improved legal status of colonial women by comparison to what still obtained in the mother country.[6] Many of his conclusions seem to make a good fit with conditions in Plymouth Colony. The baseline here is the common law tradition of England, which at this time accorded to women only the most marginal sort of recognition. The married woman, indeed, was largely subsumed under the legal personality of her husband; she was virtually without rights to own property, make contracts, or sue for damages on her own account. But in the New World this situation was perceptibly altered.

Consider, for example, the evidence bearing on the property rights of Plymouth Colony wives. The law explicitly recognized their part in the accumulation of a family's estate, by the procedures it established for the treatment of widows. It was a basic principle of inheritance in this period—on both sides of the Atlantic—that a widow should have the use or profits of one-third of the land owned by her husband at the time of his death and full title to one-third of his movable property. But at least in Plymouth, and perhaps in other colonies as well, this expressed more than the widow's need for an adequate living allowance. For the laws also prescribed that "if any man do make an irrational and unrighteous Will, whereby he deprives his Wife of her reasonable allowance for her subsistency," the Court may "relieve her out of the estate, notwithstanding by Will it were otherwise disposed; especially in such case where the Wife brought with her good part of the Estate in Marriage, or hath by her diligence and industry done her part in the getting of the Estate, and was otherwise well deserving."[7] Occasionally the Court saw fit to alter the terms of a will on this account. In 1663, for example, it awarded to widow Naomi Silvester a larger share of her late husband's estate than the "inconsiderable pte" he had left her, since she had been "a frugall and laborious woman in the procuring of the said estate."[8] In short, the widow's customary "thirds" was not a mere dole; it was her *due*.

But there is more still. In seventeenth-century England women were denied the right to make contracts, save in certain very exceptional instances. In Plymouth Colony, by contrast, one finds the Court sustaining certain kinds of contracts involving women on a fairly regular basis. The most common case of this type was the agreement of a widow and a new husband, made *before* marriage, about the future disposition of their respective properties. The contract drawn up by John Phillips of Marshfield and widow Faith Doty of Plymouth in 1667 was fairly standard. It stipulated that "the said Faith Dotey is to enjoy all her house and land, goods and cattles, that shee is now possessed of, to her owne proper use, to dispose of them att her owne free will from time to time, and att any time, as shee shall see cause." Moreover this principle of separate control extended beyond the realm of personal property. Phillips and widow Doty each had young children by their previous marriages, and their agreement was "that the children of both the said pties shall remaine att the free and proper and onely dispose of theire owne naturall parents, as they shall see good to dispose of them."[9] Any woman entering marriage on terms such as these would seem virtually an equal partner, at least from a legal standpoint. Much rarer, but no less significant, were contracts made by women *after* marriage. When Dorothy Clarke wished to be free of her husband Nathaniel in 1686, the Court refused a divorce but allowed a separation. Their estate was then carefully divided up by contract to which the wife was formally a party.[10] Once again, no clear precedents for this procedure can be found in contemporary English law.

The specific terms of some wills also help to confirm the rights of women to a limited kind of ownership even within marriage. No husband ever included his wife's clothing, for example, among the property to be disposed of after his death. And consider, on the other side, a will like that of Mistress Sarah Jenny, drawn up at Plymouth in 1655. Her husband had died just a few months earlier, and she wished simply to "Despose of som smale thinges that is my owne proper goods leaveing my husbands will to take place according to the true Intent and meaning thereof."[11] The "smale thinges" included not only her wardrobe, but also a bed, some books, a mare, some cattle and sheep. Unfortunately, married women did not usually leave wills of their own (unless they had been previously widowed); and it is necessary to infer that in most cases there was some sort of informal arrangement for the transfer of their personal possessions. One final indication of these same patterns comes from wills which made bequests to a husband and wife separately. Thus, for example, Richard Scalis of Scituate conferred most of his personal possessions on the families of two married daughters, carefully specifying which items should go to the daughters themselves and which to their husbands.[12] Thomas Rickard, also of Scituate, had no family of his own and chose therefore to distribute his property among a variety of friends. Once again spouses were treated separately: "I give unto Thomas Pincin my bedd and Rugg one paire of sheets and pilloty . . . I give and bequeath unto Joane the wife of the aforsaid Thomas Pincin my bason and fouer sheets . . . I give and bequeath unto Joane Stanlacke my Chest . . . unto Richard Stanlacke my Chest . . . unto Richard Stanlacke my best briches and Dublit and ould Coate."[13]

The questions of property rights and of the overall distribution of authority within a marriage do not necessarily coincide; and modern sociologists interested in the latter subject usually emphasize the process of decision-making.[14] Of course, their use of live samples gives them a very great advantage; they can ask their informants, through questionnaires or interviews, which spouse decides where to go on vacation, what kind of car to buy, how to discipline the children, when to have company in, and so forth. The historian simply cannot draw out this kind of detail, nor can he contrive any substantial equivalent. But he is able sometimes to make a beginning in this direction; for example, the records of Plymouth do throw light on two sorts of family decisions of the very greatest importance. One of these involves the transfer of land, and illustrates further the whole trend toward an expansion of the rights of married women to hold property. The point finds tangible expression in a law passed by the General Court in 1646: "It is enacted &c. That the Assistants or any of them shall have full power to take the acknowledgment of a bargaine and sale of houses and lands . . . And that the wyfe hereafter come in & consent and acknowledg the sale also; but that all bargaines and sales of houses and lands made before this day to remayne firm to the buyer notwithstanding the wife did not acknowledge the same."[15] The words "come in" merit special attention: the authorities wished to confront the wife personally (and even, perhaps, privately?) in order to minimize the possibility that her husband might exert undue pressure in securing her agreement to a sale.

The second area of decision-making in which both spouses shared important *joint* responsibility was the "putting out" of children into foster families. For this there was no statute prescribing a set line of procedure, but the various written documents from specific cases make the point clearly enough. Thus in 1660 "An Agreement appointed to bee Recorded" affirmed that "Richard Berry of Yarmouth with his wifes Concent and other frinds; hath given unto Gorge Crispe of Eastham and his; wife theire son Samuell Berry; to bee att the ordering and Disposing of the said Gorge and his wife as if hee were theire owne Child."[16] The practice of formally declaring the wife's consent is evident in all such instances, when both parents were living. Another piece of legal evidence describes an actual deathbed scene in which the same issue had to be faced. It is the testimony of a mother confirming the adoption of her son, and it is worth quoting in some detail. "These prsents Witnesse that the 20th of march 1657-8 Judith the wife of William Peaks acknowlidged that her former husband Lawrance Lichfeild lying on his Death bedd sent for John Allin and Ann his wife and Desired to give and bequeath unto them his youngest son Josias Lichfeild if they would accept of him and take him as theire Child; then they Desired to know how long they should have him and the said Lawrance said for ever; but the mother of the child was not willing then; but in a short time after willingly Concented to her husbands will in the thinge."[17] That the wife finally agreed is less important here than the way in which her initial reluctance sufficed to block the child's adoption, in spite of the clear wishes of her husband.

Another reflection of this pattern of mutual responsibility appears in certain types of business activity—for instance, the management of inns and taverns ("ordinaries" in the language of the day). All such establishments were licensed by the General Court; hence their history can be followed, to a limited degree, in the official Colony Records. It is interesting to learn that one man's license was revoked because he had recently "buryed his wife, and in that respect not being soe capeable of keeping a publicke house."[18] In other cases the evidence is less explicit but still revealing. For many years James Cole ran the principal ordinary in the town of Plymouth, and from time to time the Court found it necessary to censure and punish certain violations of proper decorum that occurred there. In some of these cases Cole's wife Mary was directly implicated. In March 1669 a substantial fine was imposed "for that the said Mary Cole suffered divers psons after named to stay drinking on the Lords day . . . in the time of publicke worshipp."[19] Indeed the role of women in all aspects of this episode is striking, since two of the four drinking customers, the "divers psons after named," turned out to be female. Perhaps, then, women had considerable freedom to move on roughly the same terms with men even into some of the darker byways of Old Colony life.

The Court occasionally granted liquor licenses directly to women. Husbands were not mentioned, though it is of course possible that all of the women involved were widows. In some cases the terms of these permits suggest retail houses rather than regular inns or taverns. Thus in 1663 "Mistris Lydia Garrett" of Scituate was licensed to "sell liquors, alwaies provided . . . that shee sell none but to house keepers, and not lesse than a gallon att a time;"[20] and the agreement with another Scituate lady, Margaret Muffee, twenty years later, was quite similar.[21] But meanwhile in Middlebury one "Mistress Mary Combe" seems to have operated an ordinary of the standard type.[22] Can we proceed from these specific data on liquor licensing to some more general conclusion about the participation of women in the whole field of economic production and exchange? Unfortunately there is little additional hard evidence on one side or the other. The Court Records do not often mention other types of business activity, with the single exception of milling; and no woman was ever named in connection with this particular enterprise. A few more wills could be cited—for instance, the one made by Elizabeth Poole, a wealthy spinster in Taunton, leaving "my pte in the Iron workes" to a favorite nephew.[23] But this does not add up to very much. The economy of Plymouth was, after all, essentially simple— indeed "underdeveloped"—in most important respects. Farming claimed the energies of all but a tiny portion of the populace; there was relatively little opportunity for anyone, man *or* woman, to develop a more commercial orientation. It is known that in the next century women played quite a significant role in the business life of many parts of New England,[24] and one can view this pattern as simply the full development of possibilities that were latent even among the first generations of settlers. But there is no way to fashion an extended chain of proof.

Much of what has been said so far belongs to the general category of the rights and privileges of the respective partners to a marriage. But what of their duties, their basic responsibilities to one another? Here, surely, is another area of major importance in any assessment of the character of married life. The writings of John Robinson help us to make a start with these questions, and especially to recover the framework of ideals within which most couples of Plymouth Colony must have tried to hammer out a meaningful day-to-day relationship. We have noted already that Robinson prescribed "subjection" as the basic duty of a wife to her husband. No woman deserved praise, "how well endowed soever otherwise, except she frame, and compose herself, what may be, unto her husband, in conformity of manners."[25] From the man, by contrast, two things were particularly required: "love . . . and wisdom." His love for his wife must be "like Christ's to his church: holy for quality, and great for quantity," and it must stand firm even where "her failings and faults be great." His wisdom was essential to the role of the family "head"; without it neither spouse was likely to find the way to true piety, and eventually to salvation.

It is a long descent from the spiritual counsel of John Robinson to the details of domestic conflict as noted in the Colony Records. But the Records are really the only available source of information about the workings of actual marriages in this period. They are, to be sure, a negative type of source; that is, they reveal only those cases which seemed sufficiently deviant and sufficiently important to warrant the attention of the authorities. But it is possible by a kind of reverse inference to use them to reconstruct the norms which the community at large particularly wished to protect. This effort serves to isolate three basic obligations in which both husband and wife were thought to share.

There was, first and most simply, the obligation of regular and exclusive cohabitation. No married person was permitted to live apart from his spouse except in very unusual and temporary circumstances (as when a sailor was gone to sea). The Court stood ready as a last resort to force separated couples to come together again, though it was not often necessary to deal with the problem in such an official way. One of the few recorded cases of this type occurred in 1659. The defendant was a certain Goodwife Spring, married to a resident of Watertown in the Bay Colony and formerly the wife and widow of Thomas Hatch of Scituate. She had, it seems, returned to Scituate some three or four years earlier, and had been living "from her husband" ever since. The Court ordered that "shee either repaire to her husband with all convenient speed, . . . or . . . give a reason why shee doth not."[26] Exactly how this matter turned out cannot be determined, but it seems likely that the ultimate sanction was banishment from the Colony. The government of Massachusetts Bay is known to have imposed this penalty in a number of similar cases. None of the extant records describe such action being taken at Plymouth, but presumably the possibility was always there.

Moreover, the willful desertion of one spouse by the other over a period of several years was one of the few legitimate grounds for divorce. In 1670, for example, the Court granted the divorce plea of James Skiffe "haveing received sufficient testimony that the late wife of James Skiffe hath unlawfully forsaken her lawfull husband . . . and is gone to Roanoke, in or att Verginnia, and there hath taken another man for to be her husband."[27] Of course, bigamy was always sufficient reason in itself for terminating a marriage. Thus in 1680 Elizabeth Stevens obtained a divorce from her husband when it was proved that he had three other wives already, one each in Boston, Barbadoes, and a town in England not specified.[28]

But it was not enough that married persons should simply live together on a regular basis; their relationship must be relatively peaceful and harmonious. Once again the Court reserved the right to interfere in cases where the situation had become especially difficult. Occasionally both husband and wife were judged to be at fault, as when George and Anna Barlow were "severly reproved for theire most ungodly liveing in contension one with the other, and admonished to live otherwise."[29] But much more often one or the other was singled out for the Court's particular attention. One man was punished for "abusing his wife by kiking her of from a stoole into the fier,"[30] and another for "drawing his wife in an uncivell manor on the snow."[31] A more serious case was that of John Dunham, convicted of "abusive carriage towards his wife in continuall tiranising over her, and in pticulare for his late abusive and uncivill carryage in endeavoring to beate her in a deboist manor."[32] The Court ordered a whipping as just punishment for these cruelties, but the sentence was then suspended at the request of Dunham's wife. Sometimes the situation was reversed and the woman was the guilty party. In 1655, for example, Joan Miller of Taunton was charged with "beating and reviling her husband, and egging her children to healp her, bidding them knock him in the head, and wishing his victuals might coak him."[33] A few years later the wife of Samuel Halloway (also of Taunton) was admonished for "carryage towards her husband . . . soe turbulend and wild, both in words and actions, as hee could not live with her but in danger of his life or limbs."[34]

It would serve no real purpose to cite more of these unhappy episodes—and it might indeed create an erroneous impression that marital conflict was particularly endemic among the people of the Old Colony. But two general observations are in order. First, the Court's chief aim in this type of case was to restore the couple in question to something approaching tranquility. The assumption was that a little force applied from the outside might be useful, whether it came in the form of an "admonition" or in some kind of actual punishment. Only once did the Court have to recognize that the situation might be so bad as to make a final reconciliation impossible. This happened in 1665 when John Williams, Jr., of Scituate, was charged with a long series of "abusive and harsh carriages" towards his wife Elizabeth, "in speciall his sequestration of himselfe from the marriage bed, and his accusation of her to bee a whore, and that especially in reference unto a child lately borne of his said wife by him denied to bee legittimate."[35] The case was frequently before the Court during the next two years, and eventually all hope of a settlement was abandoned. When Williams persisted in his "abuses," and when too he had "himself . . . [declared] his insufficiency for converse with weomen,"[36] a formal separation was allowed—though not a full divorce. In fact, it may be that his impotence, not his habitual cruelty, was the decisive factor in finally persuading the Court to go this far. For in another case, some years later, a separation was granted on the former grounds alone.[37]

The second noteworthy aspect of all these situations is the equality they seem to imply between the sexes. In some societies and indeed in many parts of Europe at this time, a wife was quite literally at the mercy of her husband—his prerogatives extended even to the random use of physical violence. But clearly this was not the situation at Plymouth. It is, for example, instructive to break down these charges of "abusive carriage" according to sex: one finds that wives were accused just about as often as husbands. Consider, too, those cases of conflict in which the chief parties were of opposite sex but not married to one another. Once again the women seem to have held their own. Thus we have, on the one side, Samuel Norman punished for "strikeing Lydia, the wife of Henery Taylor,"[38] and John Dunham for "abusive speeches and carriages"[39] toward Sarah, wife of Benjamin Eaton; and, on the other side, the complaint of Abraham Jackson against "Rose, the wife of Thomas Morton, . . . that the said Rose, as hee came from worke, did abuse him by calling of him lying rascall and rogue."[40] In short, this does not seem to have been a society characterized by a really pervasive, and operational, norm of male dominance. There is no evidence at all of habitual patterns of deference in the relations between the sexes. John Robinson, and many others, too, may have assumed that woman was "the weaker vessel" and that "subjection" was her natural role. But as so often happens with respect to such matters, actual behavior was another story altogether.

The third of the major obligations incumbent on the married pair was a normal and exclusive sexual union. As previously indicated, impotence in the husband was one of the few circumstances that might warrant a divorce. The reasoning behind this is nowhere made explicit, but most likely it reflected the felt necessity that a marriage produce children. It is worth noting in this connection some of the words used in a divorce hearing of 1686 which centered on the issue of a man's impotence. He was, according to his wife, "always unable to perform the act of generation.[41] The latter phrase implies a particular view of the nature and significance of the sexual act, one which must have been widely held in this culture. Of course, there were other infertile marriages in the same period which held together. But perhaps the cause of the problem had to be obvious—as with impotence—for the people involved to consider divorce. Where the sexual function appeared normal in both spouses, there was always the hope that the Lord might one day grant the blessing of children. Doubtless for some couples this way of thinking meant year after year of deep personal disappointment.

The problem of adultery was more common—and, in a general sense, more troublesome. For adultery loomed as the most serious possible distortion of the whole sexual and reproductive side of marriage. John Robinson called it "that most foul and filthy sin, . . . the disease of marriage," and concluded that divorce was its necessary "medicine."[42] In fact, most of the divorces granted in the Old Colony stemmed from this one cause alone. But adultery was not only a strong *prima facie* reason for divorce; it was also an act that would bring heavy punishment to the guilty parties. The law decreed that "whosoever shall Commit Adultery with a Married Woman or one Betrothed to another Man, both of them shall be severely punished, by whipping two several times . . . and likewise to wear two Capital Letters A.D. cut out in cloth and sewed on their uppermost Garments . . . and if at any time they shall be found without the said Letters so worne . . . to be forthwith taken and publickly whipt, and so from time to time as often as they are found not to wear them."[43]

But quite apart from the severity of the prescribed punishments, this statute is interesting for its definition of adultery by reference to a married (or betrothed) *woman*. Here, for the first time, we find some indication of difference in the conduct expected of men and women. The picture can be filled out somewhat by examining the specific cases of adultery prosecuted before the General Court down through the years. To be sure, the man involved in any given instance was judged together with the woman, and when convicted their punishments were the same. But there is another point to consider as well. All of the adulterous couples mentioned in the records can be classified in one of two categories: a married woman and a married man, or a married woman and a single man. There was, on the other hand, no case involving a married man and a single woman. This pattern seems to imply that the chief concern, the essential element of sin, was the woman's infidelity to her husband. A married man would be punished for his part in this aspect of the affair—rather than for any wrong done to his own wife.

However, this does not mean that a man's infidelities were wholly beyond reproach. The records, for example, include one divorce plea in which the wife adduced as her chief complaint "an act of uncleanes" by her husband with another woman.[44] There was no move to prosecute and punish the husband—apparently since the other woman was unmarried. But the divorce was granted, and the wife received a most favorable settlement. We can, then, conclude the following. The adultery of a wife was treated as both a violation of her marriage (hence grounds for divorce) *and* an offense against the community (hence cause for legal prosecution). But for comparable behavior by husbands only the former consideration applied. In this somewhat limited sense the people of Plymouth Colony do seem to have maintained a "double standard" of sexual morality.

Before concluding this discussion of married life in the Old Colony and moving on to other matters, one important area of omission should at least be noted. Very little has been said here of love, affection, understanding—a whole range of positive feelings and impulses—between husbands and wives. Indeed the need to rely so heavily on Court Records has tended to weight the balance quite conspicuously on the side of conflict and failure. The fact is that the sum total of actions of divorce, prosecutions for adultery, "admonitions" against habitual quarreling, does not seem terribly large. In order to make a proper assessment of their meaning several contingent factors must be recognized: the long span of time they cover, the steady growth of the Colony's population (to something like 10,000 by the end of the century),[45] the extensive jurisdiction of the Court over many areas of domestic life. Given this overall context, it is clear that the vast majority of Plymouth Colony families never once required the attention of the authorities. Elements of disharmony were, at the least, controlled and confined within certain limits.

But again, can the issue be approached in a more directly affirmative way? Just how, and how much, did feelings of warmth and love fit into the marriages of the Old Colony? Unfortunately our source materials have almost nothing to say in response to such questions. But this is only to be expected in the case of legal documents, physical remains, and so forth. The wills often refer to "my loveing wife"—but it would be foolish to read anything into such obvious set phrases. The records of Court cases are completely mute on this score. Other studies of "Puritan" ideals about marriage and the family have drawn heavily on literary materials—and this, of course, is the biggest gap in the sources that have come down from

Plymouth Colony. Perhaps, though, a certain degree of extrapolation is permissible here; and if so, we must imagine that love was quite central to these marriages. If, as Morgan has shown, this was the case in Massachusetts Bay, surely it was also true for the people of Plymouth.[46]

There are, finally, just a few scraps of concrete evidence on this point. As previously noted, John Robinson wrote lavishly about the importance of love to a marriage—though he associated it chiefly with the role of the husband. And the wills should be drawn in once again, especially those clauses in which a man left specific instructions regarding the care of his widow. Sometimes the curtain of legal terms and style seems to rise for a moment and behind it one glimpses a deep tenderness and concern. There is, for example, the will written by Walter Briggs in 1676. Briggs's instructions in this regard embraced all of the usual matters—rooms, bedding, cooking utensils, "lyberty to make use of ye two gardens." And he ended with a particular request that his executors "allow my said wife a gentle horse or mare to ride to meeting or any other occasion she may have, & that Jemy, ye neger, catch it for her."[47] Surely this kind of thoughtfulness reflected a larger instinct of love—one which, nourished in life, would not cease to be effective even in the face of death itself.

NOTES

1. The first occurred in 1661, in Marshfield. A girl named Dinah Silvester accused the wife of William Holmes of being a witch, and of going about in the shape of a bear in order to do mischief. The upshot, however, was a suit for defamation against Dinah. The Court convicted her and obliged her to make a public apology to Goodwife Holmes. *Plymouth Colony Records,* III, 205, 207, 211. The second case (at Scituate, in 1677) resulted in the formal indictment of one Mary Ingham—who, it was said, had bewitched a girl named Mehitable Woodworth. But after suitable deliberations, the jury decided on an acquittal. *Plymouth Colony Records,* V, 223-24.
2. From a series of depositions bearing on the estate of Samuel Ryder, published in *Mayflower Descendant,* XI, 52. The case is discussed in greater detail below, pp. 165-66.
3. *The Works of John Robinson,* ed. Robert Ashton (Boston, 1851), I, 236.
4. *Ibid.,* 239-40.

5. *Ibid.*, 240.
6. Richard B. Morris, *Studies in the History of American Law* (New York, 1930), Chapter III, "Women's Rights in Early American Law."
7. Brigham, *The Compact with the Charter and Laws of the Colony of New Plymouth*, 281.
8. *Plymouth Colony Records*, IV, 46.
9. *Ibid.*, 1643-64. For another agreement of this type, see *Mayflower Descendant*, XVII, 49 (the marriage contract of Ephraim Morton and Mistress Mary Harlow). The same procedures can be viewed, retrospectively, in the wills of men who had been married to women previously widowed. Thus when Thomas Boardman of Yarmouth died in 1689 the following notation was placed near the end of his will: "the estate of my wife brought me upon marriage be at her dispose and not to be Invintoried with my estate." *Mayflower Descendant*, X, 102. See also the will of Dolar Davis, *Mayflower Descendant*, XXIV, 73.
10. *Mayflower Descendant*, VI, 191-92.
11. *Mayflower Descendant*, VIII, 171.
12. *Mayflower Descendant*, XIII, 94-96.
13. *Mayflower Descendant*, IX, 155.
14. See, for example, Robert O. Blood, Jr., and Donald M. Wolfe, *Husbands and Wives* (Glencoe, Ill., 1960), esp. ch. 2.
15. Brigham, *The Compact with the Charter and Laws of the Colony of New Plymouth*, 86.
16. *Mayflower Descendant*, XV, 34.
17. *Mayflower Descendant*, XII, 134.
18. *Plymouth Colony Records*, IV, 54.
19. *Plymouth Colony Records*, V, 15.
20. *Plymouth Colony Records*, IV, 44.
21. *Plymouth Colony Records*, VI, 187.
22. *Ibid.*, 141.
23. *Mayflower Descendant*, XIV, 26.
24. Elizabeth Anthony Dexter, *Colonial Women of Affairs* (Boston, 1911).
25. *The Works of John Robinson*, I, 20.
26. *Plymouth Colony Records*, III, 174.
27. *Plymouth Colony Records*, V, 33.
28. *Plymouth Colony Records*, VI, 44-45.
29. *Plymouth Colony Records*, IV, 10.
30. *Plymouth Colony Records*, V, 61.
31. *Plymouth Colony Records*, IV, 47.
32. *Ibid.*, 103-4.
33. *Plymouth Colony Records*, III, 75.
34. *Plymouth Colony Records*, V, 29.
35. *Plymouth Colony Records*, IV, 93.
36. *Ibid.*, 125.

37. *Plymouth Colony Records*, VI, 191.
38. *Plymouth Colony Records*, V, 39.
39. *Ibid.*, 40.
40. *Plymouth Colony Records*, IV, 11.
41. *Plymouth Colony Records*, VI, 191.
42. *The Works of John Robinson*, I, 241.
43. Brigham, *The Compact with the Charter and Laws of the Colony of New Plymouth*, 245-46.
44. *Plymouth Colony Records*, III, 221.
45. There are three separate investigations dealing with this question: Bowen, *Early Rehoboth*, I, 15-24; Joseph B. Felt, "Population of Plymouth Colony," in American Statistical Association *Collections*, I, Pt. ii (Boston, 1845), 143-44; and Bradford, *Of Plymouth Plantation*, xi.
46. See Edmund Morgan, *The Puritan Family* (New York, 1966), esp. 46 ff.
47. *Plymouth Colony Records*, VI, 134-35.

Article 3

Participation in Public Affairs

Julia Cherry Spruill

Wifehood and motherhood . . . were held before the colonial woman as the purpose of her being, and home as the sphere of all her actions. Her mission in life was, first, to get a husband and then to keep him pleased, and her duties were bearing and rearing children and caring for her household. Her education, directed to these ends, consisted of instructions in morality, training in household occupations, and, among the upper classes, the acquirement of the social amenities. But while homemaking was the one occupation for which women were trained and was probably the sole business of a large majority, it did not absorb all the energies of some women and was by no means the only employment required of others. Quite a few gentlewomen interested themselves in affairs beyond their households, and a much larger number than is generally known were forced by necessity into performing services outside their own families.

Women, it will be remembered, had an active part in founding the southern colonies. Not only did wives accompany their husbands to the New World and share with them the hardships and responsibilities of subduing the wilderness, but single women came on their own ventures, bringing in new settlers, and establishing plantations.[1] It is true that women were desired as colonists chiefly to provide comfortable homes for the masculine settlers and to bear children to increase the population, but while performing these functions the more energetic were active also in public affairs. In the early records appear the names of a number who distinguished themselves in matters of common concern and of some who, while not deliberately championing the principle of political rights for their sex, were drawn into the public arena by their exertions in behalf of friends or relatives or in the protection of their own private estates.

From *Women's Life and Work in the Southern Colonies* (Chapel Hill: University of North Carolina Press, 1938), 232-246. Reprinted by permission.

Among the "women of figure" at Jamestown at an early date was the wife of Thomas Nuice, whose strenuous efforts in relieving the needs of the poor and suffering inhabitants of the little colony during the war and famine of 1622 were commended to the Virginia Company in London and inscribed in the public documents.[2] Another notable Virginia dame was remembered for her courage and independence during the same evil times. The historian Stith relates that during the fearful days following the Indian massacre the authorities, "much frightened at this lamentable and unexpected Disaster," decided to abandon the outlying plantations and assemble all the inhabitants into five or six of the most defensible places. It was impossible, naturally, on sudden notice for the planters to transfer their cattle and other goods, and several of the most daring, unwilling to leave their plantations to be pillaged by the Indians, refused to move themselves and their people. Among them was Mistress Alice Proctor, a widow, described as "a proper, civil, and modest Gentlewomen," who "with an heroic spirit" defended her plantation against the assaults of the Indians for over a month. Later she continued in her refusal to obey the order of the council to abandon her house for a safer place at Jamestown until the officers threatened to burn it down.[3]

A Virginia matron who at an early period left her housekeeping to interfere in political matters was Elizabeth Pott, wife of John Pott, one of Virginia's earliest physicians. Dr. Pott was acting governor of Virginia in 1629 and was later chief agitator against unpopular Governor Harvey. Soon after the arrival of Harvey in Virginia, Dr. Pott was charged with cattle stealing and tried before the general court. He was found guilty, but the question of his punishment was referred to the king of England. Mistress Pott, in defiance of authorities, boarded a vessel and traveled all the way to London to defend her husband before the king. There she pleaded his cause so earnestly that she secured a pardon for him.[4]

A few decades later, women were among the most zealous participants in the popular uprising known as Bacon's Rebellion. The wife of Anthony Haviland, one of the first to help gather the people together, was sent posthaste up and down the country as Bacon's emissary to carry his "declaration papers." Sarah Drummond, wife of William Drummond, Bacon's leading adviser, by her fiery speeches denouncing and defying Governor Berkeley, spurred the wavering to action. Sarah Grendon, wife of Colonel Thomas Grendon, was charged with being "a great encourager and assister in the late horrid Rebellion" and was the only woman excepted from the pardon in the act of indemnity and free pardon passed by the Assembly in February, 1677.[5]

Another instigator of rebellion was Lydia, wife of Major Edmund Chiesman, an insurgent who after Bacon's death was condemned to death by Berkeley. One of the chroniclers of the time gives this dramatic account of Mistress Chiesman's gallant defence of her husband: "When that the Major was brought into the Governours presence, and by him demanded, what made him to ingage in Bacon's designes? Before that the Major could frame an answer to the Governours demand; his Wife steps in and tould his honour that it was her provocations that made her husband joyne in the case that Bacon contended for; ading; that if he had not bin enfluenced by her instigations, he had never don that which he had done. Therefore (upon her bended knees) she desired of his honour, that since what her husband had done, was by her meanes, and so, by consequence, she most guilty, that she might be hanged and he pardoned. Though the Governour did know, that what she had saide, was neare to the truth, yet he said little to her request. . . ."[6] Mistress Chiesman's courageous shouldering of responsibility did not save her husband, for he escaped the gallows only by dying in prison before the governor's vengeance could be executed.

Other gentlewomen, wives of Berkeley's supporters, were impressed by the rebels into service in a unique manner. An Cotton, one of the leading chroniclers of the rebellion, gives this account of Bacon's extraordinary tactics: "He was no sooner arrived at Towne [Jamestown] but by several small partyes of Horse (2 or 3 in a party, for more he could not spare) he fetcheth into his little League, all the prime mens wives, whose Husbands were with the Governour, (as coll. Bacon's Lady, Madm. Bray, Madm. Page. Mdm. Ballard, and others) which the next morning he presents to the view of their husbands and ffriends in towne, upon the top of the small worke hee had cast up in the night; where he caused them to tarey till hee had finished his defence against his enemies shott. . . ."[7] Another annalist wrote of Bacon's placing the gentlewomen atop his breastworks: "The poor Gentlwomen were mightily astonished at this project; neither were their husbands voide of amazements at this subtill invention. If Mr. Fuller thought it strange, that the Divells black guard should be enrouled Gods shoulders, they made it no less wonderful, that their innocent and harmless wives should thus be entred a white garde to the Devill. This action was a method in war, that they were not well acquainted with (no not those the best inform'd in military affaires) that before they could com to pearce their enemies sides, they must be obliged to dart their weapons through their wives brest."[8] Naturally Berkeley's supporters refused to fire upon their wives. So, concluded the narrator, "these Ladyes white Aprons" proved to be of greater protection to Bacon and his men than all his fortifications.

Lady Berkeley was not among the "white aprons." Neither was she at home attending to household occupations. According to a letter written by Mistress Bacon to her sister, June 29, 1676, the governor had sent his lady to England with "great complaints" against Bacon, relying upon her, apparently, to represent to those in authority his side of the troublous events.[9]

Though the complaints carried by Dame Berkeley were first to reach the ears of the king, those of Bacon's female followers later also crossed the Atlantic and helped to bring royal censure and reproof upon the governor. When, after Bacon's sudden death and the subsequent disorganization of his supporters Berkeley regained power, he charged the chief of his opponents with treason, confiscated their estates, and had twenty-three hanged. Among these was William Drummond, husband of the spirited Sarah. Mistress Drummond did not bow in calm resignation to the governor's orders. Determined to justify her husband and proclaim Berkeley's harshness as well as to regain her property, she sent a petition to the Lords for Trade and Plantations, explaining that her husband had been sentenced to die by martial law and executed, though he had never borne arms or any military office, and that the governor had seized his plantation and goods and forced her and her five children to fly from their habitation. Her case was reported to the king, who ordered that her property be restored and announced that her husband had been put to death contrary to the laws of the kingdom.[10]

In Maryland as in Virginia, women took part in political and religious struggles and were active in other public matters. An account of the quarrel and battle between Governor Stone and the Puritan Party in 1655 mentions women among the participants. It tells of the Puritans' capture of the governor and all his company and relates that the victors condemned ten to death, executed four, and would have executed all had it not been for the incessant pleading of some good women, which saved some, and the petitions of the soldiers, which saved others.[11] The Puritans, endeavoring to prevent stories of their brutality from getting abroad and determined to have only favorable accounts of their actions presented before Cromwell, immediately sent dispatches to England and attempted to keep their prisoners incommunicado. But the governor's wife, Virlinda, who had not been allowed to see her wounded husband, was determined that he and his followers should not suffer from the misrepresentation of Puritan messengers. She wrote at once to Lord Baltimore, describing the armed conflict and explaining the issues from the governor's point of view. Her letter shows not merely a keen interest in her husband's predicament but also an understanding of the whole political situation.[12] Another Maryland matron to plead her husband's cause before his enemies could "make their owne tale" in England was Barbara Smith, wife of Captain Richard Smith of Calvert County. During the Revolution of 1689, when her husband was imprisoned for refusing to take part with the insurgents, Mistress Smith hurried to England to lay his case before the authorities there.[13]

The outstanding woman in early Maryland, however, was not a devoted wife, but, as she appears repeatedly in the records, "Mistresse Margarett Brent, Spinster." This remarkable woman was not only the most conspicuous of her sex, but was one of the most prominent personages in the colony, whose business and public activities fill many pages of court records and suggest a career which the most ambitious of modern feminists might envy. Margaret Brent was of distinguished family and apparently a person of means, but as a Catholic she suffered persecution in England. Dissatisfied, probably, with the disabilities of her family under the English laws and encouraged by Lord Baltimore's extraordinary offers of land and privileges in Maryland, she decided to emigrate, and, with her brothers Giles and Fulke and her sister Mary, arrived in the province in November 1638.

Though accompanied by their brothers, the Mistresses Brent came on their own ventures, bringing in servants, patenting large tracts of land in their own rights, and establishing plantations. As owners of manorial estates, they had the right to hold courts-baron, where controversies relating to manor lands were tried and tenants did fealty for their lands, and courts-leet, where residents on their manors were tried for criminal offences. One of the few surviving records of a court-baron is of that held at St. Gabriel's Manor by the steward of Mistress Mary Brent, where the tenant appeared, "did fealty to the Lady," and took possession of thirty-seven acres according to the custom of the manor.[14] Whether Mistress Margaret exercised such feudal rights over her tenants does not appear, but the many references to her in the minutes of the provincial court bear witness to her diligence and perseverance in prosecuting her debtors. Between the years 1642 and 1650 her name occurs no less than one hundred and thirty-four times in the court records, and during these eight years there was hardly a court at which she did not have at least one case. Occasionally she appeared as defendant, but oftener as plaintiff, and, it is interesting to know, a majority of these cases were decided in her favor.

Her successful handling of her own affairs probably accounts for her being called upon often to act on behalf of her friends and members of her family. When her brother Fulke returned to England, he gave her a power of attorney to conduct his affairs, and on several occasions she acted for her older brother, Giles.[15] As guardian of the little Indian princess, Mary Kittamaquund, daughter of the Piscataway Emperor, she brought suits and collected debts due her, and she also acted as agent for other gentlewomen.[16] Because she so frequently transacted business for others by power of attorney, it has been mistakenly assumed that she was an attorney at law, but no evidence appears to show that she made any claim to membership in the legal profession.

During the first eight years of her residence in Maryland, Mistress Brent's energies were exerted largely in the conduct of private business, but rapidly moving events following the civil wars thrust her into a position of great public responsibility and for a time placed in her hands the destiny of the whole colony. Leonard Calvert, the governor, went to England in April, 1643, to consult with his brother, Lord Baltimore, about affairs in the province and, on his return in September, 1644, found the colony on the verge of an insurrection. Led by William Claiborne and Richard Ingle, a band of rebels soon took possession of Kent Island, invaded the western shore, and established themselves at St. Mary's. Governor Calvert with a large number of the councillors fled to Virginia, leaving Maryland in a state of anarchy. Toward the end of 1646 he returned with a small force of Virginians and Maryland refugees, entered St. Mary's, and established his authority over the province. But he had hardly restored order when on June 9, 1647, he died, leaving Maryland once more without a strong hand to direct her affairs.[17] On his deathbed, by a nuncupative will, he named Thomas Greene to succeed him as governor and appointed Margaret Brent his executrix with the enigmatical instruction, "Take all and pay all."[18]

With her appointment as executrix of Governor Calvert, Margaret Brent's public career began. She was summoned into court to answer numerous suits for his debts and found it necessary to start legal proceedings for sums due his estate. The most urgent matter before her was the satisfaction of debts due the soldiers of Fort Inigoes. Governor Calvert had brought these volunteers from Virginia to help regain the government from the rebels, and, in order to secure their much needed services, had pledged his entire estate and that of the Lord Proprietor to pay them. Before his executrix could complete her inventory, the captain of the fort, on behalf of the soldiers, demanded their back wages and secured an attachment upon the whole Calvert estate.[19]

Mistress Brent now found herself confronted by a grave and critical situation. Leonard Calvert's estate was inadequate to meet the demands upon it. The price of corn was soaring higher and higher and famine threatened. Enemies of the existing government were just outside the borders of the province, awaiting an opportunity for a new invasion, and the hungry soldiers in the fort, frightened by the rise in prices and the scarcity of food, became unruly and threatened mutiny. Realizing the necessity for prompt and decisive measures, she demanded and obtained a power to act as attorney for the Lord Proprietor and quieted the clamorous soldiers by promising to send to Virginia for corn and by selling enough of the proprietary's cattle to pay them. Thus she rescued the struggling little colony from certain disaster and very probably saved it from all the evils of another civil war.

One of Maryland's historians, commenting upon her courageous handling of the situation, suggests that Leonard Calvert might have done better had he reversed his testamentary dispositions and made Margaret Brent governor and Thomas Greene executor.[20] But it was not a day of political rights for women, as Mistress Margaret soon discovered. On January 21, 1647, probably in order to be in a better position to look after the Calvert interests, she went before the assembly and demanded a seat, thereby unconsciously distinguishing herself as the first woman in America to claim the right to vote. The minutes of the proceedings for the day state: "Came Mrs Margarett Brent and requested to have vote in the howse for herselfe and voyce also for that att the last Court 3d: Jan: it was ordered that the said Mrs. Brent was to be looked upon and received as his Lordships

Attorney. The Governor denied that the sd Mrs Brent should have any vote in the howse."[21] She did not submit quietly to this decision, however, for, according to the record, she protested against all the proceedings in the assembly unless she might be present and vote.

The members of the assembly, while unwilling to allow a woman within the sacred precincts of their ordained sphere, nevertheless appreciated her public services and commended her to the Lord Proprietor. Lord Baltimore, ignorant of the succession of disturbances in his colony and hearing of the bold manner in which Margaret Brent had taken matters into her own hands and disposed of his cattle, wrote to the assembly, complaining of her highhandedness. In answer, the assembly wrote him a long letter describing the calamities and disorders they had suffered and concluding with this earnest justification of their countrywoman: ". . . as for Mrs Brents undertaking and medling with your Lordships Estate here (whether she procured it with her own and others importunity or no) we do Verily Believe and in Conscience report that it was better for the Collonys safety at that time in her hands than in any mans else in the whole Province after your Brothers death for the Soldiers would never have treated any other with that Civility and respect and though they were even ready at times to run into mutiny yet she still pacified them till at the last things were brought to that straight that she must be admitted and declared your Lordships Attorney by an order of Court (the Copy whereof is herewith inclosed) or else all must go to ruin Again and then the second mischief had been doubtless far greater than the former so that if there hath not been any sinister use made of your Lordships Estate by her from what it was intended and engaged for by Mr Calvert before his death, as we verily Believe she hath not, then we conceive from that time she rather deserved favour and thanks from your Honour for her so much Concurring to the Public Safety then to be liable to all those bitter invectives you have been pleased to express against her."[22] Lord Baltimore was not moved by this spirited defence to withdraw his accusations or to express any appreciation of Mistress Brent's services, but continued distrustful and hostile.

Margaret Brent's fall from grace, however, was not due altogether to her selling the proprietary cattle. She and her family were the victims of a new policy which the proprietor was observing in order to meet the change in English politics. A shrewd politician, Lord Baltimore warily watched the undercurrents of popular feeling in England, determined to gain the good will of those in power and thereby save his proprietary estates by whatever means he found expedient. Perceiving the rise of the Puritans to power in Parliament, he sought to conciliate them by showing disfavor to prominent Catholics and granting concessions to Protestants in Maryland.[23] Deprived of the Maryland Proprietor's favor, the Brents moved down to Westmoreland County in Virginia, where they patented land and established a plantation, giving it the significant name "Peace." Though Mistress Margaret continued active in the conduct of business for other people and for herself, she was no longer prominent in political affairs and after about 1650 her name disappears from the public records.

The idea of a woman's conducting business enterprises and having a hand in public matters was not new to the early colonists. It was customary for English women of the aristocracy to be interested in national affairs and for those of the lower classes to be engaged in what today we call gainful occupations. Family letters and other records present gentlewomen as active participants on both sides of the political and religious struggles of the first half of the seventeenth century.[24] Among the nobility, the management of the family estate was often left to the care of the wife while the husband was detained at court, was devoting himself to politics, science or religion, or was abroad for business or pleasure. The wife of the English husbandman looked after the farm during his absence and at his death frequently took over its entire management. Poorer women labored for wages in the fields at almost every kind of farm work. Women of means sometimes carried on enterprises requiring considerable capital, and wives of shopkeepers and tradesmen, whose places of business were ordinarily in the home, commonly assisted their husbands in their shops. Women also practiced medicine and surgery and had almost a complete monopoly in the field of obstetrics.[25]

But with the advance of the seventeenth century, English women of the upper classes came to be less concerned with business and other affairs. The great increase in wealth and the vogue for frivolous entertainments following the Restoration discouraged the exercise of initiative, energy, and independence in the conduct of practical affairs and brought about a rapid deterioration in the physique, the morale, and the general efficiency of upper-class women.[26] Their whole education in the eighteenth century stressed sex differences, encouraged the development of passive rather than active qualities, opposed robustness of mind and body as vulgar, and emphasized the importance of ornamental rather than utilitarian accomplishments. In the southern colonies also the eighteenth century saw a decline in the vigor and self-reliance of women in wealthier families and a lessening of their influence in public matters. Because of the rural character of their lives and the general influence of the frontier, American ladies were less idle and artificial than those in England, but compared with the daring and independent matrons of the preceding century, they appear somewhat effeminate and timid.

In the back settlements and on the frontier, women continued to be valued for their strength and valor, and though their exploits seldom got into the records, they were probably busy with many matters beyond their cabins. The early records of Georgia tell of the important part played by Mary Musgrove [later Matthews], daughter of an Indian mother and an English father, and wife of a Carolina trader.[27] Finding that she could speak the Creek language as well as English and that she had a great influence over the Indians and was a skillful diplomat, Oglethorpe secured her services as interpreter and adviser on Indian affairs, agreeing to allow her an annual stipend of one hundred pounds. That he relied upon her advice is evident in many references to her like the following in the secretary's journal: "Matthews Wife has always been in great Esteem with the General, and not without good Reason; for being half Indian by Extract, she has a very great influence upon many of them, particularly the Creek Nation, our next neighbours . . . and the General would advise with her in many Things, for his better dealing with the Indians; taking her generally for his Interpreter, and using her very kindly on all Occasions."[28]

Mary was a person of means as well as influence. She owned broad acres of valuable land and had many Indian traders under her command. When food was scarce, she supplied the hungry colonists with provisions and at her own expense furnished Indian warriors to serve Oglethorpe. When trouble threatened with the neighboring Spanish colony of Florida, Oglethorpe sent her to the border to establish a trading post on the Altamaha River, from which she could watch the Spaniards and acquaint him with their movements and at the same time treat with the Indians and keep them on friendly terms with the Georgia colonists. When hostilities began, she rallied her war Indians to Oglethorpe's side and sent her traders to the conflict. Until her marriage with Thomas Bosomworth, an avaricious and unscrupulous English clergyman, who attempted to use her influence over the Indians and in the colony to acquire wealth and power for himself, she continued to be of incalculable help to Oglethorpe and the colonists.[29] One of Georgia's historians writes of her services: "Her assistance was invaluable, and her aid, not only in concluding treaties but also in securing warriors from the Creek confederacy during the conflict between Georgia and Florida, indispensable. Promptly did she respond on all occasions to any request made of her. . . . She was certainly of great use to him [Oglethorpe] and to the colony."[30]

Other women in pioneer communities probably played important rôles which were not committed to record, and . . . many throughout the colonies were occupied with making a living. But those who enjoyed the advantages of wealth and refinement came more and more to be content to be "shining ornaments" in their families. A comparison of petitions presented by the undaunted dames of the first years of the colonies with the requests of the more modest ladies of the next century reveals a consciousness of sex and an unnatural prudishness in the latter not observable in their pioneer grandmothers. Sarah Drummond, Virlinda Stone, and Margaret Brent stated their requests confidently and boldly, professed no ignorance of politics, and made no attempt to excuse their interference in public matters. Their petitions disclose no doubts regarding their ability to understand and explain the political issues of the time or their right to interpose in matters of public concern. The women of the later period appear disinclined to admit any interest in public policy and anxious lest their private requests be mistaken for an unwomanly meddling in politics. One petitioner, for instance, soliciting Governor Martin of North Carolina regarding some requirements made of her husband, was very careful to preface her entreaty with this modest declaration: "It is not for me, unacquainted as I am with the politics and laws, to say with what propriety this was done."[31] A petition of some ladies of Wilmington, North Carolina, asking the governor to rescind an order regarding the removal of the wives and children of Tories from the state, declares apologetically, "It is not the province of our sex to reason deeply upon the policy of the order," and justifies their "earnest supplication" on the grounds that it was prompted by the distress of the innocent and helpless.[32]

These petitioners had evidently been carefully educated in the eighteenth-century ideals of female character. They had doubtless read in their *Spectators* that participating in politics was "repugnant to the softness, the modesty, and those other endearing qualities . . .

natural to the fair sex," and agreed that gentlewomen should "distin-guish themselves as tender mothers and faithful wives rather than as furious partisans."[33] In many admonitions like the following from one of their textbooks on behavior, they had been warned against pre-suming to understand political matters: "It [politics] is a subject entirely above your sphere. I would not willingly resign any of the privileges that properly belong to our sex; but, I hope, I shall have all the sensible part of it on my side, when I affirm that the conduct and management of state affairs is a thing with which we have no concern. Perhaps our natural abilities are not equal to such an arduous task; at any rate, our education, as it is now conducted, is too slight and superficial to render us competent judges of these matters; and I have always thought it as ridiculous for a woman to put herself in a passion about political disputes, as it would be for a man to spend his time haranguing upon the colour of a silk, or the water of a diamond."[34]

During the Revolution, women emerged for a time from their circumscribed sphere. Moralists who had maintained that woman's interests should be confined to her family, as soon as serious national difficulties threatened, sought to arouse her patriotism and began to apprise her of her public duty. Journalists who previously had com-mended the sex for their retiring modesty, now praised the more daring female patriots for their display of zeal. Women who joined themselves into associations and gave public demonstrations of their patriotism were applauded loudly and even had their names printed in the papers.[35] The lively protests of the ladies of the famous Edenton tea party, which provoked the customary ridicule from male wits in England, were commended by neighboring journalists.[36] The voluntary association of "the young ladies of the best families of Mecklenburg County" in North Carolina and their public declara-tions not to receive the addresses of any gentleman who had failed to do his military duty were acclaimed by the newspapers as signifi-. cant and exemplary proceedings,[37] and similar resolutions adopted by the ladies of Rowan County were entered into the minutes of the Committee of Safety as "worthy the imitation of every young lady in America."[38] Enthusiastic matrons plunged into the conflict and wrote fiery articles for the newspapers inciting their countrywomen to action. One of these ardent patriots wrote that when she reflected on the American grievances she was ready to start up with sword in hand to fight by the side of her husband.[39] Other correspondents urged their countrywomen not to be "tame spectators" and reminded them that "much, very much depends on the public virtue the ladies will exert at this critical juncture."[40]

But the Revolution had no permanent effect on the status of women. The author of the Declaration of Independence believed that woman's place was the home and hoped that American women would be "too wise to wrinkle their foreheads with politics."[41] The popular phrases, "rights of man," and "all men are created free and equal," so often on the lips of men and women of the period, were generally applied to men only. Glancing into the future, we find the founders of the republic no more ready to permit their wives and daughters to have a hand in public affairs than were the founders of the colonies.

In church affairs as in those of government, while women were generally supposed to be meek and quiet onlookers, they were sometimes persons of influence. The Anglican Church, the established form of worship in all the southern colonies, held strictly to the Pauline doctrine regarding woman, maintaining her inferiority and subjection in the creation and her exclusion from all church offices. Representative of the views of orthodox divines, were those of the author of *The Ladies Calling.* While regarding woman as the "weaker vessel," he allowed her a soul "of as Divine an Original" and as "endless a Duration" as that of man. Indeed, "in respect to their eternal well-being," he believed God gave women advantages over men, for he implanted in them "some native propensions" toward virtue and "closelier fenced them in" from temptations and "those wider excursions, for which the customary liberties of the other Sex afford a more open way." Piety was a virtue enjoined especially on woman and irreligion was more odious in her than in man. But, though possessing "peculiar aptness" toward piety, she should not presume to lift her voice in the church. The silence enjoined upon the sex by the apostle, he declared, was based "not only on the inferiority of the Woman in regard of the creation and first sin ... but also on the presumption that they needed instruction."[42] Nonconformists, though holding somewhat different views of her natural tendency toward virtue, agreed that woman should not presume to understand theology, pass judgment on the sermons, or teach in the church. But they all expected her to understand the fundamental principles of religion well enough to teach them to her children and servants, and, if her husband were an unbeliever, to reclaim him by persuasive arguments as well as by her good example. Also, though she had no voice in church business, it was taken for granted that she was a more faithful attendant at divine services than her husband, and a generous contributor. . . .

NOTES

1. See Spruill, *Women's Life and Work in the Southern Colonies,* p. 11.
2. *Records of the Virginia Company of London,* II, 383.
3. William Stith, *History of Virginia,* pp. 235-36; *William and Mary Quarterly,* XV, 39.
4. *Ibid.,* XIV, 99.
5. *Ibid.,* XV, 41.
6. "Narrative of the Indian and Civil Wars in Virginia, in the Years 1675 and 1676." *Force Tracts,* I (No. 11), 34.
7. "An Account of Our Late Troubles in Virginia," *Force Tracts,* I (No. 9), 8.
8. "Narrative of the Indian and Civil Wars in Virginia," *Force Tracts,* I, (No. 11), 22.
9. *William and Mary Quarterly,* IX, 5.
10. *Virginia Magazine,* XXII, 235-36; Neill, *Virginia Carolorum,* p. 380.
11. John Langford, "Refutation of Babylon's Fall," *Narratives of Early Maryland,* p. 264.
12. The whole of her letter is given in the *Narratives of Maryland,* pp. 265-67.
13. *Archives of Maryland,* VIII, 153; *Maryland Magazine,* II, 374.
14. *Archives of Maryland,* IV, 417.
15. *Ibid.,* IV, 192, 228, 357, 477, 481; X, 28, 49.
16. *Ibid.,* IV, 259, 264, 265, 487-88.
17. William Hand Browne, *Maryland: A History of a Palatinate* (Boston and New York, 1884), pp. 58-64.
18. *Archives of Maryland,* IV, 314.
19. *Ibid.,* p. 338.
20. Browne, *op. cit.,* p. 64.
21. *Archives of Maryland,* I, 215.
22. *Ibid.,* I, 216-17.
23. Matthew Page Andrews, *History of Maryland: Province and State* (New York, 1929), p. 93.
24. Alice Clark, *Working Life of Women in the Seventeenth Century* (London and New York, 1919), pp. 23-28.
25. *Ibid.,* pp. 14-23, 29-35, 44-92, 150-289.
26. *Ibid.,* pp. 35-41.
27. After Musgrove's death, Mary married Jacob Matthews, and as a third husband married Rev. Thomas Bosomworth.

28. *Colonial Records of Georgia*, IV, 518.
29. Merton Coulter, "Mary Musgrove, Queen of the Creeks," *Georgia Historical Quarterly*, XI, 1–30.
30. Charles C. Jones, *History of Georgia* (2 vols. Boston and New York, 1883), I, 384.
31. *State Records of North Carolina*, XVI, 389–90.
32. *Ibid.*, pp. 467–79.
33. Nos. 57, 81, 342.
34. *The Polite Lady*, pp. 266–67.
35. Articles of this type appear in the *Virginia Gazette*, December 24, 1767, February 18, 1768, July 27, 1769, January 20 and 27, 1774, June 9 and November 3, 1774; *South Carolina Gazette*, April 3, 1775; *South Carolina Gazette and Country Journal*, January 7, 1766, August 2, 1774; *Georgia Gazette*, January 6, 1768; (Fayetteville) *North Carolina Gazette*, September 14, 1789.
36. *Virginia Gazette*, November 3, 1774. Postscript.
37. *South Carolina and American General Gazette*, February 9, 1776.
38. *Colonial Records of North Carolina*, X, 594.
39. *Virginia Gazette*, September 21, 1776.
40. *Ibid.*, September 15, 1774.
41. *Writings of Thomas Jefferson* (ed., Ford), V, 390–91. Also Randolph, *Domestic Life of Thomas Jefferson*, p. 158.
42. (2d ed., 1673), pp. 8–9, 81, 101.

Article 4

The Dynamics of Interracial Sex in Colonial America

Winthrop D. Jordan

When Europeans met Africans in America the result was slavery, revolt, the sociability of daily life, and, inevitably, sexual union. The blending of black and white began almost with the first contact of the two peoples and has far outlasted the institution of chattel slavery. It became, in some English colonies, almost an institution in itself. It rivaled the slave revolt as a source of tension. It may even have equaled the pressure of daily contact as a mechanism of cultural fusion. Most important, however, was the reticular complex of tensions which arose concerning interracial mixture.

These tensions may be viewed in several interrelated ways. The Englishmen who came to America brought with them not merely a prevalent social mood but also certain specific sexual mores and certain more or less definite ideas about African sexuality. Many of them came with more or less explicit intentions as to the proper character of the communities they wished to establish in the wilderness. These intentions were not always, or perhaps ever, fully realized; they were deflected—again sometimes more, sometimes less— by conditions in the New World. One of the most important deflectors was the development of a racial slavery which itself became one of the New World's "conditions," though of course the character of this condition was not everywhere the same. Presumably all Englishmen would have had similar reactions (allowing for enormous and significant variations among individuals and groups) to the attributes which set the Negro apart if they had perceived these attributes in similar contexts. But of course the Negro was encountered in very different contexts in the various English colonies. Particularly important in making for such differences was the demographic pattern which matured during the first quarter of the eighteenth century;

From *White Over Black: American Attitudes Toward the Negro, 1550-1812* (Chapel Hill: University of North Carolina Press, 1968), 136-150. Reprinted by permission.

variations in the numbers of the races and of the sexes in the English colonies may be shown to be almost determinative in shaping certain attitudes. These attitudes did not of course spring full blown from demographic tables, but demographic conditions did do a great deal to shape attitudes by imparting to racial intermixture distinct social functions and meanings in various regions. Within these varying social contexts, moreover, English colonials acted and reacted in revealing ways which serve to expose how powerfully and pervasively the most basic human biological and psychic energies were in operation and how, too, these energies affected the character of the emergent English communities in America.

1. REGIONAL STYLES IN RACIAL INTERMIXTURE

Miscegenation was extensive in all the English colonies, a fact made evident to contemporaries by the presence of large numbers of mulattoes. It is impossible to ascertain how much intermixture there actually was, though it seems likely there was more during the eighteenth century than at any time since.[1] Although miscegenation was probably most common among the lower orders, white men of every social rank slept with Negro women.[2] The colonists, as well as European travelers in the colonies, frequently pointed to this facet of American life.

No one thought intermixture was a good thing. Rather, English colonials were caught in the push and pull of an irreconcilable conflict between desire and aversion for interracial sexual union. The perceptual prerequisite for this conflict is so obvious as to be too easily overlooked: desire and aversion rested on the bedrock fact that white men perceived Negroes as being *both alike and different* from themselves. Without perception of similarity, no desire and no widespread gratification was possible. Without perception of difference, on the other hand, no aversion to miscegenation nor tension concerning it could have arisen. Without perception of difference, of course, the term *miscegenation* had no meaning. Given the simultaneous feelings of desire and aversion, it seems probable that of the two the latter is more demanding of explanation. The sexual drive of human beings has always, in the long run, overridden even the strongest sense of difference between two groups of human beings and, in some individuals, has even overridden the far stronger sense which men have of the difference between themselves and animals. What demands explanation, in short, is why there was any aversion among the white colonists to sexual union with Negroes. More than desire, aversion was a manifestation of cultural rather than biological patterns, so that the answers may be looked for in the qualities of the various cultural settings which were emerging in English America and to the prevailing patterns of miscegenation which constituted important elements in New World cultural styles.

In most colonies virtually all the offspring of these unions were illegitimate, but legally sanctified interracial marriages did occur, especially though not exclusively in New England. Miscegenation in colonial America, as has been true since, typically involved fornication between white men and Negro women, though the inverse combination was common, far more common than is generally supposed. Probably a majority of interracial marriages in New England involved Negro men and white women of "the meaner sort."[3] In the plantation colonies, though there were occasional instances of white women marrying Negroes, legitimization of this relationship was unusual. Yet white men were sometimes left to ponder indignities such as that suffered (and in return imposed) by a Maryland man who advertised in 1759 that he would no longer be responsible for his wife's debts because "*Mary Skinner,* my Wife, has, after all the Love and Tenderness which could possibly be shown by Man to a Woman, polluted my Bed, by taking to her in my Stead, her own Negro Slave, by whom she hath a Child, which hath occasioned so much Disgrace to me and my Family, that I have thought proper to forbid her my Sight any more."[4]

Public feeling about miscegenation was strong enough to force itself over the hurdles of the legislative process into the statute books of many English continental colonies. As early as the 1660's the Maryland and Virginia assemblies had begun to lash out at miscegenation in language dripping with distaste and indignation. By the turn of the century it was clear in many continental colonies that the English settlers felt genuine revulsion for interracial sexual union, at least in principle. About 1700 the Chester County Court in Pennsylvania ordered a Negro "never more to meddle with any white woman more uppon paine of his life."[5] Statutory prohibitions roughly similar to those of the tobacco colonies and Bermuda were adopted by Massachusetts in 1705, North Carolina in 1715, South Carolina in 1717, Pennsylvania in 1726, and by Georgia when Negroes were admitted to the colony in 1750. Delaware enacted no

outright prohibition but prescribed heavier fines for interracial bas-
tardy cases than for such cases involving two white persons. Thus
two northern and all the plantation colonies legally prohibited miscegenation.[6] Community feeling was of course not monolithically
arrayed against interracial union: in 1699 several citizens petitioned
the Virginia Council for repeal of the intermarriage prohibition, and
as late as 1755 the North Carolina Assembly responded favorably to
a petition by inhabitants from several counties asking repeal of the
laws in which "free Negroes and Mulatto's Intermarrying with white
women are obliged to pay taxes for their wives and families."[7] In
general, though, the weight of community opinion was set heavily
against the sexual union of white and black, as the long-standing
statutory prohibitions indicated. Even in South Carolina, where
interracial liaisons were less carefully concealed than elsewhere on
the continent, a grand jury in 1743 publicly condemned "THE TOO
COMMON PRACTICE of CRIMINAL CONVERSATION with
NEGRO and other SLAVE WENCHES IN THIS PROVINCE, as
an Enormity and Evil of general Ill-Consequence." In significant
contrast, none of the West Indian assemblies prohibited extramarital
miscegenation and only one took the probably unnecessary step of
banning racial intermarriage.[8]

In the West Indian colonies especially, and less markedly in
South Carolina, the entire pattern of miscegenation was far more
inflexible than in the other English settlements. White women in the
islands did not sleep with Negro men, let alone marry them. Nor did
white men actually marry Negroes or mulattoes: as one usually
temperate planter declared, "The very idea is shocking."[9] Yet white
men commonly, almost customarily, took Negro women to bed with
little pretense at concealing the fact. Colored mistresses were kept
openly. "The Planters are in general rich," a young traveler wrote,
"but a set of dissipating, abandoned, and cruel people. Few even of
the married ones, but keep a Mulatto or Black Girl in the house or at
lodgings for certain purposes."[10] Edward Long of Jamaica described
the situation more vividly: "He who should presume to shew any
displeasure against such a thing as simple fornication, would for his
pains be accounted a simple blockhead; since not one in twenty can
be persuaded, that there is either sin; or shame in cohabiting with
his slave."[11] Negro concubinage was an integral part of island life,
tightly interwoven into the social fabric.

It is scarcely necessary to resort to speculation about the influence of tropical climate in order to explain this situation, for life in

the islands was in large degree shaped by the enormous dispropor-
tion of Negroes to white settlers and characterized by the concomitant brutal nakedness of planter domination over the slaves. In the
West Indian islands and to less extent South Carolina, racial slavery
consisted of unsheathed dominion by relatively small numbers of
white men over enormous numbers of Negroes, and it was in these
colonies that Negro men were most stringently barred from sexual
relations with white women. Sexually as well as in every other way,
Negroes were utterly subordinated. White men extended their dominion over their Negroes to the bed, where the sex act itself served
as ritualistic re-enactment of the daily pattern of social dominance.
In New England, at the other extreme, white men had no need for
agressive assertion of their dominance in order to sustain slavery on
a major scale and hence in New England Negro men were accorded
some measure of sexual freedom.

Congruent to these regional differences in slavery and interracial relationships were the bedrock demographic facts which so
powerfully influenced, perhaps even determined, the kind of society
which emerged in each colony. With Negroes overwhelmingly outnumbering white men in the various islands (ten to one in Jamaica),
and with white men outnumbering Negroes everywhere on the
continent except South Carolina, it was inevitable that radically
dissimilar social styles should have developed in the two areas. As a
French traveler perceptively epitomized this dissimilarity in 1777,
when it had become so evident in the pattern of revolt against Great
Britain: "In the colonies of the Antilles, most of the colonists are
people who have left their homeland with the intention of rebuilding
their fortunes. Far from settling in the islands, they look upon them
merely as a land of exile, never as a place where they plan to live,
prosper, and die. On the other hand, the Anglo-American colonists
are permanent, born in the country and attached to it; they have no
motherland save the one they live in; and, although London formerly was so considered, they have clearly proved that they held it
in less esteem than they did the prosperity, tranquility, and freedom
of their own country."[12] The West Indian planters were lost not so
much in the Caribbean as in a sea of blacks. They found it impossible to re-create English culture as they had known it. They were
corrupted by living in a police state, though not themselves the
objects of its discipline. The business of the islands was business, the
production of agricultural staples; the islands were not where one
really lived, but where one made one's money. By contrast, the

American colonists on the continent maintained their hold upon their English background, modifying it less for accommodating slavery than for winning the new land. They were sufficiently numerous to create a new culture with a self-evident validity of its own, complete with the adjustments necessary to absorb non-English Europeans. Unlike the West Indian planters, they felt no need to be constantly running back to England to reassure themselves that they belonged to civilization. Because they were conscious of having attained a large measure of success in transplanting their own society, they vehemently rejected any trespass upon it by a people so alien as the Negroes. The islanders could hardly resent trespass on something which they did not have. By sheer weight of numbers their society was black and slave.

It was precisely this difference which made the Negro seem so much more alien on the continent than on the islands and miscegenation accordingly less common. For a West Indian to have declared, with Samuel Sewall of Boston, that Negroes "cannot mix with us and become members of society, . . . never embody with us, and grow up into orderly Families, to the Peopling of the Land" would have been false by reason of the extensive blending of the races in the islands and meaningless because the "peopling" of the islands had already been accomplished—by Negroes. Americans on the continent stood poised for a destiny of conquering a vast wilderness while Englishmen in the little crowded islands looked forward down a precipice of slave rebellion or at best a slippery slope of peaceful but inevitable defeat. It was geography rather than culture which in the last analysis placed South Carolina closer to Massachusetts than to the islands. Certainly the bustling communities on the continent had good reason to feel that they had successfully established a beachhead of English civilization in America. They possessed optimism, self-confidence, and a well-defined sense of Englishness, a sense which came automatically to bear when they were confronted with peoples who for whatever reason seemed appreciably dissimilar. When large numbers of very dissimilar people threatened the identity of the continental colonists, their response was rejection of those people in the mind and a tendency to perceive them as being more dissimilar than ever. For the sense of dissimilarity fed on itself: once the cycle was started, the differences between Americans and "others," which first sparked anxiety and rejection, loomed progressively larger and generated further anxiety and rejection.

Certainly many Americans on the continent became convinced that the American people were not intended to be Negroes. Benjamin Franklin, who was as fully attuned to American destiny as anyone, nervously expressed this feeling in his famous *Observations Concerning the Increase of Mankind* (1751), where one of his main purposes was demonstration that the American continent was of all regions upon the globe the most conducive to population growth. After throwing querulous aspersions at the Germans in Pennsylvania, he pointed out (as has been frequently pointed out since) that "the Number of purely white People in the World is proportionably very small." Even most Europeans, including the Germans, he declared, "are generally of what we call a swarthy Complexion." The Saxons and the English "make the principal Body of White People on the Face of the Earth." And though Benjamin Franklin plainly felt awkward in expressing the idea and consequently presented it in fanciful terms, he was convinced that America should belong to the "White People." "I could wish their Numbers were increased. And while we are, as I may call it, *Scouring* our Planet, by clearing America of Woods, and so making this Side of our Globe reflect a brighter Light to the Eyes of Inhabitants in Mars or Venus, why should we in the Sight of Superior Beings, darken its People? Why increase the Sons of Africa, by Planting them in America, where we have so fair an Opportunity, by excluding all Blacks and Tawneys, of increasing the lovely White and Red? But perhaps I am partial to the Complexion of my Country," he concluded with his usual self-conscious good sense, "for such Kind of Partiality is natural to Mankind." With all his puns and despite his apologetics, Franklin was expressing an important feeling, one which a famous Virginian, William Byrd, expressed more directly: "They import so many Negros hither, that I fear this Colony will some time or other be confirmed by the Name of New Guinea."[13]

It was more than a matter of colonial Americans not wanting to give their country over to the Africans. Miscegenation probably did not seem so much a matter of long-term discoloration as an immediate failure to live up to immemorial standards. Here again, the intentions which drove English overseas expansion were of crucial importance. The colonists' conviction that they must sustain their civilized condition wherever they went rendered miscegenation *ipso facto* a negation of the underlying plan of settlement in America. Simply because most Negroes were chattel slaves, racial amalgamation was stamped as irredeemably illicit; it was irretrievably associated with loss of control over the baser passions, with weakening of traditional family ties, and with breakdown of proper social ordering. Judge Sewall's "orderly Families" were rendered a mockery by fathers taking slave wenches to bed.

At the same time it would be absurd to suppose that the status of Negroes in itself aroused American aversion to intermixture and that the physical difference in Negroes was of slight importance. Without that difference there could never have developed well-formulated conceptions about sexual relations between Africans and Europeans in America. Although perhaps there was some feeling that the laws which prevented racial intermingling helped prevent Negroes, as one astute foreign observer put it, "from forming too great opinions of themselves," the underlying reason for their passage was that these mixtures were "disagreeable" to white men. Probably it was this feeling which prompted the prominent Boston merchant, James Bowdoin, to ship one of his Negroes to the West Indies in exchange for produce or another Negro boy, explaining that "my Man Caesar has been engaged in an amour with some of the white ladies of the Town." When Mrs. Anne Grant recalled her early years in the colony of New York she daintily reported that the citizens of Albany possessed a particular "moral delicacy" on one point: "they were from infancy in habits of familiarity with these humble friends [the Negroes], yet being early taught that nature had placed between them a barrier, which it was in a high degree criminal and disgraceful to pass, they considered a mixture of such distinct races with abhorrence, as a violation of her laws."[14]

2. MASCULINE AND FEMININE MODES IN CAROLINA AND AMERICA

While the "laws" of nature seem to have appeared in abundant clarity in Albany, New York, they were very dimly perceived in Charleston, South Carolina, where white persons were surrounded by so many more "humble friends." On the face of things it seems paradoxical that the one region on the continent which had become demographically most like a new Guinea should have been the one in which white men seemed least anxious about interracial sexual activity. While permanent unions between persons of the two races normally were quiet or secretive affairs elsewhere on the continent, in South Carolina and particularly in Charleston they were not. It was the only city worthy of the name in the plantation colonies. It was an elegant, gay, extravagant city, where men took advantage of certain of their opportunities in more overt, more relaxed, and probably more enterprising fashion than in the colonies to the northward. They possessed an abundance of Negro women. The result may best be described in the words of two travelers from different backgrounds. As young Josiah Quincy of Boston reported on his tour through North and South Carolina, "The enjoyment of a negro or mulatto woman is spoken of as quite a common thing: no reluctance, delicacy or shame is made about the matter."[15] A visiting merchant from Jamaica, where the atmosphere surrounding interracial sex was so utterly different from New England, wrote from Charleston in 1773, "I know of but one Gentleman who professedly keeps a Mulatto Mistress and he is very much pointed at: There are swarms of Negroes about the Town and many Mulattoes, and by the Dress of the Girls, who mostly imitate their Mistresses, I have no doubt of their Conversations with the whites, but they are carried on with more privacy than in our W. India Islands." (Josiah Quincy would scarcely have appreciated the niceness of the distinction.) "As I travell'd further North," the Jamaican visitor continued, concerning his trip from Charleston to North Carolina, "there were fewer Negroes about the Houses, and these taken less notice of, and before I finish'd my Journey North, I found an empty House, the late Tenant of which had been oblig'd by the Church Wardens to decamp on Account of his having kept a Black Woman. Dont suppose Fornication is out of Fashion here," he added reassuringly about North Carolina, "more than in other Places, No! the difference only is, that the White Girls monopolize it."[16]

Here was an important regional difference in social "fashion." Charleston was the only English city on the continent where it was at all possible to jest publicly concerning miscegenation. In 1732 the *South-Carolina Gazette* published a verse which touched off a round robin on the subject.

The Cameleon Lover

If what the Curious *have observ'd be true,*
That the Cameleon *will assume the* Hue
Of all the Objects *that approach its* Touch;

No Wonder then, that the Amours *of* such
Whose Taste *betrays them to a close Em-*
    brace
With the dark *Beauties of the* Sable *Race*
(Stain'd with the Tincture of the Sooty
    Sin,)
Imbibe the Blackness *of their* Charmer's
    Skin.[17]

This "little smattering of Wit" greatly offended one serious-minded citizen who, pointedly signing himself "ALBUS," declared that he was "one of those, who are not a little fired at any Instance of this Kind." "ALBUS" caustically admitted that "it is too well known, that I need not be under any great Apprehension of pointing at *One* Man only. Were that the Case, he would not be worth our Notice, and we might silently contemn both the *Offence* and the *Offender.* But it is too shocking to see an *Evil* of this *Kind,* spreading it self among us. Too gross to be suffered to pass in Silence!" Unfortunately, the impact of Albus's lengthy admonition was somewhat dampened by the presence of a poem defending miscegenation in the very same issue of the *Gazette.*[18] And four years later the paper published some frank advice to the bachelors and widowers of Charleston ostensibly from some ladies newly arrived from Bermuda: "that if they are in a Strait for Women, to wait for the next Shipping from the Coast of Guinny. Those African Ladies are of a strong, robust Constitution: not easily jaded out, able to serve them by Night as well as Day. When they are Sick, they are not costly, when dead, their funeral Charges are but *viz* an old Matt, one Bottle Rum, and a lb. Sugar[.] The cheapness of a Commo-di-ty becomes more taking when it fully Answers the end, or T——1." Next week another writer replied in obvious determination not to be outdone in indelicacy of expression: "in my Opinion, our Country-Women are full as capable for Service either night or day as any African Ladies whatsoever, unless their native Constitution is much alter'd. In all Companies wheresoever I have been, my Country-Women have always the praise for their Activity of Hipps and humoring a Jest to the Life in what Posture soever their Partners may fancy, which makes me still hope that they'll have the Preference before the black Ladies in the Esteem of the Widowers and Batchelors at C—— *town.*" Next week the *Gazette* published still another verse.[19]

If these contributions to the *South-Carolina Gazette* were a trifle raw by the standards of a modern family newspaper, they reflected more than eighteenth-century literary frankness about sex. Newspapers elsewhere on the continent did not publish similar discussions of interracial sex, though everywhere (including Boston) they published some none-too-delicate pieces concerning sexual matters. Only in Charleston was it possible to debate publicly, "Is sex with Negroes right?" In other colonies the topic was not looked upon as being open.

The reasons for this distinctiveness are apparent in the mosaic of South Carolina's economic and social history. The original colonization of South Carolina had been intimately linked with the English experience in the Caribbean islands. Although staple crops (rice and indigo) and large plantations in the low country made for aristocratic control along the Virginia pattern, the presence of Charleston, which served as entrepôt for the back country as well as the social and commercial center of the low country, made for less political responsibility, for more absenteeism on the plantations, and for a gayer, less serious-minded style of life among the aristocracy.[20] More important, the preponderance of slaves in the low country tended to give white men a queasy sense that perhaps they were marooned, a feeling that their society was irrevocably committed to Negro slavery and that somehow their mere Englishness had lost its savor in the shuffle for plantation prosperity. The effect of this uneasiness was to make men feel like both fleeing and embracing Negro slavery all at once: hence the common annual flights from the plantations to Charleston and from South Carolina to northern cities and England, the negation of cherished traditional liberties in the slave codes, the importation of more and more slaves, the continual efforts to encourage white immigration, and not least, the simultaneous embracing of Negro women and rejection of the ensuing offspring. Caught as they were in powerful crosscurrents, it is no wonder that white men in Charleston joked nervously about their sexual abandon.

For white women the situation was different, and here again the Charleston area seems to have been characterized by attitudes somewhere mid-way between those of the West Indies and further north. In the islands, where English settlers were most thoroughly committed to a Negro slave society and where strenuous attempts to attract more white settlers had been unavailing, white women were, quite literally, the repositories of white civilization. White men tended to place them protectively upon a pedestal and then run off to gratify their passions elsewhere. For their part white women, though they might propagate children, inevitably held themselves aloof from the world of lust and passion, a world which reeked of infidelity and Negro slaves. Under no circumstances would they have attempted, any more than they would have been allowed, to clamber down from their pedestal to seek pleasures of their own across the racial line. In fact white women in the West Indies tended to adhere rigidly to the double sexual standard which characterized English sexual mores and to refrain more than in the continental colonies from infidelity with white men.[21] The oppressive presence of slavery itself tended to inhibit the white woman's capacity for emotional, sexual, and intellectual commitment. She served principally an ornamentive function, for everything resembling work was done by Negro slaves. Visitors to the islands were almost universally agreed in describing her life as one of indolence and lassitude, though some were impressed by a formal, superficial gaiety. Her choices were to withdraw from the world or to create an unreal one of her own. She withdrew from the colored race and, perhaps not entirely because of prevailing notions about health, scrupulously shielded her face from the darkening effects of the tropic sun.[22] A tanned skin implied an affinity which she had to deny.

The white women of the Charleston area were less tightly hemmed in. Nevertheless, they rarely if ever established liaisons with Negro men, as happened in the South Carolina back country. Some visitors to the city were struck by their dessicated formality, which seems now to betray the strains imposed by the prevailing pattern of miscegenation. A New Jersey lawyer who moved to Charleston just after the Revolution described his initial impressions of aristocratic circles there in the following terms:

> It is hard that hospitality should thus want its most essential part (sociability) and that a person cannot be made an object of politeness without being also made an object of formality. The ladies carry formality and scrupulosity to a considerable extreme; a stranger makes his female acquaintance by slow gradations interspersed with niceties and punctilios which often disconcert the forward and intimidate the bashful. The maxims of the country have taught them and custom has forced them to almost consider a sociability on their part with gentlemen as an unbecoming forwardness—and they are by this means circumscribed within such narrow bounds as exclude the frankness and care which are necessary to put people on the most agreeable footing and constitutes the principal charms of Society.

The gentlemen are more sociable and I must confess as agreeable as any I have ever seen after a person has made an acquaintance with them. But they are generally very dissipated, little inclined to study and less to business.[23]

The dissipation of the white gentleman was as much a tragedy for his white lady as for him. A biracial environment warped her affective life in two directions at once, for she was made to feel that sensual involvement with the opposite sex burned bright and hot with unquenchable passion and at the same time that any such involvement was utterly repulsive. Accordingly, as the above passage suggests so clearly, she approached her prospective legitimate sexual partners as if she were picking up a live coal in one hand and a dead rat in the other.

If women were particularly affected by the situation in South Carolina, white persons of both sexes in *all* the English colonies were affected in a more general way by the tensions involved in miscegenation. Though these tensions operated in white men rather differently than in white women, it seems almost self-evident that the emergent attitudes toward Negroes possessed a unity which transcended differences between the two sexes. Put another way, out of a pattern of interracial sexual relationships which normally placed white men and white women in very different roles, there arose a common core of belief and mythology concerning the Negro which belonged to neither sex but to white American culture as a whole. The emergence of common beliefs out of divergent experiences was of course principally a function of the homogenizing effect of culture upon individual experience, but it is important to bear in mind that the functional significance of beliefs about the Negro may have been very different for white women than for white men even when the beliefs themselves were identical. Since the English and colonial American cultures were dominated by males, however, sexually-oriented beliefs about the Negro in America derived principally from the psychological needs of men and were to a considerable extent shaped by specifically masculine modes of thought and behavior. This is not to say that American attitudes toward the Negro were *male* attitudes but merely that when one talks about *American* attitudes toward anything (the frontier, the city, money, freedom, the Negro) one is using a shorthand for attitudes common to both sexes but predominantly male in genesis and tone.[24]

NOTES

1. My own impression and that of Edward B. Reuter, *The Mulatto in the United States; Including a Study of the Role of Mixed-Blood Races throughout the World* (Boston, 1918), 112. An interesting but over-eager world-wide treatment is Joel A. Rogers, *Sex and Race; Negro-Caucasian Mixing in All Ages and All Lands,* 3 vols. (N. Y., 1940-44).
2. Explicit references to gentlemen fathering mulattoes were uncommon in the continental colonies; for example, Samuel Thornely, ed., *The Journal of Nicholas Cresswell, 1774-1777* (N. Y., 1924), 164-65; Thomas Anburey, *Travels through the Interior Parts of America,* 2 vols. (Boston, 1923), II, 223.
3. Greene, *Negro in New England,* 200-202. For intermarriages involving white women elsewhere, Anne Grant, *Memoirs of an American Lady; With Sketches of Manners and Scenes in America As They Existed Previous to the Revolution,* ed. James Grant Wilson, 2 vols. (N. Y., 1901), I, 86; Arthur W. Calhoun, *A Social History of the American Family from Colonial Times to the Present,* 3 vols. (Cleveland, 1917-19), I, 211; Catterall, ed., *Judicial Cases,* II, 11; Duc de La Rochefoucauld-Liancourt, *Travels through the United States of North America . . . 1795, 1796, and 1797 . . .,* 2 vols. (London, 1799), I, 602; Annapolis *Md. Gaz.,* July 31, 1794. For this combination outside marriage, see extracts from Box 16, bundle: Court of General Sessions of the Peace [Suffolk Co., Mass.], Apr. 4, 1704, Oct. 2, 1705, Apr. 6, 1708, July 4, 1710, Apr. 6, 1714. Parish Transcripts, N. Y. Hist. Soc; Morse, "Lemuel Haynes," *Jour. Negro Hist.,* 4 (1919), 22; [Horsmanden], *Journal of the Proceedings,* 2, 4; *Boston News-Letter,* June 25, 1741; Calhoun, *Family,* I, 211; Catterall, ed., *Judicial Cases,* I, 89-91, II, 12, IV, 28, 32; Annapolis *Md. Gaz.,* Aug. 19, 1746; James H. Johnston, Race Relations in Virginia and Miscegenation in the South, 1776-1860 (unpubl. Ph.D. diss., University of Chicago, 1937), 199-202; John H. Franklin, *The Free Negro in North Carolina, 1790-1860* (Chapel Hill, 1943), 37, 39; Saunders, ed., *Col. Recs. N. C.,* II, 704; Klaus G. Loewald, Beverly Starika, and Paul S. Taylor, trans. and eds., "Johann Martin Bolzius Answers a Questionnaire on Carolina and Georgia," *Wm. and Mary Qtly.,* 3d Ser., 14 (1957), 235.
4. Annapolis *Md. Gaz.,* Oct. 12, 1769, also Apr. 22, 1773.
5. Turner, *Negro in Pa.,* 3on.
6. Hening, ed., *Statutes Va.,* II, 170, III, 86-87, 452-54; *Archives Md.,* I, 533-34, VII, 204-5, XIII, 546-49, XXII, 552, XXVI, 259-60, XXX, 289-90, XXXIII, 112. XXXVI, 275-76; Lefroy, comp., *Memorials Bermudas,* II, 190; *Acts and Resolves Mass.,* I, 578-79; Clark, ed., *State Recs. N. C.,* XXIII, 65, 106, 160, 195; Cooper and McCord, eds., *Statutes S. C.,* III, 20; Mitchell *et al.,* eds., *Statutes Pa.,* IV, 62-63; Candler, comp.,

Col. Recs. Ga., I, 59-60; *Laws Del.,* I, 105-9. For circumstances surrounding the Massachusetts and Pennsylvania acts, *Diary of Sewall,* II, 143; Herrick, *White Servitude in Pennsylvania,* 92. The 18th-century laws barred all licit unions, illicit unions involving white women, and in most cases illicit unions involving white men, but Maryland and Virginia arrived at this position by different routes, Maryland at first barring only interracial fornication and Virginia only interracial marriage.

7. Henry R. McIlwaine, ed., *Legislative Journals of the Council of Colonial Virginia,* 3 vols. (Richmond, 1918-19), I, 262; Box 2, bundle: N. C., Minutes of Council in Assembly (1732-55), Minutes of House of Burgesses (1733-46) 19, Parish Transcripts, N.Y. Hist. Soc.

8. Charleston *S.-C. Gaz.,* Mar. 28, 1743. For the West Indies, Jordan, "American Chiaroscuro: The Status and Definition of Mulattoes in the British Colonies," *Wm. and Mary Qtly.,* 3d Ser., 19 (1962), 194-95. The one West Indian law (Montserrat's) was probably disallowed: CO 391/ 69, 51, P.R.O.

9. Edwards, *History of British West Indies,* II, 26.

10. Thornely, ed., *Journal of Nicholas Cresswell,* 39. There is a vivid picture of an overseer's life in the West Indies in O. A. Sherrard, *Freedom from Fear: The Slave and His Emancipation* (London, 1959), chap. 9.

11. [Edward Long], *The History of Jamaica . . . ,* 3 vols. (London, 1774), II, 328.

12. Edward D. Seeber, trans., *On the Threshold of Liberty: Journal of a Frenchman's Tour of the American Colonies in 1777* (Bloomington, Ind., 1959). 123-24.

13. Samuel Sewall, *The Selling of Joseph, a Memorial* (Boston, 1700), 2; Labaree *et al.,* eds., *Papers of Franklin,* IV, 225-34; William Byrd to Lord Egmont, Virginia, July 12, 1736. "Colonel William Byrd on Slavery and Indentured Servants," *Amer. Hist. Rev.,* I (1895), 88-89.

14. Adolph B. Benson, trans. and ed., *The America of 1750: Peter Kalm's Travels in North America. The English Version of 1770,* 2 vols. (N. Y., 1937), I, 209; James Bowdoin to George Scott, Boston, Oct. 14, 1763, Bowdoin-Temple Papers, XXVIII, 56, Massachusetts Historical Society, Boston; Grant, *Memoirs,* ed. Wilson, I, 85.

15. Mark Anthony De Wolfe Howe, ed., "Journal of Josiah Quincy, Junior, 1773," Mass. Hist. Soc., *Proceedings,* 49 (1915-16), 463.

16. G. Moulton to ?, Charles Town, Jan. 23, 1773, Additional Manuscripts, 22677, 75, British Museum, London. For reference to this letter I am indebted to Pitman, *British West Indies,* 1700-1763, 28.

17. Charleston *S.C. Gaz.,* Mar. 11, 1732.

18. *Ibid.,* Mar. 18, 1732.

19. *Ibid.,* July 17, 24, 31, 1736.

20. The best introduction is Carl Bridenbaugh, *Myths and Realities: Societies of the Colonial South* (Baton Rouge, La., 1952), chap. 2.

21. Stated emphatically, for example, by Luffman. *Brief Account of Antigua*, 37, also 168-70. For sexual mores in England, see Keith J. Thomas, "The Double Standard," *Journal of the History of Ideas*, 20 (1959), 195-216.

22. John Singleton, *A General Description of the West-Indian Islands . . .* (Barbados, 1767), 146-51; [Schaw], *Journal of a Lady of Quality*, eds. Andrews, 114-15, 123-24; [Long], *Jamaica*, II, 413; Luffman, *Brief Account of Antigua*, 35. For this in the southern colonies, John Lawson, *A New Voyage to Carolina . . .* (London, 1709), 84; entry of June 22, 1781, in Military Journal of William Feltman, May, 26, 1781, to Apr. 25, 1782, Hist. Soc. Pa.

23. Joseph W. Barnwell, ed., "Diary of Timothy Ford, 1785-1786," *South Carolina Historical and Genealogical Magazine*, 13 (1912), 190-91.

24. A closely related problem is discussed by David M. Potter, "American Women and the American Character," *Stetson University Bulletin*, 62 (1962), 1-22.

Part Two

The Victorian Image

The rapid industrialization and increased geographic mobility characteristic of the nineteenth century had special implications for American women. The dynamic economic order reinforced the social distinctions which had appeared in the post-Revolutionary period. In the context of extreme competitiveness and dizzying social change, the Victorian home lost many of its earlier functions and came to serve as a haven of tranquility and order. "As the larger society lost structural coherence, the family was cut adrift from its old institutional moorings."[1] The roles of husband and wife were becoming more neatly differentiated than ever before and the size of American families declined. Particularly for the middle classes, men worked on farms and in factories while women ruled the home and served as the custodians of civility and culture. The intimacy of colonial marriage was rended and a social distance grew between husbands and wives that at times seemed unbridgable.[2]

The variety of economic roles colonial women performed virtually disappeared in the early nineteenth century. As Gerda Lerner explains, work roles became differentiated along class lines. The middle class woman displaced by professionalization emerged in the role of "the lady." In "The Cult of True Womanhood" Barbara Welter details the idealization of "the lady" and relates how this set of social values insured the middle class woman's dependency. She was the object of both adoration and domination. The paradox of the cult was nowhere more evident than in the glorification of "the southern lady" whom Anne Firor Scott describes as an immensely hard working administrator and domestic drudge.

Ironically at the same time that middle class culture worshipped the cult of domesticity, increasing numbers of women moved into the labor force. The vast majority of working women were domestics until the end of the nineteenth century, but the factory system from its beginning employed large numbers of women and children. Although romantics extolled the "freedom of the factory," the labor of these women was usually necessary for the family to attain the minimum necessities of life. Thousands worked for a pittance, enduring long hours in the cotton and woolen mills of New England and the sweat shops of New York. It was estimated that in 1865 New York alone had 75,000 women workers struggling on the edge of poverty.[3]

From the beginning, women in the factories resisted oppression and demanded better working conditions, shorter hours, and an end to wage differentials. Unfamiliar with organizational problems, women often accepted more experienced male leaders who generally failed to sustain arguments for equal pay. Women's attempts at unionization during this period failed, but they laid the foundation for later successful organization. However, "mill girls" and "ladies" were distinct social types during the Jacksonian era and social stratification prevented their alliance. The feminist movement which did appear in the antebellum period grew out of the acute status deprivation experienced by middle class women aware that in a time when lip service was being paid to their purity and virtue, they remained disfranchised and bereft of property rights, able to exercise little control over their own destinies.

Expanded opportunities for education drew middle class women out of the home and into some professions.[4] Under the leadership of Emma Willard and Catherine Beecher the movement for secondary education spread. In 1837 Mary Lyon founded Mount Holyoke Female Seminary, which set an example for such post-Civil War women's colleges as Vassar, Wellesley, and Smith. Co-education on the college level emerged first in the Midwest when Oberlin College in Ohio opened its doors to women in the 1830s; and between 1858 and 1870 midwestern state universities followed Oberlin's example. The number of women doctors increased as medical education (in sexually segregated classes) became increasingly available to women. However, with several prominent exceptions women were restricted from the ministry and few entered the legal profes-

sion. Most women college graduates became either nurses or teachers—both low status, low paying positions.

Middle class women, many of whom were educated in the
professions and well understood the discriminations against their sex,
banded together in the growing feminist movement. Feminism was
part of the general ferment of humanitarian reform which appeared
in the 1830s. Religious enthusiasm attracted increasing numbers of
women to abolitionism, temperance, the campaign for public
schools, prison reform, and other causes of the antebellum years.[5]
Quaker women, in particular, whose theology taught them there was
something of God in every man and woman, took active part in
efforts at social amelioration. Of particular interest to these women
reformers was the slave and particularly the enslaved black woman
whose degradation and stoic beauty are recounted by E. Franklin
Frazier in "Hagar and Her Children."

Within the abolition and temperance movements these women
often found men objecting to their activity on the grounds that it
was inappropriate for women to speak publicly. This situation
prompted Sarah Grimké to write her *Letters on the Equality of the
Sexes,* and other women reformers to contemplate separate action to
secure for women civil and political rights equal to those of men. In
the selection from her biography of the Grimké sisters, Gerda Lerner
recounts the struggle of these well known abolitionists who when
subject to much abuse struck back at their critics and claimed that
women's subjection was comparable to slavery. Sarah Grimké's insistence upon equal status and equal opportunities defined most of the
major issues which dominated the feminist movement for over a
century.

Eventually women's rights advocates acted independently from
the abolition movement. Barred from taking their seats at the World
Anti-Slavery Convention in 1840 simply because they were women,
Lucretia Mott and Elizabeth Cady Stanton planned taking action to
secure women's rights. In 1848, at a convention in Seneca Falls,
New York, women issued their own Declaration of Independence
which proclaimed that "all men *and* women are created equal." In a
pathetically long list of grievances presented to an audience of
factory women and small town reformers they protested that they
had been denied their basic human rights and discriminated against
by the legal, moral, and social order.

Although the Civil War raised feminist expectations, the passage of the Fourteenth and Fifteenth Amendments during Recon-

struction created a crisis in feminist ranks. Because of their wartime activities as civil servants, nurses, and teachers, and because of the support of the Thirteenth Amendment by organizations such as the National Women's Loyal League, women assumed that reformers would rally to the cause of woman suffrage. However, many male abolitionists thought black male suffrage was vital to the freedmen and that tying it to woman suffrage meant inevitable defeat. Elizabeth Cady Stanton and Susan B. Anthony refused to accept this theory or to sacrifice woman suffrage to the cause of the black male and consequently broke with the moderates who thought it was indeed "the Negro's hour." Subsequently the feminist movement split into two groups. The more radical National Woman Suffrage Association, led by Stanton and Anthony, concerned itself with a variety of reform causes and held that only by changing the entire structure of society could women achieve full equality. The more conservative American Woman Suffrage Association, headed by Lucy Stone, stuck closer to the single issue of the vote.

In subsequent years both groups agitated for woman suffrage with little success. Even when women did secure the vote, as in Wyoming, success was the product of social forces over which women in general, and the eastern feminist movement in particular, had little control. The suffrage victory was the product of an effort to re-establish eastern ideas of order, refinement, and culture in the West.[6]

Thus, even the success of woman suffrage in Wyoming reaffirmed the pervasiveness of the Victorian image of woman as the guardian of culture and civilization. Throughout this entire period most Americans, men and women, treated feminist demands with apathy or disgust. In his book *Sex and Education* E. M. Clarke argued that college education would "desex" women. Similarly, opponents of equal suffrage insisted it would undermine the family and endanger the entire social order. Women such as Eliza Francis Andrews agreed that woman's "business is to refine and elevate society ... her mission is moral rather than intellectual, domestic rather than political."[7] The feminine intellect was deemed incapable of dealing with civic affairs. Until the twentieth century the advocates of woman suffrage scored few successes precisely because of the opposition of their own sex as well as the hostility of males.

NOTES

1. Rowland Berthoff, *An Unsettled People: Social Order and Disorder in American History* (New York: Harper and Row, 1971), 204. See also William E. Bridges, "Family Patterns and Social Values in America, 1825-1875," *American Quarterly*, XVII (Spring, 1965), 3-11.
2. William R. Taylor and Christopher Lasch, "Two 'Kindred Spirits': Sorority and Family in New England, 1839-1846," *New England Quarterly*, XXXVI (March, 1963), 23-41.
3. Allan Nevins, *The Emergence of Modern America, 1865-1878* (New York: Macmillan, 1927), 324.
4. Merle Curti, *Social Ideas of American Educators* (Totowa, N.J.: Littlefield Adams, 1959), 169-193.
5. Two suggestive analyses of women reformers in the nineteenth century are: Carroll Smith Rosenberg, "Beauty, the Beast and the Militant Woman: A Case Study of Sex Roles and Social Stress in Jacksonian America," *American Quarterly*, XXIII (October, 1971), 562-584; and Christopher Lasch, "Emancipated Women," *New York Review of Books* (July 13, 1967), 28-32.
6. Alan P. Grimes, *The Puritan Ethic and Woman Suffrage* (New York: Oxford University Press, 1967).
7. Quoted in Mary Elizabeth Massey, *Bonnet Brigades* (New York: Alfred A. Knopf, 1966), 359.

Article 1

The Lady and the Mill Girl: Changes in the Status of Women in the Age of Jackson

Gerda Lerner

The period 1800-1840 is one in which decisive changes occurred in the status of American women. It has remained surprisingly unexplored. With the exception of a recent, unpublished dissertation by Keith Melder and the distinctive work of Elisabeth Dexter, there is a dearth of descriptive material and an almost total absence of interpretation.[1] Yet the period offers essential clues to an understanding of later institutional developments, particularly the shape and nature of the women's rights movement. This analysis will consider the economic, political and social status of women and examine the changes in each area. It will also attempt an interpretation of the ideological shifts which occurred in American society concerning the "proper" role for women.

Periodization always offers difficulties. It seemed useful here, for purposes of comparison, to group women's status before 1800 roughly under the "colonial" heading and ignore the transitional and possibly atypical shifts which occurred during the American Revolution and the early period of nationhood. Also, regional differences were largely ignored. The South was left out of consideration entirely because its industrial development occurred later.

From *Midcontinent American Studies Journal,* X (Spring, 1969), 5-14. Reprinted by permission of the author and publisher.

Research for this article was facilitated by a research grant provided by Long Island University, Brooklyn, N. Y., which is gratefully acknowledged.

The generalizations in this article are based on extensive research in primary sources, including letters and manuscripts of the following women: Elizabeth Cady Stanton, Susan B. Anthony, Abby Kelley, Lucretia Mott, Lucy Stone, Sarah and Angelina Grimké, Maria Weston Chapman, Lydia Maria Child and Betsey Cowles. Among the organizational records consulted were those of the Boston Female Anti-Slavery Society, the Philadelphia Female Anti-Slavery Society, Anti-Slavery Conventions of American Women, all the Woman's Rights Conventions prior to 1870 and the records of various female charitable organizations.

The status of colonial women has been well studied and described and can briefly be summarized for comparison with the later period. Throughout the colonial period there was a marked shortage of women, which varied with the regions and always was greatest in the frontier areas.[2] This (from the point of view of women) favorable sex ratio enhanced their status and position. The Puritan world view regarded idleness as sin; life in an underdeveloped country made it absolutely necessary that each member of the community perform an economic function. Thus work for women, married or single, was not only approved, it was regarded as a civic duty. Puritan town councils expected single girls, widows and unattached women to be self-supporting and for a long time provided needy spinsters with parcels of land. There was no social sanction against married women working; on the contrary, wives were expected to help their husbands in their trade and won social approval for doing extra work in or out of the home. Needy children, girls as well as boys, were indentured or apprenticed and were expected to work for their keep.

The vast majority of women worked within their homes, where their labor produced most articles needed for the family. The entire colonial production of cloth and clothing and partially that of shoes was in the hands of women. In addition to these occupations, women were found in many different kinds of employment. They were butchers, silversmiths, gunsmiths, upholsterers. They ran mills, plantations, tan yards, shipyards and every kind of shop, tavern and boarding house. They were gate keepers, jail keepers, sextons, journalists, printers, "doctoresses," apothecaries, midwives, nurses and teachers. Women acquired their skills the same way as did the men, through apprenticeship training, frequently within their own families.[3]

Absence of a dowry, ease of marriage and remarriage and a more lenient attitude of the law with regard to woman's property rights were manifestations of the improved position of wives in the colonies. Under British common law, marriage destroyed a woman's contractual capacity; she could not sign a contract even with the consent of her husband. But colonial authorities were more lenient toward the wife's property rights by protecting her dower rights in her husband's property, granting her personal clothing and upholding pre-nuptial contracts between husband and wife. In the absence of the husband, colonial courts granted women "femme sole" rights, which enabled them to conduct their husband's business, sign contracts and sue. The relative social freedom of women and the esteem in which they were held was commented upon by most early foreign travelers in America.[4]

But economic, legal and social status tell only part of the story. Colonial society as a whole was hierarchical, and rank and standing in society depended on the position of the men. Women did not play a determining role in the ranking pattern; they took their position in society through the men of their own family or the men they married. In other words, they participated in the hierarchy only as daughters and wives, not as individuals. Similarly, their occupations were, by and large, merely auxiliary, designed to contribute to family income, enhance their husbands' business or continue it in case of widowhood. The self-supporting spinsters were certainly the exception. The underlying assumption of colonial society was that women ought to occupy an inferior and subordinate position. The settlers had brought this assumption with them from Europe; it was reflected in their legal concepts, their willingness to exclude women from political life, their discriminatory educational practices. What is remarkable is the extent to which this felt inferiority of women was constantly challenged and modified under the impact of environment, frontier conditions and a favorable sex ratio.

By 1840 all of American society had changed. The Revolution had substituted an egalitarian ideology for the hierarchical concepts of colonial life. Privilege based on ability rather than inherited status, upward mobility for all groups of society and unlimited opportunities for individual self-fulfillment had become ideological goals, if not always realities. For men, that is; women were, by tacit consensus, excluded from the new democracy. Indeed their actual situation had in many respects deteriorated. While, as wives, they had benefitted from increasing wealth, urbanization and industrialization, their role as economic producers and as political members of society differed sharply from that of men. Women's work outside of the home no longer met with social approval; on the contrary, with two notable exceptions, it was condemned. Many business and professional occupations formerly open to women were now closed, many others restricted as to training and advancement. The entry of large numbers of women into low status, low pay and low skill industrial work had fixed such work by definition as "woman's work." Women's political status, while legally unchanged, had deteriorated relative to the advances made by men. At the same time the genteel lady of fashion had become a model of American femininity and the definition of "woman's proper sphere" seemed narrower and more confined than ever.

Within the scope of this article only a few of these changes can be more fully explained. The professionalization of medicine and its impact on women may serve as a typical example of what occurred in all the professions.

In colonial America there were no medical schools, no medical journals, few hospitals and few laws pertaining to the practice of the healing arts. Clergymen and governors, barbers, quacks, apprentices and women practiced medicine. Most practitioners acquired their credentials by reading Paracelsus and Galen and serving an apprenticeship with an established practitioner. Among the semi-trained "physics," surgeons and healers the occasional "doctoress" was fully accepted and frequently well rewarded. County records of all the colonies contain references to the work of the female physicians. There was even a female Army surgeon, a Mrs. Allyn, who served during King Philip's war. Plantation records mention by name several slave women who were granted special privileges because of their useful service as midwives and "doctoresses."[5]

The period of the professionalization of American medicine dates from 1765, when Dr. William Shippen began his lectures on midwifery in Philadelphia. The founding of medical faculties in several colleges, the standardization of training requirements and the proliferation of medical societies intensified during the last quarter of the eighteenth century. The American Revolution dramatized the need for trained medical personnel, afforded first hand battlefield experience to a number of surgeons and brought increasing numbers of semi-trained practitioners in contact with the handful of European-trained surgeons working in the military hospitals. This was an experience from which women were excluded. The resulting interest in improved medical training, the gradual appearance of graduates of medical colleges and the efforts of medical societies led to licensing legislation. In 1801 Maryland required all medical practitioners to be licensed; in 1806 New York enacted a similar law, providing for an examination before a commission. By the late 1820's all states except three had set up licensing requirements. Since most of these laws stipulated attendance at a medical college as one of the prerequisites for licensing, women were automatically excluded.[6] By the 1830's the few established female practitioners who might have continued their practice in the old ways had probably died out.

Whatever vested interest they had had was too weak to assert itself against the new profession.

This process of pre-emption of knowledge, institutionalization of the profession and legitimation of its claims by law and public acceptance is standard for the professionalization of the sciences, as George Daniels has pointed out.[7] It inevitably results in the elimination of fringe elements from the profession. It is interesting to note that women had been pushed out of the medical profession in sixteenth-century Europe by a similar process.[8] Once the public had come to accept licensing and college training as guarantees of up-to-date practice the outsider, no matter how well qualified by years of experience, stood no chance in the competition. Women were the casualties of medical professionalization.

In the field of midwifery the results were similar, but the process was more complicated. Women had held a virtual monopoly in the profession in colonial America. In 1646 a man was prosecuted in Maine for practicing as a midwife.[9] There are many records of well trained midwives with diplomas from European institutions working in the colonies. In most of the colonies midwives were licensed, registered and required to pass an examination before a board. When Dr. Shippen announced his pioneering lectures on midwifery, he did it to "combat the widespread popular prejudice against the man-midwife" and because he considered most midwives ignorant and improperly trained.[10]

Yet he invited "those women who love virtue enough, to own their Ignorance, and apply for instruction" to attend his lectures, offering as an inducement the assurance that female pupils would be taught privately. It is not known if any midwives availed themselves of the opportunity.[11]

Technological advances, as well as scientific, worked against the interests of female midwives. In sixteenth-century Europe the invention and use of the obstetrical forceps had for three generations been the well-kept secret of the Chamberlen family and had greatly enhanced their medical practice. Hugh Chamberlen was forced by circumstances to sell the secret to the Medical College in Amsterdam, which in turn transmitted the precious knowledge to licensed physicians only. By the time the use of the instrument became widespread it had become associated with male physicians and midwives. Similarly in America, introduction of the obstetrical forceps was associated with the practice of male midwives and served to their advantage. By the end of the eighteenth century a number of male physicians advertised their practice of midwifery. Shortly thereafter female midwives also resorted to advertising, probably in an effort to meet the competition. By the early nineteenth century male physicians had virtually monopolized the practice of midwifery on the Eastern seaboard. True to the generally delayed economic development in the Western frontier regions, female midwives continued to work on the frontier until a much later period. It is interesting to note that the concepts of "propriety" shifted with the prevalent practice. In seventeenth-century Maine the attempt of a man to act as a midwife was considered outrageous and illegal; in mid-nineteenth-century America the suggestion that women should train as midwives and physicians was considered equally outrageous and improper.[12]

Professionalization, similar to that in medicine with the elimination of women from the upgraded profession, occurred in the field of law. Before 1750, when law suits were commonly brought to the courts by the plaintiffs themselves or by deputies without specialized legal training, women as well as men could and did act as "attorneys-in-fact." When the law became a paid profession and trained lawyers took over litigation, women disappeared from the court scene for over a century.[13]

A similar process of shrinking opportunities for women developed in business and in the retail trades. There were fewer female storekeepers and business women in the 1830's than there had been in colonial days. There was also a noticeable shift in the kind of merchandise handled by them. Where previously women could be found running almost every kind of retail shop, after 1830 they were mostly found in businesses which served women only.[14]

The only fields in which professionalization did not result in the elimination of women from the upgraded profession were nursing and teaching. Both were characterized by a severe shortage of labor. Nursing lies outside the field of this inquiry since it did not become an organized profession until after the Civil War. Before then it was regarded peculiarly as a woman's occupation, although some of the hospitals and the Army during wars employed male nurses. These bore the stigma of low skill, low status and low pay. Generally, nursing was regarded as simply an extension of the unpaid services performed by the housewife—a characteristic attitude that haunts the profession to this day.

Education seems, at first glance, to offer an entirely opposite pattern from that of the other professions. In colonial days women had taught "Dame schools" and grade schools during summer sessions. Gradually, as educational opportunities for girls expanded, they advanced just a step ahead of their students. Professionalization of teaching occurred between 1820-1860, a period marked by a sharp increase in the number of women teachers. The spread of female seminaries, academies and normal schools provided new opportunities for the training and employment of female teachers.

This trend which runs counter to that found in the other professions can be accounted for by the fact that women filled a desperate need created by the challenge of the common schools, the ever-increasing size of the student body and the westward growth of the nation. America was committed to educating its children in public schools, but it was insistent on doing so as cheaply as possible. Women were available in great numbers and they were willing to work cheaply. The result was another ideological adaptation: in the very period when the gospel of the home as woman's only proper sphere was preached most loudly, it was discovered that women were the natural teachers of youth, could do the job better than men and were to be preferred for such employment. This was always provided, of course, that they would work at the proper wage differential—30-50% of the wages paid male teachers was considered appropriate. The result was that in 1888 in the country as a whole 63% of all teachers were women, while the figure for the cities only was 90.04%.[15]

It appeared in the teaching field, as it would in industry, that role expectations were adaptable provided the inferior status group filled a social need. The inconsistent and peculiar patterns of employment of black labor in the present-day market bear out the validity of this generalization.

There was another field in which the labor of women was appreciated and which they were urged to enter—industry. From Alexander Hamilton to Matthew Carey and Tench Coxe, advocates of industrialization sang the praises of the working girl and advanced arguments in favor of her employment. The social benefits of female labor particularly stressed were those bestowed upon her family, who now no longer had to support her. Working girls were "thus happily preserved from idleness and its attendant vices and crimes" and the whole community benefitted from their increased purchasing power.[16]

American industrialization, which occurred in an underdeveloped economy with a shortage of labor, depended on the labor of women and children. Men were occupied with agricultural work and were not available or willing to enter the factories. This accounts for the special features of the early development of the New England textile industry: the relatively high wages, the respectability of the job and relatively high status of the mill girls, the patriarchal character of the model factory towns and the temporary mobility of women workers from farm to factory and back again to farm. All this was characteristic only of a limited area and of a period of about two decades. By the late 1830's the romance had worn off; immigration had supplied a strongly competitive, permanent work force willing to work for subsistence wages; early efforts at trade union organization had been shattered and mechanization had turned semiskilled factory labor into unskilled labor. The process led to the replacement of the New England-born farm girls by immigrants in the mills and was accompanied by a loss of status and respectability for female workers.

The lack of organized social services during periods of depression drove ever greater numbers of women into the labor market. At first, inside the factories distinctions between men's and women's jobs were blurred. Men and women were assigned to machinery on the basis of local need. But as more women entered industry the limited number of occupations open to them tended to increase competition among them, thus lowering pay standards. Generally, women regarded their work as temporary and hesitated to invest in apprenticeship training, because they expected to marry and raise families. Thus they remained untrained, casual labor and were soon, by custom, relegated to the lowest paid, least skilled jobs. Long hours, overwork and poor working conditions would characterize women's work in industry for almost a century.[17]

Another result of industrialization was in increasing differences in life styles between women of different classes. When female occupations, such as carding, spinning and weaving, were transferred from home to factory, the poorer women followed their traditional work and became industrial workers. The women of the middle and upper classes could use their newly gained time for leisure pursuits: they became ladies. And a small but significant group among them chose to prepare themselves for professional careers by advanced education. This group would prove to be the most vocal and troublesome in the near future.

As class distinctions sharpened, social attitudes toward women became polarized. The image of "the lady" was elevated to the accepted ideal of femininity toward which all women would strive. In this formulation of values lower class women were simply ignored. The actual lady was, of course, nothing new on the American scene; she had been present ever since colonial days. What was new in the 1830's was the cult of the lady, her elevation to a status symbol. The advancing prosperity of the early nineteenth century made it possible for middle class women to aspire to the status formerly reserved for upper class women. The "cult of true womanhood" of the 1830's became a vehicle for such aspirations. Mass circulation newspapers and magazines made it possible to teach every woman how to elevate the status of her family by setting "proper" standards of behavior, dress and literary tastes. *Godey's Lady's Book* and innumerable gift books and tracts of the period all preach the same gospel of "true womanhood"—piety, purity, domesticity.[18] Those unable to reach the goal of becoming ladies were to be satisfied with the lesser goal—acceptance of their "proper place" in the home.

It is no accident that the slogan "woman's place is in the home" took on a certain aggressiveness and shrillness precisely at the time when increasing numbers of poorer women *left* their homes to become factory workers. Working women were not a fit subject for the concern of publishers and mass media writers. Idleness, once a disgrace in the eyes of society, had become a status symbol. Thorstein Veblen, one of the earliest and sharpest commentators on the subject, observed that it had become almost the sole social function of the lady "to put in evidence her economic unit's ability to pay." She was "a means of conspicuously unproductive expenditure," devoted to displaying her husband's wealth.[19] Just as the cult of white womanhood in the South served to preserve a labor and social system based on race distinctions, so did the cult of the lady in an egalitarian society serve as a means of preserving class distinctions. Where class distinctions were not so great, as on the frontier, the position of women was closer to what it had been in colonial days; their economic contribution was more highly valued, their opportunities were less restricted and their positive participation in community life was taken for granted.

In the urbanized and industrialized Northeast the life experience of middle class women was different in almost every respect from that of the lower class women. But there was one thing the society lady and the mill girl had in common—they were equally disfranchised and isolated from the vital centers of power. Yet the political status of women had not actually deteriorated. With very few exceptions women had neither voted nor stood for office during the colonial period. Yet the spread of the franchise to ever wider groups of white males during the Jacksonian age, the removal of property restrictions, the increasing numbers of immigrants who acquired access to the franchise, made the gap between these new enfranchised voters and the disfranchised women more obvious. Quite naturally, educated and propertied women felt this deprivation more keenly. Their own career expectations had been encouraged by widening educational opportunities; their consciousness of their own abilities and of their potential for power had been enhanced by their activities in the reform movements of the 1830's; the general spirit of upward mobility and venturesome entrepreneurship that pervaded the Jacksonian era was infectious. But in the late 1840's a sense of acute frustration enveloped these educated and highly spirited women. Their rising expectations had met with frustration, their hopes had been shattered; they were bitterly conscious of a relative lowering of status and a loss of position. This sense of frustration led them to action; it was one of the main factors in the rise of the woman's rights movement.[20]

The women, who in 1848 declared boldly and with considerable exaggeration that "the history of mankind is a history of repeated injuries and usurpations on the part of man toward woman, having in direct object the establishment of an absolute tyranny over her," did not speak for the truly exploited and abused working woman.[21] As a matter of fact, they were largely ignorant of her condition and, with the notable exception of Susan B. Anthony, indifferent to her fate. But they judged from the realities of their own life experience. Like most revolutionaries, they were not the most downtrodden but rather the most status-deprived group. Their frustrations and traditional isolation from political power funneled their discontent into fairly utopian declarations and immature organizational means. They would learn better in the long, hard decades of practical struggle. Yet it is their initial emphasis on the legal and political "disabilities" of women which has provided the framework for most of the historical work on women. For almost a hundred years sympathetic historians have told the story of women in America from the feminist viewpoint. Their tendency has been to reason from the position of middle class women to a generalization concerning all American women. This distortion has obscured the actual and continuous contributions of women to American life.[22] To avoid such a distortion, any valid generalization concerning American women after the 1830's should reflect a recognition of class stratification.

For lower class women the changes brought by industrialization were actually advantageous, offering income and advancement opportunities, however limited, and a chance for participation in the ranks of organized labor. They, by and large, tended to join men in their struggle for economic advancement and became increasingly concerned with economic gains and protective labor legislation. Middle and upper class women, on the other hand, reacted to actual and fancied status deprivation by increasing militancy and the formation of organizations for women's rights, by which they meant especially legal and property rights.

The four decades preceding the Seneca Falls Convention were decisive in the history of American women. They brought an actual deterioration in the economic opportunities open to women, a relative deterioration in their political status and a rising level of expectation and subsequent frustration in a privileged elite group of educated women. The ideology still pervasive in our present-day society regarding woman's "proper" role was formed in those decades. Later, under the impact of feminist attacks this ideology would grow defensive and attempt to bolster its claims by appeals to universality and pretentions to a history dating back to antiquity or, at least, to *The Mayflower*. Women, we are told, have always played a restricted and subordinate role in American life. In fact, however, it was in mid-nineteenth-century America that the ideology of "woman's place is in the home" changed from being an accurate description of existing reality into a myth. It became the "feminine mystique"—a longing for a lost, archaic world of agrarian family self-sufficiency, updated by woman's consumer function and the misunderstood dicta of Freudian psychology.

The decades 1800-1840 also provide the clues to an understanding of the institutional shape of the later women's organizations. These would be led by middle class women whose self-image, life experience and ideology had largely been fashioned and influenced by these early, transitional years. The concerns of middle class women—property rights, the franchise and moral uplift—would dominate the women's rights movement. But side by side with it, and at times cooperating with it, would grow a number of organizations serving the needs of working women.

American women were the largest disfranchised group in the nation's history, and they retained this position longer than any other group. Although they found ways of making their influence felt continuously, not only as individuals but as organized groups, power eluded them. The mill girl and the lady, both born in the age of Jackson, would not gain access to power until they learned to cooperate, each for her own separate interests. It would take almost six decades before they would find common ground. The issue around which they finally would unite and push their movement to victory was the "impractical and utopian" demand raised at Seneca Falls—the means to power in American society—female suffrage.

NOTES

1. Keith E. Melder, "The Beginnings of the Women's Rights Movement in the United States: 1800-1840" (Diss. Yale, 1963). Elisabeth A. Dexter, *Colonial Women of Affairs: Women in Business and Professions in America before 1776* (Boston, 1931); *Career Women of America: 1776-1840* (Francestown, N.H., 1950).

2. Herbert Moller, "Sex Composition and Corresponding Culture Patterns of Colonial America," *William and Mary Quarterly,* Ser. 3, II (April, 1945), 113-153.

3. The summary of the status of colonial women is based on the following sources: Mary Benson, *Women in 18th Century America: A Study of Opinion and Social Usage* (New York, 1935); Arthur Calhoun, *A Social History of the American Family,* 3 vols. (Cleveland, 1918); Dexter, *Colonial Women;* Dexter, *Career Women;* Edmund S. Morgan, *Virginians at Home: Family Life in the 18th Century* (Williamsburg, 1952); Julia C. Spruill, *Women's Life and Work in the Southern Colonies* (Chapel Hill, 1938).

4. E. M. Boatwright, "The political and legal status of women in Georgia: 1783-1860," *Georgia Historical Quarterly,* XXV (April, 1941). Richard B. Morris, *Studies in the History of American Law* (New York, 1930), Chap. 3. A summary of travelers' comments on American women may be found in: Jane Mesick, *The English Traveler in America: 1785-1835* (New York, 1922), 83-99.

5. For facts on colonial medicine the following sources were consulted: Wyndham B. Blanton, *Medicine in Virginia,* 3 vols. (Richmond, 1930); N. S. Davis, M.D., *History of Medical Education and Institutions in the United States. . . .* (Chicago, 1851); Dexter, *Career Women;* K. C. Hurd-Mead, M.D., *A History of Women in Medicine: from the earliest Times to the Beginning of the 19th Century* (Haddam, Conn., 1938); Geo. W. Norris, *The Early History of Medicine in Philadelphia* (Phila-

delphia, 1886); Joseph M. Toner, *Contributions to the Annals of Medical Progress in the United States before and during the War of Independence* (Washington, D.C., 1874). The citation regarding Mrs. Allyn is from Hurd-Mead, *Women in Medicine,* 487.

6. Fielding H. Garrison, M.D., *An Introduction to the History of Medicine* (Philadelphia, 1929). For licensing legislation: Davis, 88–103.

7. George Daniels, "The Professionalization of American Science: the emergent period, 1820–1860," paper delivered at the joint session of the History of Science Society and the Society of the History of Technology, San Francisco, December 28, 1965.

8. Hurd-Mead, *Women in Medicine,* 391.

9. *Ibid.,* 486.

10. Betsy E. Corner, *William Shippen Jr.: Pioneer in American Medical Education* (Philadelphia, 1951), 103.

11. *Ibid.*

12. Benjamin Lee Gordon, *Medieval and Renaissance Medicine* (New York, 1959), 689–691. Blanton, *Medicine,* II, 23–24; Hurd-Mead, *Women in Medicine,* 487–88; Annie Nathan Meyer, *Woman's Work in America* (New York, 1891). Harriot K. Hunt, M.D., *Glances and Glimpses or Fifty Years Social including Twenty Years Professional Life* (Boston, 1856), 127–140. Eleanor Flexner, *Century of Struggle: The Woman's Rights Movement in the United States* (Cambridge, Mass., 1959), 115–119.

13. Sophie H. Drinker, "Women Attorneys of Colonial Times," *Maryland Historical Society Bulletin,* LVI, No. 4 (Dec., 1961).

14. Dexter, *Colonial Women,* 34–35, 162–165.

15. Harriet W. Marr, *The Old New England Academies* (New York, 1959), Chap. 8; Thomas Woody, *A History of Women's Education in the United States,* 2 vols. (New York, 1929) H, 100–109, 458–460, 492–493.

16. Matthew Carey, *Essays on Political Economy . . .* (Philadelphia, 1822), 459.

17. The statements on women industrial workers are based on the following sources: Edith Abbot, *Women in Industry* (New York, 1910), 66–80; Edith Abbot, "Harriet Martineau and the Employment of Women in 1836," *Journal of Political Economy,* XIV (Dec., 1906), 614–626; Matthew Carey, *Miscellaneous Essays* (Philadelphia, 1830), 153–203; Helen L. Sumner, *History of Women in Industry in the United States,* in *Report on Condition of Woman and Child Wage-Earners in the United States,* 19 vols. (Washington, D.C., 1910), IX. Also: Elizabeth F. Baker, *Technology and Woman's Work* (New York, 1964), Chaps. 1–5.

18. Emily Putnam, *The Lady: Studies of certain significant Phases of her History* (New York, 1910), 319–320. Barbara Welter, "The Cult of True Womanhood: 1820–1860," *American Quarterly,* XVIII, No. 2, Part I (Summer, 1966), 151–174.

19. Veblen generalized from his observations of the society of the Gilded

Age and fell into the usual error of simply ignoring the lower class women, whom he dismissed as "drudges ... fairly content with their lot," but his analysis of women's role in "conspicuous consumption" and of the function of women's fashions is unsurpassed. For references see: Thorstein Veblen, *The Theory of the Leisure Class* (New York, 1962, first printing, 1899), 70-71, 231-232. Thorstein Veblen, "The Economic Theory of Woman's Dress," *Essays in Our Changing Order* (New York, 1934), 65-77.

20. Like most groups fighting status oppression women formulated a compensatory ideology of female superiority. Norton Mezvinsky has postulated that this was clearly expressed only in 1874; in fact this formulation appeared in the earliest speeches of Elizabeth Cady Stanton and in the speeches and resolutions of the Seneca Falls Conventions and other pre-Civil War woman's rights conventions. Rather than a main motivating force, the idea was a tactical formulation, designed to take advantage of the popularly held male belief in woman's "moral" superiority and to convince reformers that they needed the votes of women. Those middle class feminists who believed in woman's "moral" superiority exploited the concept in order to win their major goal—female equality. For references see: Norton Mezvinsky, "An Idea of Female Superiority," *Midcontinent American Studies Journal*, II, No. I (Spring, 1961), 17-26. E. C. Stanton, S. B. Anthony and M. J. Gage, eds., *A History of Woman Suffrage*, 6 vols. (New York, 1881-1922), I, 72, 479, 522, 529 and *passim*. Alan P. Grimes, *The Puritan Ethic and Woman Suffrage* (New York, 1967), Chaps. 2 and 3.

21. Stanton *et al*, *History of Woman Suffrage*, I, 70.

22. Mary R. Beard, *Woman as Force in History: A Study of Traditions and Realities* (New York, 1946).

Article 2

The Cult of True Womanhood: 1820-1860

BARBARA WELTER

The nineteenth-century American man was a busy builder of bridges and railroads, at work long hours in a materialistic society. The religious values of his forebears were neglected in practice if not in intent, and he occasionally felt some guilt that he had turned this new land, this temple of the chosen people, into one vast counting-house. But he could salve his conscience by reflecting that he had left behind a hostage, not only to fortune, but to all the values which he held so dear and treated so lightly. Woman, in the cult of True Womanhood[1] presented by the women's magazines, gift annuals and religious literature of the nineteenth century, was the hostage in the home.[2] In a society where values changed frequently, where fortunes rose and fell with frightening rapidity, where social and economic mobility provided instability as well as hope, one thing at least remained the same—a true woman was a true woman, wherever she was found. If anyone, male or female, dared to tamper with the complex of virtues which made up True Womanhood, he was damned immediately as an enemy of God, of civilization and of the Republic. It was a fearful obligation, a solemn responsibility, which the nineteenth-century American woman had—to uphold the pillars of the temple with her frail white hand.

The attributes of True Womanhood, by which a woman judged herself and was judged by her husband, her neighbors and society could be divided into four cardinal virtues—piety, purity, submissiveness and domesticity. Put them all together and they spelled mother, daughter, sister, wife—woman. Without them, no matter whether there was fame, achievement or wealth, all was ashes. With them she was promised happiness and power.

From *American Quarterly*, XVIII (Summer, 1966), 151-174. Copyright 1966, Trustees of the University of Pennsylvania. Reprinted by permission of the author and publisher.

Religion or piety was the core of woman's virtue, the source of her strength. Young men looking for a mate were cautioned to search first for piety, for if that were there, all else would follow.[3] Religion belonged to woman by divine right, a gift of God and nature. This "peculiar susceptibility" to religion was given her for a reason: "the vestal flame of piety, lighted up by Heaven in the breast of woman" would throw its beams into the naughty world of men.[4] So far would its candle power reach that the "Universe might be Englightened, Improved, and Harmonized by WOMAN!!"[5] She would be another, better Eve, working in cooperation with the Redeemer, bringing the world back "from its revolt and sin."[6] The world would be reclaimed for God through her suffering, for "God increased the cares and sorrows of woman, that she might be sooner constrained to accept the terms of salvation."[7] A popular poem by Mrs. Frances Osgood, "The Triumph of the Spiritual Over the Sensual" expressed just this sentiment, woman's purifying passionless love bringing an erring man back to Christ.[8]

Dr. Charles Meigs, explaining to a graduating class of medical students why women were naturally religious, said that "hers is a pious mind. Her confiding nature leads her more readily than men to accept the proffered grace of the Gospel."[9] Caleb Atwater, Esq., writing in *The Ladies' Repository*, saw the hand of the Lord in female piety: "Religion is exactly what a woman needs, for it gives her that dignity that best suits her dependence."[10] And Mrs. John Sandford, who had no very high opinion of her sex, agreed thoroughly: "Religion is just what woman needs. Without it she is ever restless or unhappy...."[11] Mrs. Sandford and the others did not speak only of that restlessness of the human heart, which St. Augustine notes, that can only find its peace in God. They spoke rather of religion as a kind of tranquilizer for the many undefined longings which swept even the most pious young girl, and about which it was better to pray than to think.

One reason religion was valued was that it did not take a woman away from her "proper sphere," her home. Unlike participation in other societies or movements, church work would not make her less domestic or submissive, less a True Woman. In religious vineyards, said the *Young Ladies' Literary and Missionary Report*, "you may labor without the apprehension of detracting from the charms of feminine delicacy." Mrs. S. L. Dagg, writing from her chapter of the Society in Tuscaloosa, Alabama, was equally reassuring: "As no sensible woman will suffer her intellectual pursuits to clash with her domestic duties" she should concentrate on religious work "which promotes these very duties."[12]

The women's seminaries aimed at aiding women to be religious, as well as accomplished. Mt. Holyoke's catalogue promised to make female education "a handmaid to the Gospel and an efficient auxiliary in the great task of renovating the world."[13] The Young Ladies' Seminary at Bordentown, New Jersey, declared its most important function to be "the forming of a sound and virtuous character."[14] In Keene, New Hampshire, the Seminary tried to instill a "consistent and useful character" in its students, to enable them in this life to be "a good friend, wife and mother" but more important, to qualify them for "the enjoyment of Celestial Happiness in the life to come."[15] And Joseph M' D. Mathews, Principal of Oakland Female Seminary in Hillsborough, Ohio, believed that "female education should be preeminently religious."[16]

If religion was so vital to a woman, irreligion was almost too awful to contemplate. Women were warned not to let their literary or intellectual pursuits take them away from God. Sarah Josepha Hale spoke darkly of those who, like Margaret Fuller, threw away the "One True Book" for others, open to error. Mrs. Hale used the unfortunate Miss Fuller as fateful proof that "the greater the intellectual force, the greater and more fatal the errors into which women fall who wander from the Rock of Salvation, Christ the Saviour. . . ."[17]

One gentleman, writing on "Female Irreligion" reminded his readers that "Man may make himself a brute, and does so very often, but can woman brutify herself to his level—the lowest level of human nature—without exerting special wonder?" Fanny Wright, because she was godless, "was no woman, mother though she be." A few years ago, he recalls, such women would have been whipped. In any case, "woman never looks lovelier than in her reverence for religion" and, conversely, "female irreligion is the most revolting feature in human character."[18]

Purity was as essential as piety to a young woman, its absence as unnatural and unfeminine. Without it she was, in fact, no woman at all, but a member of some lower order. A "fallen woman" was a "fallen angel," unworthy of the celestial company of her sex. To contemplate the loss of purity brought tears; to be guilty of such a crime, in the women's magazines at least, brought madness or death. Even the language of the flowers had bitter words for it: a dried white rose symbolized "Death Preferable to Loss of Innocence."[19]

The marriage night was the single great event of a woman's life, when she bestowed her greatest treasure upon her husband, and from that time on was completely dependent upon him, an empty vessel,[20] without legal or emotional existence of her own.[21]

Therefore all True Women were urged, in the strongest possible terms, to maintain their virtue, although men, being by nature more sensual than they, would try to assault it. Thomas Branagan admitted in *The Excellency of the Female Character Vindicated* that his sex would sin and sin again, they could not help it, but woman, stronger and purer, must not give in and let man "take liberties incompatible with her delicacy." "If you do," Branagan addressed his gentle reader, "You will be left in silent sadness to bewail your credulity, imbecility, duplicity, and premature prostitution."[22]

Mrs. Eliza Farrar, in *The Young Lady's Friend,* gave practical logistics to avoid trouble: "Sit not with another in a place that is too narrow; read not out of the same book; let not your eagerness to see anything induce you to place your head close to another person's."[23]

If such good advice was ignored the consequences were terrible and inexorable. In *Girlhood and Womanhood: Or Sketches of My Schoolmates,* by Mrs. A. J. Graves (a kind of mid-nineteenth-century *The Group*), the bad ends of a boarding school class of girls are scrupulously recorded. The worst end of all is reserved for "Amelia Dorrington: The Lost One." Amelia died in the almshouse "the wretched victim of depravity and intemperance" and all because her mother had let her be "high-spirited not prudent." These girlish high spirits had been misinterpreted by a young man, with disastrous results. Amelia's "thoughtless levity" was "followed by a total loss of virtuous principle" and Mrs. Graves editorializes that "the coldest reserve is more admirable in a woman a man wishes to make his wife, than the least approach to undue familiarity."[24]

A popular and often-reprinted story by Fanny Forester told the sad tale of "Lucy Dutton." Lucy "with the seal of innocence upon her heart, and a rose-leaf on her cheek" came out of her vine-covered cottage and ran into a city slicker. "And Lucy was beautiful and trusting, and thoughtless: and he was gay, selfish and profligate. Needs the story to be told? . . . Nay, censor, Lucy was a child—consider how young, how very untaught—oh! her innocence was no match for the sophistry of a gay, city youth! Spring came and shame was stamped upon the cottage at the foot of the hill." The baby died; Lucy went mad at the funeral and finally died herself. "Poor, poor Lucy Dutton! The grave is a blessed couch and pillow to the wretched. Rest thee there, poor Lucy!"[25] The frequency with which derangement follows loss of virtue suggests the exquisite sensibility of woman, and the possibility that, in the women's magazines at least, her intellect was geared to her hymen, not her brain.

If, however, a woman managed to withstand man's assaults on her virtue, she demonstrated her superiority and her power over him. Eliza Farnham, trying to prove this female superiority, concluded smugly that "the purity of women is the everlasting barrier against which the tides of man's sensual nature surge."[26]

A story in *The Lady's Amaranth* illustrates this dominance. It is set, improbably, in Sicily, where two lovers, Bianca and Tebaldo, have been separated because her family insisted she marry a rich old man. By some strange circumstance the two are in a shipwreck and cast on a desert island, the only survivors. Even here, however, the rigid standards of True Womanhood prevail. Tebaldo unfortunately forgets himself slightly, so that Bianca must warn him: "We may not indeed gratify our fondness by caresses, but it is still something to bestow our kindest language, and looks and prayers, and all lawful and honest attentions on each other." Something, perhaps, but not enough, and Bianca must further remonstrate: "It is true that another man is my husband, but you are my guardian angel." When even that does not work she says in a voice of sweet reason, passive and proper to the end, that she wishes he wouldn't but "still, if you insist, I will become what you wish; but I beseech you to consider, ere that decision, that debasement which I must suffer in your esteem." This appeal to his own double standards holds the beast in him at bay. They are rescued, discover that the old husband is dead, and after "mourning a decent season" Bianca finally gives in, legally.[27]

Men could be counted on to be grateful when women thus saved them from themselves. William Alcott, guiding young men in their relations with the opposite sex, told them that "Nothing is better calculated to preserve a young man from contamination of low pleasures and pursuits than frequent intercourse with the more refined and virtuous of the other sex." And he added, one assumes in equal innocence, that youths should "observe and learn to admire, that purity and ignorance of evil which is the characteristic of well-educated young ladies, and which, when we are near them, raises us above those sordid and sensual considerations which hold such sway over men in their intercourse with each other."[28]

The Rev. Jonathan F. Stearns was also impressed by female

chastity in the face of male passion, and warned woman never to compromise the source of her power: "Let her lay aside delicacy, and her influence over our sex is gone."[29]

Women themselves accepted, with pride but suitable modesty, this priceless virtue. *The Ladies' Wreath,* in "Woman the Creature of God and the Manufacturer of Society" saw purity as her greatest gift and chief means of discharging her duty to save the world: "Purity is the highest beauty—the true pole-star which is to guide humanity aright in its long, varied, and perilous voyage."[30]

Sometimes, however, a woman did not see the dangers to her treasure. In that case, they must be pointed out to her, usually by a male. In the nineteenth century any form of social change was tantamount to an attack on woman's virtue, if only it was correctly understood. For example, dress reform seemed innocuous enough and the bloomers worn by the lady of that name and her followers were certainly modest attire. Such was the reasoning only of the ignorant. In another issue of *The Ladies' Wreath* a young lady is represented in dialogue with her "Professor." The girl expresses admiration for the bloomer costume—it gives freedom of motion, is healthful and attractive. The "Professor" sets her straight. Trousers, he explains, are "only one of the many manifestations of that wild spirit of socialism and agrarian radicalism which is at present so rife in our land." The young lady recants immediately: "If this dress has any connexion with Fourierism or Socialism, or fanaticism in any shape whatever, I have no disposition to wear it at all . . . no true woman would so far compromise her delicacy as to espouse, however unwittingly, such a cause."[31]

America could boast that her duaghters were particularly innocent. In a poem on "The American Girl" the author wrote proudly:

> Her eye of light is the diamond bright,
> Her innocence the pearl,
> And these are ever the bridal gems
> That are worn by the American girl.[32]

Lydia Maria Child, giving advice to mothers, aimed at preserving that spirit of innocence. She regretted that "want of confidence between mothers and daughters on delicate subjects" and suggested a woman tell her daughter a few facts when she reached the age of twelve to "set her mind at rest." Then Mrs. Child confidently hoped that a young lady's "instinctive modesty" would "prevent her from

dwelling on the information until she was called upon to use it."[33] In
the same vein, a book of advice to the newly-married was titled
Whisper to a Bride.[34] As far as intimate information was concerned,
there was no need to whisper, since the book contained none at all.

A masculine summary of this virtue was expressed in a poem
"Female Charms":

> *I would have her as pure as the snow on*
> *the mount—*
> *As true as the smile that to infamy's*
> *given—*
> *As pure as the wave of the crystalline*
> *fount,*
> *Yet as warm in the heart as the sunlight of*
> *heaven.*
> *With a mind cultivated, not boastingly*
> *wise,*
> *I could gaze on such beauty, with exquisite*
> *bliss;*
> *With her heart on her lips and her soul in*
> *her eyes—*
> *What more could I wish in dear woman*
> *than this.*[35]

Man might, in fact, ask no more than this in woman, but she
was beginning to ask more of herself, and in the asking was threaten-
ing the third powerful and necessary virtue, submission. Purity,
considered as a moral imperative, set up a dilemma which was hard
to resolve. Woman must preserve her virtue until marriage and
marriage was necessary for her happiness. Yet marriage was, literally, an end to innocence. She was told not to question this dilemma,
but simply to accept it.

Submission was perhaps the most feminine virtue expected of
women. Men were supposed to be religious, although they rarely
had time for it, and supposed to be pure, although it came awfully
hard to them, but men were the movers, the doers, the actors.
Women were the passive, submissive responders. The order of dialogue was, of course, fixed in Heaven. Man was "woman's superior
by God's appointment, if not in intellectual dowry, at least by official
decree." Therefore, as Charles Elliott argued in *The Ladies' Repository,* she should submit to him "for the sake of good order at least."[36]

In *The Ladies Companion* a young wife was quoted approvingly as saying that she did not think woman should "feel and act for herself" because "When, next to God, her husband is not the tribunal to which her heart and intellect appeals—the golden bowl of affection is broken."[37] Women were warned that if they tampered with this quality they tampered with the order of the Universe.

The Young Lady's Book summarized the necessity of the passive virtues in its readers' lives: "It is, however, certain, that in whatever situation of life a woman is placed from her cradle to her grave, a spirit of obedience and submission, pliability of temper, and humility of mind, are required from her."[38]

Woman understood her position if she was the right kind of woman, a true woman. "She feels herself weak and timid. She needs a protector," declared George Burnap, in his lectures on *The Sphere and Duties of Woman*. "She is in a measure dependent. She asks for wisdom, constancy, firmness, perseverance, and she is willing to repay it all by the surrender of the full treasure of her affections. Woman despises in man every thing like herself except a tender heart. It is enough that she is effeminate and weak; she does not want another like herself."[39] Or put even more strongly by Mrs. Sandford: "A really sensible woman feels her dependence. She does what she can, but she is conscious of inferiority, and therefore grateful for support."[40]

Mrs. Sigourney, however, assured young ladies that although they were separate, they were equal. This difference of the sexes did not imply inferiority, for it was part of that same order of Nature established by Him "who bids the oak brave the fury of the tempest, and the alpine flower lean its cheek on the bosom of eternal snows."[41] Dr. Meigs had a different analogy to make the same point, contrasting the anatomy of the Apollo of the Belvedere (illustrating the male principle) with the Venus de Medici (illustrating the female principle). "Woman," said the physician, with a kind of clinical gallantry, "has a head almost too small for intellect but just big enough for love."[42]

This love itself was to be passive and responsive. "Love, in the heart of a woman," wrote Mrs. Farrar, "should partake largely of the nature of gratitude. She should love, because she is already loved by one deserving her regard."[43]

Woman was to work in silence, unseen, like Wordsworth's Lucy. Yet, "working like nature, in secret" her love goes forth to the world "to regulate its pulsation, and send forth from its heart, in pure and temperate flow, the life-giving current."[44] She was to work only for pure affection, without thought of money or ambition. A poem, "Woman and Fame," by Felicia Hemans, widely quoted in many of the gift books, concludes with a spirited renunciation of the gift of fame:

> *Away! to me, a woman, bring*
> *Sweet flowers from affection's spring.*[45]

"True feminine genius," said Grace Greenwood (Sara Jane Clarke) "is ever timid, doubtful, and clingingly dependent; a perpetual childhood." And she advised literary ladies in an essay on "The Intellectual Woman"—"Don't trample on the flowers while longing for the stars."[46] A wife who submerged her own talents to work for her husband was extolled as an example of a true woman. In *Women of Worth: A Book for Girls,* Mrs. Ann Flaxman, an artist of promise herself, was praised because she "devoted herself to sustain her husband's genius and aid him in his arduous career."[47]

Caroline Gilman's advice to the bride aimed at establishing this proper order from the beginning of a marriage: "Oh, young and lovely bride, watch well the first moments when your will conflicts with his to whom God and society have given the control. Reverence his *wishes* even when you do not his *opinions.*"[48]

Mrs. Gilman's perfect wife in *Recollections of a Southern Matron* realizes that "the three golden threads with which domestic happiness is woven" are "to repress a harsh answer, to confess a fault, and to stop (right or wrong) in the midst of self-defense, in gentle submission." Woman could do this, hard though it was, because in her heart she knew she was right and so could afford to be forgiving, even a trifle condescending. "Men are not unreasonable," averred Mrs. Gilman. "Their difficulties lie in not understanding the moral and physical nature of our sex. They often wound through ignorance, and are suprised at having offended." Wives were advised to do their best to reform men, but if they couldn't, to give up gracefully. "If any habit of his annoyed me, I spoke of it once or twice, calmly, then bore it quietly."[49]

A wife should occupy herself "only with domestic affairs—wait till your husband confides to you those of a high importance—and do not give your advice until he asks for it," advised the *Lady's Token.* At all times she should behave in a manner becoming a woman, who had "no arms other than gentleness." Thus "if he is abusive, never retort."[50] *A Young Lady's Guide to the Harmonious Development of a Christian Character* suggested that females should "become as little children" and "avoid a controversial spirit."[51] *The Mother's Assistant and Young Lady's Friend* listed "Always Conciliate" as its first commandment in "Rules for Conjugal and Domestic Happiness." Small wonder that these same rules ended with the succinct maxim: "Do not expect too much."[52]

As mother, as well as wife, woman was required to submit to fortune. In *Letters to Mothers* Mrs. Sigourney sighed: "To bear the evils and sorrows which may be appointed us, with a patient mind, should be the continual effort of our sex. . . . It seems, indeed, to be expected of us; since the passive and enduring virtues are more immediately within our province." Of these trials "the hardest was to bear the loss of children with submission" but the indomitable Mrs. Sigourney found strength to murmur to the bereaved mother: "The Lord loveth a cheerful giver."[53] *The Ladies' Parlor Companion* agreed thoroughly in "A Submissive Mother," in which a mother who had already buried two children and was nursing a dying baby saw her sole remaining child "probably scalded to death. Handing over the infant to die in the arms of a friend, she bowed in sweet submission to the double stroke." But the child "through the goodness of God survived, and the mother learned to say 'Thy will be done.' "[54]

Woman then, in all her roles, accepted submission as her lot. It was a lot she had not chosen or deserved. As *Godey's* said, "the lesson of submission is forced upon woman." Without comment or criticism the writer affirms that "To suffer and to be silent under suffering seems the great command she has to obey."[55] George Burnap referred to a woman's life as "a series of suppressed emotions."[56] She was, as Emerson said, "More vulnerable, more infirm, more mortal than man."[57] The death of a beautiful woman, cherished in fiction, represented woman as the innocent victim, suffering without sin, too pure and good for this world but too weak and passive to resist its evil forces.[58] The best refuge for such a delicate creature was the warmth and safety of her home.

The true woman's place was unquestionably by her own fireside—as daughter, sister, but most of all as wife and mother. Therefore domesticity was among the virtues most prized by the women's magazines. "As society is constituted," wrote Mrs. S. E. Farley, on the "Domestic and Social Claims on Woman," "the true dignity and beauty of the female character seem to consist in a right understanding and faithful and cheerful performance of social and family duties."[59] Sacred Scripture re-enforced social pressure: "St. Paul knew what was best for women when he advised them to be domestic," said Mrs. Sandford. "There is composure at home; there is something sedative in the duties which home involves. It affords security not only from the world, but from delusions and errors of every kind."[60]

From her home woman performed her great task of bringing men back to God. *The Young Ladies' Class Book* was sure that "the domestic fireside is the great guardian of society against the excesses of human passions."[61] *The Lady at Home* expressed its convictions in its very title and concluded that "even if we cannot reform the world in a moment, we can begin the work by reforming ourselves and our households—It is woman's mission. Let her not look away from her own little family circle for the means of producing moral and social reforms, but begin at home."[62]

Home was supposed to be a cheerful place, so that brothers, husbands and sons would not go elsewhere in search of a good time. Woman was expected to dispense comfort and cheer. In writing the biography of Margaret Mercer (every inch a true woman) her biographer (male) notes: "She never forgot that it is the peculiar province of woman to minister to the comfort, and promote the happiness, first, of those most nearly allied to her, and then of those, who by the Providence of God are placed in a state of dependence upon her."[63] Many other essays in the women's journals showed woman as comforter: "Woman, Man's Best Friend," "Woman, the Greatest Social Benefit," "Woman, A Being to Come Home To," "The Wife: Source of Comfort and the Spring of Joy."[64]

One of the most important functions of woman as comforter was her role as nurse. Her own health was probably, although regrettably, delicate.[65] Many homes had "little sufferers," those pale children who wasted away to saintly deaths. And there were enough other illnesses of youth and age, major and minor, to give the nineteenth-century American woman nursing experience. The sickroom called for the exercise of her higher qualities of patience, mercy and gentleness as well as for her housewifely arts. She could thus fulfill her dual feminine function—beauty and usefulness.

The cookbooks of the period offer formulas for gout cordials, ointment for sore nipples, hiccough and cough remedies, opening pills and refreshing drinks for fever, along with recipes for pound cake, jumbles, stewed calves head and currant wine.[66] *The Ladies'*

New Book of Cookery believed that "food prepared by the kind hand of a wife, mother, sister, friend" tasted better and had a "restorative power which money cannot purchase."[67]

A chapter of *The Young Lady's Friend* was devoted to woman's privilege as "Ministering spirit at the couch of the sick." Mrs. Farrar advised a soft voice, gentle and clean hands, and a cheerful smile. She also cautioned against an excess of female delicacy. That was all right for a young lady in the parlor, but not for bedside manners. Leeches, for example, were to be regarded as "a curious piece of mechanism ... their ornamental stripes should recommend them even to the eye, and their valuable services to our feelings." And she went on calmly to discuss their use. Nor were women to shrink from medical terminology, since "If you cultivate right views of the wonderful structure of the body, you will be as willing to speak to a physician of the bowels as the brains of your patient."[68]

Nursing the sick, particularly sick males, not only made a woman feel useful and accomplished, but increased her influence. In a piece of heavy-handed humor in *Godey's* a man confessed that some women were only happy when their husbands were ailing that they might have the joy of nursing him to recovery "thus gratifying their medical vanity and their love of power by making him more dependent upon them."[69] In a similar vein a husband sometimes suspects his wife "almost wishes me dead—for pleasure of being utterly inconsolable."[70]

In the home women were not only the highest adornment of civilization, but they were supposed to keep busy at morally uplifting tasks. Fortunately most of housework, if looked at in true womanly fashion, could be regarded as uplifting. Mrs. Sigourney extolled its virtues: "The science of housekeeping affords exercise for the judgment and energy, ready recollection, and patient self-possession, that are the characteristics of a superior mind."[71] According to Mrs. Farrar, making beds was good exercise, the repetitiveness of routine tasks inculcated patience and perservance, and proper management of the home was a surprisingly complex art: "There is more to be learned about pouring out tea and coffee, than most young ladies are willing to believe."[72] *Godey's* went so far as to suggest coyly, in "Learning vs. Housewifery" that the two were complementary, not opposed: chemistry could be utilized in cooking, geometry in dividing cloth, and phrenology in discovering talent in children.[73]

Women were to master every variety of needlework, for, as Mrs. Sigourney pointed out, "Needle-work, in all its forms of use, elegance, and ornament, has ever been the appropriate occupation of woman."[74] Embroidery improved taste; knitting promoted serenity and economy.[75] Other forms of artsy-craftsy activity for her leisure moments included painting on glass or velvet, Poonah work, tussy-mussy frames for her own needlepoint or water colors, stands for hyacinths, hair bracelets or baskets of feathers.[76]

She was expected to have a special affinity for flowers. To the editors of The Lady's Token "A Woman never appears more truly in her sphere, than when she divides her time between her domestic avocations and the culture of flowers."[77] She could write letters, an activity particularly feminine since it had to do with the outpourings of the heart,[78] or practice her drawingroom skills of singing and playing an instrument. She might even read.

Here she faced a bewildering array of advice. The female was dangerously addicted to novels, according to the literature of the period. She should avoid them, since they interfered with "serious piety." If she simply couldn't help herself and read them anyway, she should choose edifying ones from lists of morally acceptable authors. She should study history since it "showed the depravity of the human heart and the evil nature of sin." On the whole, "religious biography was best."[79]

The women's magazines themselves could be read without any loss of concern for the home. Godey's promised the husband that he would find his wife "no less assiduous for his reception, or less sincere in welcoming his return" as a result of reading their magazine.[80] The Lily of the Valley won its right to be admitted to the boudoir by confessing that it was "like its namesake humble and unostentatious, but it is yet pure, and, we trust, free from moral imperfections."[81]

No matter what later authorities claimed, the nineteenth century knew that girls could be ruined by a book. The seduction stories regard "exciting and dangerous books" as contributory causes of disaster. The man without honorable intentions always provides the innocent maiden with such books as a prelude to his assault on her virtue.[82] Books which attacked or seemed to attack woman's accepted place in society were regarded as equally dangerous. A reviewer of Harriet Martineau's Society in America wanted it kept out of the hands of American women. They were so susceptible to persuasion, with their "gentle yielding natures" that they might listen to "the bold ravings of the hard-featured of their own sex." The frightening result: "such reading will unsettle them for their true station and pursuits, and they will throw the world back again into confusion."[83]

The debate over women's education posed the question of whether a "finished" education detracted from the practice of housewifely arts. Again it proved to be a case of semantics, for a true woman's education was never "finished" until she was instructed in the gentle science of homemaking.[84] Helen Irving, writing on "Literary Women," made it very clear that if women invoked the muse, it was as a genie of the household lamp. "If the necessities of her position require these duties at her hands, she will perform them nonetheless cheerfully, that she knows herself capable of higher things." The literary woman must conform to the same standards as any other woman: "That her home shall be made a loving place of rest and joy and comfort for those who are dear to her, will be the first wish of every true woman's heart."[85] Mrs. Ann Stephens told women who wrote to make sure they did not sacrifice one domestic duty. "As for genius, make it a domestic plant. Let its roots strike deep in your house. . . ."[86]

The fear of "blue stockings" (the eighteenth-century male's term of derision for educated or literary women) need not persist for nineteenth-century American men. The magazines presented spurious dialogues in which bachelors were convinced of their fallacy in fearing educated wives. One such dialogue took place between a young man and his female cousin. Ernest deprecates learned ladies ("A *Woman* is far more lovable than a *philosopher*") but Alice refutes him with the beautiful example of their Aunt Barbara who "although she *has* perpetrated the heinous crime of writing some half dozen folios" is still a model of "the spirit of feminine gentleness." His memory prodded, Ernest concedes that, by George, there was a woman: "When I last had a cold she not only made me a bottle of cough syrup, but when I complained of nothing new to read, set to work and wrote some twenty stanzas on consumption."[87]

The magazines were filled with domestic tragedies in which spoiled young girls learned that when there was a hungry man to feed French and china painting were not helpful. According to these stories many a marriage is jeopardized because the wife has not learned to keep house. Harriet Beecher Stowe wrote a sprightly piece of personal experience for *Godey's,* ridiculing her own bad housekeeping as a bride. She used the same theme in a story "The Only Daughter," in which the pampered beauty learns the facts of domestic life from a rather difficult source, her mother-in-law. Mrs.

Hamilton tells Caroline in the sweetest way possible to shape up in the kitchen, reserving her rebuke for her son: "You are her husband—her guide—her protector—now see what you can do," she admonishes him. "Give her credit for every effort: treat her faults with tenderness; encourage and praise whenever you can, and depend upon it, you will see another woman in her." He is properly masterful, she properly domestic and in a few months Caroline is making lumpless gravy and keeping up with the darning. Domestic tranquillity has been restored and the young wife moralizes: "Bring up a girl to feel that she has a responsible part to bear in promoting the happiness of the family, and you make a reflecting being of her at once, and remove that lightness and frivolity of character which makes her shrink from graver studies."[88] These stories end with the heroine drying her hands on her apron and vowing that *her* daughter will be properly educated, in piecrust as well as Poonah work.

The female seminaries were quick to defend themselves against any suspicion of interfering with the role which nature's God had assigned to women. They hoped to enlarge and deepen that role, but not to change its setting. At the Young Ladies' Seminary and Collegiate Institute in Monroe City, Michigan, the catalogue admitted few of its graduates would be likely "to fill the learned professions." Still, they were called to "other scenes of usefulness and honor." The average woman is to be "the presiding genius of love" in the home, where she is to "give a correct and elevated literary taste to her children, and to assume that influential station that she ought to possess as the companion of an educated man."[89]

At Miss Pierce's famous school in Litchfield, the students were taught that they had "attained the perfection of their characters when they could combine their elegant accomplishments with a turn for solid domestic virtues."[90] Mt. Holyoke paid pious tribute to domestic skills: "Let a young lady despise this branch of the duties of woman, and she despises the appointments of her existence." God, nature and the Bible "enjoin these duties on the sex, and she cannot violate them with impunity." Thus warned, the young lady would have to seek knowledge of these duties elsewhere, since it was not in the curriculum at Mt. Holyoke. "We would not take this privilege from the mother."[91]

One reason for knowing her way around a kitchen was that America was "a land of precarious fortunes," as Lydia Maria Child pointed out in her book *The Frugal Housewife: Dedicated to Those Who Are Not Ashamed of Economy.* Mrs. Child's chapter "How To

Endure Poverty" prescribed a combination of piety and knowledge—the kind of knowledge found in a true woman's education, "a thorough religious *useful* education."[92] The woman who had servants today, might tomorrow, because of a depression or panic, be forced to do her own work. If that happened she knew how to act, for she was to be the same cheerful consoler of her husband in their cottage as in their mansion.

An essay by Washington Irving, much quoted in the gift annuals, discussed the value of a wife in case of business reverses: "I have observed that a married man falling into misfortune is more apt to achieve his situation in the world than a single one . . . it is beautifully ordained by Providence that woman, who is the ornament of man in his happier hours, should be his stay and solace when smitten with sudden calamity."[93]

A story titled simply but eloquently "The Wife" dealt with the quiet heroism of Ellen Graham during her husband's plunge from fortune to poverty. Ned Graham said of her: "Words are too poor to tell you what I owe to that noble woman. In our darkest seasons of adversity, she has been an angel of consolation—utterly forgetful of self and anxious only to comfort and sustain me." Of course she had a little help from "faithful Dinah who absolutely refused to leave her beloved mistress," but even so Ellen did no more than would be expected of any true woman.[94]

Most of this advice was directed to woman as wife. Marriage was the proper state for the exercise of the domestic virtues. "True Love and a Happy Home," an essay in *The Young Ladies' Oasis,* might have been carved on every girl's hope chest.[95] But although marriage was best, it was not absolutely necessary. The women's magazines tried to remove the stigma from being an "Old Maid." They advised no marriage at all rather than an unhappy one contracted out of selfish motives.[96] Their stories showed maiden ladies as unselfish ministers to the sick, teachers of the young, or moral preceptors with their pens, beloved of the entire village. Usually the life of single blessedness resulted from the premature death of a fiancé, or was chosen through fidelity to some high mission. For example, in "Two Sisters," Mary devotes herself to Ellen and her abandoned children, giving up her own chance for marriage. "Her devotion to her sister's happiness has met its reward in the consciousness of having fulfilled a sacred duty."[97] Very rarely, a "woman of genius" was absolved from the necessity of marriage, being so extraordinary that she did not need the security or status of being a wife.[98] Most often, however, if girls proved "difficult," marriage and a family were regarded as a cure.[99] The "sedative quality" of a home could be counted on to subdue even the most restless spirits.

George Burnap saw marriage as "that sphere for which woman was originally intended, and to which she is so exactly fitted to adorn and bless, as the wife, the mistress of a home, the solace, the aid, and the counsellor of that ONE, for whose sake alone the world is of any consequence to her."[100] Samuel Miller preached a sermon on women: "How interesting and important are the duties devolved on females as WIVES . . . the counsellor and friend of the husband; who makes it her daily study to lighten his cares, to soothe his sorrows, and to augment his joys; who, like a guardian angel, watches over his interests, warns him against dangers, comforts him under trials; and by her pious, assiduous, and attractive deportment, constantly endeavors to render him more virtuous, more useful, more honourable, and more happy."[101] A woman's whole interest should be focused on her husband, paying him "those numberless attentions to which the French give the title of *petits soins* and which the woman who loves knows so well how to pay . . . she should consider nothing as trivial which could win a smile of approbation from him."[102]

Marriage was seen not only in terms of service but as an increase in authority for woman. Burnap concluded that marriage improves the female character "not only because it puts her under the best possible tuition, that of the affections, and affords scope to her active energies, but because it gives her higher aims, and a more dignified position."[103] *The Lady's Amaranth* saw it as a balance of power: "The man bears rule over his wife's person and conduct. She bears rule over his inclinations: he governs by law; she by persuasion. . . . The empire of the woman is an empire of softness . . . her commands are caresses, her menaces are tears."[104]

Woman should marry, but not for money. She should choose only the high road of true love and not truckle to the values of a materialistic society. A story "Marrying for Money" (subtlety was not the strong point of the ladies' magazines) depicts Gertrude, the heroine, rueing the day she made her crass choice: "It is a terrible thing to live without love. . . . A woman who dares marry for aught but the purest affection, calls down the just judgments of heaven upon her head."[105]

The corollary to marriage, with or without true love, was motherhood, which added another dimension to her usefulness and her prestige. It also anchored her even more firmly to the home. "My

Friend," wrote Mrs. Sigourney, "If in becoming a mother, you have reached the climax of your happiness, you have also taken a higher place in the scale of being ... you have gained an increase of power."[106] The Rev. J. N. Danforth pleaded in *The Ladies' Casket*, "Oh, mother, acquit thyself well in thy humble sphere, for thou mayest affect the world."[107] A true woman naturally loved her children; to suggest otherwise was monstrous.[108]

America depended upon her mothers to raise up a whole generation of Christian statesmen who could say "all that I am I owe to my angel mother."[109] The mothers must do the inculcating of virtue since the fathers, alas, were too busy chasing the dollar. Or as *The Ladies' Companion* put it more effusively, the father "weary with the heat and burden of life's summer day, or trampling with unwilling foot the decaying leaves of life's autumn, has forgotten the sympathies of life's joyous springtime. ... The acquisition of wealth, the advancement of his children in worldly honor—these are his self-imposed tasks." It was his wife who formed "the infant mind as yet untainted by contact with evil ... like wax beneath the plastic hand of the mother."[110]

The Ladies' Wreath offered a fifty-dollar prize to the woman who submitted the most convincing essay on "How May An American Woman Best Show Her Patriotism." The winner was Miss Elizabeth Wetherell who provided herself with a husband in her answer. The wife in the essay of course asked her husband's opinion. He tried a few jokes first—"Call her eldest son George Washington," "Don't speak French, speak American"—but then got down to telling her in sober prize-winning truth what women could do for their country. Voting was no asset, since that would result only in "a vast increase of confusion and expense without in the smallest degree affecting the result." Besides, continued this oracle, "looking down at their child," if "we were to go a step further and let the children vote, their first act would be to vote their mothers at home." There is no comment on this devastating male logic and he continues: "Most women would follow the lead of their fathers and husbands," and the few who would "fly off on a tangent from the circle of home influence would cancel each other out."

The wife responds dutifully: "I see all that. I never understood so well before." Encouraged by her quick womanly perception, the master of the house resolves the question—an American woman best shows her patriotism by staying at home, where she brings her influence to bear "upon the right side for the country's weal." That woman will instinctively choose the side of right he has no doubt. Besides her "natural refinement and closeness to God" she has the "blessed advantage of a quiet life" while man is exposed to conflict and evil. She stays home with "her Bible and a well-balanced mind" and raises her sons to be good Americans. The judges rejoiced in this conclusion and paid the prize money cheerfully, remarking "they deemed it cheap at the price."[111]

If any woman asked for greater scope for her gifts the magazines were sharply critical. Such women were tampering with society, undermining civilization. Mary Wollstonecraft, Frances Wright and Harriet Martineau were condemned in the strongest possible language—they were read out of the sex. "They are only semi-women, mental hermaphrodites." The Rev. Harrington knew the women of America could not possibly approve of such perversions and went to some wives and mothers to ask if they did want a "wider sphere of interest" as these nonwomen claimed. The answer was reassuring. " 'NO!' they cried simultaneously, 'Let the men take care of politics, *we will take care of the children!*' " Again female discontent resulted only from a lack of understanding: women were not subservient, they were rather "chosen vessels." Looked at in this light the conclusion was inescapable: "Noble, sublime is the task of the American mother."[112]

"Women's Rights" meant one thing to reformers, but quite another to the True Woman. She knew her rights,

> *The right to love whom others scorn,*
> *The right to comfort and to mourn,*
> *The right to shed new joy on earth,*
> *The right to feel the soul's high worth . . .*
> *Such women's rights, and God will bless*
> *And crown their champions with suc-*
> *cess.*[113]

The American woman had her choice—she could define her rights in the way of the women's magazines and insure them by the practice of the requisite virtues, or she could go outside the home, seeking other rewards than love. It was a decision on which, she was told, everything in her world depended. "Yours it is to determine," the Rev. Mr. Stearns solemnly warned from the pulpit, "whether the beautiful order of society . . . shall continue as it has been" or whether "society shall break up and becomes a chaos of disjointed and unsightly elements."[114] If she chose to listen to other voices than those of her proper mentors, sought other rooms than those of her home, she lost both her happiness and her power—"that almost magic power, which, in her proper sphere, she now wields over the destinies of the world."[115]

But even while the women's magazines and related literature encouraged this ideal of the perfect woman, forces were at work in the nineteenth century which impelled woman herself to change, to play a more creative role in society. The movements for social reform, westward migration, missionary activity, utopian communities, industrialism, the Civil War—all called forth responses from woman which differed from those she was trained to believe were hers by nature and divine decree. The very perfection of True Womanhood, moreover, carried within itself the seeds of its own destruction. For if woman was so very little less than the angels, she should surely take a more active part in running the world, especially since men were making such a hash of things.

Real women often felt they did not live up to the ideal of True Womanhood: some of them blamed themselves, some challenged the standard, some tried to keep the virtues and enlarge the scope of womanhood.[116] Somehow through this mixture of challenge and acceptance, of change and continuity, the True Woman evolved into the New Woman—a transformation as startling in its way as the abolition of slavery or the coming of the machine age. And yet the stereotype, the "mystique" if you will, of what woman was and ought to be persisted, bringing guilt and confusion in the midst of opportunity.[117]

The women's magazines and related literature had feared this very dislocation of values and blurring of roles. By careful manipulation and interpretation they sought to convince woman that she had the best of both worlds—power and virtue—and that a stable order of society depended upon her maintaining her traditional place in it. To that end she was identified with everything that was beautiful and holy.

"Who Can Find a Valiant Woman?" was asked frequently from the pulpit and the editorial pages. There was only one place to look for her—at home. Clearly and confidently these authorities proclaimed the True Woman of the nineteenth century to be the Valiant Woman of the Bible, in whom the heart of her husband rejoiced and whose price was above rubies.

NOTES

1. Authors who addressed themselves to the subject of women in the mid-
nineteenth century used this phrase as frequently as writers on religion
mentioned God. Neither group felt it necessary to define their favorite
terms; they simply assumed—with some justification—that readers
would intuitively understand exactly what they meant. Frequently
what people of one era take for granted is most striking and revealing
to the student from another. In a sense this analysis of the ideal woman
of the mid-nineteenth century is an examination of what writers of
that period actually meant when they used so confidently the vague
phrase True Womanhood.

2. The conclusions reached in this article are based on a survey of almost
all of the women's magazines published for more than three years
during the period 1820-60 and a sampling of those published for less
than three years; all the gift books cited in Ralph Thompson, *American
Literary Annuals and Gift Books, 1825-1865* (New York, 1936) depos-
ited in the Library of Congress, the New York Public Library, the
New-York Historical Society, Columbia University Special Collections,
Library of the City College of the University of New York, Pennsylvania Historical Society, Massachusetts Historical Society, Boston Public
Library, Fruitlands Museum Library, the Smithsonian Institution and
the Wisconsin Historical Society; hundreds of religious tracts and
sermons in the American Unitarian Society and the Galatea Collection
of the Boston Public Library; and the large collection of nineteenth-
century cookbooks in the New York Public Library and the Academy
of Medicine of New York. Corroborative evidence not cited in this
article was found in women's diaries, memoirs, autobiographies and
personal papers, as well as in all the novels by women which sold over
75,000 copies during this period, as cited in Frank Luther Mott,
Golden Multitudes: The Story of Best Sellers in the United States
(New York, 1947) and H. R. Brown, *The Sentimental Novel in America, 1789-1860* (Durham, N. C., 1940). This latter information also
indicated the effect of the cult of True Womanhood on those most
directly concerned.

3. As in "The Bachelor's Dream," in *The Lady's Gift: Souvenir for All
Seasons* (Nashua, N. H., 1849), p. 37.

4. *The Young Ladies' Class Book: A Selection of Lessons for Reading in
Prose and Verse,* ed. Ebenezer Bailey, Principal of Young Ladies' High
School, Boston (Boston, 1831), p. 168.

5. A Lady of Philadelphia, *The World Enlightened, Improved, and Harmonized by WOMAN!!! A lecture, delivered in the City of New
York, before the Young Ladies' Society for Mutual Improvement, on
the following question, proposed by the society, with the offer of $100*

for the best lecture that should be read before them on the subject proposed;—What is the power and influence of woman in moulding the manners, morals and habits of civil society? (Philadelphia, 1840), p. 1.

6. The Young Lady's Book: A Manual of Elegant Recreations, Exercises, and Pursuits (Boston, 1830), p. 29.

7. Woman As She Was, Is, and Should Be (New York, 1849), p. 206.

8. "The Triumph of the Spiritual Over the Sensual: An Allegory," in Ladies' Companion: A Monthly Magazine Embracing Every Department of Literature, Embellished With Original Engravings and Music, XVII (New York) (1842), 67.

9. Lecture on Some of the Distinctive Characteristics of the Female, delivered before the class of the Jefferson Medical College, Jan. 1847 (Philadelphia, 1847), p. 13.

10. "Female Education," Ladies' Repository and Gatherings of the West: A Monthly Periodical Devoted to Literature and Religion, I (Cincinnati), 12.

11. Woman, in Her Social and Domestic Character (Boston, 1842), pp. 41–42.

12. Second Annual Report of the Young Ladies' Literary and Missionary Association of the Philadelphia Collegiate Institution (Philadelphia, 1840), pp. 20, 26.

13. Mt. Holyoke Female Seminary: Female Education. Tendencies of the Principles Embraced, and the System Adopted in the Mt. Holyoke Female Seminary (Boston, 1839), p. 3.

14. Prospectus of the Young Ladies' Seminary at Bordentown, New Jersey (Bordentown, 1836), p. 7.

15. Catalogue of the Young Ladies' Seminary in Keene, New Hampshire (n.p., 1832), p. 20.

16. "Report to the College of Teachers, Cincinnati, October, 1840" in Ladies' Repository, I (1841), 50.

17. Woman's Record: or Sketches of All Distinguished Women from 'The Beginning' Till A. D. 1850 (New York, 1853), pp. 665, 669.

18. "Female Irreligion," Ladies' Companion, XIII (May–Oct. 1840), 111.

19. The Lady's Book of Flowers and Poetry, ed. Lucy Hooper (New York, 1842), has a "Floral Dictionary" giving the symbolic meaning of floral tributes.

20. See, for example, Nathaniel Hawthorne, The Blithedale Romance (Boston, 1852), p. 71, in which Zenobia says: "How can she be happy, after discovering that fate has assigned her but one single event, which she must contrive to make the substance of her whole life? A man has his choice of innumerable events."

117

21. Mary R. Beard, *Woman As Force in History* (New York, 1946) makes this point at some length. According to common law, a woman had no legal existence once she was married and therefore could not manage property, sue in court, etc. In the 1840s and 1850s laws were passed in several states to remedy this condition.

22. *Excellency of the Female Character Vindicated: Being an Investigation Relative to the Cause and Effects on the Encroachments of Men Upon the Rights of Women, and the Too Frequent Degradation and Consequent Misfortunes of The Fair Sex* (New York, 1807), pp. 277, 278.

23. By a Lady (Eliza Ware Rotch Farrar), *The Young Lady's Friend* (Boston, 1837), p. 293.

24. *Girlhood and Womanhood: or, Sketches of My Schoolmates* (Boston, 1844), p. 140.

25. Emily Chubbuck, *Alderbrook* (Boston, 1847), 2nd. ed., II, 121, 127.

26. *Woman and Her Era* (New York, 1864), p. 95.

27. "The Two Lovers of Sicily," *The Lady's Amaranth: A Journal of Tales, Essays, Excerpts—Historical and Biographical Sketches, Poetry and Literature in General* (Philadelphia), II (Jan. 1839), 17.

28. *The Young Man's Guide* (Boston, 1833), pp. 229, 231.

29. *Female Influence: and the True Christian Mode of Its Exercise; a Discourse Delivered in the First Presbyterian Church in Newburyport, July 30, 1837* (Newburyport, 1837), p. 18.

30. W. Tolles, "Woman The Creature of God and the Manufacturer of Society," *Ladies' Wreath* (New York), III (1852), 205.

31. Prof. William M. Heim, "The Bloomer Dress," *Ladies' Wreath*, III (1852), 247.

32. *The Young Lady's Offering: or Gems of Prose and Poetry* (Boston, 1853), p. 283. The American girl, whose innocence was often connected with ignorance, was the spiritual ancestress of the Henry James heroine. Daisy Miller, like Lucy Dutton, saw innocence lead to tragedy.

33. *The Mother's Book* (Boston, 1831), pp. 151, 152.

34. Mrs. L. H. Sigourney, *Whisper to a Bride* (Hartford, 1851), in which Mrs. Sigourney's approach is summed up in this quotation: "Home! Blessed bride, thou art about to enter this sanctuary, and to become a priestess at its altar!," p. 44.

35. S. R. R., "Female Charms," *Godey's Magazine and Lady's Book* (Philadelphia), XXXIII (1846), 52.

36. Charles Elliott, "Arguing With Females," *Ladies' Repository,* I (1841), 25.

37. *Ladies' Companion,* VIII (Jan. 1838), 147.

38. *The Young Lady's Book* (New York, 1830), American edition, p. 28.

(This is a different book than the one of the same title and date of publication cited in note 6.)

39. *Sphere and Duties of Woman* (5th ed., Baltimore, 1854), p. 47.

40. *Woman*, p. 15.

41. *Letters to Young Ladies* (Hartford, 1835), p. 179.

42. *Lecture*, p. 17.

43. *The Young Lady's Friend*, p. 313.

44. Maria J. McIntosh, *Woman in America: Her Work and Her Reward* (New York, 1850), p. 25.

45. *Poems and a Memoir of the Life of Mrs. Felicia Hemans* (London, 1860), p. 16.

46. Letter "To an Unrecognized Poetess, June, 1846" (Sara Jane Clarke), *Greenwood Leaves* (2nd ed.; Boston, 1850), p. 311.

47. "The Sculptor's Assistant: Ann Flaxman," in *Women of Worth: A Book for Girls* (New York, 1860), p. 263.

48. Mrs. Clarissa Packard (Mrs. Caroline Howard Gilman), *Recollections of a Housekeeper* (New York, 1834), p. 122.

49. *Recollections of a Southern Matron* (New York, 1838). pp. 256, 257.

50. *The Lady's Token: or Gift of Friendship*, ed. Colesworth Pinckney (Nashua, N. H., 1848), p. 119.

51. Harvey Newcomb, *Young Lady's Guide to the Harmonious Development of Christian Character* (Boston, 1846), p. 10.

52. "Rules for Conjugal and Domestic Happiness," *Mother's Assistant and Young Lady's Friend*, III (Boston), (April 1843), 115.

53. *Letters to Mothers* (Hartford, 1838), p. 199. In the diaries and letters of women who lived during this period the death of a child seemed consistently to be the hardest thing for them to bear and to occasion more anguish and rebellion, as well as eventual submission, than any other event in their lives.

54. "A Submissive Mother," *The Ladies' Parlor Companion: A Collection of Scattered Fragments and Literary Gems* (New York, 1852), p. 358.

55. "Woman," *Godey's Lady's Book*, II (Aug. 1831), 110.

56. *Sphere and Duties of Woman*, p. 172.

57. Ralph Waldo Emerson, "Woman," *Complete Writings of Ralph Waldo Emerson* (New York, 1875), p. 1180.

58. As in Donald Fraser, *The Mental Flower Garden* (New York, 1857). Perhaps the most famous exponent of this theory is Edgar Allan Poe who affirms in "The Philosophy of Composition" that "the death of a beautiful woman is unquestionably the most poetical topic in the world. . . ."

59. "Domestic and Social Claims on Woman," *Mother's Magazine*, VI (1846), 21.

60. *Woman*, p. 173.

61. *The Young Ladies' Class Book*, p. 166.

62. T. S. Arthur, *The Lady at Home: or, Leaves from the Every-Day Book of an American Woman* (Philadelphia, 1847), pp. 177, 178.

63. Caspar Morris, *Margaret Mercer* (Boston, 1840), quoted in *Woman's Record*, p. 425.

64. These particular titles come from: *The Young Ladies' Oasis: or Gems of Prose and Poetry*, ed. N. L. Ferguson (Lowell, 1851), pp. 14, 16; *The Genteel School Reader* (Philadelphia, 1849), p. 271; and *Magnolia*, I (1842), 4. A popular poem in book form, published in England, expressed very fully this concept of woman as comforter: Coventry Patmore, *The Angel in the Home* (Boston, 1856 and 1857). Patmore expressed his devotion to True Womanhood in such lines as:

> *The gentle wife, who decks his board*
> *And makes his day to have no night,*
> *Whose wishes wait upon her Lord,*
> *Who finds her own in his delight.* (p. 94)

65. The women's magazines carried on a crusade against tight lacing and regretted, rather than encouraged, the prevalent ill health of the American woman. See, for example, *An American Mother, Hints and Sketches* (New York, 1839), pp. 28 ff. for an essay on the need for a healthy mind in a healthy body in order to better be a good example for children.

66. The best single collection of nineteenth-century cookbooks is in the Academy of Medicine of New York Library, although some of the most interesting cures were in hand-written cookbooks found among the papers of women who lived during the period.

67. Sarah Josepha Hale, *The Ladies' New Book of Cookery: A Practical System for Private Families in Town and Country* (5th ed.; New York, 1852), p. 409. Similar evidence on the importance of nursing skills to every female is found in such books of advice as Willam A. Alcott, *The Young Housekeeper* (Boston, 1838), in which, along with a plea for apples and cold baths, Alcott says "Every female should be trained to the angelic art of managing properly the sick," p. 47.

68. *The Young Lady's Friend*, pp. 75–77, 79.

69. "A Tender Wife," *Godey's* II (July 1831), 28.

70. "MY WIFE! A Whisper," *Godey's*, II (Oct. 1831), 231.

71. *Letters to Young Ladies*, p. 27. The greatest exponent of the mental and moral joys of housekeeping was the *Lady's Annual Register and Housewife's Memorandum Book* (Boston, 1838), which gave practical advice on ironing, hair curling, budgeting and marketing, and turning cuffs—all activities which contributed to the "beauty of usefulness" and "joy of accomplishment" which a woman desired (I, 23).

72. *The Young Lady's Friend*, p. 230.

73. "Learning vs. Housewifery," *Godey's*, X (Aug. 1839), 95.

74. *Letters to Young Ladies*, p. 25. W. Thayer, *Life at the Fireside* (Bos-

ton, 1857), had an idyllic picture of the woman of the house mending her children's garments, the grandmother knitting and the little girl taking her first stitches, all in the light of the domestic hearth.

75. "The Mirror's Advice," *Young Maiden's Mirror* (Boston, 1858), p. 263.
76. Mrs. L. Maria Child, *The Girl's Own Book* (New York, 1833).
77. P. 44.
78. T. S. Arthur, *Advice to Young Ladies* (Boston, 1850), p. 45.
79. R. C. Waterston, *Thoughts on Moral and Spiritual Culture* (Boston, 1842), p. 101. Newcomb's *Young Lady's Guide* also advised religious biography as the best reading for women (p. 111).
80. *Godey's,* I (1828), 1. (Repeated often in *Godey's* editorials.)
81. *The Lily of the Valley,* n. v. (1851), p. 2.
82. For example, "The Fatalist," *Godey's,* IV (Jan. 1834), 10, in which Somers Dudley has Catherine reading these dangerous books until life becomes "a bewildered dream . . . O passion, what a shocking perverter of reason thou art!"
83. Review of *Society in America* (New York, 1837) in *American Quarterly Review* (Philadelphia), XXII (Sept. 1837), 38.
84. "A Finished Education," *Ladies' Museum* (Providence), I (1825), 42.
85. Helen Irving, "Literary Women," *Ladies' Wreath,* III (1850), 93.
86. "Women of Genius," *Ladies' Companion,* XI (1839), 89.
87. "Intellect vs. Affection in Woman," *Godey's,* XVI (1846), 86.
88. "The Only Daughter," *Godey's,* X (Mar. 1839), 122.
89. *The Annual Catalogue of the Officers and Pupils of the Young Ladies' Seminary and Collegiate Institute* (Monroe City, 1855), pp. 18, 19.
90. *Chronicles of a Pioneer School from 1792 to 1833: Being the History of Miss Sarah Pierce and Her Litchfield School,* Compiled by Emily Noyes Vanderpoel; ed. Elizabeth C. Barney Buel (Cambridge, 1903), p. 74.
91. *Mt. Holyoke Female Seminary,* p. 13.
92. *The American Frugal Housewife* (New York, 1838), p. 111.
93. "Female Influence," in *The Ladies' Pearl and Literary Gleaner: A Collection of Tales, Sketches, Essays, Anecdotes, and Historical Incidents* (Lowell), I (1841), 10.
94. Mrs. S. T. Martyn, "The Wife," *Ladies' Wreath,* II (1848–49), 171.
95. *The Young Ladies' Oasis,* p. 26.
96. "On Marriage," *Ladies' Repository,* I (1841), 133; "Old Maids," *Ladies' Literary Cabinet* (Newburyport), II (1822) (Microfilm), 141; "Matrimony," *Godey's,* II (Sept. 1831), 174; and "Married or Single," *Peterson's Magazine* (Philadelphia) IX (1859), 36, all express the belief that while marriage is desirable for a woman it is not essential. This attempt to reclaim the status of the unmarried woman is an example of the kind of mild crusade which the women's magazines sometimes carried on. Other examples were their strictures against an overly-

genteel education and against the affectation and aggravation of ill health. In this sense the magazines were truly conservative, for they did not oppose all change but only that which did violence to some cherished tradition. The reforms they advocated would, if put into effect, make woman even more the perfect female, and enhance the ideal of True Womahood.

97. *Girlhood and Womanhood*, p. 100. Mrs. Graves tells the stories in the book in the person of an "Old Maid" and her conclusions are that "single life has its happiness too" for the single woman "can enjoy all the pleasures of maternity without its pains and trials" (p. 140). In another one of her books, *Woman in America* (New York, 1843), Mrs. Graves speaks out even more strongly in favor of "single blessedness" rather than "a loveless or unhappy marriage" (p. 130).

98. A very unusual story is Lela Linwood, "A Chapter in the History of a Free Heart," *Ladies' Wreath*, III (1853), 349. The heroine, Grace Arland, is "sublime" and dwells "in perfect light while we others struggle yet with the shadows." She refuses marriage and her friends regret this but are told her heart "is rejoicing in its *freedom.*" The story ends with the plaintive refrain:

> But is it not a happy thing,
>   All fetterless and free,
> Like any wild bird, on the wing,
>   To carol merrily?

But even in this tale the unusual, almost unearthly rarity of Grace's genius is stressed; she is not offered as an example to more mortal beings.

99. Horace Greeley even went so far as to apply this remedy to the "dissatisfactions" of Margaret Fuller. In his autobiography, *Recollections of a Busy Life* (New York, 1868) he says that "noble and great as she was, a good husband and two or three bouncing babies would have emancipated her from a deal of cant and nonsense" (p. 178).

100. *Sphere and Duties of Woman*, p. 64.

101. *A Sermon: Preached March 13, 1808, for the Benefit of the Society Instituted in the City of New-York, For the Relief of Poor Widows with Small Children* (New York, 1808), pp. 13, 14.

102. *Lady's Magazine and Museum: A Family Journal* (London) IV (Jan. 1831), 6. This magazine is included partly because its editorials proclaimed it "of interest to the English speaking lady at home and abroad" and partly because it shows that the preoccupation with True Womahood was by no means confined to the United States.

103. *Sphere and Duties of Woman*, p. 102.

104. "Matrimony," *Lady's Amaranth*, II (Dec. 1839), 271.

105. Elizabeth Doten, "Marrying for Money," *The Lily of the Valley*, n. v. (1857), p. 112.

106. *Letters to Mothers,* p. 9.
107. "Maternal Relations," *Ladies' Casket* (New York, 1850?), p. 85. The importance of the mother's role was emphasized abroad as well as in America. *Godey's* recommended the book by the French author Aimeé-Martin on the education of mothers to "be read five times," in the original if possible (XIII, Dec. 1842, 201). In this book the highest ideals of True Womanhood are upheld. For example: "Jeunes filles, jeunes épouses, tendres mères, c'est dans votre âme bien plus que dans les lois du législateur que reposent aujourd'hui l'avenir de l'Europe et les destinées du genre humain," L. Aimeé-Martin, *De l'Education des Meres de famille ou De la civilisation du genre humain par les femmes* (Bruxelles, 1857), II, 527.
108. *Maternal Association of the Amity Baptist Church:* Annual Report (New York, 1847), p. 2: "Suffer the little children to come unto me and forbid them not, is and must ever be a sacred commandment to the Christian woman."
109. For example, Daniel Webster, "The Influence of Woman," in *The Young Ladies' Reader* (Philadelphia, 1851), p. 310.
110. Mrs. Emma C. Embury, "Female Education." *Ladies' Companion,* VIII (Jan. 1838), 18. Mrs. Embury stressed the fact that the American woman was not the "mere plaything of passion" but was in strict training to be "the mother of statesmen."
111. "How May An American Woman Best Show Her Patriotism?" *Ladies' Wreath* III (1851), 313. Elizabeth Wetherell was the pen name of Susan Warner, author of *The Wide Wide World* and *Queechy.*
112. Henry F. Harrington, "Female Education," *Ladies Companion,* IX (1838), 293, and "Influence of Woman—Past and Present," *Ladies' Companion,* XIII (1840), 245.
113. Mrs. E. Little, "What Are the Rights of Women?" *Ladies' Wreath,* II (1848-49), 133.
114. *Female Influence,* p. 18.
115. *Ibid.,* p. 23.
116. Even the women reformers were prone to use domestic images, i.e. "sweep Uncle Sam's kitchen clean," and "tidy up our country's house."
117. The "Animus and Anima" of Jung amounts almost to a catalogue of the nineteenth-century masculine and female traits, and the female hysterics whom Freud saw had much the same training as the nineteenth-century American woman. Betty Friedan, *The Feminine Mystique* (New York, 1963), challenges the whole concept of True Womanhood as it hampers the "fulfillment" of the twentieth-century woman.

Article 3

Reality and the Southern Lady

Anne Firor Scott

The mythology assured every young woman that she was a belle, endowed with magic powers to attract men and bend them to her will. This was comforting, since she was also assured that God had created her to be a wife and mother, and men did the proposing. Parents, boarding schools, advice books, and friends tried to help her make up for any natural deficiencies by emphasizing the power of manner, charm, "accomplishments," and virtue. And since God had created women to be wives and mothers it was logical that he had also, as George Fitzhugh cheerfully asserted, designed a lord and master for every woman.

In spite of the combined efforts of nature and nurture, however, girls might well be discouraged by their real life experience. To be sure, in areas where there were enough men to go around, most women did marry, and marry young, but romantic expectations and the myth of the southern gentleman might hinder rather than help in reaching that all-important goal. One young woman put the matter bluntly in her diary:

> Shall I say here if not aloud why I have never yet fallen in love? Simply because I have yet to meet the man I would be willing to acknowledge as my lord and master. For unconfessed to myself, and until very recently, I have dressed up an image in my heart and have unconsciously worshipped it under the name of Beau Ideal ... my lord and master must be some one I shall never have to blush for, or be ashamed to acknowledge, the one that after God I shall most venerate and respect. ... He must be as brave as a man can be.[1]

If the neighborhood failed to yield a Beau Ideal, or if the magic spell turned out to be inadequate to attract him, romantic images of

From *The Southern Lady: From Pedestal to Politics 1830-1930* (Chicago: University of Chicago Press, 1970), 23-39. Reprinted by permission.

love gave way to more pragmatic considerations. Proximity, a thoughtful consideration of land and family connections, or the painful fear of being an old maid were often the basis for marriage. A South Carolina matron demonstrated a mother's view of these matters when she noted in her diary that all the world seemed to be getting married except her own children. "I wish a suitable offer would come Elizabeth's way . . . and that Berkeley would find some nice girl with a little money to get married to."[2] And when her brother married she observed with pleasure that his wife was of good family, would have $40,000 in peacetime, and "is a sensible woman, quite accustomed to society, and will manage Charles and take care of his money & make him very happy."[3]

Also in the privacy of a diary, a wealthy North Carolina matron reflected upon the order of concerns her recently widowed sister might feel. Her brother-in-law had been good company, but more important, the "position and political importance she derived from him and in which she took such pride" would make the bereavement severe.[4]

A great lady in Charleston, a sophisticated observer of society wherever she went, took a cynical view of all talk of romantic love.

> It is an odd thing. In all my life how many persons have I seen in love? Not a half-dozen, and yet I am a tolerably close observer, a faithful watcher of men and manners. Society has been for me only an enlarged field for character study. Flirtation is the business of society. That is play at love making; it begins in vanity, it ends in vanity. It is spurred on by idleness and a want of other excitement. . . . it is a pleasant but very foolish game.[5]

In private letters and diaries, as opposed to fiction and poetry, pragmatic considerations loomed larger than romance. A Methodist minister in North Carolina decided after the death of his parents that he should find a wife, lest he lose touch with humanity. He looked over the available girls, chose one, and after a few months noted in his diary that there was no disadvantage to a minister in having a wife as long as she was the right kind.[6] A young student at the University of North Carolina recorded his intention to call upon a young lady whom he had never met with an eye to courting her, apparently because he had heard she was both beautiful and rich. After one visit he unsuccessfully begged leave to "address" her. Rejected, he turned his attention to another lady, whom he regretfully gave up when he discovered she had no dowry.[7] William Dorsey Pender, a gentleman of a slightly later generation, upbraided by his wife about an old flame, replied quickly, "I never loved her, *nor did my judgement sanction any connection with the family."* [8]

In middle Georgia, an area inhabited by solid up-country planters, girls began very early to accumulate a hope chest. Marriages at fourteen or fifteen were common. The girl who had many beaux was envied, and families with a "houseful of old maids" pitied. "If there was a prospect of plantation or slaves as a dowry there was a rush into matrimony," though such hasty decisions might lead later to regret.[9] Much of the courting was done on horseback as young people went to and from church. When land was plentiful, so that each child could have a farm, parents encouraged early marriage.[10]

For all the insistence that family life and motherhood were the central meaning of woman's life, marriages were often contracted casually. A Virginia Methodist minister took his audience to task for the haste with which both men and women rushed into matrimony only to discover when it was too late that they were "married but not mated. A marries for a freak just to be talked about; B for spite; C, to be revenged on an enemy . . . G to avoid being teased on the subject by gossips . . . and others they know not why."[11]

If pragmatism or impulse or necessity for the most part outweighed romance in the marriage market, there were enough real life love affairs to keep the myth alive. Joseph Jones, scion of an influential Georgia family who had been north for his medical education, was appointed to the faculty of the Georgia Medical College in Augusta. There he met the daughter of a local minister with whom he was soon corresponding daily. The order of virtues Jones listed in a letter to his parents is interesting: "The intelligence, charity and piety of Miss Caroline S. Davis have completely won my heart." Both Jones and his fiancée were inclined to literary expression, he resorting to Aristotle for help in making his points and she making generous use of Elizabeth Barrett Browning. They were married, and when he went into the army in 1861 the correspondence was resumed. In it they left a record of a devoted marriage, which lasted until Mrs. Jones's early death.[12]

If the actual process of finding a mate did not always follow the romantic prescription, so, too, the everyday realities of married women's lives were different from anything the image would lead one to expect. The shock of sudden transition from the life of a carefree, sought-after girl to one circumscribed by matronly responsibilities was recorded over and over. "She often told us of her distress on realising for the first time the responsibilities devolving upon the mistress of a large plantation, and the nights of sorrow and tears these thoughts had given her," a Virginia woman wrote of her mother.[13] It was two years before Thomas Dabney's shy sixteen-year old bride could summon the courage to take charge of her servants, and not all men were as patient as Dabney, who at the time of his marriage was a twenty-seven-year-old widower.[14] The wife of a South Carolina planter, similarly dismayed to find what was expected of her, went to her husband in tears saying she had no idea what to do with so many servants. In this case the husband simply pointed out that she had to begin somewhere, and that once begun she would find plenty to do. "And truly she found it so," wrote her daughter. "But it took all her own precious time to direct and plan and carry out the work. The calls to do something which seemed important and necessary were incessant."[15] "I was so young a bride, only seventeen . . . that I felt no dread whatever of my new duties as a mistress . . . and felt rather nonplussed when brought into contact with reality," wrote a North Carolina plantation mistress.[16] A South Carolina matron summed up the whole matter: "After the first year, no man can tell whether he married for love or for money."[17] Whatever had occasioned the match, the responsibilities of wives were much the same everywhere.

The precise meaning of "work" varied with station in society, economic condition, and geographic location, but women of leisure were hard to find. The ordinary planter's wife led a very demanding life, and the wife of the yeoman farmer differed from her more affluent sister chiefly in the amount of work she did with her own hands. Even the poor white woman, whose husband, according to legend, was largely employed in hunting, fishing, and whittling, worked much harder than her spouse, since someone had to keep the family alive. In *Plain Folk in the Old South,* Frank Owsley suggests that many of the people taken by casual travelers to be "poor whites" were really herdsmen who only appeared to be idle and shiftless, but he adds that their wives did not give even the appearance of idleness, as they "hoed the corn, cooked the dinner or plied the loom, or even came out and took up the ax and cut the wood with which to cook the dinner."[18]

There were a few urban great ladies whose slaves were so well trained that their own duties were largely administrative. Some wives of congressmen "boarded" in Washington and had time for a gay social existence. But such relatively idle southern women were rare.[19]

A planter's wife was, as a Virginia lady noted, a good house-keeper whether she wanted to be or not. To be so was "a necessity thrust upon her by circumstances. . . . Her large family, the immense retinue of slaves who all had to be fed, clothed, nursed, not to mention the incessant and heavy demands of hospitality, made her the real burden-bearer of the community."[20] "From supervising the sitting of turkeys to fighting a pestilence, there was nothing which was not her work," added another Virginian.[21] "Mother Williams works harder than any Northern farmer's wife I know," wrote the surprised bride of a southern planter, who had pictured herself marrying into a life of ease.[22] "This is the first leisure moment I have had for a long time," wrote a Virginia lady to her son. "I must take advantage of it. *Thank God*, I have almost gotten thro' Christmas. What a slave a holiday makes of a mistress! Indeed, she is always a slave, but doubly and trebly so at such times."[23]

Plantation wives did not work in the field as did wives of small farmers but many did their own spinning, weaving, and sewing. The son of a small slaveholder in the Colleton district of South Carolina recalled that

> my mother spun, wove cloth, cooked and occasionally went to the cow pen to milk the cows, father plowed and drove the wagon, made shoes and did other work. My mother always seed to her cooking and did a good deal of it, had her spinning and weaving done for the whole planta-tion white and black, no cloth or negro shoes were bought whilst father and mother lived, father made his own negro shoes and mother made the clothes.[24]

On one farm in a moment of crisis when the mother and all the children were ill, a Negro slave rejected in bewilderment the sugges-tion that he milk the cow, on the ground that everybody knew that to be "woman's work" and therefore impossible for him to under-take.[25]

No matter how large or wealthy the establishment, the mistress was expected to understand not only the skills of spinning, weaving, and sewing but also gardening, care of poultry, care of the sick, and all aspects of food preparation from the sowing of seed to the appearance of the final product on the table. Fine ladies thought nothing of supervising hog butchering on the first cold days in fall, or of drying fruits and vegetables for the winter. They made their own yeast, lard, and soap, set their own hens, and were expected to be able to make with equal skill a rough dress for a slave or a ball gown for themselves. It was customary for the mistress to rise at five or six, and to be in the kitchen when the cook arrived, to "overlook" all the arrangements for the day. A Virginia gentleman's bland assertion that "a considerable portion of her life must be spent in the nursery and the sickroom"[26] was a simple description of reality. The view that illness was inevitable was suggested in a diary entry of a Vicksburg woman, mother of a new baby: "I have felt rather depressed this evening, fearing a long summer of heat & sickness— even if I keep well how can I nurse baby and my sick too?"[27]

Even extraordinary wealth could not buy leisure for a planter's wife. Thomas Dabney owned a thousand acres and five hundred slaves, and until the Civil War was one of the wealthiest men in Mississippi. His wife bore sixteen children, carried on all the normal responsibilities of a plantation mistress, and moved her large menage of children and house slaves to the Gulf coast each summer.[28] The childless mistress of a rich Roanoke River plantation combined wine-making, peach-pruning, canning, and gardening with reading, study, and assistance to her husband. It was her custom to ride over their various plantations with him, and to keep his account books. In 1860 she promised herself "by energy and self-denial and strict attention to detail to master this debt."[29]

A South Carolina matron recorded, somewhat breathlessly:

A Plantation life is a very active one. This morning I got up late having been disturbed in the night, hurried down to have something arranged for breakfast, Ham & eggs, ... wrote a letter to Charles ... had prayers, got the boys off to town. Had work cut out, gave orders about dinner, had the horse feed fixed in hot water, had the box filled with cork: went to see about the carpenters working at the negro houses.... these carpenters Mr. Grimball told me he wished me to see about every day, & now I have to cut out the flannel jackets.[30]

She does not indicate how she found time to keep a diary in addition.

A middle Georgia matron supervised a milk dairy, a loom house, and a meat house, as well as a large poultry yard in which she included geese for feather beds. Withal she bore eleven children and raised nine to maturity.[31]

An Alabama planter's wife described her days in a laconic diary:

October 20, 1859. Put in quilt for Olivia
    Oct. 21st. Spent the day in quilting. Some hog drovers spent the night here.
    Nov. 2. Preparing a web of cloth for the loom . . . .
    Nov. 5. Went to Yellow Creek. Mr. Flood preached on the election and did his subject credit I thought.
    Dec. 7. This has been a busy day. We slaughtered 15 hogs, large ones. It is my birthday and I sit this evening by a fire, recording the fact—44 I have seen
    Dec. 8. . . . I dried up 22 gallons of lard
    Dec. 10. . . . finished our sausage, made up and to press some cheese souse.[32]

The work of town-dwelling women was very much like that of their country cousins, except that there were fewer slaves to supervise. A doctor's wife in Salisbury, North Carolina, administered the equivalent of a small farm within the city limits and "a home unit of industry to carry on all those processes which are now delegated to the baker, the grocer, and a dozen other trades."[33] Similarly, the widow of a United States senator living on six acres in Columbia, South Carolina, supervised all the work inside and outside the house, taught sewing to slave girls and her own daughters, and carried the responsibility for a plantation in the country as well.[34] The wife of a Vicksburg railroad official sewed continually and was so burdened with household cares that she felt guilty about sitting in the parlor talking to guests unless she had sewing in her hands. She, too, planted her own garden, took up carpets in the spring, cooked and washed, and cared for children, despite the fact that she was never without house slaves. The indefatigable Mrs. Grimball showed no more sign of taking her ease during her winter sojourns in Charleston than in her summer ones on the plantation.[35]

From the earliest settlement of the South some women had been planters in their own right. In 1807 a pioneer in the Louisiana territory reported upon returning from a trip east: "I found my family well and my Plantation affairs better conducted than if I had been at home. Mrs. B. has acquired a high reputation as a cotton planter."[36] Another Louisiana woman took full charge of a plantation because her husband was a surveyor and often away from home, and many wives of professional men or politicians were part-time planters. Congressman Clement Clay, Sr., of Alabama took it for granted that his wife would make plantation decisions when he was in Washington, and when he finally decided that he wanted her with him it was she who wrote letters home to overseers and relatives to make sure that all the details were attended to.[37]

The skill with which many widows carried on plantations suggests that women knew a good deal more about the planting operation than has generally been supposed. A widow in Wilkinson County, Louisiana, ran a plantation from the time her husband died until her son was old enough to assume responsibility. Her correspondence with a New Orleans factor is filled with careful detail and astute negotiation.[38] Another young widow moved to Louisiana, bought land, and established a profitable sugar plantation, while she carried on all the normal duties of a plantation, wife as well.[39] When a South Carolina planter died toward the end of the war his widow "suddenly had to plan and arrange for the 100 people on the farms in North Carolina, as well as for the 500 down on the plantations. It was perfectly wonderful to see how she rose to the requirements of the moment, and how strong and level her mind was."[40]

The belief that woman was created to be a wife and mother did not allow much room for spinsters, but of course there were some. In the families of yeoman farmers, single women performed agricultural labor and, according to the manuscript census returns, sometimes owned and operated farms independently.[41] Others hired out to do housework or sewed for more prosperous neighbors. Women of all classes sold surplus produce, and some ran millinery shops and bakeshops, inns and boardinghouses, as well as small schools. By the 1850s travelers commented on the fact that a few white girls were working in small cotton mills in Augusta, Athens, and Graniteville— a slight forecast of the future. A spinster of good family had very few options. Even if she had money of her own, respectability required a family, so she was apt to live with relatives, performing unpaid labor in return for the requisite social sanction. A woman with no such home available might go out as governess or housekeeper, though the average wage of four dollars a month which prevailed in North Carolina just before the Civil War could not have been a great incentive. Not all incentives were monetary, however. One North Carolina woman, an orphan, consulted friends and relatives about the propriety of taking such a housekeeper's job in a widower's family. A few months later she married her employer and eventually bore him a dozen children.[42]

Few aspects of women's work accorded so poorly with the image of delicate, frivolous, submissive women than the responsibility for managing slaves. Slavery influenced the lives and thoughts of southern women in many ways, not least in the kinds of work it created. Supervising slaves was difficult, demanding, frustrating, and above all never-ending. The wife allocated duties among house servants, who on a large plantation might number dozens of slaves. In addition the mistress was often responsible for dealing out weekly rations to all the slaves, and for making sure that they were clothed according to the standards of her plantation.

The mistress was usually chief medical officer, responsible for the health of family and slaves, and for the delivery of babies. On a large plantation someone was nearly always sick, and epidemics were not infrequent. The fertility of slave women was economically important to the master, but it added to the burdens of the mistress. One plantation wife recorded every few days the birth of a slave child over which she had presided.[43]

Supervising slaves raised problems of controlling and guiding behavior. The mistress had to dispense justice, settle small personal feuds, and cajole those who did not want to work into doing so. Women gifted in human relations had little difficulty and their household affairs ran smoothly even when there was much work to be done. Others, less gifted, had constant problems with recalcitrant, defiant, slovenly slaves, some of whom were skilled at intimidating their mistresses. Such personal relationships ran the gamut from that typified by one diary note, "Business negligently done & much altogether neglected, some disobedience, much idleness, sulleness, slovenliness. . . . Used the rod," to those of the warm, peaceful Smedes household, based upon Mrs. Smedes's injunction to her daughters, "They are not machines, they are just like you, made from the same flesh and blood."[44]

One of the most persistent threads in the romanticization of woman was the glorification of motherhood, with its great possibilities for beneficent influence on the coming generation. Nothing in the myth emphasized the darker side of maternity. In the face of the idealization of the family and the aura of sanctity surrounding the word "mother," only in private could women give voice to the misery of endless pregnancies, with attendant illness, and the dreadful fear of childbirth, a fear based on fact. The number of women who died in childbirth was high. When the mother survived the family tended to be large. "Family on the increase continually, and every one added increased labor and responsibility. And this was the case with the typical southern woman," wrote one upper-class wife.[45] "My heart almost sinks within me at the thought of feeding another child," a pregnant woman wrote her mother.[46] "I have never been so opposed to having children as many women I know," wrote a Georgia woman discussing her husband's objection to any further increase in the family, and inadvertently throwing light on the views of her friends.[47]

The depth of the fear of pregnancy came out clearly in much husband-wife correspondence. "Please let me know if your hopes as to your condition the day you left Richmond turned out to be as you thought or if it was a false alarm," wrote General William Dorsey Pender to his wife, who had just spent seven weeks with him in camp. "I sincerely hope it was bona fide, for we all have enough to contend with in these times even when we are free from continuous nausea and do not have to look forward to nine months of pain and general ill feeling." And, a year later, "Indeed I did sincerely hope that you had escaped this time, but darling it must be the positive and direct will of God that it should be so." Notwithstanding this pious observation, he enclosed some pills which the camp surgeon thought might bring on a spontaneous abortion.[48]

A North Carolina planter's wife found constant childbearing such a trial that she began making longer and longer visits to her own family, to the point, finally, that her husband ordered her to come home. Her unhappiness at the thought of frequent pregnancy did not diminish, and in 1862 when he went off to one of the Virginia springs for his health she wrote that her only hope was to die young: "Some wifes are nothing but trouble, and I am one, I'm not fit for anything but to have children, and that is nothing but trouble and sorrow." Her wish for early death was not granted, and in 1867 when he went to the legislature she was still worrying: "Willis, I have not seen anything of my monthlies yet, and I am afraid your going to Raleigh and coming home will make me suffer. . . . you know I hate even to think of such a thing." To which he unfeelingly replied, "I was never hopeful that you would not have more children, you come of a breed too prolific to stop at your age and if its the Lords will why we must submit to it."[49] This after thirteen years of marriage.

The absence of effective contraception created a strain on the domestic relationship. This, more than a commitment to ladylike decorum, may have been responsible for the widespread but erroneous view that eroticism was a thing unknown among southern ladies.

NOTES

1. Sarah Morgan Diary, 6 May 1862, MS Dept., Duke.
2. Diary of Meta Morris Grimball, 10 December 1860, SHC UNC.
3. *Ibid.,* 19 October 1862.
4. Catherine Edmonston, "Diary of Looking Glass Plantation," ed. James Patton and Beth Crabtree; typescript in Dr. Patton's possession. Original 4-vol. manuscript in N.C. Dept. of Archives and History, Raleigh.
5. Mary Boykin Chesnut, *A Diary from Dixie* (Boston: Houghton Mifflin, Sentry edition, 1951), p. 463.
6. Diary of Sidney Bumpas, SHC UNC.
7. John L. Sanders, ed., "Diary of Ruffin Wirt Tomlinson," *North Carolina Historical Review* 30 (January–April 1953).
8. William W. Hassler, ed., *The General to His Lady: The Civil War Letters of William Dorsey Pender to Fanny Pender* (Chapel Hill: University of North Carolina Press, 1966), p. 206. Italics added.
9. Rebecca Latimer Felton, *Country Life in Georgia in the Days of My Youth* (Atlanta: Index Printing Co. 1919), pp. 62–63.
10. Judge Garnett Andrews, *Reminiscences of an Old Georgia Lawyer* (Atlanta: Franklin Steam Printing House, 1870), passim.
11. John C. Bayley, *Marriage As It Is and Should Be* (New York: M. W. Dodd, 1857), pp. 43–44.
12. Joseph Jones to C. C. Jones, 17 February 1859, C. C. Jones Papers, Manuscripts Division, Howard Tilton Memorial Library, Tulane University. Both sides of the Jones-Davis correspondence have been preserved. Some of the letters are in the C. C. Jones Papers at Tulane and others in the Joseph Jones Papers at LSU.
13. Letitia Burwell, *A Girl's Life in Virginia before the War* (New York: Frederick A. Stokes, 1895), p. 23.
14. Susan Dabney Smedes, *Memorials of a Southern Planter,* ed. Fletcher Green (New York: Knopf, 1965), p. 19.
15. Elizabeth Allston Pringle, *Chronicles of Chicora Wood* (New York: Charles Scribner's Sons, 1922), p. 61.
16. Margaret Devereux, *Plantation Sketches* (Cambridge, Mass.: Privately printed, 1946), p. 5.
17. Chesnut, *Diary from Dixie,* p. 177.

18. Owsley, *Plain Folk in the Old South* (Baton Rouge: Louisiana State University Press, 1949), p. 35.
19. Mary Boykin Chesnut is an excellent example of the first, and her leisure was greater because she had no children. Virginia Clay-Clopton described life in the congressional circle of which both she and Mrs. Chesnut were a part in that decade. See *A Belle of the Fifties: Memoirs of Mrs. Clay of Alabama, covering Social and Political Life in Washington and the South 1853-66. Put into narrative form by Ada Sterling* (New York: William Heinemann, 1905).
20. Sally McCarty Pleasants, *Old Virginia Ways and Days* (Menasha, Wis., 1916), p. 34.
21. Thomas Nelson Page, *Social Life in Old Virginia* (New York: Charles Scribner's Sons, 1897), p. 38.
22. James C. Bonner, ed., "Plantation Experiences of a New York Woman," *North Carolina Historical Review* 33 (July 1956): 384-412.
23. L. Minor Blackford, *Mine Eyes Have Seen the Glory* (Cambridge, Mass., 1954), p. 7, quoting his grandmother Lucy Carter Minor.
24. David Garvin Diary, 31 May 1865, SHC UNC.
25. A Southern Country Minister, *Old Pine Farm* (Nashville: Southwestern Publishing House, 1860), pp. 93-94. This is an unusual book in that it depicts, apparently autobiographically, the life of a minister's family living in a log cabin with two slaves. Its author intended, he says, to "show up some of the features of Southern Ministerial life among the country churches." His livelihood came, of course, not from his preaching but from the farm.
26. Thomas R. Dew in the *Southern Literary Messenger* 1 (May 1835): 497.
27. Diary of Mahala P. Roach, 15 May 1859, typescript, SHC UNC.
28. Smedes, *Memorials,* passim.
29. Edmonston, "Diary of Looking Glass Plantation," 13 July 1860.
30. Meta Morris Grimball Diary, 29 December 1860, SHC UNC.
31. Felton, *Country Life in Georgia*, p. 29.
32. Private Journal of Mrs. Sarah R. Espy, 20 October 1859. Alabama Department of Archives, quoted in M. C. Boyd, *Alabama in the Fifties* (New York: Columbia University Press, 1931), pp. 116-18.
33. Hope Summerell Chamberlain, *This Was Home* (Chapel Hill: University of North Carolina Press, 1938), p. 43.
34. Grace Elmore Diary, typescript, vol. 2, Covering 1864-65, passim, SHC UNC.
35. Mahala P. Roach Diary and Meta Morris Grimball Diary, passim, SHC UNC.
36. David Bradford Papers, 30 November 1807, Dept. of Archives, LSU.
37. Mrs. Andrew McCollum Diary, SHC UNC; C. C. Clay Papers, MS Dept., Duke; Ruth Ketring Nuremberger, *The Clays of Alabama* (Lexington: University of Kentucky Press, 1958).

38. Nancy Pinson Papers, Dept. of Archives, LSU; see also Diary of Sarah Witherspoon Erwin McIver, Coker Papers, SHC UNC, and the collection of papers of women planters at LSU.

39. *Brockenburn: The Journal of Kate Stone,* ed. John Q. Anderson (Baton Rouge: Louisiana State University Press, 1955).

40. Pringle, *Chronicles of Chicora Wood,* p. 212.

41. Owsley, *Plain Folk,* pp. 11–13.

42. Lucy Cole Burwell Papers, MS Dept., Duke; for the $4 wage see Guion G. Johnson, *Ante-Bellum North Carolina* (Chapel Hill: University of North Carolina Press, 1937), p. 247.

43. Sarah McIver Diary, SHC UNC.

44. Lucilla McCorkle Diary, 5 July 1846, SHC UNC; Smedes, *Memorials,* p. 88. The relation of women and slaves is discussed more fully in the following chapter.

45. V. V. Clayton, *White and Black under the Old Regime* (Milwaukee: Young Churchmen Co., 1899), p. 124.

46. Laura Norwood to Mrs. L. L. Lenoir, 1 May 1845, Lenoir Papers, SHC UNC.

47. E. G. Thomas Diary 29 November 1870, MS Dept., Duke. See also Johnson, *Ante-Bellum North Carolina,* p. 237.

48. Hassler, ed., *The General to His Lady,* p. 114, 21 February 1862, and ibid., p. 202, 10 March 1863.

49. Willis Williams to his wife Harriet, 18 January 1858; Harriet Williams to Willis Williams, 23 October 1862; same to same 26 January 1867; Willis Williams to Harriet Williams, 31 January 1867, all in Willis Williams Papers, SHC UNC.

Article 4

Hagar and Her Children

E. Franklin Frazier

To pregnant women who formed a part of the slave caravans motherhood meant only a burden and an accentuation of their miseries. Maternal feeling was choked and dried up in mothers who had to bear children, in addition to loads of corn or rice, on their backs during marches of eight to fourteen hours. Nor did life in the slave pens on the coast, where they were chained and branded and sometimes starved, mitigate the sufferings of motherhood.

In the selection of Negroes for the cargoes of the slave ships, their physical condition and their suitability for the specific requirements of the trade were the only factors of moment to the traders. When William Ellery, the father of one of the signers of the Declaration of Independence, instructed the captain of his slaver: "If you have a good Trade for Negroes may purchase forty or Fifty Negroes. get most of them mere Boys and Girl, some Men, let them be Young, No very small Children," it is unlikely that the faithful captain in obeying his orders cared much about the feelings of the Negro mothers who had to surrender their children. During the Middle Passage that followed the gathering of slaves on the coast, the last spark of maternal feeling was probably smothered in the breasts of many mothers who were packed spoon fashion between decks and often gave birth to children in the scalding perspiration from the human cargo. Then whatever was left of maternal sentiment had to undergo another ordeal in the slave markets of the New World.

Scarcely more regard was shown for the humanity of the slaves in the American markets than in those of Africa. To be sure, humanitarian sentiment was more likely to make itself felt in the American communities than among the adventurers and criminals who frequented the slave markets of Africa. Moreover, in the slave markets of Charleston and Richmond it was to the economic advantage of

From *The Negro Family in the United States* (Chicago: University of Chicago Press), 34-42, 49-59, 63-66. Reprinted by permission.

those who bought and sold slaves to see that infants did not die because of the lack of maternal care. But since, as a South Carolina court held in 1809, "the young of slaves. . . . stand on the same footing as other animals," the relation of mothers to their children was recognized not because of its human or social significance but because of the property interests involved in the relationship.

In some cases the affectional ties between mother and children survived the ordeals of the slave markets and the Middle Passage and were perhaps strengthened by common suffering. But the characteristic attitudes and sentiments which the slave mother developed in America grew out of her experiences with pregnancy and childbirth and her relations with her offspring in the new environment. Where slave women were maintained as breeders and enjoyed certain indulgences and privileges because of their position, the experience of pregnancy and childbirth was likely to cause them to look upon their children as the source of these favors.

The following instructions were sent to an agent for the management of a plantation in Virginia in 1759: "The breeding wenches particularly, you must instruct the overseers to be kind and indulgent to, and not to force them when with child upon any service or hardship that will be injurious to them and that they have every necessary when in that condition that is needful for them, and the children to be well looked after and to give them every spring and fall the jerusalem oak seed for a week together and that none of them suffer in time of sickness for want of proper care."[1]

On the other hand, where slave women were forced into cohabitation and pregnancy, and childbirth brought no release from labor, they might develop a distinct antipathy toward their offspring. A former slave, Moses Grandy, wrote the following concerning the treatment of women by the overseer:

> On the estate I am speaking of, those women who had sucking children suffered much from their breasts becoming full of milk, the infants being left at home; they therefore could not keep up with the other hands: I have seen the overseer beat them with raw hide, so that the blood and milk flew mingled from their breasts. A woman who gives offence in the field, and is large in the family way, is compelled to lie down over a hole made to receive her corpulency, and is flogged with the whip, or beat with a paddle, which had holes in it; at every stroke comes a blister. One of my sisters was so severely punished in this way, that labor was brought on, and the child was born in the field. This very overseer, Mr. Brooks,

killed in this manner a girl named Mary: her father and mother were in the field at the time.[2]

Even under the more normal conditions of slavery, childbirth could not have had the same significance for the slave mother as for the African mother. In Africa tribal customs and taboos tended to fix the mother's attitude toward her child before it was born. In America this traditional element in the shaping of maternal feeling was absent. Consequently, the development of maternal feeling was dependent largely upon the physiological and emotional responses of the mother to her child.

Concerning the biologically inherited elements in the so-called "maternal instinct," L. L. Bernard writes:

It is difficult to separate early acquirements through the imitation process from biological inheritance without considerable intensive investigation. But it is doubtful if more than the response to touch, temperature and odor stimuli from the child by fondling, holding and licking or kissing, a more or less vague unorganized emotional response to its cries, which chiefly manifests itself in movement toward the child, vague answering cries and the discharge of milk upon certain definite stimuli of pressure upon the breast, can be said to be inherited by the human mother.[3]

Generally, during the period of pregnancy, the slave woman's labor was reduced, and on the birth of a child she received additional clothes and rations. But the following letter of an overseer indicates that the needs of the mothers and their newborn children were not always promptly met:

Charlotte & Venus & Mary & Little Sary have all had children and have not received their baby clothes also Hetty & Sary & Coteler will want baby clothes. I see a Blanket for the old fellow Sampson he is dead. I thought I wrote to you that he was dead. Little Peggy Sarys daughter has not ever drawn any Blanket at all, and when they come I think it would be right to give her the Blanket that was sent to Sampson.[4]

As soon as possible after childbirth, the mother was required to return to the fields, often taking her unweaned child along. A former slave describes the situation as follows:

The bell rings, at four o'clock in the morning, and they have half an hour to get ready. Men and women start together, and the women must work as steadily as the men, and perform the same tasks as the men. If the plantation is far from the house, the sucking children are taken out and kept in the field all day. If the cabins are near, the women are permitted to go in two or three times a day to their infant children. The mother is driven out when the child is three to four weeks old.[5]

In some cases the mothers were permitted to return to the cabin in order to nurse the infant who was left either alone or in the charge of a child. "At this period," writes a former slave, John Brown, "my principal occupation was to nurse my little brother whilst my mother worked in the field. Almost all the slave children have to do the nursing; the big taking care of the small, who often come poorly off in consequence. I know this was my little brother's case. I used to lay him in the shade, under a tree, sometimes, and go to play, or curl myself up under a hedge, and take a sleep."

The following situation described by Frances A. Kemble in her *Journal* was typical of many plantations:

> It is true that every able-bodied woman is made the most of in being driven afield as long as, under all and any circumstances, she is able to wield a hoe; but, on the other hand, stout, hale, hearty girls and boys, of from eight to twelve and older, are allowed to lounge about, filthy and idle, with no pretense of an occupation but what they call "tend baby," i.e., see to the life and limbs of the little slave infants, to whose mothers, working in distant fields, they carry them during the day to be suckled, and for the rest of the time leave them to crawl and kick in the filthy cabins or on the broiling sand which surrounds them.[6]

Consequently, where such limitations were placed upon the mother's spontaneous emotional responses to the needs of her children and where even her suckling and fondling of them were restricted, it was not unnatural that she often showed little attachment to her offspring.

A slaveholder, who loved "to recall the patriarchal responsibility and tenderness" which her father "felt for his poor, ignorant, dependent slaves," tells the following story to "show that the master's feelings are sometimes even deeper than the mother's":

> One of my slaves had an infant child two months old who was attacked with an affection of the windpipe. I never saw such extreme suffering; it was one continual spasm and struggle for breath. The physician visited it several times every day, but could give no relief. The poor little sufferer

seemed as if it would neither live nor die. These extreme tortures lasted a whole week before it breathed its last; and my own mind was so excited by its sharp and constant convulsive shrieks, that I never left it night or day, and could not sleep, even a moment, sitting by its side; and yet its own mother slept soundly at the foot of the bed, not because she was fatigued, for she was required to do nothing but nurse the dying child.[7]

While the pathos expressed here is understandable, one would require a knowledge of the mother's experience during pregnancy and childbirth and her subsequent relations with her infant in order to decide whether her behavior was unnatural or extraordinary. However, one might ask: Why were these slave women, in the words of the same informant, "the most enthusiastically fond foster-mothers, when they [were] called upon to nurse the infant child of their owners"?

Often the relations of the foster-mother or "mammy" to her "white children" offered greater scope for the expression of the emotions and impulses characteristic of maternal love than the contacts which she had with her own offspring. The attachment and devotion which the "mammy" showed for the white children began before the children were born. The "mammy," who was always an important member of the household, attended her mistress during pregnancy and took under her care the infant as soon as it was born. Often she, instead of the mother, suckled the child and if the child was a girl, was never separated from her until she was grown. Miss Bremer has left a picture of one of these foster-mothers sitting "like a horrid specter, black and silent by the altar," during the wedding of her foster-child from whom she "could not bear the thought of parting." If these black foster-mothers showed more maternal affection and devotion for their charges than they or their black sisters showed for their own offspring, it was due to the emotional and biological dependence that developed between them as the result of this intimate association. Moreover, where this intimate association extended over several generations and the "mammy" became assimilated into the master's household, tradition tended to define her role and to inculcate in her sentiments proper to her status.

It should not be inferred from what has been said concerning the Negro woman's devotion to the children of the master race that she never developed a deep and lasting sentiment for her own children. In the slave cabin, where she was generally mistress, she often gathered about her a numerous progeny, in spite of miscarriages and a high infant mortality. Miss Kemble enters in her *Journal,* pp. 190-91, the following information relative to the size of slave families, miscarriages, and infant mortality:

> "*Fanny* has had six children; all dead but one. She came to beg to have her work in the field lightened.
>
> "*Nanny* has had three children; two of them dead. She came to implore that the rule of sending them into the field three weeks after their confinement might be altered.
>
> "*Leah,* Caesar's wife, has had six children; three are dead.
>
> "*Sophy,* Lewis's wife, came to beg for some old linen. She is suffering fearfully; has had ten children; five of them are dead. The principal favor she asked was a piece of meat, which I gave her.
>
> "*Sally,* Scipio's wife, has had two miscarriages and three children born, one of whom is dead. She came complaining of incessant pain and weakness in her back. This woman was a mulatto daughter of a slave called Sophy, by a white man of the name of Walker, who visited the plantation.
>
> "*Charlotte,* Renty's wife, had had two miscarriages, and was with child again. She was almost crippled with rheumatism, and showed me a pair of poor swollen knees that made my heart ache. I have promised her a pair of flannel trowsers, which I must forthwith set about making.
>
> "*Sarah,* Stephen's wife—this woman's case and history were alike deplorable. She had had four miscarriages, had brought seven children into the world, five of whom were dead, and was again with child. She complained of dreadful pains in the back, and an internal tumor which swells with the exertion of working in the fields; probably, I think, she is ruptured."

The following entries concerning births and deaths of children were made by an overseer on a plantation in Florida, 1851.

BIRTHS ON THE PLANTATION IN 1851

Florer was confined this morning with a male Child, Jany. 27, 1851.

May 28th, Cate was delivered of a Female Child this morning.

June 4th, Martha was delivered of a male child at 12 o'clock today.

June 13th, Long Mariah was delivered of a male Child today at twelve o'clock.

August 17th, B. Mariah was delivered of a male child this morning.

DEATHS ON THE PLANTATION IN 1851

August 4th, Catherine, a child departed this life today at 2 oclock.

September 18th, one Child Departed this life today at ten oclock; by the name of Amy.

December 31. B. Mariers Child Billy died this morning.

After the day's labor in the field under an unsympathetic over-seer, she could find warmth and sympathy and appreciation among her children and kinsmen. There the mother could give full rein to her tender feelings and kindly impulses. "One of my earliest recol-lections," writes Booker T. Washington, "is that of my mother cooking a chicken late at night, and awakening her children for the purpose of feeding them." The devotion of the mothers to their own children was often demonstrated in their sacrifices to see them when they were separated from them. Douglass' childhood recollections of his mother, who lived twelve miles from him, were of "a few hasty visits made in the night on foot, after the daily tasks were over, and when she was under the necessity of returning in time to respond to the driver's call to the field in the early morning."

It is not surprising, then, to find that slave mothers, instead of viewing with indifference the sale, or loss otherwise, of their chil-dren, often put up a stubborn resistance and suffered cruel punish-ments to prevent separation from them. The fact that slave families were often divided when it was to the economic advantage of the owners is too well established to take seriously the denials of those who have idealized slavery. Washington Irving, who regarded the separation of children from their parents as a peculiar evil of slavery, rationalized thus: "But are not white people so, by schooling, mar-riage, business, etc. . . ."[8]

Generally speaking, the mother remained throughout slavery the dominant and important figure in the slave family. Although tradition has represented her as a devoted foster-parent to her master's children and indifferent to her own, it appears that, where this existed, the relations between the slave woman and the white child were similar to the relations which normally exist between mother and child. On the other hand, pregnancy and childbirth often meant only suffering for the slave mother who, because of her limited contacts with her young, never developed that attachment which grows out of physiological and emotional responses to its needs. Nevertheless, there is abundant evidence that slave mothers developed a deep and permanent love for their children, which often caused them to defy their masters and to undergo suffering to prevent separation from their young. This is only a part of the story

143

of the slave mother, for there was another mother who bore children for the men of the master race. . . .

Nowhere did human impulses and human feelings and sentiments tend to dissolve the formal relations between master and slave as in their sexual association, from which sprang those anomalous family groups consisting mainly of slave mother and mulatto offspring. But it was often in these very cases of human solidarity created by ties of blood that the ideas and sentiments embodied in the institution of slavery prevailed over the promptings of human feeling and sympathy. Where sexual association between master and slave was supported by personal attachment and in many cases genuine sentiment, we find the black, and more often mulatto, woman, under the protection of her master's house, playing a double role—a wife without the comfirmation of the law and a mistress without the glamour of romance. Where the slave woman was only the means of satisfying a fleeting impulse, we find her rearing her mulatto offspring on the fare of slaves or being sold at a premium on the auction block because of her half-white brood. But whether her children were doomed to servitude or nurtured under the guidance of a solicitous father, they were not unconscious of their relation to the master race.

The admonition contained in the sermon preached at Whitechapel in 1609 for the benefit of adventurers and planters bound for Virginia, that "Abrams posteritie [must] keepe to themselves," was ignored in regard to the Negro as well as to the Indian. But the added injunction that "they may not marry nor give in marriage to the heathen, that are uncircumcised" became, except in rare instances, the inexorable policy of the whites in their relation with both of the subordinate races. Intercourse between whites and Negroes began as soon as the latter were introduced into America. In the beginning the sexual association between the two races was not confined to white males and the women of the black race. Colonial records furnish us with numerous instances of bastard children by Negro men and indentured white women. Two instances of this nature are reported by Helen Tunnicliff Catterall. A case brought into the Virginia courts in 1769 by a mulatto in suing for his freedom begins thus:

A Christian white woman between the year of 1723 and 1765, had a daughter, Betty Bugg, by a negro man. This daughter was by deed indented, bound by the churchwardens to serve till thirty-one. Before the expiration of her servitude, she was delivered of the defendant Bugg, who never was bound by the churchwardens, and was sold by his master to the plaintiff. Being now twenty-six years of age, and having cause of complaint against the plaintiff, as being illy provided with clothes and diet, he brought an action in the court to recover his liberty, founding his claim on three points.

Another case for the following year states that

the plaintiff's grandmother was a mulatto, begotten on a white woman by a negro man, after the year 1705, and bound by the churchwardens, under the law of that date, to serve to the age of thirty-one.

There is also good evidence that intercourse between Negro males and white servant women was sometimes encouraged by white masters who desired to increase the number of their bound servants. Marriages of Negroes and whites, most of whom were indentured servants, seem to have been numerous enough to require the enactment of severe laws for their prevention. But, when the principle of racial integrity and white domination became fixed in the minds of the whites, social censure and severe penalties were reserved, with rare exceptions, for the association of Negro men and white women. Calhoun has given us the following items from the court records of Chester County, Pennsylvania, in 1698:

For that hee . . . contrary to the lawes of the government and contrary to his masters consent hath . . . got with child a certain mulato woman called swart Anna. . . .

David Lewis Constable of Haverford returned a negro man of his and a white woman for haveing a baster childe . . . the negro said she intised him and promised to marry him; she being examined, confest the same . . . the court ordered that she shall receive twenty-one lashes on her beare backe . . . and the court ordered the negroe man never to meddle with any white woman more uppon paine of his life.

As slavery developed into an institution, neither the segregation of the great body of slaves from the masses of the whites nor the mutual antagonism between the "poor whites" and the blacks was an effectual check on the sexual association between the two races. In the cities, especially, where the slaves were released from the control under which they lived on the plantations, and there were many free Negroes, association between the women of the subordinate race and white men assumed in the majority of cases a casual and debasing character. In fact, a traffic in mulatto women especially for prostitution became a part of the regular slave trade in southern cities. The following item appeared in the *Memphis Eagle and Enquirer,* June 26, 1857: "A slave woman is advertised to be sold in St. Louis who is so surpassingly beautiful that $5,000 has been already offered for her, at private sale, and refused."

Prostitution of slave women became in many cases a private affair and, when in such cases it led to the formation of more or less permanent associations, it merged into that developed and almost socially approved system of concubinage which was found in Charleston, Mobile, and New Orleans. The cities were not, however, the only places where widespread intermixture of the races occurred. Although it is difficult to estimate the extent to which the slaveholders entered into sexual associations with their slaves, there is abundance of evidence of both concubinage and polygamy on the part of the master class. Moreover, although the intercourse between the masters and slave women on the plantations assumed as a rule a more permanent form than similar relations in the cities, the character of these associations varied considerably. Therefore, we shall examine the character of the different types of associations and try to determine the nature of the family groups that grew out of them.

In view of the relations of superordination and subordination between the two races, how far did these associations originate in mere physical compulsion? How far did the women of the subordinate race surrender themselves because they were subject to the authority of the master race? Or was the prestige of the white race sufficient to insure compliance on the part of the black and mulatto women, both slave and free? How far was mutual attraction responsible for acquiescence on the part of the woman?

All these factors were effective in creating the perplexing relationships in which men of the master race and women of the subject race became entangled. That physical compulsion was necessary at times to secure submission on the part of black women, both slave and free, is supported by historical evidence and has been preserved in the traditions of Negro families. A young man in a Negro college writes concerning the birth of his great-great-grandfather on his mother's side:

> Approximately a century and a quarter ago, a group of slaves were picking cotton on a plantation near where Troy, Alabama, is now located.

Among them was a Negro woman, who, despite her position as a slave, carried herself like a queen and was tall and stately. The over-seer (who was the plantation's owner's son) sent her to the house on some errand. It was necessary to pass through a wooded pasture to reach the house and the over-seer intercepted her in the woods and forced her to put her head between the rails in an old stake and rider fence, and there in that position my great-great-grandfather was conceived.

In the family history of another college student the story of the circumstances under which the Negro woman had been forced to yield to the sexual assault by her white master had become a sort of family skeleton, well guarded because of the sensitive feelings and pride of the victim. Of her great-grandmother, our informant writes:

As young as I was when I knew her, I remember distinctly her fierce hatred of white people, especially of white men. She bore marks of brutal beatings she received for attempted escapes, or for talking back to her master or mistress. One mark in particular stands out in my memory, one she bore just above her right eye. As well as she liked to regale me with stories of her scars, this is one she never discussed with me. Whenever I would ask a question concerning it, she would simply shake her head and say, "White men are as low as dogs, child. Stay away from them." It was only after her death, and since I became a woman that I was told by my own mother that she received that scar at the hands of her master's youngest son, a boy of about eighteen years at the time she conceived their child, my grandmother, Ellen. She belonged to a family of tobacco planters I believe, for she often spoke of tobacco, and liked very much to smoke it in an old pipe, which seems to have been almost as old as she. During the time she was carrying Ellen, she was treated more brutally than before, and had to work even harder than ever. But strange to say, after the child was born, and was seen to be white, in appearance at least, the attitude of the whole C——family seemed to soften toward her somewhat, and after this she became a house servant and was taught to sew, and became the family seamstress.

It seems that at times resistance to the white man's passion resulted in sadistical revenge upon the women. The form of punishment administered in the following case bears this implication.

Thomas James, Jep's second son, had cast his eyes on a handsome young negro girl, to whom he made dishonest overtures. She would not submit to him, and finding he could not overcome her, he swore he would be revenged. One night he called her out of the gin-house, and then bade me and two or three more, strip her naked; which we did. He then made us throw her down on her face, in front of the door, and hold her whilst he flogged her—the brute—with the bullwhip, cutting great gashes of flesh out of her person, at every blow, from five to six inches long. The poor unfortunate girl screamed most awfully all the time, and writhed under our strong arms, rendering it necessary for us to use our united strength to hold her down. He flogged her for half an hour, until he nearly killed her, and then left her to crawl away to her cabin.[9]

However, in many instances men of the master race did not meet much resistance on the part of the slave women. The mere prestige of the white race was sufficient to secure compliance with their desires. As Miss Kemble observed, the slaves accepted the contempt of their masters to such an extent that "they profess, and really seem to feel it for themselves, and the faintest admixture of white blood in their veins appears at once, by common consent of their own race, to raise them in the scale of humanity." The following incident related by John Thompson, a former slave indicates compliance on the part of a woman who was married to a slave:

Soon after my arrival in the family, Mr. Thomas let me to one of his sons, named Henry, who was a doctor, to attend his horse. This son was unmarried, lived a bachelor, and kept a cook and waiter. The cook belonged neither to him nor his father, but was hired. She was a good looking mulatto, and was married to a right smart, intelligent man, who belonged to the doctor's uncle. One night, coming home in haste, and wishing to see his wife, he sent me up stairs to request her to come down. Upon going up I found she was in a room with the doctor, the door of which was fast. This I thoughtlessly told her husband, who, upon her coming down a moment after, upbraided her for it. She denied it, and afterwards told the doctor. . . . The doctor was a very intemperate man. As soon as his cook told him her story, he came to his father with the complaint that I had left him without his consent; upon which his father told him to flog me.[10]

Moreover, there were often certain concrete advantages to be gained by surrendering themselves to the men of the master race that overcame any moral scruples these women might have had. In some cases it meant freedom from the drudgery of field labor as well as better food and clothing. Then there was the prospect that her half-white children would enjoy certain privileges and perhaps in time be emancipated.

Mutual attraction also played a part in securing the compliance of the woman. In many cases the intimacies that developed began in the household where the two races lived in close association. The historian of Alabama, who attempts to place the responsibility for these illicit unions upon the slave woman, refers to the seductiveness of the latter. But it appears that, aside from the prestige of the white race and the material advantages to be gained, these slave women were as responsive to the attractiveness of the white males as the latter were to the charms of the slave women. Hence, slave women were not responsive to the approaches of all white men and often showed some discrimination and preference in the bestowal of their favors. The following incident is from the life of Bishop Loguen's mother, who was the mistress of a white man near Nashville, Tennessee:

> When she was about the age of twenty-four or five, a neighboring planter finding her alone at the distillery, and presuming upon the privileges of his position, made insulting advances, which she promptly repelled. He pursued her with gentle force, and was still repelled. He then resorted to a slaveholder's violence and threats. These stirred all the tiger's blood in her veins. She broke from his embrace, and stood before him in bold defiance. He attempted again to lay hold of her—and careless of caste and slave laws, she grasped the heavy stick used to stir the malt, and dealt him a blow which made him reel and retire. But he retired only to recover and return with the fatal knife, and threats of vengeance and death. Again she aimed the club with unmeasured force at him, and hit the hand which held the weapon, and dashed it to a distance from him. Again he rushed upon her with the fury of a madman, and she then plied a blow upon his temple, which laid him, as was supposed, dead at her feet.[11]

The relations between the white men and the slave women naturally aroused the jealousy and antagonism of the women of the master race. Because of the patriarchal character of the family, it was probably true to some extent, as one traveler related, that "a Southern wife, if she is prodigally furnished with dollars to 'go shopping,' apparently considers it no drawback to her happiness if some brilliant mulatto or quadroon woman ensnares her husband." But, frequently, the wife visited her resentment not only upon the slave woman but upon her husband's mulatto children. In some cases white women arranged marriages for their female slaves as a means of breaking off their husband's attachment. . . .

The resentment of the white woman was likely to be manifested toward the offspring of her husband's relations with the slave woman. A mulatto former slave, after remarking that white women were "always revengeful toward the children of slaves that [had] any of the blood of their husbands in them," tells of his mother's anxiety when he, because of his relation to his master, became the object of the mistress' resentment. Calhoun cites the case of a mistress who, "out of ungrounded jealousy, had slaves hold a negro girl down while she cut off the forepart of the victims's feet."

All classes of whites in the South were involved in these associations with the slave women. Some have attempted to place the burden upon the overseers and the landless poor whites, the class from which they were recruited. But there is no evidence that the poor whites were more involved than the men of the master class. In fact, there was always considerable antagonism between the slaves and the overseers and the class to which they belonged. Concubinage was the privilege of those classes in the South that were economically well off. In Charleston, South Carolina, and in New Orleans, where the system of concubinage reached its highest development, wealthy bachelors included beautiful mulatto women among their luxuries. Sometimes they developed a serious and permanent affection for these women that culminated in marriage. . . .

. . . More often, it seems, the women developed real affection for the men; for, when they were abandoned by the white men who entered legal marriage, these women seldom entered new relationships and in some cases committed suicide. . . .

When men of the slaveholding aristocracy renounced the conventional society of their peers, withdrew to the seclusion of their feudal estates, and took as their companions mulatto women, it was natural that deep and permanent sentiment should develop between them and their colored mistresses and children. This was the case with those anomalous family groups in which the woman enjoyed the protection of her master and paramour and occupied a dignified and respected position in relation to her children and other slaves on the plantation. It is not surprising, then, to find in the court cases, contesting the wills of masters who emancipated their mistresses and mulatto children and left them their estates, that the fact of the woman's having "had the influence over him of a white woman and a wife" was cited to show undue influence on her part.

That such associations undermined the moral order upon which slavery rested and made possible the gradual assimilation of the Negro as his blood became more and more diluted by white blood cannot be denied. Within the intimacy of these family groups color caste was dissolved, and the children, who were often scarcely distinguishable from white, took over the ideals, sentiments, and ambitions of their white fathers. Their mothers, who were generally mulattoes and already possessed some of the culture and feeling of the master race, were further assimilated into the white group by their close association with the cultured classes of the South.

NOTES

1. Arthur W. Calhoun, *A Social History of the American Family from Colonial Times to the Present,* Cleveland, 1917-18, I, 327.
2. Moses Grandy, *Narrative of the Life of Moses Grandy; Late a Slave in the United States of America,* Boston, 1844, p. 18.
3. L. L. Bernard, *Instinct: A Study in Social Psychology,* New York, 1924, p. 326.
4. Letter of Elisha Cain, overseer, on Retreat Plantation, Jefferson County, Georgia, to his employer, Miss Mary Telfair, Savannah, November 20, 1836, in Phillips, *Documentary History of American Industrial Society: Plantation and Frontier,* Cleveland, I, 333-34.
5. Lewis Clarke, *Narrative of the Sufferings of Lewis and Milton Clarke, Sons of a Soldier of the Revolution,* Boston, 1846, p. 127.
6. Frances A. Kemble, *Journal of a Residence on a Georgian Plantation,* New York, 1863, pp. 121-22.
7. H. B. Schoolcraft, *By A Southern Lady: Letters on the Condition of the African Race in the United States,* Philadelphia, 1852, pp. 13-14.
8. *The Journals of Washington Irving,* ed. William P. Trent and George S. Hellman, Boston, 1919, III, 115.
9. John Brown, *Slave Life in Georgia,* ed., L. A. Chameroozow (London, 1855), pp. 132-33.
10. John Thompson, *The Life of John Thompson, a Fugitive Slave; Containing His History of Twenty-five Years in Bondage, and His Providential Escape, Written by Himself* (Worcester, 1856), pp. 30-31.
11. J. W. Loguen, *The Rev. J. W. Loguen, as a Slave and as a Freeman* (Syracuse, N. Y., 1859), pp. 20-21.

Article 5

The Grimké Sisters: Women and the Abolition Movement

Gerda Lerner

We have given great offense on account of our womanhood, which seems to be as objectionable as our abolitionism. The whole land seems aroused to discussion on the province of woman, and I am glad of it. We are willing to bear the brunt of the storm, if we can only be the means of making a break in that wall of public opinion which lies right in the way of woman's rights, true dignity, honor and usefulness.

Angelina E. Grimké,
July 25, 1837.

This was the way Angelina saw their situation. It was quite true that from their first speech before "mixed audiences" they had been attacked as women and as abolitionists. Such attacks should not have been unexpected. As it happened, all during their tour they published serialized articles in the reform press, agitating their two favorite causes in such a way that it was impossible to ignore their connection. Angelina, in her *Letters to Catherine Beecher,* was making herself one of the foremost spokesmen for abolition, while Sarah, in her *Letters on the Equality of the Sexes,* was bringing the woman's rights question squarely before the public. Whether by accident or design, the Grimké sisters had come to represent in the public mind the fusion of abolition and woman's rights. It was this that precipitated an ideological crisis among reformers.

Early in 1837, Catherine Beecher, eldest daughter of Rev.

Lyman Beecher, had published *An Essay on Slavery and Abolitionism with reference to the Duty of American Females,* which she had addressed to Angelina Grimké.[1] In a foreword, the director of the Hartford Female Seminary, whose learning Angelina had once so greatly admired, explained that Angelina's *Appeal* had come to her notice while she was preparing an essay against abolition societies, and had struck her as deserving an answer. In her essay, Catherine Beecher defended the Colonization Society and gradualism as against the radicalism of the abolitionists. In particular, she declared herself against any effort to organize women in abolition societies, since the subordination of women to men was "a beneficent and immutable Divine law." And this pioneer of woman's education, who in her own life exemplified the ability of women to achieve independence through a career, declared that women's influence must be confined to the "domestic and social circle." Lecturing Angelina Grimké as though she were, indeed, the scholar at her academy she had once wished to be, Catherine Beecher declared herself strongly against women petitioning Congress: "Men are the proper persons to make appeals to the rulers whom they appoint, and if their female friends, by arguments and persuasions, can induce them to petition, all the good that can be done by such measures will be secured. But if females cannot influence their nearest friends, to urge forward a public measure in this way, they surely are out of their place in attempting to do it themselves."[2]

Angelina had decided, early in May, to answer this essay, a decision in which Weld strongly encouraged her.[3] She wrote a series of letters during the longer stops on her tour and sent them off, one by one, to be published in *The Emancipator* and *The Liberator.* The finished series was later revised and reprinted in book form.

In her *Letters to Catherine Beecher* she offered a forceful defense of abolitionist tactics and theory and demolished every argument offered by Colonizationists. In this she followed the arguments developed by Theodore Weld during the Lane Seminary debates and gave respectful attention to the opinion of leaders of the free Negro community of Philadelphia, men such as James Forten and Robert Purvis who had attacked the Colonization Society as an instrument for depriving free Negroes of their rights.[4] She wrote:

> That the Colonization Society is a *benevolent* institution we deny. . . . And it is a perfect mystery to me how men and women can *conscientiously* persevere in upholding an association, which the very objects of its

153

professed benevolence have repeatedly, solemnly, constantly and universally condemned. ... Yes, the free colored people are to be exiled,
because public opinion is crushing them into the dust; instead of their
friends protesting against that corrupt and unreasonable prejudice, and
living it down by a practical acknowledgement of their right to *every*
privilege, social, civil and religious which is enjoyed by the white man.

Surely you never want to "get rid" of people whom you *love*. ... It is
because I love the colored Americans, that I want them to stay in this
country; and in order to make it a happy home to them, I am trying to
talk down, and write down, and live down this horrible prejudice. Send-
ing a few to Africa cannot destroy it. No—we must dig up the weed by
the roots out of each of our hearts. . . .[5]

This strong and uncompromising attack on race prejudice as the
chief buttress of slavery was central to Angelina Grimké's thought
and led her directly to an acceptance of immediate emancipation.
She suggested that gradualism stemmed essentially from race prejudice. Defining what she understood by emancipation she listed a
series of concrete steps: freedom for the slave, payment of wages for
his labor, his right to marriage and to guardianship over his children,
legal rights, education and the protection of equitable laws. Then
she asked: Now, why should not all this be done immediately?
Which of these things is to be done next year, and which the year
after? . . . I have seen too much of slavery to be a gradualist.[6]

She discussed immediatism, the connection between North and
South, the lesson to be drawn from the British Emancipation Movement. Quoting from an interesting collection of letters and anecdotes, she endeavored to show the effectiveness of abolitionist doctrine in converting individual slaveholders and discussed in detail
every point of attack made by Miss Beecher on abolitionist methods.
This clearcut and strong defense of abolitionism occupied ten separate letters. Only in two letters did she answer Miss Beecher's
strictures on "women's sphere" and develop her defense of woman's
rights as a citizen into a full-fledged feminist argument.

The right of petition is the only political right that women have: why not
let them exercise it whenever they are aggrieved?

The fact that women are denied the right of voting for members of
Congress, is but a poor reason why they should also be deprived of the
right to petition. If their numbers are counted to swell the number of
Representatives in our State and National Legislatures, the *very least* that
can be done is to give them the right of petition in all cases whatsoever;

and without any abridgement. If not, they are mere slaves, known only through their masters. . . .

Now, I believe it is woman's right to have a voice in all the laws and regulations by which she is to be governed, whether in Church or State: and that the present arrangements of society, on these points, are a *violation of human rights, a rank usurpation of power*, a violent seizure and confiscation of what is sacredly and inalienably hers. . . . If Ecclesiastical and Civil governments are ordained of God, *then* I contend that woman has just as much right to sit in solemn counsel in Conventions, Conferences, Associations and General assemblies, as man—just as much right to sit upon the throne of England, or in the Presidential Chair of the United States.[7]

And, boldly linking the causes of slaves and women, Angelina Grimké charted the path of common struggle for greater democracy: "The discussion of the rights of the slave has opened the way for the discussion of other rights, and the ultimate result will most certainly be the breaking of *every* yoke, the letting the oppressed of every grade and description go free,—an emancipation far more glorious than any the world has ever yet seen. . . ."[8]

Meanwhile, starting in July, Sarah's *Letters on the Equality of the Sexes* appeared in the New England *Spectator* and were reprinted in *The Liberator*. These letters were addressed to Mary Parker, the President of the Boston Female Anti-Slavery Society, at whose suggestion the topic had been chosen as "The Province of Woman." It was she who had suggested to the editor of *The Spectator* that the Grimké sisters write such a series of articles—a suggestion the sisters considered "providential."[9] Since Angelina was already occupied with her rebuttal to Miss Beecher, Sarah undertook to write the series for *The Spectator*.[10]

The growing irritation of the New England churches with the abolitionists had been further aggravated by several articles in *The Liberator* which smacked of theological subversion. Garrison had not only reprinted J. H. Noyes' heretical doctrines, but had expressed his approval of Noyes' and H. C. Wright's "no-human-government" principles.[11] These eccentricities of Garrison, which happened to appear in print just about the time the two female abolitionist agents were lecturing to approving crowds in many New England communities, seemed to conservative churchmen dangerous threats to the established order of things.

Oliver Johnson, a friend and close co-worker of Garrison, describes the prevailing mood:

The women at that day, as in the present, were the strongest allies of the clergy, and in many things their main reliance. The ladies from South Carolina were making a very deep impression upon their sex wherever they went, and proslavery ministers felt that some strong measures must be taken to counteract their influence. . . . I believe they were more afraid of those two women than they would have been of a dozen lecturers of the other sex.[12]

The 1836 resolution of the Congregational General Association against antislavery speakers had not been as effective outside of Boston as its proponents had hoped it would be. Now the Grimké sisters' tour provided the necessary impetus for another attack. Rev. Nehemiah Adams, whose friendliness to the Southern viewpoint would later earn him the sobriquet "Southside Adams," took the lead in drafting a statement which was approved and issued on July 28, 1837, as a "Pastoral Letter of the General Association of Massachusetts to the Congregational Churches under their care."

Without naming names, the Pastoral Letter berated Garrison and the Grimké sisters. In a slap at Garrison it declared: "The perplexed and agitating subjects which are now common amongst us should not be forced upon any churches as matters for debate, at the hazard of alienation and division." Stressing the importance of deference to the pastoral office, it enjoined the churches not to permit "strangers to preach on subjects the ministers do not agree with." It went on to warn all churches against "the dangers which at present seem to threaten the female character with widespread and permanent injury." Denouncing the behavior of females "who so far forget themselves as to itinerate in the character of public lecturers and teachers," it exhorted women to abide by their "appropriate duties and influence . . . as clearly stated in the New Testament." Woman's strength derived from her dependence and weakness. "But when she assumes the place and tone of man as a public reformer, our care and protection of her seem unnecessary . . . and her character becomes unnatural. If the vine, whose strength and beauty it is to lean upon the trelliswork, and half conceal its clusters, thinks to assume the independence and the overshadowing nature of the elm, it will not only cease to bear fruit, but fall in shame and dishonor into the dust."[13]

The first effect of this Pastoral Letter, which was read from the pulpits and widely published, was to split the more conservative clerical abolitionists from Garrison and thus sharpen the leadership struggle within the abolition movement. It was followed by two "Clerical Appeals," denouncing Garrison for his intemperate and indiscriminate attack on the clergy. The first, signed by five ministers who claimed to be sincere abolitionists, was more damaging to the movement than the Pastoral Letter.[14] In reply, Garrison rushed into print with a long and heated editorial, which only aggravated the division in abolition ranks.[15] The New York Committee, and particularly the Tappans, Weld and Elizur Wright, although they were highly critical of Garrison, tried to avoid further damage by playing down the controversy.

The second Clerical Appeal emanated from Andover Theological Seminary. It directly involved the Grimkés and continued, in the vein of the Pastoral Letter, to link the attack on Garrisonism and on women lecturers.

As it happened, the sisters had lectured at Andover two days before the appearance of the Pastoral Letter, speaking there to 200 women and a few men in the Methodist Church at the invitation of the Andover Female Anti-Slavery Society. A few days later, thirty-nine students and faculty members of the Seminary published a signed statement in which they expressed their opposition to slavery, but insisted that only "moral" means must be used to bring it to an end. The means they approved were: "conversation, education and prayer." They went on to condemn "certain abolitionists" for surrounding the cause of abolition with "so many foreign and repulsive associations" and concluded, "the public lectures of females we have discountenanced and condemned as improper and unwise."[16]

The Andover Female Anti-Slavery Society replied to this statement: "We wish to have it known that the lectures ... were designed for the Ladies, and those Gentlemen who were present must sustain the responsibility of a mixed meeting." They also declared they saw no reason to regret their invitation to the Grimké sisters and recommended them to other women's organizations.

Some abolitionists responded to the Pastoral Letter with a chivalrous defense of the ladies as abolitionists and Quakers. Whittier's poem, "The Pastoral Letter," set the tone.

> So this is all—the utmost reach
> Of priestly power the mind to fetter!
> When   laymen   think—when   women
>   preach—
> A war of words—a "Pastoral Letter!"

He recalled to New England the shameful history of the persecution of heretics and witches and asked these modern-day bigots to learn from the past. He urged them to honor "Carolina's high-souled daughters" and predicted that "the pure and good shall throng to hear/ and tried and manly hearts surround them."[17]

Maria Chapman's amusing poem, "The Times That Try Men's Souls," sought to reduce the impact of the Pastoral Letter by ridicule:

> Confusion has seized us, and all things go
>   wrong,
> The women have leaped from "their
>   spheres,"
> And, instead of fixed stars, shoot as comets
>   along,
> And are setting the world by the ears!
> In courses erratic they're wheeling through
>   space,
> In brainless confusion and meaningless
>   chase. . . .
> They've taken a notion to speak for them-
>   selves,
> And are wielding the tongue and the pen;
> They've mounted the rostrum; the terma-
>   gant elves!
> And—oh horrid!—are talking to men!
> With faces unbalanced in our presence,
>   they come
> To harangue us, they say, in behalf of the
>   dumb. . . .[18]

Women rallied to the support of the sisters. Anna Weston joined them in Groton and accompanied them to some of their lectures. Mary Parker sent word that the Boston women would stand by them "if everyone else forsook them."[19] Most encouraging of all were the women in their audiences, who responded warmly to every allusion to the rights of women. That many of them walked six and eight miles to hear the sisters was better proof than words could give that they were expressing the hopes and aspirations of many.

It was Sarah Grimké with her *Letters on the Equality of the*

Sexes who "preached up woman's rights most nobly and fearlessly."[20] Attacking the Bible argument, which was the strongest point of those who claimed woman's inferiority was God-given, she held that the Scriptures had necessarily reflected the patriarchal society which had produced them. She claimed that women had been created by God as man's companion, in all respects his equal. "I ask no favors for my sex. . . . All I ask our brethren is, that they will take their feet from off our necks, and permit us to stand upright on that ground which God designed us to occupy."[21]

She characterized the Pastoral Letter as of a piece with Cotton Mather's pronouncements on witchcraft. As for its injunction that women must be instructed by their ministers before listening to speakers of their choice, she dismissed it harshly. "This I utterly defy. I have suffered too keenly from the teaching of man to lead anyone to him for instruction."[22]

After a historical and worldwide survey of the condition of women, she devoted one chapter to their situation in the United States. She decried the inferior, marriage-centered education given women, and cited Thomas Grimké in support of her demand for equal educational opportunities for women. In a survey of laws which worked to the detriment of women and deprived them of their rights as citizens Sarah Grimké anticipated by a dozen years the main arguments of the feminist movement. She even demanded equal pay for equal work and wrote at length and with bitterness about the low wages paid to women workers. She drew parallels between the status of the slave and that of women, and attacked with particular sharpness the degradation of slave women.

Addressing herself directly to women, she urged them to abandon all frivolity, love of fashion and the false protection of chivalry. Instead, they must become conscious of their own dignity and worth. "Woman must feel that she is the equal, and is designed to be the fellow laborer of her brother."[23] While she charged men with most of the responsibility for holding women in subjection, she pointed to specific examples of women acquiescing in their own degradation. The practice of having ministers open a meeting of a woman's organization she considered "ludicrous." Women were perfectly capable of taking charge of their own meetings. Women, who in sewing circles earned money to supply ministerial students, would do better to work for the advancement of their own sex.[24] She urged full and active participation of women in all the moral and social reform movements of the day. ". . . whatsoever it is morally

159

right for a man to do, it is morally right for a woman to do."[25] Men and women have the same rights and duties.

She ended her appeal with a strong bid to men. Equality of the sexes would be to their benefit: they would find woman as their equal "unspeakably more valuable than woman as their inferior."

In their abolition speeches and writings the Grimké sisters had often given a new and different emphasis from that of other abolitionists. But they had not originated theoretical or legal arguments; their strength lay in their approach and their incisive presentation of tried and tested material. But their feminist argument was original. Its strongly religious derivation made it particularly adapted to the American scene. Considering that it appeared ten years before the Seneca Falls Convention and seven years before Margaret Fuller's *Woman in the Nineteenth Century,* the outraged reaction with which so many of even the most radical reformers greeted it, is quite understandable.

NOTES

1. Catherine Beecher, *An Essay on Slavery and Abolitionism with reference to the Duty of American Females* (Philadelphia: Henry Perkins, 1837).
2. *Ibid.,* p. 101.
3. Gilbert H. Barnes and Dwight L. Dumond, eds., *Letters of Theodore Dwight Weld, Angelina Grimké Weld and Sarah Grimké, 1822-1844* (New York: D. Appleton-Century Co., 1938), I, 391.
4. Aptheker, *Documentary History,* pp. 71-72, 145-46. Also R. Billington (ed.), *A Free Negro in the Slave Era: Journal of Charlotte Forten* (New York: Collier Books, 1961), introduction.
5. Angelina E. Grimké, *Letters to Catherine E. Beecher, in Reply to an Essay on Slavery and Abolitionism, Addressed to A. E. Grimké, Revised by the Author* (Boston: Isaac Knapp, 1838), pp. 35-36, 40.
6. *Ibid.,* pp. 12-13.
7. *Ibid.,* pp. 112-13, 119.
8. *Ibid.,* p. 126.
9. *Weld-Grimké Letters,* I, 428.
10. Sarah M. Grimké, *Letters on the Equality of the Sexes and the Condition of woman: Addressed to Mary S. Parker, President of the Boston Female Anti-Slavery Society* (Boston: Isaac Knapp, 1838).
11. *The Liberator,* June 23, 1837, quoted in W. and F. Garrison, II, 150.

12. Allen Johnson and Dumas Malone, *Dictionary of American Biography* (22 vols.; New York: Scribner's & Sons, 1928-44), VII, 261.
13. Stanton, *et al., History of Woman Suffrage*, I, 81.
14. The New England *Spectator*, Aug. 2, 1837, reprinted in *The Liberator*, Aug. 11, 1837.
15. *The Liberator*, Aug. 18, 1837.
16. *Ibid.*, Aug. 25, 1837.
17. Stanton, *et al., History of Woman Suffrage*, I, 84-86.
18. *Ibid.*, pp. 82-83.
19. *Weld-Grimké Letters*, I, 419.
20. A. Grimké to J. Smith, July 25, 1837, Weld MSS.
21. S. Grimké, *Letters on Equality*, p. 10.
22. *Ibid.*, p. 19.
23. *Ibid.*, p. 116.
24. *Ibid.*, p. 120. In 1836, Lucy Stone, then sixteen and a schoolteacher, was sewing a shirt for a young man in theological seminary, when her church sewing circle was addressed by Mary Lyon, who was then trying to raise funds for Mount Holyoke Female Seminary. Lucy Stone, coming to the same conclusion as Sarah Grimké, "left the shirt unfinished and hoped that no one would ever complete it." See Alice Blackwell, *Lucy Stone: Pioneer of Woman's Rights* (Boston: Little, Brown & Co., 1930), p. 20. There is no known connection between the two incidents.
25. S. Grimké, *Letters on Equality*, p. 122.

Part Three

The Progressive Impulse

Throughout the latter part of the nineteenth century, urbanization and industrialization proceeded at an ever increasing pace. Women followed the general migration pattern from country to city, from farm to factory. Women at all levels of society were breaking out of the confines of the home. For the new immigrants and lower class women in general this process brought the dubious emancipation of the sweat shop and the shirtwaist factory. Other women for whom social change meant increased leisure were often horrified by the multiplying slums and the conditions under which the poor labored, and frustrated by a nearly pervasive sense of helplessness. As a consequence the Progressive era witnessed the activity of such women in a growing tangle of organizations which confronted a wide range of social ills from contaminated food and water to prostitution.

Although the percentage of women in industry declined, the number of working women increased with every census. By 1900 working women represented 20 per cent of the total female population over sixteen years of age. For the most part they remained domestics or farm workers and many still labored in the textile mills; however, new white collar jobs such as telephone and telegraph operators, stenographers, and secretaries employed increasing numbers of women. The lot of most working women was a hard one that improved little until the enactment of Progressive measures setting minimum wages and controlling hours and conditions of labor. In

1910 the bureau of labor reported that most working women were "paid very low wages—wages in many cases inadequate to supply a reasonable standard of living for women dependent upon their own earnings for support."[1] These women had little leisure time to devote to any form of organized activity. Only a few women in select areas, such as the garment industry, moved into the labor movement. After 1903 the Women's Trade Union attempted, with limited success, to bring women into the trade union movement, but for the most part working class women contributed little to Progressive reform.

Women from the middle and upper classes were also moving outside the home and becoming increasingly involved in reform projects. The growth of cities led directly to the shrinking of the physical dimensions of the home and the decline in family size. Aided by birth control[2] these women had fewer children than their mothers or grandmothers, and increasingly tended to seek release from unfortunate liaisons through divorce. At the same time the appearance of the sewing machine, pre-packaged foods, and electronic devices such as toasters and vacuum cleaners lightened the burdens of housework and increased the leisure time of these women. The new "leisure class" of wives of professionals and businessmen were joined in their reform activities by the group of women whom Vida D. Scudder termed "the first generation of college women."[3] Rich and well born, fewer than half of these young women ever married; they devoted themselves to serving others, whether in missions overseas or settlement houses in urban slums. Typically they were women whose education, intelligence, and sympathies outran the confines of the roles they were expected to play. Leisure made reform activity possible; frustration and sympathy gave it its dynamic impulse.

In "Woman as Alien," an excerpt from *The New Radicalism in America,* Christopher Lasch analyzes the appearance of discontented women of leisure as a social type, and relates their alienation from family and culture to both the feminist revolt of this period and the emergence of modern American liberalism. For Lasch the alienated woman reformer was epitomized by Jane Addams, but his general analysis also fits the foremost intellectual leader of early twentieth century feminism, Charlotte Perkins Gilman. Carl Degler's discussion of her main work, *Women and Economics,* hints at those aspects of nineteenth century America which feminists of her day rebelled against and reveals the depth of their critique.

Although the majority of alienated women were far less radical than Charlotte Gilman, their energies fired a succession of reform enterprises. The settlement house activities of Lillian Wald and Jane Addams are well known,[4] but the women's organizations which appeared in increasing numbers after 1890 were more typical of the Progressive era. These organizations, which often shared member-ship and sometimes worked together, ranged from the numerous women's clubs which focused on civic improvement and were only loosely united after 1901 under the egis of the General Federation of Women's Clubs (GFWC) to the older political organizations like the Women's Christian Temperance Union (WCTU) and the National American Woman Suffrage Association (NAWSA).

By 1890 a good many of the legal discriminations against which women earlier protested had been removed. Educational and eco-nomic opportunities had greatly expanded, but women still lacked elemental political rights. Increasingly women who wished to reform the social order felt their disfranchisement as a great handicap, and woman suffrage became the major focus of the feminist movement. In "The 'New Women' in the New South," Anne Firor Scott traces the expanding reform impulse in the South. Beginning with the WCTU, southern reformers gradually moved into a succession of community activities and finally joined the quest for the vote.

A similar pattern could be traced in the country as a whole as women became active in nearly all aspects of Progressive social reform. By 1920 women reformers had reason to be proud of their accomplishments and to be optimistic about the future. The two major reforms which had agitated women since the nineteenth cen-tury had been achieved with the enactment of Prohibition and the acceptance of woman suffrage. Women had been an important force in securing restrictions on child labor, the passage of more effective pure food and drug legislation, and conservation measures. They had also influenced the movements to curb prostitution[5] and to reform the divorce laws. Both of these movements sought to emancipate women from degrading situations. However, their success was based, as Christopher Lasch has noted, "not [on] the image of women as equals . . . but [on] the image of women as victims."[6]

Women reformers very often connected these issues with de-mands for suffrage and insisted that a purification of the political process would follow the entrance of women into the polling place. Alice Stone Blackwell, the activist daughter of Lucy Stone, believed that "in the main suffrage and prohibition have the same friends and the same enemies," and urged clergymen to support suffrage because it would augment the power of the churches in "the welfare against the liquor traffic, the white slave traffic, child labor, impure food, and many other existing evils . . ."[7] Aileen S. Kraditor summarizes the strengths and weaknesses of the movement in "Woman Suffrage in Perspective," the final chapter of her model study, *The Ideas of the Woman Suffrage Movement, 1890-1920.* She makes clear the truly democratic nature of the suffragist argument and yet shows that the increasing concern for tactics undermined the idealism of the movement.

The Nineteenth Amendment was finally recommended by President Woodrow Wilson, ironically as a war measure in response to women's wholehearted support of World War I. Traditionally women had made up a sizable element of the American peace movement, and at first organizations such as the NAWSA opposed American entrance into the war. Once war was declared, however, the marjoity of women supported the administration. Dr. Anna Howard Shaw, former president of NAWSA served as head of the National Women's Committee of the Council of National Defense during the war. Although she had little effect within the government, her organization, working through state and local branches, rolled bandages for the Red Cross and provided food and clothing to the soldiers. Many other women took over men's jobs in factories and the civil service or actually worked in Europe with the Red Cross and the Salvation Army. Such activities drew wide praise and contributed positively to the attainment of suffrage.

However, the achievement of these reforms was not without cost to the feminist movement. In order to gain the unity necessary for effective political pressure, the major women's organizations had to disavow their more militant elements such as Alice Paul's Women's party, and ignore the needs and desires of black women. Certainly there were black Progressives such as Ida B. Wells-Barnett, who is best remembered for her crusade against lynching, and white women who took a special interest in racial equality like Mary Hall Ovington, one of the founders of the National Association for the Advancement of Colored People. But for the most part the interests of black women were sacrificed to attain southern support. The GFWC and the WCTU were built upon sectional reconciliation and were strong in the South, but even NAWSA, whose roots stretched back into the abolition movement, tolerated racist arguments and gave in to the racist demands of their southern members.

NOTES

1. Quoted in Harold Underwood Faulkner, *The Quest for Social Justice, 1898-1914* (New York: Macmillan, 1931), 154.
2. David M. Kennedy, *Birth Control in America: The Career of Margaret Sanger* (New Haven: Yale University Press, 1970), 136, reports a study made in 1922 showing 75 per cent of a sample of college women and women's club members used contraceptives.
3. Quoted in Arthur Mann, *Yankee Reformers in the Urban Age* (Cambridge, Mass.: Harvard University Press, 1954), 201. This includes an excellent essay on Professor Scudder and her environment.
4. Allan Davis, *Spearheads for Reform: The Social Settlements and the Progressive Movement, 1890-1914* (New York: Oxford University Press, 1967).
5. In this connection see Egal Feldman, "Prostitution, the Alien Woman and the Progressive Imagination, 1910-1915," *American Quarterly,* XIX (Summer, 1967), 192-206; and Roy Lubove, "The Progressives and the Prostitute," *The Historian,* XXV (May, 1962), 308-330.
6. Christopher Lasch, "Divorce and the Family in America," *Atlantic* (November, 1966), 59.
7. Quoted in Aileen S. Kraditor, *The Ideas of the Woman Suffrage Movement, 1890-1920* (New York: Columbia University Press, 1965), 47-48.

Article 1

Woman as Alien

Christopher Lasch

Restlessness! Restlessness!" cried the novelist Margaret Deland in 1910. Everywhere one found "a prevailing discontent among women," "a restlessness infinitely removed from the old content of a generation ago."[1] The figure of the "neurasthenic" woman haunted the period—"the woman of privilege, the woman of sane and sheltered life,"[2] whose possessions included everything except happiness. "One meets wives, young or mature, apparently happy, gay; suddenly they confide in you that they are bored to death. . . . Others . . . merely want a 'change.' If they live in California, they want to live in New York. . . . Many . . . fall into a state of depression, develop nerves, lose the taste of life."[3]

A literature of reproach and alarm sprang up around the discontented woman of leisure. For psychologists, called in when the symptoms defied medical explanation, she was an object of intense concern; indeed, so familiar were the symptoms of women—ennui, fatigue, inexplicable illnesses, fits of crying over the most trivial causes, "nerves," "melancholia"—that psychologists for a long time assumed that hysterical neuroses were purely feminine manifestations. Students of society found a portent of disaster in the "parasitism" of the educated woman of the leisure class—the "fine lady," as Olive Schreiner called her, "the effete wife, concubine or prostitute, clad in fine raiment, the work of others' fingers; fed on luxurious viands, the result of others' toil, waited on and tended by the labor of others."[4] To people already troubled by thoughts of overcivilization, the appearance of the female parasite seemed to herald an age of imperial decadence, a second Rome.

The fiction of the period abounds in speculation about the "emancipated" woman, whose new found freedom seemed to be so much heavier a burden than her centuries of slavery. Robert Her-

Excerpts from *The New Radicalism in America* 1889-1963, by Christopher Lasch. Copyright © 1965 by Christopher Lasch. Reprinted by permission of Alfred A. Knopf, Inc.

rick, the most interesting of the so-called problem novelists around the turn of the century, saw in the restlessness of the modern woman the key to the social disorder about him: for it was the woman of fashion, he thought, freed by wealth and leisure to devote all her energies to competitive consumption, who drove her husband to sacrifice everything to the accumulation of wealth. Only by seeing economic competition as at bottom not economic at all, but social, could Herrick continue to deplore the "fierce competitive struggle" while at the same time celebrating the virtues of the old-fashioned entrepreneur. The entrepreneur might appear at first sight to have been himself implicated in the competitive struggle. But by distinguishing between the competition which centers on the production of goods and that which centers on consumption, and by investing the distinction with a moral value, Herrick avoided the utterly pessimistic conclusions to which his analysis so often seemed about to lead.[5]

"You drive him to the market-place," Herrick shouts at the despised "intellectual women" who were at once the objects of his censure and the most faithful readers of his fictions.[6] And in *Together,* his most ambitious production, he presented a whole gallery of restless, striving women, of the kind who leave destruction wherever their influence is felt: Bessie Falkner, whose social ambitions drive her husband first to bankruptcy and then to adultery; Connie Woodyard, the new intellectual whose first question is always, "What does it mean for *me?*"; Isabelle Lane, neurasthenic and effete, "too finely organized for the plain animal duties" of matrimony and motherhood, a victim, like the others, of the cult of "self-fulfillment."[7] Strangers to their husbands (as in the novels of William Dean Howells, the growing separation of the wife's and husband's spheres, she in the social whirl, he absorbed with business, is a persistent theme in Herrick's work), strangers to any conception of the traditional obligations of their sex, these women pass their lives in the pursuit of their own pleasure. They live in fear of pregnancy and have learned to prate of the family as an enslaving institution. The "atmosphere of the age" is epitomized for Herrick in Margaret Pole's adulterous affair with Rob Falkner—after which, however, he arranges her repentance and renunciation (not unlike similar renunciations in the novels of Henry James), an event which serves to throw into bolder contrast the unregeneracy of the others. Even in her moment of sin, Margaret distinguishes herself from the rest of Herrick's women by wishing nothing more than utterly to submit to her lover. She retains that intuitive sense of sexual differentiation the loss of which, in the others, is for Herrick the most telling sign of their depravity. "You," she sighs to her lover, "are the Man!"[8]. . . .

A further indication of the contemporary confusion surrounding the new woman is the fact that the opinions of anti-feminists such as Herrick coincided in so many particulars with those of the feminists themselves. The feminists did not of course share the view that feminism embodied the "arrant individualism" of the times, but they were equally convinced that the fierce pursuit of self-fulfillment was the source of the social unrest deplored by feminists and anti-feminists alike. They were at one with Herrick in regarding the problem of the modern woman as essentially a labor problem; a problem, that is, created by the sudden superabundance of leisure, or as the feminists were fond of putting it, by woman's evolution from producer to consumer. In the latter role she was condemned, it seemed, to live on the labor of others. It was this condition that feminists like Olive Schreiner and Charlotte Perkins Gilman called "parasitism." As Olive Schreiner noted, the fact that feminism had "essentially taken its rise among women of the more cultured and wealthy classes"[9] seemed to confirm this theory about its origins. Feminism apparently was a response—and an alternative—to the useless idleness which afflicted leisure-class women most immediately but which with the further advance of industrialism threatened to spread throughout modern society.

Rather than regarding this condition as originating in a moral flaw, the feminists reasoned that although it indisputably gave rise to uninhibited self-indulgence, its origins themselves were primarily economic. The family, they thought, once the most important unit of production, had gradually surrendered its functions to institutions outside the home—manufacturing to the factory, control over property to the state, the education of children to the public schools. This development, rather than the more obvious invasion of the home by labor-saving devices, was what the feminists had mainly in mind when they claimed that women's work had passed out of the home. The tasks formerly performed by the housewife and by the family in general were now performed elsewhere, and the function of the housewife in consequence was reduced to the passive role of consumption. The feminists did not regret the passing of the family; on the contrary, as staunch evolutionists, they regarded it as highly desirable, a necessary step in the "socialization" of mankind. They quarreled only with the refusal of their adversaries to see what these developments implied for the future role of women.

It was not only feminists who analyzed the problem this way. So common was the view that the family had lost its economic functions that by the turn of the century it was already a sociological truism.[10] Nor did it necessarily lead to feminist conclusions. More often it led to conclusions midway between those of the feminists, who welcomed the demise of the patriarchal family but insisted that it dictated a larger role for women outside the home, and those of the anti-feminists, who held that women's claim to a larger role was itself the cause of the whole problem. More common than either of these arguments was the characteristically "progressive" contention that the emergence of woman as a consumer demanded above all that she learn to play her new role more effectively. Those who took this line did not urge her to adopt a new role altogether, to "follow her work out of the home," as the feminists put it. Rather, they wanted her to stay at home as before, but to learn to use her new "profession" as consumer as a strategic position through which to influence and finally control the national destiny. This argument was a somewhat more sophisticated version of the old cliché that women as wives and mothers ruled the world from behind the scenes. Now women were urged to see that the most humdrum details of marketing and household economics had repercussions felt in distant capitals of trade and commerce, repercussions which profoundly altered the course of public affairs.

It was this position—what one might call the pseudo-feminist position—that was expounded by the more advanced of the women's magazines and in particular by *Good Housekeeping* and *Harper's Bazar*. The former devoted itself to the premise that housekeeping ought to be seen as a science; it was an unofficial organ of the home-economics movement, which achieved its first successes around the turn of the century. *Harper's Bazar* was more genteel in tone, and concerned itself not only with household affairs but with fashions, "society," and the arts and letters. It addressed itself precisely to the woman of leisure and cultivation who was presumed to be the chief victim of technological unemployment. Politically more adventurous than *Good Housekeeping* or the *Ladies' Home Journal,* the latter of which, under the editorship of Edward Bok, was strongly anti-feminist, the *Bazar* favored woman suffrage and other progressive reforms. For Bok, on the other hand, even the women's club movement represented a threat to the family. "Twenty years ago," he wrote, "a change in economic conditions, caused chiefly by the invention of labor-saving devices, found thousands of women suddenly thrown with leisure on their hands." But instead of using this leisure to combat such evils as the laxity of the divorce laws or the public drinking-cup, club women wasted their time on activities that drew them still further away from the "great and fundamental problems directly touching the marriage relation and the home."[11]

Compared with *Ladies' Home Journal, Harper's Bazar* was a model of enlightened progressivism. Nevertheless, it rejected the feminist demand for the socialization of womanhood. To women in search of excitement, in search of careers, the *Bazar* replied that the most ancient and honorable of professions was the home. A typical article, of the kind one can find in any issue of the magazine for these years, deplores "the spirit of unrest in the drawing-room" and enjoins on women the higher fulfillment of "wifehood and mother-hood."[12]

> Home life in our busy day [the writer regretfully notes] . . . is passing out of vogue. . . . Each [daughter] has her fad or mission, keeping her for hours abroad, or else when in-doors bent over a desk heaped with notes to answer, minutes to be made up, reports to be prepared . . . papers to be written. . . . At breakfast she is too absorbed in tearing open and digesting her correspondence to be able to diffuse around her the aroma of gracious and sympathizing young womanhood which would help to arm the men of the family for their fight with circumstance downtown.

But at the same time—and this is what is so characteristic of the pseudo-feminist position—the writer makes it clear that she does not advocate a return to the family of former times. "Far be it from me to suggest a relapse to those dark ages of home life when a girl strummed on the piano or worked the cross-stitch tapestry what time she was not engaged in dressing or receiving 'beaux,' until she married and passed into a new arena." Not a "relapse" into culture and courtship, but modern motherhood, the ideal of "home life as a profession," ought henceforth to be the goal of women's efforts.

Full-blown feminists naturally had no patience with such counsel. To the home economists they replied that it was no use trying to make home industry a science. "It is just because it is home industry that all this trouble is necessary."[13] Home industry was inherently inefficient because it required the housewife, unspecialized and untrained, to perform a multitude of tasks each of which could better be performed by a specialist. It followed that homemade clothes were inferior to those made by a tailor, home cooking inferior to the products of the factory, home-baked bread inferior to the baker's. Bread, Mrs. Gilman noted, had "risen greatly in excellence as we make less and less at home."[14] In every sphere, progress came from without. If the home was safe, it owed its safety to the police; if it was clean, it had public sanitation to thank. And if such services as these were already "socialized," with obvious advantage to all, why not socialize the rest?—the education of children above all else. The kindergarten and the day nursery were encouraging signs. "There is no more brilliant hope on earth to-day than this new thought about the child . . . the recognition of 'the child,' children as a class, children as citizens with rights to be guaranteed only by the state; instead of our previous attitude toward them of absolute personal ownership—the unchecked tyranny, or as unchecked indulgence, of the private home."[15]

If selfishness was the disease of modern society, in short, it was precisely because of the survival of the patriarchal family into an age in which it had no place. The family institutionalized selfishness; it gave sanction to every anti-social impulse. "Civilization and Christianity teach us to care for 'the child,' motherhood stops at 'my child.' "[16] Mrs. Gilman, who like so many radicals of the time tended to equate technological with cultural advancement, the division of labor with the progress of the spirit, analyzed the evolution of "love" as follows.

The primitive father, to feed the child, went forth himself and killed some rabbit—and the primitive mother cooked it: love, in grade A. The modern father, to feed his child, takes his thousandth part in some complex industry, and receives his thousand-fold share of the complex products of others' industry, and so provides for the child far more richly than could the savage: love, in grade Z.

But the modern mother, she complained, to feed her child still did nothing but cook for it. The modern mother "still loves in grade A, and the effect of that persistence of grade A is to retard the development of grade Z." "Mother-love," Mrs. Gilman concluded, "is the fountain of all our human affection, but mother-love, *as limited by the home,* does not have the range and efficacy proper to our time."[17]

What the feminists wanted to make clear was that not only women and the family, but society as a whole, would benefit from

173

the changes they proposed. Indeed, they managed at times to convince themselves that woman had as much to lose as to gain—looking at the matter in terms of her narrow and immediate self-interest—from her emancipation. She would be called on to make heavy sacrifices of leisure and comfort. It was "not for herself, not even for fellow women alone, but for the benefit of humanity at large, [that] she must seek to readjust herself to life"; and it was this fact, Olive Schreiner argued, that excused even the "passionate denunciations, not always wisely thought out," which some feminists leveled at the opposite sex.[18] It was woman's nature, after all, to work for others. Social consciousness was preeminently a feminine trait, and men acquired it, if they acquired it at all, through contact with women. The difference between men and women in this regard was inherent in the respective roles men and women, from time immemorial, had been required to perform. Women, as mothers, developed a sense of responsibility for others. Men, as providers, were necessarily dominated by the spirit of gain. As Rheta Childe Dorr put it: "Man, in the aggregate, thinks in terms of money profit and money loss, and try as he will, he cannot yet think in any other terms." But women had been trained for "constant service," and they were accustomed to look for "purely a spiritual reward."[19]

This line of argument was not without its difficulties. If it was domesticity that bred in women the social sense, would not women lose the social sense when they were no longer domestic? When exposed to the man's world, would they not take on what Mrs. Dorr called the "commercial habit of thought"? Answers to the question varied. Mrs. Dorr conceded that the danger existed and that in another age women might have been contaminated by contact with the world affairs. But it happened, she contended, that the new woman came into a world which was "already losing faith in the commercial ideal, and which is endeavoring to substitute in its place a social idea."[20] The time was singularly propitious, in other words, for woman's entry into the larger sphere of her responsibilities.

Others were not content to rest their case on the existing enlightenment of the age, perhaps because they could not concede that any age was enlightened which still discriminated against women. At the same time they insisted that women would not lose their womanly qualities by doing men's work. But that put them in the position of saying that woman's nature was unchanging and thus implied a rejection of the environmentalism to which feminists professed to be devoted. At this point, one begins to suspect that for many feminists the doctrine of evolution merely served to give scientific respectability to existing clichés about the nature of woman—her essential purity, her freedom from coarse or selfish motives, her "habit of service." A strict environmentalism would have forced them to reckon with the possibility that the nature of women, no less than that of men, might be changed, as Ellen Key observed, "by different vocations and surroundings." If women now believed they could achieve the "strength of men" without sacrificing something of the harmony of their lives, Ellen Key warned her more complacent colleagues, they believed "their sex capable of possibilities which thus far have been granted rarely and then only to the exceptional in both sexes."[21] But that was exactly what many American feminists did believe.

It is an added irony that the ideas about woman's nature to which some feminists still clung, in spite of their opposition to the enslavement of woman in the home, were the very clichés which had so long been used to keep her there. The assumption that women were morally purer than men, better capable of altruism and self-sacrifice, was the core of the myth of domesticity against which the feminists were in revolt. Once again, feminist and anti-feminist assumptions seemed curiously to coincide . . .

As propaganda, all this was enormously effective. As an explanation of the sources of feminism, it left something to be desired. What neither the pleas of the feminists nor, for that matter, the despairing cries of their adversaries accounted for was the violence of the debate about the new woman. It was well to point out that the patriarchal family had lost its economic and social reasons for being, but that did not explain why women should have turned with such fury on an institution which according to their own reasoning was already defunct. One could argue, again, that women's eagerness to serve humanity excused their sweeping assault on the male sex, but that did not explain why the assault took place; it did not account for the enormous amount of sexual antipathy generated by the feminist movement. Nor did the evolutionist theories of Mrs. Gilman and Olive Schreiner throw any light on what in retrospect appears so marked a characteristic of American feminism, its preoccupation with the question of sexual identity. The whole "woman question," as it was debated in the United States, turned on the issue not simply of what roles women and men ought respectively to play, but of the respective *nature* of the sexes. What did it mean to be masculine or feminine? What did the adjectives signify? The inten-

175

sity of the speculation about these questions discloses anxieties which lie much deeper than anything associated with the greater leisure of the modern woman or the flight of housework from the home. Those developments doubtless took place, but why they should have left such bitterness and passion behind them neither the feminists nor the sociologists and historians who adopted their theories about the family were able to explain.

Whatever one thinks of the justice of the feminists' cause, one has to admit that the envy of men was very pronounced in American feminism. Sometimes it amounted to outright antagonism. The feminists talked a great deal about the need for a freer and more spontaneous companionship between men and women, but in practice they often seemed to assume a state of perpetual war. Even when the envy of men did not reach the point of hostility—and it is possible to exaggerate the Lesbian and castrating aspects of the feminist revolt—the envy nevertheless remained. So did the unconcealed abhorrence of everything connected with the middle-class family and with middle-class life in general, an abhorrence of which the envy of men, in fact, was probably a single facet. Consider, for example, the autobiographical essays of Inez Haynes Gillmore, which she published under the deliberate and revealing title, "Confessions of an Alien."[22] In these memoirs one encounters at once the sense of superfluity that more than anything else identifies the feminist impulse. It was this "feeling of alienage," Mrs. Gillmore says, together with "a feeling of sex discontent" (i.e., envy of men), which pushed her into the "discoveries in regard to the life of woman" that made her a feminist.

> For several years now I have felt myself alien to this world, and alien not because of race or color, but alien because of changing economic conditions. It seems to me that sociologically, so to speak, I hang in a void midway between two spheres—the man's sphere and the woman's sphere. A professional career ... puts me beyond the reach of the average woman's duties and pleasures. The conventional limitations of the female lot put me beyond the reach of the average man's duties and pleasures.

But whereas her sense of alienation was "a comparatively recent growth," "that other feeling—sex discontent—has oppressed me all my life."

Not since I started to do my own thinking have I been in any doubt as to which sphere most attracted me. The duties and pleasures of the average woman bore and irritate. The duties and pleasures of the average man interest and allure. This seemed the most shameful of my discoveries. But I soon found that it was a feeling which I shared with the majority of my kind. I have never met a man who at any time wanted to be a woman. I have met very few women who have not at some time or other wanted to be men.

To uncover the reasons for her discontent, Mrs. Gillmore had to "go back to the very beginning" of her life. She grew up, a bookish and imaginative child, in genteel poverty, "poor enough to be dull, poor enough to be put to all the threadbare makeshifts of a faded gentility, but not poor enough to enjoy the hearty, vulgar social promiscuity of the frankly poverty-stricken." At first she attributed her unhappiness to her family's poverty. Then she discovered that poverty, "that strangling gray fog," bore harder on her than it bore on her brothers. "They were always escaping, not like me to an imaginative world, but to an actual, if invisible, world—that scarlet-and-gold country of the foot-loose male." She yearned for adventure, but "custom had decreed" that she could not go out in search of it; she must wait for adventure to come to her. Sometimes she was overwhelmed with a sense of the possibilities that lay before her, the sense that "almost anything can happen."

But "almost anything" did not happen. . . . "Almost anything" can happen to men. . . . But to women adventure, excepting always what must be for most of them the only adventure—love and marriage—comes in the most casual way, comes, if at all, at such long intervals that it often finds them unready and afraid. Even the adventure of marriage is accidental. They cannot demand it of life.

At college she took courses in literature and philosophy and developed "an enormous curiosity about life." She and her friends argued and debated endlessly. But all the evidence on which they based their speculations came from books. "It never occurred to us that we were studying a second-hand world, that we were getting our life in translation, that we never really had a face-to-face encounter with it." Men, she thought—there was a men's college in the same town—didn't read as much and almost certainly didn't talk so well, but they *lived*.[23] "They were talking all the time to the man in the street, the cabman, the barber, the policeman. They were talking a great deal to the woman in industry, the shop-girl, the waitress, the stenographer." The world, she concluded, had "set up a double standard of experience—one for men, one for women."[24]

Eventually Mrs. Gillmore rebelled against her lot and determined to "play the man's game." She became a journalist and a writer. She went where she pleased and chose her own friends. Life favored her "above most women." "It has permitted me to do the man's work and it has paid me the man's pay." But she wondered whether she had not "paid high for my independence—in that feeling of alienage to which I have confessed." At the same time she continued to be tormented by the thought that after all, in spite of her exertions, she had not yet managed to confront experience for herself. "The fact that I've never seen life in the raw gives me an odd sense of bafflement. I am certain that . . . I shall at the end feel as much an amateur at life as I feel now."[25]

These "confessions" are not an isolated and solitary cry of despair. They were the common complaint of a certain kind of American woman in the period around the turn of the century—the middle-class woman of intellectual ambitions. Jane Addams, when she wrote of her own early sufferings, was describing the same experience exactly—the yearning for "adventure"; the sense of living at second hand and of "getting life in translation"; the fear of finding oneself "unready and afraid" in the face of experience. Few of the feminists of this period seem to have escaped the kind of nervous crisis described by Jane Addams—a period of utter aimlessness, in which all one's powers seemed to atrophy. Often the crisis was precipitated by marriage. Thus Charlotte Perkins Gilman, after tasting independence at twenty-one—a "tremendous surge of free energy"—stumbled into a disastrous marriage with Charles Stetson, a painter, in spite of her premonition that she was entering "a future of failure and suffering."[26] Immediately she sank into an inexplicable illness. "A sort of gray fog drifted across my mind, a cloud that grew and darkened."[27] She bore a daughter, a "heavenly baby"; her husband was more attentive, more considerate than ever; but the gloom deepened day by day. "Here was a charming home; a loving and devoted husband; an exquisite baby, healthy, intelligent and good; a highly competent mother to run things; a wholly satisfactory servant—and I lay all day on the lounge and cried."[28] But when she went to California to visit friends, her spirits lifted at once. "From the moment the wheels began to turn, the train to move, I felt better."[29] She came home and within a month "was as low as before leaving."[30] One could not find a more conclusive application of the feminist contention that family life inhibited creative effort. Mrs. Gilman divorced her husband and went on to a brilliant career as writer and agitator.

Likewise Margaret Sanger, encouraged by the example of a revered father to develop her talents, embarked on a medical career, only to cut it off by an impulsive marriage to a young painter. Almost immediately she fell sick; in her case, with a real sickness, tuberculosis, from which she made a slow recovery. Thereafter she and her husband lived in Greenwich Village, cultivated the society of the artists and radicals whom they met at Mabel Dodge's salon, and to outward appearances led a busy life. Yet Mrs. Sanger was not happy, and as she grew older she realized that she had wasted too much of her life in "inactive, incoherent brooding." "I could not contain my ideas, I wanted to get on with what I had to do in the world."[31] Like Charlotte Gilman, she had to leave her husband in order to do so.

For women such as these, conscious of their intellectual gifts but unable, it seemed, to make use of them within the sphere of women's traditional duties, life, experience, "growth" were always *out there,* they belonged to the great world beyond the household and the family. But the sense of "alienage" was by no means confined to women. When one sees the feminist impulse as an aspect of a more general development—the revolt of intellectuals against the middle class—one begins to understand the feminists' acute fear that life had passed them by. For this conviction that life lay always outside the narrow confines of one's own experience was common to all those, of whatever sex, who felt themselves imprisoned in the stale room of a borrowed culture.

The envy with which women looked on men had its counterpart in the envy of intellectuals in general of what they conceived to be the richer life of the proletariat (an envy which in our own time has been transferred to Negroes).[32] Women also, when they were not lost in wonder at the masculine world of activity and adventure, often gave vent to this mingled fear and envy of the working class. But when Inez Gillmore spoke of "the hearty, vulgar social promiscuity" of the poor, to which her own "faded gentility" made so poignant a contrast, she spoke not as a woman but as a middle-class intellectual gazing wistfully across the social chasm. She said no more than what every intellectual of the age must at one time or another have suspected, that his own class had somehow lost contact with life. To live fully, directly, spontaneously; to live to the outer limits of one's capacities; to immerse oneself in the stream of experience—all this was no longer something one took for granted as the essence of the human condition, but had become rather an objective to be strived after with all one's powers, an objective one was yet fated always to fall pitiably short of. It was precisely this mystical sense of the sanctity of experience, life, growth, and development that rendered the men and women of the period incapable of setting up an alternative to the cult of "self-fulfillment" the destructuve possibilities of which they were so quick to discern. Charlotte Gilman could deplore the unbridled individualism which she saw as the curse of modern society and at the same time insist that personal "growth" was the law of life and the only goal worth pursuing.[33] And the "new religion" that Robert Herrick insisted was the alternative to the triumph of egotism turned out to be nothing more than the "religion of life"—a "faith in life apart from our own personal fate."[34]

The cultural and even the political history of the period, looked at in such a light, seems always to shine back some reflected facet of this religion of experience. One sees it in the vogue of literary naturalism; in muckraking journalism, with its celebration (under the guise of censure) of the teeming life of the cities; in the assumption, common to both, that "reality" was at once sordid and romantic, dirty and unspeakably exciting—whatever in short was the antithesis of genteel respectability. One sees it in the deep ambivalence with which men and women who called themselves progressives contemplated the doings of the "malefactors of great wealth"; their mingled fascination and horror, their outraged envy. Above all, one sees it in the discontent of intellectuals not only with the old conception of culture but with intellectual life itself; in their eagerness to escape from the isolation to which intellectuality seemed to condemn them; in the self-effacement and self-contempt which made them yearn to put their abilities at the service of the community. Nothing could have been more revealing than the pervasiveness of the ideal of "service" among the very people one might have expected to have been its most outspoken critics. Disinterested inquiry and speculation could no longer suffice. Intellectuals, like everybody else—even the poor, notwithstanding the full-blooded sensuality with which the intellectuals in their own minds endowed them—could find comfort and meaning, it appeared, only in large, encompassing movements of masses of people, of which they could imagine themselves a part.

But if all these things were true, why, it must be asked, did so many women ignore them? Why did they see only the "sexual question"? If, in fact, women shared with men of the same class this yearning for a larger life and for more direct encounters with experience, why did they not perceive the existence of this common ground? Why did they persist in attributing their sufferings not to class but to sex, not to their being middle-class intellectuals in rebellion against what had come to seem a sterile and meaningless existence, but to the simple fact of their being women? It is true, of course, that women such as Jane Addams saw the class issue as well as the sexual issue and in fact gave precedence to the first, but it is also true that the discussion of the new woman, considered as a whole, had a way always of coming back to the fact of "sex discontent," to the recital of women's age-old hardships and deprivations. Even Jane Addams could not altogether escape this resentment. Nor could she escape the suspicion that obsessed the feminist imagination: that in pursuing a masculine ideal she had betrayed her own feminity.

The resentment and the suspicion were inescapable because of the peculiar conditions of American life—or perhaps more accurately the peculiar conditions of life in English-speaking countries. In America the idea of culture was predominantly feminine to begin with. The care and preservation of culture had early been entrusted to women. Not only art but religion was considered to belong to woman's sphere, the more practical pursuits to man's, and in no other country in the world was the distinction between the two, in the popular mind, so uncompromisingly rigid. Women were the moral custodians of society. In a society that felt itself on the verge of chaos—a "frontier" in the broadest sense of the term—they came to represent cohesion, decency, and self-restraint; and the cult of the home, over which they presided, became the national religion. Under those circumstances the rebellion against culture necessarily became a rebellion also against the definition of woman's "place" with which the nineteenth-century concept of culture was so closely bound up.[35]

The association of moral and aesthetic refinement with femininity was more than an expression of the sentimental myth of woman's purity. It seems at one time to have served a more immediate and practical purpose. Artistic and intellectual accomplishments in a

181

young woman, in the eighteenth and nineteenth centuries, were regarded as indispensable to her success in the marriage market, toward which from girlhood all her energies were supposed to be devoted. The feminists suspected, and with good reason, that not only the genteel ideal of culture but the whole system of genteel social intercourse had as its essential function the auctioning off of young girls to the most eligible bidders. When an eligible marriage was considered for one's daughters the *summum bonum* of existence, a vast body of convention grew up designed at once to facilitate and to regulate the frantic competitive quest for husbands which inevitably ensued. Fashion, "society," "culture" were all aspects of the same process. Their purpose, it seemed, was to cultivate a girl's attractions and then to provide a setting for their display. Even the business life of the middle class, if novelists like Robert Herrick were to be believed, came eventually to be pervaded by the social ambitions of American women; and the complaints one so often encounters around the turn of the century, that all life had been "womanized," would seem to reflect the degree to which social intercourse of every kind, at a certain level of society, had come to revolve inexorably around the demands of competitive matchmaking.

It is not surprising that images of slavery and prostitution figured so prominently in the rhetoric of feminism. The analogy between the condition of women and the condition of Negro slaves was always a favorite of feminists. It expressed the sense that women were legally the slaves of their husbands, but it may also have referred, more obliquely, to this sense of society as a kind of auction block, to which girls were bred (like Negro wenches) from birth. As for prostitution, the reference was perfectly obvious. When the feminists referred to the "parasitism" of the modern woman, they meant, among other things, that her only function in life was to be pleasing to men. Thus the difference between marriage and prostitution was hardly more than a legal nicety. There was "no sharp, clear, sudden-drawn line," Olive Schreiner maintained, between the "kept wife," living "by the exercise of her sex functions alone," and the prostitute.[36]

The practical effect of all this, for young girls of intellectual interests and serious disposition, was to make the society of their contemporaries almost intolerable. The lowest common denominator of the feminist revolt was simply a revulsion, formed early in life, against the sheer silliness of the life which a girl was expected to lead and which most girls apparently did lead. "My aim," said one feminist, "is . . . to make myself a true woman, one worthy of the name, and not to be one of the delicate little dolls or the silly fools who make up the bulk of American women, slaves to society and fashion."[37] One of Jane Addams's schoolgirl friends cried: "If anyone wishes to make himself particularly disagreeable to me just let him call me a *school girl.*" Sentimental, "gushing, and *young*"; everlastingly "afflicted with the giggles"; having "nothing excepting the affairs of their neighbors to interest them"; lacking altogether the "faculty of reviewing what they read and enlarging upon it: digesting and discussing"—such were her companions. "How unhappy the quiet girl is deemed; she that can talk the most and gossip in an *easily hateful* [way] (do you understand?) is the popular girl."[38]

Another letter to Jane Addams, from a friend at a girls' seminary, captures at once the conditions against which the feminists rebelled and the difficulties inherent in the rebellion.

> The girls here are afflicted with the same sentimental "spooning" malady, which, you say, infests Rockford. I heartily agree with you, old fellow, that it is both disgusting & horrible, & demoralizing to us as women. . . . Indeed, the girls carried the thing so far as to actually *flirt* with *one another,* in a way similar to the different sexes. For a time there was quite an excitement over the affair. Miss Bently brought it up in gen[eral] ex[ercises] in such a sarcastic yet sad & reproving way, that we were all filled with shame. I believe in kissing one's friends at the proper time, but as to bestowing them—the kisses—promiscuously on one & all, the sacredness of a kiss loses its charm. I believe that the true, deep friendship & loves are those which make no obstreperous demonstrations—as it were. Dear Pythias, I think that in you, I have found my affinity & I picture to myself the delightful, quiet times we might have "of an evening," reading aloud to each other, & holding earnest conversations.[39]

It is touching and revealing that in their mutual revulsion against the vanity and frivolity of their classmates—whose casual flirtations among themselves, rehearsals for the more important flirtations to come, were the logical end-product of a system which elevated the drama of courtship to so central a position—and in their pursuit of a life that would not be "demoralizing to us as women," girls of more serious habits should have found themselves addressing each other as "old fellow," as "Damon" and "Pythias." It is an unimportant detail in itself, this assumption of masculine pseudonyms; but it symbolizes the feminist dilemma. The determination to be a "true woman" forced one in effect to lead a man's life. That was exactly the point made by the most uncomprehending critics of the feminist movement. What was so maddening was that there was finally no answer to this easiest of clichés. The search for woman's nature led always in circles.

NOTES

1. Margaret Deland: "The Change in the Feminine Ideal," *Atlantic*, CV (March, 1910), pp. 290-1.
2. Ibid., p. 290.
3. Gertrude Atherton: "The Woman in Love," *Harper's Bazar*, XLIV (May, 1910), p. 305.
4. Olive Schreiner: *Woman and Labor* (New York: Frederick A. Stokes; 1911), pp. 79-80.
5. Herrick was by no means the only novelist who wrote of the American woman in this light. The works of both Howells and James abound in matrons whose social ambitions and lust for power come to focus on the consumption of goods. Mrs. Westgate, in James's "An International Episode," is an example:
   > "An American woman who respects herself," said Mrs. Westgate, turning to Beaumont with her bright expository air, "must buy something every day of her life. If she cannot do it herself, she must send out some member of her family for the purpose." (Leon Edel, ed.: *The Complete Tales of Henry James* [London: Rupert Hart-Davis; 1962], Vol. IV, p. 275.)
6. Robert Herrick: *Together* (New York: Macmillan; 1908), p. 499.
7. Ibid., pp. 220, 155.
8. Ibid., p. 390.
9. Schreiner: *Woman and Labor*, p. 124.
10. See, for example, William E. Carson: *The Marriage Revolt: A Study of Marriage and Divorce* (New York: Hearst's International Library Co.; 1915), pp. 21-2; Orison Swett Marden: *Woman and Home* (New York: Thomas Y. Crowell; 1915), pp. 23-31.
11. Edward Bok: "My Quarrel with Women's Clubs," *Ladies' Home Journal*, XXVII (Jan., 1910), pp. 5-6.
12. Mrs. Burton Harrison: "Home Life as a Profession," *Harper's Bazar*, XXXIII (May 19, 1900), pp. 148-50.
13. Charlotte Perkins Gilman: *The Home: Its Work and Influence* (New York: McClure, Phillips & Co.; 1903), p. 93.
14. Ibid., p. 331.

15. Ibid., p. 335. On the discovery of the child see below, chapter 3.

16. Ibid., p. 165.

17. Ibid., p. 167.

18. Schreiner: *Woman and Labor,* pp. 125-6.

19. Rheta Childe Dorr: *What Eight Million Women Want* (Boston: Small, Maynard & Co.; 1910), pp. 6, 11.

20. Ibid., pp. 12-13.

21. Ellen Key: *The Woman Movement* (New York: G. P. Putnam's Sons; 1912), p. 105.

22. *Harper's Bazar,* XLVI (April, 1912), pp. 17ff.; another installment appeared in the following issue. The editors published these articles with the explanation that the author's opinions "are not the opinions of the editors, nor are they in harmony with the editorial policy of the BAZAR."

23. For the very similar comments of Randolph Bourne—but with the sexes exactly reversed—see below, p. 101.

24. There were a few experiences, she admitted, that were "essentially sexed," like fatherhood and motherhood. "But between those two classes there is a broad mass of experience essentially sexless, essentially human. My quarrel with life is that women are permitted to enjoy so few of the human experiences." Cf. Charlotte Perkins Gilman (*The Home,* p. 217): "It can never be too frequently insisted upon . . . that the whole area of human life is outside of, and irrelevant to, the distinctions of sex. Race characteristics belong in equal measure to either sex, and the misfortune of the house-bound woman is that she is denied time, place, and opportunity to develop those characteristics. She is feminine . . . but she is not human."

25. See also Inez Haynes Gillmore: "The Life of an Average Woman," *Harper's Bazar,* XLVI (June, 1912), pp. 281ff.: "Woman is, after all, only a supernumerary in the great drama of the world. . . . The picture which, in imagination, I always draw of her is a slim, weak, pale, bowed, weary figure—weak, humorless, inarticulate, standing timidly on the threshold of life, peering through the open door, but not daring to enter."

26. Charlotte Perkins Gilman: *The Living of Charlotte Perkins Gilman, An Autobiography* (New York: Appleton-Century; 1935), pp. 72, 84.

27. Ibid., p. 198.

28. Ibid., p. 89.

29. Ibid., p. 92.

30. Ibid., p. 95.

31. Margaret Sanger: *An Autobiography* (New York: Norton; 1938), pp. 104-5.

32. See, e.g., Norman Mailer: *The White Negro* (San Francisco: City Lights Books; n.d. [1957]). See below, pp. 344-5.

33. Zona Gale, foreword to Gilman: *Living,* p. xiii.

34. Herrick: *Together,* pp. 500-1.

35. On the feminization of American culture, see Denis Brogan: *The American Character* (New York: Alfred A. Knopf; 1944), part I, *passim;* Geoffrey Gorer: *The American People: A Study in National Character* (New York: W. W. Norton; 1948); Margaret Mead: *Male and Female: A Study of the Sexes in a Changing World* (New York: W. Morrow; 1949); Leslie A. Fiedler: *Love and Death in the American Novel* (New York: Criterion Press; 1960).

36. Schreiner: *Woman and Labor,* p. 104.

37. Caroline L. Hunt: *The Life of Ellen H. Richards, 1842-1911* (Boston: Whitcomb & Barrows; 1912), p. 57.

38. Vallie E. Beck to Jane Addams, Feb. 5, 1897, Addams MSS.

39. Unidentified correspondent to [Jane Addams], Dec. 5, 1877, Addams MSS.

Article 2

The "New Woman" in the New South

Anne Firor Scott

In 1884 a distinguished lady in New Orleans was made chairman of a committee of the New Orleans Education Society. When she came to make the report of her committee, over which she had labored long, the Society decreed that it must be read for her by one of the male members. The lady resigned in protest—but even her protest required male co-operation: "I requested my husband," she recorded, "to cease paying my dues!" Here, in miniature, was the "woman problem" as it began to take shape in the post-Civil-War South.

Northern women had begun in the 1830's to raise their voices against legal and social discrimination, to protest the lack of equal educational and professional opportunity. In the South the institution of chivalry had held firm. It seems to have been characterized by a widespread legal and theoretical acceptance of the premise that woman was an inferior creature and a widespread practical expectation that she would perform as a superior one. The acceptable goals for southern women were to please their husbands and to please God, and to this end they were supposed to be beautiful, mildly literate, gracious, hardworking, and church going. "Woman's sphere," as they called it, was well marked out. This description applies to the minority of women who belonged to the pace-setting plantation families. For the rest, our information is small, but such as we have indicates that they worked hard and knew their place.

Testimony is unanimous that slavery did not make for leisure as far as plantation mistresses were concerned. They carried large responsibilities and did as well much physical work. Open protest against their disabilities was infrequent, and genuine rebels such as the Grimké sisters found it necessary to leave the South altogether.

From *South Atlantic Quarterly*, LXV (Autumn, 1962), 473–483. Reprinted by permission of the publisher. Copyright 1962, Duke University Press, Durham, North Carolina.

Then came the war. Southern women were thrust into new public and private responsibilities, ranging from running whole plantations to providing food, clothing, bandages, and nursing care for the Confederate army. With the men away "woman's sphere" suddenly became very elastic. If the fire-eaters had foreseen this particular consequence, perhaps they would have been less eager for secession—for as far as women were concerned Pandora's box was opened. Reconstruction offered other challenges, including for many the necessity of making one's way in a world in which women outnumbered men. With the whole South to rebuild, every pair of hands was needed, and while the legend of the southern lady was tended along with other more or less accurate legends of the old South, the lady herself had not much time for acting her prescribed role. In addition, the whole structure of women's lives was being changed by the multiplication of factory-made products which lightened domestic burdens immeasurably. The single invention of the sewing machine was an immense emancipation of mothers. For southern women there was an additional emancipation in the freeing of the slaves. Nearly all who recorded their opinions rejoiced that slavery was ended.

The culture pattern, of course, remained strong and was faithfully reflected by the law. In some southern states a married woman could not make a will, collect her own wages, or claim possession of any property, real or personal. Guardianship rights were often vested wholly in the husband. In 1879 Louisiana women were outraged when a generous bequest by a woman to an orphan asylum was lost because all the witnesses to the will were women. They were, declared the Chief Justice of the North Carolina Supreme Court, "slaves of despots."

There was plenty of evidence that any change would be difficult. A traveling organizer for the national woman's suffrage organization found her way to Mississippi and found discouragement on every hand. In some towns she was not permitted to lecture on suffrage at all, and had to content herself with a discourse on "Literature and Modern Tendencies" into which she bootlegged as much talk of the forbidden subject as she dared. "Death and education have much to do to redeem the southland," she concluded. A prominent Baptist minister declared that a woman who went into politics "violated the womanly instinct and defied God's law as certainly as did the painted woman who walks the streets and invites the noonday sun to witness her shame." The University of Georgia trustees found a petition for the admission of women so unfitting that they agreed to expunge all mention of it from the record. In Louisville, Henry Watterson announced that votes for women would imperil the whole human species.

The contrary forces stirred up by the war, reinforced by material and intellectual influences from the North, would not have an easy time. They were too strong, however, to be downed. The end of slavery and intellectual and material influences from the North were catalytic forces. They could not have had a significant influence without a corresponding change in the way southern women were viewing the world. Here and there such a change was taking place. In Kentucky in 1874, a twenty-five-year-old daughter of the Clay family recorded her "rebelliousness to the inequality set between men and women in this world" and decided that God had called her to help further Women's Rights. In North Carolina, a busy planter's wife, with a house full of children, was writing that "the greatest need in the world is educated, vigorous and unhampered womanhood. . . ." In Mississippi, a planter's daughter, forbidden by her father to undertake a career, felt "a constant and unceasing rebellion" at "the injustice that had always been heaped upon my sex." Another Mississippi woman mocked the favorite male palliative for discontented women—"the hand that rocks the cradle is the hand that rules the world"—as nonsense, saying that if men did not respect women, children would not either.

These were the women who now began to emerge as leaders in the southern version of what was inelegantly called the Woman Movement. Most of them were women of such impeccable family that they could, as it were, afford to be radical. They were generally in outward appearance the very model of Southern Ladies, described by their contemporaries as beautiful, charming, poised, intelligent, and brave. They were educated women, and not solely because they had been to school. All were voracious readers and writers. A long intimacy with the English classics had produced in them a pungent English style. Many were married and had children. They were women with enough energy to travel outside the South, who very early established contact with women leaders in other parts of the country, as well as with each other. They listened to and were influenced by Frances Willard, Susan B. Anthony, Elizabeth Cady Stanton, and later Anna Howard Shaw and Carrie Chapman Catt. All of them were deeply religious. Perhaps most significant, all were women of talent who had at some time in their lives felt that their talents might well be wasted for lack of opportunity to use them. As one of them put it: ". . . of all the unhappy sights the most pitiable is that of a human life, rich in possibilities and strong with divine yearnings for better things than it has known, atrophying in the prison house of blind and palsied custom."

Leaders are indispensable, but to produce a major social change many ordinary people must also be involved. In the face of the strong cultural pattern with its narrowly defined role for women, how could anything in the way of a following emerge? Not for southern women was any such blatant call to action as the "Declaration of Rights" flung to the shocked world by the Woman's Rights Convention at Seneca Falls in 1848. On the contrary, to the eye of the casual observer the southern home and fireside seemed as safe from radical modernism and the dangerous "new woman" in the eighties as it had been in the forties.

An acute observer, however, might have been led to look closely at such respectable and safe groups as the women's missionary societies of the various churches. It was here that many women first had a taste of running their own affairs. The minister who had opposed the organization of a separate prayer meeting on the grounds that if they were alone "who knows what the women will pray for?" was perhaps more prescient than he seemed. For it was in precisely such groups that the intense soul searching which had characterized southern religion before the war began to be transformed into a demand for social reform. In what was euphemistically called "home and foreign mission work" women encountered the disinherited of the post-war world, and began to question the political and social arrangements which permitted them to exist. In these church societies, natural leaders had a chance to lead, to learn to stand on their feet and make speeches, to keep records, and to organize. Yet because they were doing "church work," it was all very respectable and the most suspicious husband or father could hardly forbid attendance.

Equally respectable—for what could be more proper than a concern for Christianity and temperance?—was the Woman's Christian Temperance Union. Yet no group did more to subvert the traditional role of women, or to implant in its southern members a sort of unself-conscious radicalism which would have turned the conservative southern male speechless if he had taken the trouble to listen to what the ladies were saying. Between efforts to secure prohibition laws, the women of the WCTU worked in various southern states for prison reform, child labor regulation, shorter hours of labor, compulsory education—and cheered Frances Willard to the echo when she announced that the industrial revolution must be made to benefit the average working man and added "If to teach this is to be socialist, then so let it be."

Part of the influence of the WCTU in the lives of emerging southern women came from the quality of its national leader. Frances Willard was one of the most magnetic personalities of the nineteenth century and her tours of the South, during which she expounded a comprehensive program for reform (for which, one is tempted to think, demon rum was only a respectable front), were vastly influential. "For the local and denominational" one southern woman wrote, "she substituted the vision of humanity." "The W.C.T.U.," said another, "was the generous liberator, the joyous iconoclast, the discoverer, the developer of southern women."

The woman who penned this flowery description of the WCTU spoke from personal experience. Belle Kearney had been born into an aristocratic Mississippi family which had been so impoverished by the war that for a time she and her mother did sewing for their former slaves. She yearned for education, but the idea of a girl working her way through school was so foreign to her father's view of life that it was never even discussed. Over his vigorous protests she opened a school in her bedroom, and attained thereby her first small measure of independence. Public opinion and family pressure were so strong, however, that she succumbed to the accepted pattern, hating herself for her weakness and abhorring the way her time was spent. Then came Frances Willard, whose ability to identify potential leaders was considerable. Before long "Miss Belle" was organizing the WCTU in Mississippi, and from her success in this endeavor she moved easily into the national suffrage movement. When women were finally enfranchised, she crowned her career by being elected first woman senator in the Mississippi legislature. "The Woman's Christian Temperance Union," she recorded in her autobiography, "was the golden key that unlocked the prison doors of pent-up possibilities."

Hard upon the heels of the missionary societies and the WCTU came the women's clubs. This movement, which began spontaneously in many parts of the country, mushroomed in the South in the eighties after the pioneer organization in New Orleans announced its purpose to assist "the intellectual growth and spiritual ambition of the community." Literary societies, Browning and Shakespeare

191

clubs, Daughters of the American Revolution, and village improvement societies began to dot the landscape. Some began wholly as
cultural groups—what husband could object to the ladies gathering
to read Shakespeare or study Dante? And how was he to know if
they moved along to John Stuart Mill's "On the Subjugation of
Women" or read Margaret Fuller or discussed, as the Portias in New
Orleans were wont to do, the problems of organized labor?

As every authoritarian regime knows, association can be a dangerous thing. From discussion it is only a few steps to action, and by
1900 the list of things that women's clubs were doing or trying to do
in the South was staggering. They organized libraries; expanded
schools; tackled adult illiteracy; organized settlement houses; fought
child labor; supported sanitary laws, juvenile courts, pure water,
modern sewage systems; planted trees; and helped girls to go to
college. Doubtless many of these groups would have inspired the
pen of an earlier Helen Hokinson, but it is impossible to overlook
their record of achievement or the spirit in which they began to
attack the problems with which their native region was so plentifully
supplied. One has only to read their diaries and scrapbooks to catch
a sense of the seriousness of purpose and the broad ambitions which
motivated these women.

In North Carolina, Governor Elias Carr appointed a personal
friend, Mrs. Sallie Southall Cotten, to be North Carolina Lady
Manager for the Chicago World's Fair of 1893. Mrs. Cotten had
lived a quiet life as a planter's wife, raising six children, and spending most of her spare time reading and thinking, thinking especially
about the need for better educated and more independent women.
The World's Fair responsibility took her to Chicago, where she met
outstanding women from all over the country. It also took her over
the whole state of North Carolina from New Bern to Asheville, and
in many towns she found small clubs working away at village improvement or self-improvement. She came back after the Fair determined to unite the women of North Carolina in their efforts, and by
strenuous personal effort managed to bring the local groups into a
state-wide federation, which she then proceeded to lead into one
battle after another for the improvement of North Carolina.

In the nature of things it would not be long before such groups
began to have political significance. It is rare to find these women
speculating upon any philosophical analysis of the proper relationship of government to the people. But in a pragmatic way they

discovered more and more that the things they wanted to accomplish could only be accomplished through political action.

As a lobbyist, the southern lady turned new woman proved herself ingenious. The principle enunciated by one Arkansas lady, "If you don't make a friend at least don't leave an enemy," might have stood for most of these women as they journeyed to city council and state legislature armed with facts and figures to be presented with quiet dignity. "An unpleasant aggressiveness will doubtless be expected from us," a Mississippi leader told her group. "Let us endeavor to disappoint such expectations and spend the year in learning what to do and how to do it." One indignant Alabama legislator announced that the ladies had "apparently hypnotized some members of the Senate."

Occasionally more direct methods were possible, as when Miss Kate Gordon of New Orleans discovered that taxpaying women could vote in New Orleans when a question of taxes was involved. New Orleans suffered from a shortage of good water—the poorer people relied entirely upon cisterns—and an absence of a municipal sewage system. Wakened to their danger by a yellow fever epidemic, more farsighted members of the community were anxious to acquire both a water system and a sewage system, but the weight of opinion appeared to be of the "what was good enough for father is good enough for me" variety. Then Miss Gordon, with the Equal Rights Association (a pioneer woman's club) behind her, undertook to ferret out and register every woman taxpayer. The proposition to raise twenty million dollars for sewage and drainage passed handily.

It was experiences such as these, added to many others when women could *not* vote and felt the consequences, rather than an abstract belief in "women's rights," which was the real impetus behind the suffrage movement in the South. Miss Jean Gordon, a sister of the redoubtable Kate, put the case pungently in recording her battle for a Louisiana child labor law:

> The much boasted influence of the wife over the husband in matters political is one of the many theories which melt before the sun of experience. The wife of every representative present was heartily in sympathy with the child labor bill, but when the roll was called the husbands answered "no" and in that moment were sown the seeds of a belief in the potency of the ballot beyond that of woman's influence.

In 1910 Miss Mary Partridge of Alabama recorded a similar experience. "After seeing the defeat of the constitutional amendment for prohibition despite the earnest but ineffectual effort of women who beseiged the polls," she decided the time was ripe for a suffrage organization. She walked out of the hall and began organizing. Seven years later she counted eighty-seven suffrage societies in her state, and remarked that she had also converted thirty-two newspapers.

A year later Patty Blackburn Semple of Kentucky made the same point in a speech to the National American Woman Suffrage Association:

> Last year an appeal came to the Woman's Club—to the women of Louisville—to take our schools out of politics. It was a gigantic fight but we won. As the climax of our struggle we spent the greater part of election day at the polls and I think at the close of that day every one of us had exhausted all the joys of "indirect influence," which is supposed to satisfy the craving of every female heart. Our club will be twenty-one years old in November, and we want to vote!

By 1910 the woman movement in the South was moving out into the open. The missionary societies and the women's clubs, the Browning groups and the village improvement societies had laid the groundwork, and had afforded an essential period of security during which leaders were developed and followers gathered. Now the time had come to throw down the gauntlet and wage an open battle for suffrage, and for equality in the eyes of the law.

The dividing lines were not those of sex. In many states able and progressive-minded men took an equal part; Desha Breckenridge in Kentucky, Luke Lea in Tennessee, Walter Clark and Josephus Daniels in North Carolina were among the best known champions of women's rights, and in every state there were public men and newspapermen supporting the movement. On the other hand, multitudes of southern women were afraid of change and believed emancipation of women to be a threat to the stability of the home. The "new women" were asking not only rights, but responsibilities, and there were plenty of women who found the older system perfectly comfortable and satisfactory. Others were sympathetic in their hearts, but had not the courage to do battle with public opinion or to face ridicule.

From 1912 onward southern newspapers were publicly rubbing their eyes in astonishment at some of the accomplishments of the women's groups. Women were credited with "the improvement of health; the betterment of morals, the modernizing of education and the humanizing of penology." "Persistence is what carries them along," wrote another editor. "These women will secure every one of the things demanded in their program and will be no fifty years about it, either . . . their aims can no more be resisted than the tides. We believe they are really unconscious of their tremendous power to affect conditions. . . ." "Woman's day has arrived," said another, "never to depart. From the back seat of obscurity she has stepped . . . to the front rank of world activities . . . and the world is going to be a happier and brighter place because of her coming."

In spite of such recognition, and in spite of a steady increase in the number of converts to the suffrage cause, the cultural pattern in the South remained the most rigid in any part of the country. In 1918 the seventy-year-old national battle to persuade Congress to initiate a constitutional amendment for woman suffrage was finally won, and the amendment sent to the states for ratification. In every southern state there was a battle royal. The victorious opposition in North Carolina even sent reinforcements to Tennessee to encourage the opponents there. Only Texas, Kentucky, Arkansas and Tennessee of the states of the former Confederacy formed part of the required three-fourths of the states who ratified the amendment.

Despite the recalcitrance of southern legislatures, there were—thanks to the developments which have been related here—plenty of southern women ready to take advantage of suffrage when it came. Not only Miss Kearney, but Mrs. Nellie Nugent Somerville was soon sitting in the Mississippi legislature. In Georgia the ladies reported that they hardly recognized their hitherto hostile and chilly legislators who now suddenly found they had plenty of time to listen to their women constituents. In many states the suffrage groups were promptly converted to Leagues of Women Voters to finish the battle, as Carrie Chapman Catt put it, and to educate other women to their responsibilities.

The achievement of suffrage was symbolic and important, but it was only part of the larger story of the transformation, in the years after 1865, of the southern lady into the "new woman." Like the lady, the new woman represented only a small minority of all women in the South. Unlike the lady she did not become the universal ideal. At her best, she maintained the graciousness and charm which had been the sound part of the chivalric ideal, and without losing her femininity or abandoning her responsibility for the propagation of the species, became an important force in public as well as in private life.[1] She made it possible for the young women who came after her to begin at once to develop whatever talent they might have, without having first to fight a long battle for the right to education and opportunity.

This change was brought about by the unremitting efforts of a few women who longed for a chance to develop as individual and independent human beings, and who felt a responsibility for improving the quality of the larger society in which their children would grow up. For themselves and to some degree for the society at large they evolved a new conception of the proper role of women. Their efforts were reinforced by a changing economy, by the influence of the modern world, and by what that first woman's club in New Orleans in 1884 had rightly called "the irresistible spirit of the age."

In an environment basically hostile, southern women had taken on various protective colorations in their initial efforts to develop independence and maturity. In the name of temperance, or Shakespeare, or the church, they had resolutely set out to work, for themselves and for their communities. In many cases they were led into a pragmatic radicalism and had tackled problems which, had they been more sophisticated, might well have frightened them.

This analysis ends, except for an occasional glance ahead, in 1920. Whether southern women with the long-sought nineteenth amendment in their hands would live up to the promise of their accomplishments when they had no vote is another tale, for another time.

NOTE

1. In introducing Mrs. Cotten in 1913, the president of the North Carolina Federation of Women's Clubs made this point: "... probably the ideal woman is the one who combines all the graces of the golden days gone by with the highest type of the woman of the present time. She has caught step with the broadening and mighty influences which characterize her age. ... Such a woman we have with us tonight."

Article 3

Charlotte Perkins Gilman on the Theory and Practice of Feminism

Carl N. Degler

When Charlotte Perkins Gilman[1] published *Women and Economics* in 1898, the Feminist movement in America gained an advocate of uncommon intellectual power and insight. Quickly acclaimed on both sides of the Atlantic for having written "the most significant utterance" on the women's question since Mill,[2] she became the idol of radical feminists and was later judged "the most original and challenging mind which the woman *[sic]* movement produced."[3] Despite this recognition of her abilities, however, she has suffered a neglect in American intellectual history difficult to explain.[3a] The neglect becomes especially regrettable when one reads her truly thought-provoking analyses of woman's position in a man's world— in remarkable anticipation of modern writers on the subject like Simone de Beauvoir, Margaret Mead and Ashley Montagu.

Though Gilman's versatile and probing mind roamed over many subjects in the course of her forty years of active writing and lecturing, the focus here is on her thought relating to the position and nature of woman. It is hardly an exaggeration to speak of her as the major intellectual leader of the struggle for women's rights, in the broadest sense, during the first two decades of the twentieth century.[4] A confirmed suffragist, she never confined her attention to that limited goal but considered the whole large question of women in society as her province. Progress for women, she wrote in *Women and Economics,* is not to be measured only by the number of states granting suffrage to women, but rather is to be seen "in the changes legal and social, mental and physical, which mark the advance of the mother of the world toward her full place."[5]

The question of women's rights, to Gilman, was not the simple one of the democratic demand of women for equal prerogatives with

From *American Quarterly,* VIII (Spring, 1956), 21–39. Copyright 1956, Trustees of the University of Pennsylvania. Reprinted by permission of the author and publisher.

men, though this, too, was a part of her well-stocked arsenal of argument. Her concern in all her writings[6] was essentially twofold: to show the disastrous and all-pervasive effects upon women and upon society of the continued suppression of her sex; and to demonstrate in theory and practice means whereby women could assume their rightful place in society. But in doing so her arguments were never shrill or ill-tempered. The words of a modern feminist aptly describe Gilman's attitude toward the question of woman: "animated less by a wish to demand our rights than by an effort toward clarity and understanding."[7] One might add that, to Gilman, service to society was also an ingredient of her purpose.

The subjection of women originated, Gilman began, in prehistoric times[8] when the males first monopolized all social activity and women were confined to motherhood and domestic duties. Thus began the dependence of women upon men for their very food and shelter. Once this took place woman's livelihood, in the most basic sense, was a function of her ability to hold a man. "From the odalisque with the most bracelets," Gilman wrote,

> to the debutante with the most bouquets, the relation still holds good, woman's economic profit comes through the power of sex-attraction.[9]

In vain did she search the animal world for analogies to this relationship between the human sexes. For human beings, she found, were the only animal species "in which the female depends on the male for food, the only animal species in which the sex-relation is also an economic relation. . . . In no other animal species is the sex-relation for sale."[10]

Since woman's livelihood is received from men, her sexual attributes, the major attraction for men, are obviously highly developed and carefully nurtured. (Gilman compared this abnormal development in women with the over-development of the horns of a stag or the milk-giving ability of a modern milch cow: both are sexual characteristics developed to excess.) The result is that "the male human being is thousands of years in advance of the female in economic status." Whereas "men produce and distribute wealth . . . women receive it at their hands."[11] This relegating of woman to roles associated only with sexual activity—and this was Gilman's thesis— is "disadvantageous to our progress as individuals and as a race."[12] In essence, it was to the proof and illustration of this conclusion that she devoted all her public efforts between 1898 and the middle of the Twenties.

This dichotomy of the sexes, initiated in the beginnings of human society has prevailed into modern times; the man the worker in the world, the woman a parasite, beholden for every morsel of food, stitch of protective clothing, and even a bed at night, to some man—husband or father. Nor, can it be claimed, Gilman showed, that actually woman is economically independent because the husband's support is remuneration for her household labors. The very fact that each woman labors a different amount for that support— the rich as compared with the poor, for example—demonstrates that something more than a simple economic *quid pro quo* is operative. It is woman's duty to work in the home regardless of the compensation; the economic return to her bears no relation, in quantity or in quality, to the work performed.[13] No, the woman lives because the man suffers her to do so.

In other words, Gilman concluded, sex and economics go hand in hand in our world. To the young man entering the world the doors stand wide; failures only mean a new start; mistakes can be righted; all that he desires he can work to attain. To the young woman the same world is there,

> but all that she may wish to have, all that she may wish to do, must come through a single channel and a single choice. Wealth, power, social distinction, fame—not only these, but home and happiness, reputation, ease and pleasure, her bread and butter—all, must come to her through a small gold ring.[14]

Even to have amusement a girl must be sexually attractive. "The fun and pleasure of the world are so interwound with the sex-dependence of women upon men that women are forced to court 'attentions,' when not really desirous of anything but amusement." Association between men and women is always on a strictly sexual basis, "friendship between man and woman being a common laughing-stock." If a single man seeks feminine company there are two kinds: married and single. To see the former causes talk; to visit the latter frequently causes speculations of intentions; so he distributes his favors and knows none very well. Even after marriage the sexes enjoy little contact which does not have sexual overtones.[15]

Up until the nineteenth century rarely was woman allowed to break out of the restrictions imposed upon her by the economic dependence upon the male, even though "the ever-growing human impulse to create, the power and will to make, to do, to express one's new spirit in new forms"—was in her as much as in man. For her there were only the ancient, simple duties of the home to be performed "in private and alone."[16] Always "the smothering 'no' " of the male's world held her back from realizing her human characteristics as well as her female.[17]

The disabilities imposed upon women were the basic explanations in Charlotte Gilman's mind for the feminine character itself. Since, for long generations, most women have spent their whole lives in contemplation of their own family affairs "they are near-sighted, or near-minded rather; the trouble is not with the nature of their minds, but with the use of them." Men too, if they had been confined to the home would be "unlikely to manifest a high order of political intelligence."[18] Similarly, courage is not wanted in women, so they do not evidence it. "Women are not ashamed of being cowards. . . . As a man is not ashamed of licentiousness, which would be ruin to a woman, so a woman is not ashamed of cowardice which would utterly disgrace a man."[19] Woman demonstrates certain typically "feminine" traits because she occupies a special, narrow position in society: "she is merely working for her own family—in the sex-relation—not the economic relation; as a servant to the family instead of servant to the world."[20] So long as "all women have to be house servants from day to day, we are still a servile world."[21] In her capacity of family worker the woman is isolated from the rest of society, yet "social intercourse . . . is the essential condition of civilization. It is not merely a pleasure or an indulgence; it is the human necessity."[22]

The diverse material roles of the two sexes produce wholly different worlds and even outlooks for the man and the woman. "The home-bred brain of the woman continually puzzles and baffles the world-bred brain of the man. . . ."[23] "Men meet one another freely in their work, while women work alone."[24] This has the effect of producing more enduring friendships among men and explains "why they associate so much more easily and freely," for "they are further developed in race functions and . . . they *work together.*"[25] On the other hand, "every sign of weakness, timidity, inability to understand, to do, is deemed feminine and admired."[26] It is not that women are really "smaller-minded, more timid and vacillating," Gilman maintained, displaying her basic environmentalistic approach, "but that whosoever, man or woman, lives always in a small dark place, is always guarded, protected, directed and restrained, will become inevitably narrowed and weakened by it."[27] Basically, she continued, "the facts are that women are people, and act very much like other people under the same conditions. . . ."[28] Being a servant has played its role in determining the character of women. The woman as a servant "was denied the moral freedom of being mistress of her own action and of learning by the merciful law of consequences what was right and what was wrong: and she has remained, perforce, undeveloped in the larger judgment of ethics."[29]

Gilman saw in woman's consuming interest in fashion a reflection of the female's part in the sexuo-economic relation. Because of the woman's dependence on sexual attraction for a livelihood, she bears the sex decoration of the species—the reverse of that obtaining in the lower animals. Once sexual attraction is no longer the sole basis for woman's securing a living, then the feminine sex would be emancipated from its preternatural concern for sex decoration, i.e., fashion.[30]

To perpetuate these environmentally induced differences between the sexes, our man-dominated culture has compelled children to bear the indicia and limitations of the adult sexual world. Boys and girls are dressed differently "not on account of their personal needs, which are exactly similar at this period," but so that neither they nor anyone else "may for a moment forget the distinction of sex."[31] Girls' toys are mainly restricted to those associated with the future occupations of mother and housekeeper; the boys have a wide range of toys and games. "The little girl is kept forever within the limitations of her mother's 'sphere' of action; while the boy learns life, and fancies that new growth is due to his superior sex."[32]

We even expect the maternal feelings to bud in little girls, though we do not expect the boy to feel paternal. Children should not, Gilman contended, any more than kittens, be expected to be precocious in their feelings.[33] The so-called "tom-boy" is the "most normal girl . . . a healthy young creature, who is human through and through, not feminine until it is time to be."[34]

Terrible pressures, she pointed out, are exerted upon the young girl by the social fiat that marriage and the home be the sole occupation of woman. A man may expect to have home, family, love and companionship and still be an "active citizen of his age and country." The girl, on the other hand, "must 'choose'; must either live alone, unloved, uncompanied, uncared for, homeless, childless, with her work in the world for sole consolation; or give up all world

201

service for the joys of love, motherhood and domestic service."[35] Social pressure further insures that she will favor marriage, for if she does not marry, then "the scorn of male and female alike falls on this sexless thing: she is a human failure." Yet—and this is the cruelest part—through all this the girl must act as if she were not interested. "Think of the strain on a highly sensitive nervous organism to have so much hang on one thing" and, at the same time, "to be forbidden to take any step toward securing it!"[36] Even the sexual ignorance of the young girl of her day Gilman saw as a consequence of the sexuo-economic relationship. Since the husband "is the market" and he prefers her innocent of any sexual knowledge, the mother has no alternative but to preserve her daughter's ignorance in order successfully to prepare "her for the market."[37]

Unavoidably, of course, the man, too, suffers from this constriction of woman's place. "The boy with a servile mother, the man with a servile wife, cannot reach the sense of equal rights we need today."[38] Furthermore, the man has no competition in society, when the woman is his inferior, his servant. He is tempted to cruelty, he becomes selfish from having a person devoted to his welfare, he is prideful of his false position of dominance.[39] The requirement that the man support a family puts a premium on money-getters. In a relation which compels a man to support a workless wife, money must be his goal, not service or ideals; his occupation cannot be freely chosen if he also desires a wife. Dedication to science or art or other financially unrewarding pursuits becomes either a hard choice or an impossibility.[40] The maintenance of the family "multiplies a man's desire for money; but in no way multiplies his ability. . . ."[41] Since the man realizes how dependent a wife is upon him for support "marriage is deferred and avoided, to the direct injury of both sexes and society at large."[42]

The home and family also feel the manifold effects of woman's subordinate and oversexed existence. The effort to isolate the home from the world—to enhance privacy—Gilman interpreted as a reflection of the sexually-oriented character of the family:

> In our besotted exaggeration of the sex relation, we have cruelly supposed that a wish for a wider human relationship was a wish for wider sex-relationships and was therefore to be discouraged. . . .

Actually, when sex and economics are divorced, talk with mere relatives will not be enough and all members of the family will have the opportunity of interpersonal contacts so necessary to human development.[43] The genesis of frictions within the family often can be traced to the socially starved woman. The husband is her only world because he is her line of communication with the real world so she "wrings" all she can out of him to make the world she needs. She demands attention and love, but "it is not further love that she needs at all . . . it is not more man, but more world—more life—that she restlessly and dumbly craves."

Failing to get it, she pushes uneasily against this well-intentioned substitute for a world and racks him with her continual demands.

Moreover, when the marriage is unhappy, the woman suffers more than the man just "because she has no other life from which to draw strength and practical consolation." He, at least, has his work, opportunity to gratify his ambition, to make money and so forth.[44]

When woman's world is bounded by the walls of the home, society—always Gilman's principal concern—has a high price to pay. To keep women in the home is an enormous social waste in an economic sense. "While every woman is expected to follow one trade the grade of efficiency must remain at the lowest possible average," Gilman argued.[45] All women cannot, any more than all men, be trained to do the same job efficiently because "specialization is necessary to develop skill. The domestic worker, wife or servant, is eternally unspecialized."[46] Much that society has gained in economic efficiency through the specialization of man's labor has been lost in requiring women to perform nothing but the unskilled, undifferentiated labor of the home.[47] The very progress of the world has been retarded by excluding women. The housewife-mothered human race "has moved only half as fast and as far as it rightly should have done" and the heavy, time-consuming work of "the patient housewife . . . is pitifully behind the march of events."[48]

Prostitution and immorality Gilman attributed to this same "morbid excess in the exercise of" sex and the economic dependence of women. By requiring a man to support a wife before he may legitimately receive sexual gratification, he is driven to the prostitute as the cheaper alternative.[49] So long, she went on, as sex is emphasized in our society—as it is in our sexuo-economic marriage—it will encourage the over-sexed man and the over-sexed woman and perpetuate the prostitute.[50]

The double standard, of course, stands forth as the most arrogant instance of male dominance, for chastity is a human, not an exclusively female virtue in Gilman's eyes:

> Masculine ethics colored by masculine instincts, always dominated by sex, has at once recognized the value of chastity in women, which is right, punished its absence unfairly, which is wrong; and then reversed the whole matter when applied to men, which is ridiculous.[51]

In her description and analysis of the subtle and often unnoticed characteristics of a man-dominated culture, Gilman displayed both her incisive mind and her acute powers of observation. We have taken the male and his activities, she pointed out, as typical of *human* activities. Even the word virtue is derived from *"vir";* "our human scheme of things," she wrote, "rests on the same tacit assumption; man being held the human type; woman a sort of accompaniment and subordinate assistant, merely essential to the making of people."[52] In popular speech when "we wish to praise the work of a woman, we say she has a 'masculine mind,' "[53] testimony in itself of the folk belief that to be a man is to be most human.[54] When females teach boys, the students, it is often said, "become 'effeminate.' " But when men teach girls the latter do not become the masculine equivalent. "Never has it occurred to the androcentric mind to conceive of such a thing as being *too* masculine. There is no such word!"[55] So habituated are men to thinking that maleness is humanness, that each step in the economic and social humanization of women has been termed "unfeminine."[56] Woman's exclusion from human activities has been justified on just these grounds—that she is pure sex and devoid of "humanness." Education offers an excellent example of this, where for centuries woman was denied schooling with men on the assumption she must be confined "exclusively to feminine interests."[57] In a word, we have created an androcentric culture,[58] treating women as merely extraneous, child-bearing females.

But to equate male sexual attributes with human nature results in harm to society from another direction. For, after all, the "manly" attributes of size, belligerence, aggressiveness, sportsmanship, and the like, are not the sum total of human virtues. All men, even, do not possess them. The artistic, the musical, the contemplative boy also fulfills a function in society, but he is pilloried in a culture identifying the masculine characteristics with the attributes of human beings. It is necessary to realize that "the advance of civilization calls for human qualities in both men and women."[59] Too often, from the standpoint of society, "the contradictions we have forcibly bred in women react injuriously upon men and are inherited by children."[60]

A culture dominated by men, Gilman believed, is inevitably permeated, on a variety of levels, by the peculiar sexual character of the male. In literature, for example, masculine interest—*i.e.*, love, sex, combat—the interests which flow from man's sexual nature, has been apparent in the myriad stories concerned with such subjects, especially in popular fiction. Such literature ignores mother love—the more fundamental and considerably less transitory variety. Not all men wrote from this narrow viewpoint, of course, for writers like Balzac and Dickens had a truly broad, human outlook.[61] The large number of love poems, in like manner, Gilman explained by the dominance of the male and his primary interest.[62]

The dominance of man has influenced popular philosophy to accept the dictum that life is a struggle—which to man is congenial and preeminent in his existence. Actually life is also growth and a world dominated by women would, by contrast, stress that element.[63] The accent on death and the after life, so common in the great religions, similarly stems from the fact that man, the ancient hunter and killer, saw death, was concerned with it, and fitted it into the religions of his culture. To woman, on the other hand, birth and life are the crucial events of her existence.[64]

For all her exposure of the masculine influence molding our culture,[65] Gilman was no uncritical or misanthropic feminist. "There should be an end," she wrote, "to the bitterness of feeling which has arisen between the sexes in this century."[66] Her evolutionary approach was too meaningful for her to denigrate man's historic activities in behalf of civilization. The economic dependence of women, she maintained, had been necessary so that man could forsake the role of hunter, fighter, and destroyer, and become the builder of civilization. The imprisonment of women had acted as a "coiled spring"—its "intense stimulus" enabling man to move mountains.[67] But, she emphasized, by the nineteenth century that stage in evolution was at an end; man alone could no longer advance civilization; the contribution of woman was required to continue the progress of humanity.[68]

As must be apparent to anyone even cursorily reading the strictures Gilman hurled against the domestic woman, the inevitable *sine qua non* for the final and complete emancipation of woman was economic independence. The working girl, the working wife and mother became the ideal which she preached.

Given the historical period in which she wrote, this solution was neither unexpected nor, in practice, even novel. Already, by the opening years of the twentieth century, millions of women, married and single, were finding places in the industrial system. To Gilman it seemed that these women, often struggling against the old restrictions and prejudices, were the heroines of the emancipation of their sex; indeed, they were taking the only path to true freedom. By their breaking of the age-old chains forged by the dependence of woman upon man for food, clothing and shelter, they were free for the first time in modern history.[69] If women are to be anything, she proclaimed, they must cease to be merely domestic servants, nursemaids and governesses in their own homes.[70]

In the last analysis, Gilman's insistence upon work outside the home as the liberating force for women rested on her fundamental assumption that women were human beings and that "a human creative must do human work; and all women are no more to be contented as house servants and housekeepers than all men would be."[71]

The word "all" in the statement contains, by implication, the two major justifications Gilman advanced for women's entering the labor market: not only was the restriction of woman to the home crippling individually to her as a human being, but, as noted earlier, it was socially inefficient. It was not that Gilman thought that no woman would like housekeeping, for, as she said, "even cleaning, rightly understood and practised is a useful, and therefore honorable profession."[72] The error lay in expecting all women to do it.

It is noteworthy that Gilman was basing her feminist arguments on higher ground than the mere demand for freedom, privilege and power equal with men. She rested her case on the conviction that women were "heavily behind-hand in their duty to the world; holding in their gift a mighty fund of Love and Service which we can no longer do without."[73] It was society which was losing as well as women, for women, even in their female capacity, had something to contribute to the world. Their very sexual nature fitted in, according to her view, with the overarching human needs of society. "To be a teacher and leader, to love and serve, to guard and guide and help," she pointed out, "are well in line with motherhood,"[74] all of which only "makes her exclusion from human function the more mischievous."[75] The altruism of motherhood, once it is allowed to influence the world, would be a force for good.[76] The very fact that the woman's "feminine functions" are "far more akin to human functions" than are those of the male means that freedom for women "will bring into human life a more normal influence."[77]

Charlotte Gilman, as the preceding paragraph illustrates, was prepared to admit that there were real character differences between the sexes, and further, that they were the consequence of the differing physiological structure and functions of the male and the female. She saw combativeness and desire, for example, as the most obvious male traits. Even "the little male"—the boy—"would be more given to fighting and destroying," she asserted; "the little female more to caring for and constructing things."[78] This, in turn, would lead to the male's being "progressive where the female is conservative by nature."[79] Nevertheless, the important point to Gilman, it should be emphasized, was not the differences, for they are minor compared to the characteristics held in common. But, insofar as the sexes do differ, they should utilize the differences to complement each other and not to subordinate one sex to the other:[80]

Women are human beings as much as men, by nature; and as women, are even more sympathetic with human processes. To develop human life in its true powers we need full equal citizenship for women.[81]

Motherhood for women and fatherhood for men are the only occupations decreed by Nature. Outside of these two:

Every handicraft, every profession, every science, every art, all normal amusements and recreations, all government, education, religion; the whole living world of human achievement: all this is human.[82]

And all should be open to women as human beings.[83] But Gilman was sufficiently perspicacious to realize that not all work would be done by women. For after all, she cautioned, "equality is not identity. There is work of all kinds and sizes—and half of it is woman's."[84] Presumably each sex would perform work congenial to its nature. But

we can make no safe assumption as to what, if any distinctions there will be in the free human work for men and women, until we have seen generation after generation grow up under absolutely equal conditions.[85]

207

Once elevated to the position of a human being, woman will, in the natural course of things, "develop social usefulness, becoming more efficient, intelligent, experienced."[86] Furthermore, the gainful employment of women would have beneficial effects upon men and the family. There would be greater family income and marriage would not have to be postponed in order to raise the man's income sufficiently to support a wife.[87] The husband would now have a worthy, intelligent partner who would "lift him up instead of pulling him heavily downward. . . ."[88] Even romance in marriage might increase, for it is difficult "to maintain the height of romantic devotion to one's house servant—or even one's housekeeper!"[89] "We shall live," she summed up, "in a world of men and women humanly related, as well as sexually related, working together, as they were meant to do, for the common good of all."[90]

To expect women to marry and to work at the same time, Gilman was well aware, created new problems. Almost contemptuously, however, she demolished the hoary argument that if women worked they would lose their charm in the eyes of men. "The respect of the male for the female," she clearly recognized, "is based on the distinction of sex, not on political or economic disability. Men respect women because they are females, not because they are weak and ignorant and defenseless." It is more likely that as they grow in humanness and lose nothing that is essential to womanhood, "they will win and hold a far larger, deeper reverence than that hitherto vouchsafed them."[91]

Gilman readily conceded that the record showed that as more and more women enjoyed economic independence, the divorce rate continued to rise and some women refused to marry at all. But this is only to be expected, she explained, when "the character of woman is changing faster than the character of matrimony."[92] More and more women are seeking companionship in marriage, now that they are free of the sexuo-economic dependence; a "kind" husband and a good provider are not enough. After all, she wrote with a tinge of humor, when two young people love each other and spend long hours talking together, they do not "dwell in ecstatic forecast on the duties of housekeeping." They dream of "being alone, of *doing* things together."[93] The outstanding defect of the old marriage was its lack of equality—one partner out in the world, the other confined to the "smallest, oldest, lowest" work in the world.[94] Marriages will be happier and men and women happier when "both sexes realize that they are human, and that humanity has far wider duties and desires than those of the domestic relations."[95] In an age when more and more women are working, Gilman realized, we must "learn how to reconcile happy work with a happy marriage."[96] In some respects, in these passages, Charlotte Gilman was the prophet of the modern American marriage.

Even though some women who work never marry, this is not to be taken, she insisted, as a valid argument against gainful employment for women. How many illustrious men of the past, she asked, could have easily given up their work for marriage? Fortunately for them, they never had to make such a difficult choice, for as men in a man's world they could enjoy both. But some women, for a variety of reasons, cannot be both wives and workers in the world, and they choose the latter merely because they are human.[97]

Though Gilman viewed marriages as a desirable state for all human beings,[98] failure to marry was not a tragedy so long as women could work and thereby consecrate "their energies as human beings to mutual assistance and social service."[99] And on all sides there was evidence of the changing position of women in the direction she pointed; she was not a voice in the wilderness, but a leader of hosts.

Charlotte Perkins Gilman might be called a rationalistic radical, for lack of a more elegant term. Few considerations of tradition or sentiment inhibited her thinking. Recognizing this, we can understand better both the strength and weakness of Gilman's social thought. Her freedom from preconceptions and tradition allowed her to make fresh and often penetrating examinations of the human institutions around her. But that same attitude of mind also prevented her from appreciating the tenacious hold which prejudice, tradition and sentiment had upon most of the men and women she was attempting to convince. Hence when she came to offer means to attain the goals she set, her rationalism and radicalism, so incisive in analysis, merely served to vitiate her realism.

To all feminists, as to Gilman, the most stubborn obstacle to the equal participation of women in the affairs of the world was the ineluctable fact that women—someone, at least—had to take care of the home. That someone, by that very fact, was thereby removed from the usual occupations of the world, and, to the conservative, this was justification enough for the confining of women to the kitchen, nursery and cleaning closet. Since Gilman had called for women in the world, she had to offer a means to attain that objective. Unfortunately, the best she could devise was less than adequate.

Since the mother-centered home was the major obstacle to woman's employment, Gilman directed her intellectual artillery against that venerable institution. Though her view was foreshadowed in *Women and Economics,* her book *The Home,* published in 1903, was a full-scale, full battle-dress assault—a model of the completely rationalistic analysis of an ancient human institution— and a good example of her scorn for sentiment which had ceased to be functional. Her criticism was on two levels: first that the home crushed women—the argument we have followed; and second that the home as it existed was dirty, inefficient, uninteresting and retrogressive. Entertaining and clever as her latter arguments and examples were, we need not go into them here.

In substance, of course, her critique of the home was closely related to her view of woman's need, for the functions of the home, too, should be specialized. Instead of having the cooking, sewing, child care, house cleaning done by a single woman—the mother-housewife—all these services would be professionalized and performed by outside, paid workers. So completely would this be carried out, according to Gilman, that there would be no kitchens in the new homes. This in itself, she envisaged, would greatly simplify cleaning, since the kitchen by its introduction of fire, cooking, grease, and smoke constituted one of the major creators of dirt in the home. Food would be professionally and nutritiously prepared in central kitchens and served either in the dining room of the home itself or in the central dining hall of the new apartments, which would become the accepted mode of living. At last the ancient handicraft of the kitchen would disappear: "we are going to lose our kitchens as we have lost our laundries and bakeries. The cook-stove will follow the loom and wheel, the wool-carder and shears."[100] While keenly aware of the esteem in which the haloed home was held, she boldly argued that the home was outmoded, and that its lack of specialization meant inefficiency and lack of development. The housewife, she wrote, is notoriously untrained and ignorant in the fields of nutrition and child-care, yet she is entrusted exclusively with these functions. With a mixture of truth and exaggeration Gilman ridiculed the ignorant mother: "Each mother slowly acquires some knowledge of her business by practising it upon the lives and health of her family and by observing its effect on the survivors."[101] Indeed, insofar as housekeeping has progressed through the application of new techniques and implements, she pointed out, it has been the result of outside, professionalized work not that of the woman in the home.[102] Under the new arrangements there would be "a clean, pretty, quiet home—not full of smell and steam and various messy industries, but simply a place to rest in . . . with a wife as glad to be home as the husband."[103] So often and so vehemently did Gilman offer her solution, that one periodical in 1913 could say, perhaps wearily, "Mrs. Gilman's ideas on this subject are well-known."[104]

Children, too, like the home itself, would be cared for by professionals. Alert to the contemporaneous educational trend of taking children under the care of society at an increasingly younger age, Gilman maintained her plan was merely the extension of this tendency to include babyhood. It is not possible, she argued, merely to train mothers to care for babies any more than they can be trained to supplant the grammar school.[105] Nevertheless, under her program, "the mother would not be excluded, but supplemented, as she is now, by the teacher and the school."[106]

Imagining all men were as rational as herself, Gilman pointed to no other social engine for the accomplishment of such a mighty domestic revolution other than its desirability.[107] This aspect of her thought, perhaps more than any other, is hopelessly tinged with utopianism.

Obviously Charlotte Perkins Gilman's insights into the position of women, and the consequences thereof for the two sexes and for society, are of much more interest to us today than her practical solutions, to the advocacy of which she devoted much of her energy. The kitchenless apartment, the beginnings of which were apparent in her time, is uninteresting to an America now wedded to the private house. Yet, in a sense, even the private home has eliminated, in part, at least, the deficiencies Gilman found in it: ignorance of nutrition and child care is no longer condoned in middle class American families, particularly not when scientific cook books and authoritative baby books abound. She mistook a few kitchenless apartments for a trend, but she herself was part of a trend when she castigated ignorant motherhood and defended social education for the pre-school child.

Increasing occupational opportunities for women, and the growing acceptance of the working wife by both husband and society today,[108] indicate that Gilman's major contribution—the requirement that women be *in* the world as well as *of* it, was essentially sound. The working wife is not as common as Gilman hoped or expected, but the practical reasons for that discrepancy are apparent. Unless some solution similar to that tendered by her, and rejected by society—professionalized home services—is developed, it is almost a superhuman task to be both a housekeeper, cook and full-time employee.[109] For as Simone de Beauvoir has observed in our own day, "for the most part it is still the woman who bears the cost of domestic harmony" when she works outside the home.[110] By the mid-twentieth century, the bulk of women in America have not found a means whereby they can both work and marry, but the opportunity is present, for society is now willing to condone that dual role if the woman is willing and capable of assuming the double burden. If, as most would agree, America in the last fifty years has basically altered its attitude toward the working woman, then Charlotte Perkins Gilman must be assigned a significant part in the accomplishment of that change.[111] As she prophesied, to utilize the labor and skills and nature of women was to enlarge the pool of human energy and to enhance human happiness.

NOTES

1. Mrs. Gilman was born Charlotte Perkins on July 3, 1860 and died by suicide August 17, 1935. She married Charles Walter Stetson in 1882, the union ending in separation and ultimate divorce, though not before the birth of a daughter. In 1900 she married her cousin George Houghton Gilman. After her marriage her contemporaries referred to her almost invariably by the three names she used, Charlotte Perkins Gilman. See her revealing, but uneven autobiography, *The Living of Charlotte Perkins Gilman* (New York: D. Appleton Century Company, 1935) hereafter *The Living* . . .

2. *Nation,* June 8, 1899, p. 443; *The London Chronicle* cited in A. Black, "The Woman Who Saw it First." *Century* (November, 1923), 39.

3. Mary Gray Peck, *Carrie Chapman Catt* (New York: The H. W. Wilson Company, 1944), p. 454. Mrs. Catt ranked Mrs. Gilman first in a list of the twelve greatest American women. *Ibid.,* p. 455.

3a. She records in her autobiography that in the 1930's she found Connecticut College for Women uninterested in a lecture by her, though thirty years before her popularity was unsurpassed on a feminine campus like Vassar's. *The Living* . . . p. 333; Harriot Stanton Blatch and Anna Lutz, *Challenging Years; The Memoirs of Harriot Stanton Blatch* (New York: G. P. Putnam's Sons, 1940), p. 108.

4. Two historians, Charles and Mary Beard, have suggested she was just that. See their *Rise of American Civilization* (New York: The Macmillan Company, 1928), II, 431.

5. Charlotte Perkins Stetson [Gilman], *Women and Economics. A Study of the Economic Relation Between Men and Women as a Factor in Social Evolution* (2nd ed.; Boston, 1899), p. 148. Hereafter *Women*. In one place she admitted that suffragists considered her too radical and that she helped the cause only by making ordinary advocates of the ballot appear conservative. *Forerunner,* (November, 1916), p. 287.

6. Beyond a doubt, her first prose work, *Women and Economics,* both announced her entrance into the field of social thought and brought her the greatest renown. Published originally in 1898, it ultimately was translated into German, Japanese, French, Dutch, Italian, Hungarian and Russian, as well as running to seven English editions by 1911. But in the course of her busy, strenuous and often painful life, Gilman published five other books of non-fiction, a full-length utopian novel, a volume of poetry, two volumes of fiction, seven volumes of a monthly magazine, *The Forerunner,* the contents of which she wrote entirely herself, scores of articles, poems and short stories in the popular and scholarly periodicals, and an autobiography published posthumously in 1935. For the purposes of this paper, her views have been drawn only from writings up to 1923, since after that date she was not so concerned with the question of women.

7. Quoted by the translator in Simone de Beauvoir, *The Second Sex* (New York: Knopf, 1953), p. v.

8. She was not concerned with the question of origins and as a result she had no really thought-out theory of the subjugation. See *Women,* pp. 60-1.

9. *Women,* p. 63.

10. *Ibid.,* pp. 5, 95.

11. *Ibid.,* p. 9.

12. *Ibid.,* p. 33.

13. *Ibid.,* p. 15.

14. *Ibid.,* p. 71.

15. *Ibid.,* pp. 308-11.

16. *Ibid.,* pp. 66-7.

17. *Ibid.,* p. 70.

18. *Forerunner,* October, 1910, p. 12.

19. Charlotte Perkins Gilman, *His Religion and Hers, A Study of the Faith of Our Fathers and the Work of Our Mothers* (New York: The Century Co., 1923), p. 133. Hereafter *Religion.*

20. Charlotte Perkins Gilman, *The Home Its Work and Influence* (New

York: Charlton Company, 1910) p. 92. This work was first published in 1903. Hereafter *Home*.

21. *Women*, p. 262.

22. *Ibid.*, p. 295.

23. *Home*, p. 275.

24. *Women*, p. 307.

25. *Ibid.*, p. 306.

26. *Home*, p. 277.

27. *Home*, p. 277.

28. Charlotte Perkins Gilman, "Woman, the Enigma," *Harper's Bazaar*, December, 1908), 1197.

29. *Women*, p. 335.

30. Charlotte Perkins Gilman, *The Man-Made World or, Our Androcentric Culture* (New York: Charlton Company, 1911), pp. 173-4. Hereafter *Man-Made*.

31. *Women*, p. 54.

32. *Man-Made*, p. 112. An interesting example of contrasting behavior bred into the two sexes during childhood is given by Gilman in the story of a boy and a girl on a railroad train. The mother holds the girl in her seat; the boy roams the train, talks with the conductors, asks questions, "learning all the time. The boy gets five times as much out of life as the girl and he knows it." *Home*, p. 279.

33. *Man-Made*, pp. 110-11.

34. *Women*, pp. 56-7.

35. Charlotte Perkins Gilman, "Passing of Matrimony," *Harper's Bazaar*, June, 1906 p. 496.

36. *Women*, p. 88.

37. *Ibid.*, p. 86.

38. *Man-Made*, p. 42.

39. *Women*, pp. 337-8.

40. *Ibid.*, pp. 112-14.

41. *Home*, p. 320.

42. *Women*, p. 93.

43. *Ibid.*, pp. 304-5.

44. Charlotte Perkins Gilman, "All the World to Her," *Independent*, July 9, 1903, pp. 1615-16.

45. Charlotte Perkins Gilman, "Waste of Private Housekeeping," *Annals of the American Academy*, July, 1913, p. 91.

46. Gilman, "Waste of Private Housekeeping," p. 94. It should not be imagined that Gilman thought that women in the home did not work hard enough, for "the Housewife is one of the hardest workers on earth. She works unceasingly. . . ." She works harder than a man just because her work is so unspecialized. *Home*, pp. 290-1.

47. It is not out of place to observe that a few years later, in 1912, Wesley

Clair Mitchell, the economist, was issuing the same complaint against the unspecialized home. See his title essay in the collection, *The Backward Art of Spending Money,* (New York: McGraw-Hill Book Company, 1937).

48. *Home,* pp. 102–3.
49. *Women,* p. 30; Charlotte Perkins Gilman, "How Home Conditions React upon the Family," *American Journal of Sociology,* March, 1909, p. 601.
50. *Women,* pp. 96–7.
51. *Man-Made,* p. 134.
52. *Ibid.,* p. 20.
53. *Ibid.,* p. 21.
54. This was written almost fifty years before Mme Simone de Beauvoir said the same thing: "A man is in the right in being a man; it is the woman who is in the wrong. It amounts to this: just as for the ancients there was an absolute vertical with reference to which the oblique was defined, so there is an absolute human type the masculine. . . . Thus humanity is male and man defines woman not in herself but as relative to him. . . ." *The Second Sex,* pp. xv-xvi.
55. *Man-Made,* pp. 149–50.
56. *Ibid.,* p. 24.
57. *Ibid.,* p. 147.
58. This term, a favorite of Gilman's, was taken from the writings of Lester Frank Ward, whose article in *Forum* for November, 1888, "Our Better Halves," catalyzed her thinking on this subject. See *Living . . .* p. 259.
59. *Man-Made,* p. 155.
60. Gilman, "Woman, the Enigma," p. 1197.
61. *Man-Made,* pp. 95–100. In an interesting and revealing analogy Gilman compares the kind of writing a drone and a worker bee would produce. The drone's work would be replete with sex and mating—his *raison d'etre;* the worker's with activity, labor and care—its life. *Man-Made,* p. 99.
62. *Ibid.,* p. 84. Like so many reformers pushing favorite theses, Gilman often saw gold where only brass was present. At one point, for example, she contended that the trend in nineteenth-century historiography away from battles, wars and statecraft in favor of social and economic affairs, was the consequence of the rise of women. Actually, of course, that historical movement began deep in the eighteenth century at least—hardly "the women's century." *Man-Made,* p. 92. She even went so far as to lay the blame for the American party system and its battles at the feet of our man-made world and its love of combat! *Man-Made,* pp. 221–2.
63. Charlotte Perkins Gilman, "Influence of Women on Public Life," *Public,* May 31, 1919, p. 572.

64. *Religion,* p. 42. In *Man-Made World,* p. 202, she gives her view of what the male has made out of Christianity: "desire—to save one's soul. Combat—with the Devil. Self-Expression—the whole gorgeous outpouring of pageant and display, from the jewels of the high priest's breastplate to the choir of mutilated men to praise a male Deity no woman may so serve." It is interesting, though Gilman did not make the point, that the one modern religion founded by a woman, Christian Science, does deny the existence of death.

65. The great intellectual debt Charlotte Gilman owed to the Darwinian revolution of the nineteenth century is apparent in these repeated efforts to base her thinking on a kind of biological certainty.

66. *Women,* p. 129.

67. *Ibid.,* p. 133.

68. *Ibid.,* p. 122.

69. It is true, as one of her critics, I. M. Rubinow, observed, that girls working in sweatshops twelve hours a day did not feel as free as Gilman portrayed them. But the critic also lost sight of the fact at which she was driving. Though many individuals, men as well as women, might not be as free as the ideal, the real test was whether the opportunity was present or whether a large segment of society was deliberately denied opportunities for free expression in labor. Rubinow was correct, however, when he pointed out that historically the working class wife who was gainfully employed was usually shamefully exploited rather than freer for her labor. In this respect the middle class bias of Gilman was as apparent as it was in much of the women's rights movement as a whole. I. M. Rubinow, of the U. S. Bureau of Labor, made his comments in the *American Journal of Sociology,* (March, 1909), 614–9.

70. Beauvoir, p. 679, in our own day, still accepts Gilman's analysis: "It is through gainful employment that woman has traversed most of the distance that separated her from the male; and nothing else can guarantee her liberty in practice."

71. Gilman, "Passing of Matrimony," p. 498. Later she put her position into the slogan: "The New Woman is Human first, last and always. Incidentally she is female; as man is male." *Forerunner,* January 1910, 12.

72. *Women,* p. 246.

73. *Forerunner,* (January, 1911), 29.

74. *Man-Made,* pp. 238–9.

75. *Ibid.,* p. 235.

76. *Religion,* p. 47.

77. *Man-Made,* pp. 255–6. The modern anthropologist, M. F. Ashley Montague, in his *Natural Superiority of Women* (New York: Macmillan Co., 1953), devotes a chapter, "The Genius of Woman as the

Genius of Humanity," to this very point. "What the world stands so much in need of at the present . . . is more of the maternal spirit and less of the masculine." p. 147.

78. *Man-Made,* p. 112.

79. *Home,* pp. 88–9.

80. She thought she saw, as a result of this differentiation, diverse functions for men and women in some areas. For example, art "will perhaps always belong," she thought, "most to men. It would seem as if that ceaseless urge to self-expression, was at least originally, most congenial to the male." *Man-Made,* p. 250. Applied arts, on the other hand, would be an area in which women would do as well as men. It may not be coincidental that Gilman confessed to just this same latter division of talent in herself. See her autobiography, *The Living . . . ,* p. 46. Certain sports, those involving the throwing of a ball, she conjectured, "will never appeal to women"—not because they are wrong, but because "they are only masculine" not human. *Man-Made,* p. 114. Modern feminist writers have also subscribed to this conception of limited differentiation between the sexes. See Beauvoir, p. 731; Margaret Mead, *Male and Female* (New York: W. Morrow, 1949), chap. xviii.

81. *Man-Made,* p. 260.

82. *Ibid.,* p. 25.

83. Compare this statement with Margaret Mead, p. 378: "There is likewise the very simple consideration that when we have no indication that intelligence is limited to one sex, any occupational restriction that prevents gifted women from exercising their gifts leaves them, and also the world that is sorely in need of every gift, the poorer."

84. *Forerunner,* (January, 1910), 13.

85. *Man-Made,* p. 250.

86. Gilman, "How Home Conditions React upon the Family," *American Journal of Sociology,* (March, 1909), 605.

87. Charlotte Perkins Gilman, "What He Craved," *The Critic,* February, 1906, p. 188. It is appropriate to observe that since Gilman's time the proportion of working women has increased while the average age of marriage has fallen. The median ages for first marriages for men and women respectively in 1890 were 26.1 and 22.0. In 1949 the ages were: 22.7 and 20.3. L. I. Dublin, *Facts of Life* (New York: Macmillan Co., 1951), p. 42. In 1900, 13.4 per cent of the women in the United States were gainfully employed; in 1954 the figure was 30.6 per cent.

88. *Women,* p. 315.

89. *Home,* p. 281.

90. *Women,* p. 313.

91. Charlotte Perkins Gilman, "Are Women Human Beings?" *Harper's Weekly,* (May 25, 1912),11. In another place she put this in environ-

mental, relativistic terms: "A woman is a woman and attractive to men of her place and times, whether she be a beaded Hottentot, a rosy milkmaid, a pretty school ma'am, or a veiled beauty of the Zenana." *Home,* p. 280.

92. Gilman, "The Passing of Matrimony," *op. cit.,* p. 497.
93. *Women,* pp. 218-9.
94. *Ibid.,* pp. 219-20.
95. Gilman, "All the World to Her," *op. cit.,* p. 1616.
96. Charlotte Perkins Gilman, "Light on the Single Woman's Problem," *American Magazine,* (August, 1906), 428.
97. Gilman, "Passing of Matrimony," *op. cit.,* pp. 496-8.
98. "There is no real reason," she argued, "why women should not be women, wives and mothers, and also members of society, performing that social service which is our first duty as human beings." Charlotte Perkins Gilman, "Social Darwinism," *American Journal of Sociology,* (March, 1907, 714. "Motherhood," she said elsewhere,"—if anything, is woman's business." Charlotte Perkins Gilman, "Good Tidings of Women—the World's Best Hope," *Woman's Home Companion,* (February, 1906), 5.
99. *Forerunner,* July, 1916, p. 173.
100. *Women,* p. 267. It should be clearly understood that she was not advocating cooperative kitchens—a development of her time which she abominated—but rather individually purchased maid and cooking service like medical care.
101. *Ibid.,* p. 229.
102. Gilman, "Waste of Private Housekeeping," *op. cit.,* p. 91; *Home, op. cit.,* p. 94.
103. *Home, op. cit.,* p. 292.
104. "Reply to Ellen Key," *Current Opinion, op. cit.,* (March, 1913), 221.
105. *Woman,* pp. 283-4.
106. *Ibid.,* p. 287.
107. See her utopian novel, *Moving the Mountain* (New York: Charlton Company, 1911).
108. In 1890, 13.9 per cent of working women were married; fifty years later the figure was 36.4 per cent.
109. See chapter 5 in Mirra Komarovsky, *Women in the Modern World; Their Education and Their Dilemmas* (Boston: Little, Brown, 1953) for a discussion, in concrete terms, of the problems facing the modern working wife and mother.
110. Beauvoir, pp. 694-5.
111. "So stirring was her analysis" of the home, Charles and Mary Beard have written, "and so clarion was her call for freedom in mind and labor that a new school of feminist thinkers was raised up in America and Europe which sent reverberations as far afield as awakening Japan." *The Rise of American Civilization,* II, 431.

Article 4

Woman Suffrage in Perspective

Aileen S. Kraditor

The "argument from justice" and the "argument from expediency"[1] as used by the suffragists shared an important characteristic: they both expressed, in different ways, the suffragists' conception of democracy. Democracy, they contended, was incompatible with the rule of force. Justice was the rule of reason, the antithesis of force; a government concerned with legislating reforms, and consequently one that needed women's votes, could not possibly be based on force. Only a government whose electorate included all fit adults could be considered democratic.[2]

It followed that governments that excluded women from their electorates not only violated the democratic principle that demanded that they be based on the consent of the governed but also relied on force instead of consent. Suffragists' belief that force and consent were incompatible, along with their assumption that the reform they demanded would be realized in the future, provided the rationale for a theory of history that placed "government by force" at an early stage of history and "government by consent" at a later stage. Historical progress consisted partly in the replacement of the former by the latter.[3] The suffragists believed that they stood somewhere in the transition period.

This theory contrasts sharply with one argument frequently found in antisuffragist polemics. In Helen Kendrick Johnson's *Woman and the Republic,* for example, the most frequently repeated thesis was the identification of democracy with force. Mrs. Johnson, too, appealed to history. She pointed out that women voted in aristocratic countries the governments of which gave representation not to individuals but to property. An estate must not be deprived of its power in government merely because its owner happened to be a woman. The argument "No Taxation without

From *The Ideas of the Woman Suffrage Movement, 1890-1920* (New York: Columbia University Press, 1965), 249-264. Reprinted by permission.

Representation!" originated, she added, in societies in which voting was connected with property ownership. But when taxation of property ceased to be the basis for voting, women lost the vote. Government came to rely solely on the strength of individual men for its defense. Before, when kings ruled nations, men and women were taxed to pay a hired soldiery to defend the established order; at a later and more enlightened time, when every man became a king, each man became liable for the defense of the government he helped rule. Consent never replaced force and never would. A time came when men agreed to vote instead of fight, but behind the voting must stand the democratic force of the majority of men even in our enlightened American society.[4] This theory contradicted that of the suffragists in regard not only to the facts of history but, more importantly, to political and social theory. The suffragists disapproved of rule by force; the antis believed rule by force of the majority of men to be the sign of true democracy.

The suffragists agreed with the antis that a government based on the ballots of both men and women could not rest on force.[5] Inevitably, therefore, they postulated a necessary interrelation among consent, democracy, woman suffrage, and the type of government that concerned itself primarily with social welfare rather than with defense against invasions and rebellions. The stage of evolution a given society had reached, they believed, could be inferred from the degree to which consent had replaced force in government. This might be measured by the extent to which women participated in the government. Such evolution was both natural and inevitable.[6]

The women took pride in the fact that their movement was in the mainstream of American history, seeking to realize and further the ideals of the Founding Fathers, but not to replace those ideals or overthrow the government of the glorious republic brought forth by their ancestors.[7] In 1917 they announced proudly that suffragism was "A Bourgeois Movement," marching down the middle of the road, with reaction to one side and radicalism to the other. An article in the *Woman Citizen* declared:

Quite the worst epithet the mind of the radical can conjure up, in castigation for the less radical, quite the smelliest rose of yesterday he can pin on you, is *"bourgeois."* To be neither very conservative nor very radical, to be plain every-day, middle-class average, is to be just too awful for language, take it from the radical who is one degree more so than the last one. . . . So far as the suffrage is concerned the accusation might as well be faced and admitted. That is exactly what the suffrage movement is today—bourgeois, middle-class, a great middle-of-the-road movement; evidence of a slow-come mass conviction; representative of that most coherent, tightest-welded, farthest-reaching section of society—the middle.[8]

In placing their movement in the middle of the road, the suffragists were perfectly correct. They exhibited both the strengths and the weaknesses of other reform movements in American history, especially when in justifying their demand for the vote they voiced principles too extreme for their own consistent allegiance. The pioneers of the suffrage movement, living in a time when victory for their cause seemed eons away, did not have to concern themselves too much with tactics. They could afford to state their ideals in ringing declarations on democracy that would admit of no qualifications or exceptions. In fact, they had to do so, for only ideals that could inspire a martyr's dedication could sustain these women through the physical violence and almost unbearable ridicule to which they were subjected. Later, when victories could be won here and there at the cost of small concessions to political expediency, the hard facts of political life and the equivocal position in American society of these middle-class women exerted a pull away from the high ideals and ringing declarations. To win support from needed allies they compromised with those principles perhaps more than the requirements of the alliances dictated. More often than not they voiced the ideals and advocated the compromises at the same time.

In a sense, however, they were perfectly consistent. When they demanded the vote on the basis of justice and the consent of the governed, they could not intend absolutely universal suffrage, which would have given the vote to every human being. Having conceded that children, lunatics, and felons must be excluded, they had to define those categories. Such definitions, necessarily containing an element of arbitrariness, would have to be justified as serving the "good of society," and other limitations of the franchise for the same reason would appear logical enough. The right to political liberty was then identified with capacity to exercise it. In an association primarily of white, native-born, middle-class American women between 1890 and 1920, capacity for political liberty was almost automatically equated with Anglo-Saxon ancestry.[9] This assumption constitutes a unifying thread linking their anti-Negro,[10] antiforeign, frequently antilabor attitudes[11] with their defense of American democ-

racy and the principles of the Declaration of Independence.[12] Even
their Americanization programs for immigrants during and after
World War I, which the suffragists themselves believed to be motivated by a new positive attitude toward the foreign born,[13] were
actually programs to transform the immigrants so far as possible into
Anglo-Saxons and "therefore" into desirable voters.[14]

The coexistence within the suffrage movement of strong reformist motives, alleged to be proof of the movement's democracy,[15]
along with undemocratic attitudes such as white supremacy, suggests a comparison with another reform movement of the period, the
Progressive party of 1912. At the founding convention, Roosevelt
and the other leaders decided that the party in the South must be
Lily-white. They calculated that the number of Southern white votes
attracted by this policy would more than compensate for the number of Northern Negro votes the party would lose. Jane Addams
searched her soul anxiously and sincerely, and finally concluded that
in the long run American Negroes would benefit from a Progressive
party with a nationwide base, even though such a party could be
built only if its Southern wing for a time excluded Negroes.[16] Most
suffragists accepted racism within the NAWSA much more easily than
Miss Addams accepted it in the Progressive party, but both the
Progressives and the suffragists could at the same time advocate
white supremacy and democratic reforms and accept the organizational reflections of this fact.[17] When Southern suffragists coupled the
"consent of the governed" argument with appeals to white supremacy, they showed that they simply did not include Negroes in "the
people"; when Miss Addams accepted a Lily-white Progressive
party, she did not believe she was betraying the Negroes' interests,
but felt she was bringing nearer the time when Negroes would have
the right to consent to the laws by which they were governed.

This coexistence of reformist and humanitarian motives with
undemocratic attitudes links the woman suffrage movement with the
Progressive movement in still another way. Progressivism may be
seen as a broad humanitarian cause, and it may be seen as a convergence of several distinct self-interested movements challenging en-
trenched political or economic powers. Suffragism may be interpreted as one of these self-interested movements. It may also be
interpreted in this dual manner, since it contained women who
wanted the vote to enact a broad humanitarian program, as well as
women who participated in the humanitarian movement in order to
achieve their primary goal of political equality. Just as progressives

of both types (those whose main interest was broad humanitarianism and those whose main interest was the achievement of specific changes in the economic or political structure) found common ground in their demand for what they called democratic reform, so did the suffragists.

The suffragists, then, saw in the long sweep of history consent replacing force in government. The United States represented the finest expression of this progress toward universal consent. This was proved by the Declaration of Independence promulgated at its birth. Since the American Revolution, new portions of the population had received the vote in each generation. Sometimes the suffragists admitted that the sense of justice of the already-enfranchised men could not account for the enfranchisement of new groups and that political expediency exerted the decisive influence,[18] but in the long view the women emphasized the pattern of steady progress toward the ideal of true "government by consent of the governed." The last step would be the enfranchisement of women.[19]

The progress, however, although inevitable, was obviously not automatic. No one knew better than the suffragists the long years of work and struggle they must contribute to their cause before it could triumph. No one knew better than they (although the antis knew it too and frequently reminded them of it) that one of their greatest obstacles was the indifference of the majority of women to their own political equality. They consoled themselves and answered their critics in two ways. First, as Mrs. Stanton had repeatedly argued, the dulling of the desire for freedom through long centuries of suppression was the best proof of its desirability. Second, progress was always made by forward-looking minorities in the face of majority hostility or indifference.[20] This theory supported suffragist morale, particularly in the days when they were indeed a very small minority and even later when, as always, the antis confronted them with theories of woman's sphere that defined the natural as the customary. If progress was always due to the minority that saw further than the majority, then the customary was never the natural, nor the natural customary. Here again the suffrage movement proved itself a "bourgeois movement," that is, reformist rather than revolutionary, for although the theory of progress that they developed seems to imply unending change, the suffragists did not visualize any further extensions of the franchise after women had secured the vote. Nor did they approve of the efforts of other minorities to effect changes in those areas of American life in which the suffragists themselves equated the customary with the natural.[21]

Two recent historians describe the essentially conservative position of the class to which most suffragists belonged:

> While maturing industrialism was responsible for the growth of many social evils, it was also responsible for producing wealth and leisure for groups that could attack such evils. Ministers, teachers, writers, and thousands of prosperous women had no large financial stake in child and female labor, long hours, sweat-shops, saloons, tenements, and slums. . . . This class had no unity, but its members suffered in common the fear of having their independence abridged by monopolizing Titans from above or else engulfed by a surge of socialism from the ranks of labor below. Truly conservative, they opposed equally the collectivism of the great trusts and the collectivism of trade unions; and they shared a profound belief in free capitalism, equal economic opportunity, fair trade practices and the protection of property. Inheritors of the victory of the English Parliament over the Stuart kings, they insisted also upon the supremacy of laws over men or institutions, and they had a naïve belief in the efficacy of legislation to achieve their ends.[22]

Working-class women certainly needed the vote more than did leisured women, if the suffragists were correct in their opinion that the ballot represented power, self-protection, and the means whereby many wrongs could be righted. But it was the middle-class women who had, in the course of the nineteenth century, acquired education, leisure time, and the opportunity to participate in activities outside their homes, all of which made them aware of the gap between their social standing and economic status on the one hand and their political power on the other. This awareness bred a sense of grievance and a motive for the struggle to secure redress. The political power of working-class women of course lagged behind their needs, and in the last few years many such women became active suffragists, but their sense of grievance, where it existed, generally focused on more urgent demands than that for the vote. Moreover, since there was no gap between their educational and social standing and their political power, they lacked one of the motives that led the middle-class women to demand the vote.[23] When workingwomen did demand the suffrage, their arguments rarely mentioned justice or the Declaration of Independence, not because justice or democracy carried less appeal to workers than to middle-class women, but because workingwomen did not simply *want* the vote; they found they *needed* it for the same reasons as they had organized their unions. Working-class women, however, never constituted more than a small minority of organized suffragists.

The ballot was for some suffragists an end and for others a means to other ends. To Mrs. Stanton, Mrs. Gilman, and Miss Addams, it was never more than a means toward woman's all-round development or toward social regeneration. One might infer that to Miss Anthony is was an end, but only because she believed that no other reform could be achieved without women's equal participation.[24] It therefore loomed so large in her writings and speeches that it could appear to be her one goal. To many later suffragists the vote was indeed the main goal; the possibility of arguing that women's votes could help reform society made the vote seem, in their writings, a means to reform. These differences among suffragists are instructive. When Mrs. Stanton was in her prime, women had not yet won many of the rights they took for granted by 1900. To her the vote then seemed to be a means to the acquisition of precisely those rights, to their entrance into professions and graduate schools, to equal guardianship of their children, and so on. Those later suffragists to whom these rights seemed almost the sum of the equality they desired in the most desirable society imaginable could not visualize the vote as a means because it was virtually the only right they aspired to that they had not yet won. Hence it stood alone and appeared to be the "end." To Mrs. Gilman and Miss Addams, both of whom belonged to the last generation of suffragists and who in different ways were deeply dissatisfied with the society in which they lived, many rights were still to be won. The suffrage in their view remained a mere means, among others, to the achievement of these rights. The more satisfied a middle-class suffragist was with her personal lot, in the later years of the suffragist agitation, the more important the vote would probably be to her, simply because it stood alone and was not sought as a means to any drastic change in the status quo.

As women obtained one new right after another, the rights of men and women became more and more similar, just as other changes were causing their spheres to draw closer together. The social, economic, and political separation that had encouraged different ways of thinking, that had given plausibility to the assertion that innate psychological differences between the sexes were so great that women must be kept in their customary sphere, melted away.

Disfranchisement itself had bred differences in thinking and social roles between enfranchised and disfranchised that had provided arguments for maintaining the political separation. Those differences led both men and women to expect women, if and when they obtained the ballot, to vote differently from men. They gave antisuffragists an argument for keeping women out of politics; they gave women reformers an argument why men reformers should give them the vote. But when women won the ballot and in other ways continued to close the gap between their sphere and men's, all those arguments lost their plausibility. The differences produced by that very disfranchisement and exclusion from the male sphere evaporated.

The pattern of women's voting since 1920 shows that the diversity of thinking within the movement, noted at the beginning of this study, has persisted. Just as the suffragists differed among themselves in religion, politics, even the reasons for wanting the vote, they have continued to differ as voters. The addition of women to the electorate has not significantly altered American voting patterns as the suffragists predicted it would. But it would not be correct for that reason to deny that an enormous change took place with the enactment of the Nineteenth Amendment. Even those many suffragists who wanted the vote primarily to enact reforms became suffragists partly because of the intense shame they felt at being thought unfit to help govern their country. When they acquired that right they felt a new pride in American democracy and a new respect for themselves.

NOTES

1. See Kraditor, *The Ideas of the Woman Suffrage Movement*, chap. III.
2. An item in "Editorial Notes," *Woman's Journal*, June 13, 1891; Alice Stone Blackwell in *ibid.*, May 25, 1895; NAWSA, *Proceedings*, 1893, p. 84, quoting the first resolution passed at the convention; Putnam-Jacobi, *"Common Sense" Applied to Woman Suffrage*, p. 187; E. Stanton, *Suffrage a Natural Right*; NAWSA, *Proceedings*, 1907, pp. 41-43, and 1910, p. 70, quoting reports of Committee on Peace and Arbitration; Jane Addams in "Women in Public Life," *Annals* of the American Academy of Political and Social Science, LVI (November, 1914), 1-4; Shaw, *Passages from Speeches*, pp. 12-13.

3. Carrie Chapman Catt in speech (1896?) quoted in clipping in Catt Collection, NYPL (the clipping, from the Oakland *Tribune,* is in scrapbook labeled "Personal"); Susan B. Anthony in the San Francisco *Examiner,* June 21, 1896; Austin and Martin, *Suffrage and Government,* pp. 3–4; Addams, "Women, War and Suffrage," *The Survey,* November 6, 1915, p. 148.

4. This was so because, as explained on p. 28, a vicious minority that had lost an election might resort to force to achieve its ends if half the electorate were incapable of taking up arms to enforce the majority's mandate. See Johnson, *Woman and the Republic,* chaps. II, III, and X.

5. This assumption is particularly clear in Ellen Battelle Dietrick, "The Errors of Mr. John Fiske," *Woman's Journal,* December 30, 1893, in which she wrote that "the point at present is to warn the public not to accept as gospel truth the opinions of teachers who preach that government rests on physical force," implying that an assertion that government did rest on physical force would *ipso facto* constitute an argument against woman suffrage.

6. Carrie Chapman Catt expressed this thought repeatedly. See: "Evolution and Woman's Suffrage," carbon of typed manuscript speech, 1893, Catt Collection, NYPL; speech quoted in *Woman's Journal,* February 23, 1901; *President's Annual Address,* 1902, p. 3 (copy in Catt Collection, NYPL); "An Address to the Congress of the United States," NAWSA, *Proceedings,* 1917, pp. 50–52.

7. Putnam-Jacobi, *"Common Sense" Applied to Woman Suffrage,* chap. VIII; Alice Stone Blackwell in *Woman's Journal,* April 25, 1903; NAWSA, *Proceedings,* 1904, p. 19, quoting "Declaration of Principles" prepared by Mrs. Catt, Miss Shaw, Miss Blackwell, and Mrs. Harper and adopted by the convention; Catt, "An Address to the Congress of the United States," NAWSA, *Proceedings,* 1917, p. 50.

8. "A Bourgeois Movement" was the title of this unsigned editorial in the *Woman Citizen,* July 7, 1917. The *Woman Citizen* was a weekly begun in mid-1917, incorporating the former *Woman's Journal, Woman Voter,* and *National Suffrage News.* The new paper was the official organ of the NAWSA. The article noted here appeared in the sixth issue, when the editor, it may be assumed, was still carefully explaining the association's nature and policy to the public.

9. Sometimes the equation was conscious. See chap. VII for examples of the common contrast they made between the old and new immigrations. They frequently declared that only the older immigrants, from England and northern Europe, could govern themselves. See also Putnam-Jacobi, *"Common Sense" Applied to Woman Suffrage,* chap. III; Harriot Stanton Blatch in *Woman's Journal,* January 18, 1896; Catt, *President's Annual Address,* 1902, p. 10.

10. See chap. VI.

11. See chap. VII.
12. See chap. III.
13. See chap. VII.
14. See "Program of the National American Woman Suffrage Association," *National Municipal Review,* IX (January, 1920), 56–57, and various speeches of Mrs. Catt in the same period, proposing that English be made the language of instruction in all public and private schools; that an educational qualification for the vote be imposed in all states after a certain date; direct citizenship for women so that a foreign-born woman could not vote simply because her more Americanized husband became a citizen; and citizenship schools to teach Americanism to adults to make foreign-imported radicalism less attractive to them.
15. See, for example, FitzGerald, *What Is a Democracy?*: "Do you know what people are most against women's voting? It is the women of means, in comfortable circumstances, who do not need it for the good of their bodies, and do not realize that they need it for the good of their souls, and who are *afraid* to let their working sisters have it. Why? Because they are afraid of the *people,* afraid of the *workingman,* afraid of *democracy.* They think that the women's vote will strengthen the workingman's vote, the popular vote, and they are *afraid.* And they may well be afraid, if they do not trust the people, for the real people are going to *win,* and the day of their victory will be hastened when women can vote."
16. See August 1912 folder in Jane Addams Papers, FHL; Addams, "The Progressive Party and the Negro," *The Crisis,* V (November, 1912), 30–31; Mowry, "The South and the Progressive Lily White Party of 1912," *Journal of Southern History,* VI (May, 1940), 237–47. Woodward, "Progressivism—For Whites Only," chap. XIV, in *Origins of the New South,* discusses the actual compatibility of Progressivism with racism. William E. Leuchtenburg, in "Progressivism and Imperialism," *Mississippi Valley Historical Review,* XXXIX (December, 1952), 483–504, shows that the same compatibility existed in other sections of the country too. Thus the suffrage movement was in the mainstream of American intellectual history in this respect, just as its demand for the vote placed it in the mainstream of American political and social history.
17. See, for example, "Statement of Purpose," of a conference of Southern suffragists held in Memphis in 1906 (copy in Clay Papers, UK), in which Laura Clay played a leading role. Note the proximity of democracy, white supremacy, and justice to workers: "Declaring our adherence to the principles of political liberty, guaranteed to the American people by the fundamental principles of our government, we affirm that they should not be limited by sex. . . . If the women of the South were enfranchised, it would insure a permanent and enormous preponderance of the white race in politics, and would preclude the necessity for

any doubtful expedients to minimize the negro vote.

"We ask for the ballot because students of industrial conditions affirm that the lack of direct political power is a factor in the comparatively low wages of the six million wage-earning women in our country.

"We ask for the ballot as the strongest insurance against child-labor under conditions destructive to the best development of the men and women of the future."

18. See, for example, Susan B. Anthony in National Council of Women, *Transactions*, 1891, pp. 229-30; Laura Clay, "Counterparts," *Woman's Journal*, June 15, 1901; Mrs. Harper in House *Hearing*, 1912, pp. 70-71.

19. In two major respects, they believed, woman suffrage was not analogous to previous extensions of the franchise. First, they declared that no other group that had won the vote had won it as much through its own efforts as the women would. Second, they occasionally complained that the enfranchisement of other groups (Negro men, foreign-born men, Indian men) had erected new obstacles to the enfranchisement of women, inasmuch as these new voters were allegedly against woman suffrage and inasmuch as the enfranchisement of "unfit" men had made many people unwilling to extend the franchise still further. Hence, although in suffragist thinking, their movement was in the mainstream of gradually broadening American democracy, that stream turned out to have a few rapids and sharp bends.

20. Elizabeth Cady Stanton to Clara B. Colby, 1894 letter quoted in Lutz, *Created Equal*, p. 292; speech of Mrs. Catt in 1900, quoted in Anthony and Harper, eds., *History of Woman Suffrage*, IV, 369-70; Harper in her 1902 introduction to *ibid.*, p. xxii.

21. See Anna Howard Shaw's comments on anarchism and McKinley's assassination, in *Woman's Journal*, September 21, 1901; Grace Bagley in *Woman Citizen*, June 30, 1917; "A Bourgeois Movement," in *ibid.*, July 7, 1917; NAWSA, *Proceedings*, 1919, p. 59, quoting sixth resolution passed.

22. Cochran and Miller, *The Age of Enterprise*, pp. 174-75, quoted by permission of The Macmillan Company which originally published the work in 1942. The order of the two passages has been reversed.

23. Thorstein Veblen commented on the same phenomenon from a different point of view: "It is among the women of the well-to-do classes, in the communities which are farthest advanced in industrial development, that this sense of grievance to be redressed is most alive and finds most frequent expression. That is to say, in other words, there is a demand, more or less serious, for emancipation from all relations of status, tutelage, or vicarious life; and the revulsion asserts itself especially among the class of women upon whom the scheme of life handed down from the regime of status imposes with least mitigation a vicarious life, and in those communities whose economic development has departed

farthest from the circumstances to which this traditional scheme is adapted. The demand comes from that portion of womankind which is excluded by the canons of good repute from all effectual work, and which is closely reserved for a life of leisure and conspicuous consumption.

"More than one critic of this new-woman movement has misapprehended its motive. The case of the American 'new woman' has lately been summed up with some warmth by a popular observer of social phenomena: 'She is petted by her husband, the most devoted and hard-working of husbands in the world. ... She is the superior of her husband in education, and in almost every respect. She is surrounded by the most numerous and delicate attentions. Yet she is not satisfied.' ... The grievance of the new woman is made up of those things which this typical characterization of the movement urges as the reasons why she should be content. She is petted, and is permitted, or even required, to consume largely and conspicuously—vicariously for her husband or other natural guardian. She is exempted, or debarred, from vulgarly useful employment—in order to perform leisure vicariously for the good repute of her natural (or pecuniary) guardian. These offices are the conventional marks of the un-free, at the same time that they are incompatible with the human impulse to purposeful activity." *Theory of the Leisure Class* (New York, Mentor Books, 1958), pp. 231-32, quoted by permission of The Viking Press, Inc. See also pp. 120-22, 229-30, and 233.

24. See, for example, Susan B. Anthony to "Mr. Bowman," September 7, 1894, Anthony Family Collection, HL: "I am as deeply and keenly interested in the many reforms in city, State & National government as any one can possibly be—but knowing that no right solution of any great question can be reached until the whole people have a voice in it—I give all of myself to the getting the whole people inside the body politic, so as to be able to begin making even the first equation of any of the problems—"

Part Four

The Illusion of Equality

The paradox of women's position in American society became clearly evident in the twentieth century. The suffrage victory in 1920, the increase of women in industry, and women's new sexual freedom enhanced their status, yet the promise of emancipation has remained largely unfulfilled. As Max Lerner has written, "In theory, in law, and to a great extent in fact, the American woman has the freedom to compete with men on equal terms: but psychically and socially she is caught in a society still dominated by masculine power and standards."[1] Women found that gaining the suffrage did not insure an effective bloc of women voters armed with the power and determination to champion women's interests. And, in spite of new job opportunities for women, employers maintained differences in men's and women's salaries. By the mid-sixties, radicals commonly referred to the "illusion" of equality, and a new generation boldly attacked what they termed the "sexist" attitudes which have remained the last barrier to women's emancipation.

Although the percentage of working women has risen continuously in the twentieth century, most women have been segregated in low paying and routine "women's jobs." New Deal legislation provided further protection for women in relation to hours and wages, but both the National Industrial Recovery Act and the Fair Labor Standards Act tolerated wage differentials and set minimum wages for women at rates lower than those for men. After 1939, wartime production drew thirteen million women into the ranks of labor and for the first time married women exceeded single women in the working population. In spite of the fact that industry dropped one out of every four women employed at the end of the war,[2] the number of working women has grown yearly since 1947. By 1970 women constituted 40 per cent of the American labor force.

These changes in their economic role have had an emancipating effect on women, particularly on those married and working outside the home. Although great strides have been made, women continue to be employed in low status jobs and to be nearly completely excluded from certain professions. "Today, there does not seem to be much disparity between men's and women's wages for the same work, though the sexual division of labor is so nearly complete that it is difficult to find comparable jobs of the two sexes to make a definitive study."[3]

The questions involving the conditions and rights of working women have consistently troubled women's organizations. While they have generally met with a good deal of opposition, they have found it easier to obtain protective legislation based on the image of woman as victim than that which implied the equality of women. Perhaps their most conspicuous success during the 1920s was the short-lived Sheppard-Towner bill designed to ensure federal protection to mothers and children by the prevention of infant mortality. Instrumental in its passage was the Women's Joint Congressional Committee which represented the League of Women Voters and hundreds of local women's groups in lobbying on behalf of the bill. As Clarke A. Chambers makes clear in "The Campaign for Women's Rights in the 1920's," such activity typified the way in which organized women carried on the Progressive spirit during those years. Both Florence Kelley's National Consumers League (NCL) and the National Women's Trade Union League (NWTUL) pressed their campaign in the interest of working women, but little tangible success marked their efforts until the economic crisis of the thirties made possible the social legislation of the New Deal.

Even then, women were still plagued by unequal pay and job segregation, and it was not until the 1960s that they were able to force government action on these problems. In the 1920s the NCL and the NWTUL had shunned cooperation with the demand of the Women's party for an equal rights amendment, but the issue of equal pay became increasingly important to such groups. By the 1940s competition from women as cheap labor brought solid support for equal pay from the labor movement, but congressional legislation on this subject failed in 1945 and again in 1947.

Women's continuing concern with the issue of equal pay led to the Women's Bureau Conference on Equal Pay and the inclusion of the demand in the Republican and Democratic platforms of 1952, but little was done. In 1963 the report of the President's Commission on the Status of Women focused attention on this problem and recommended reform in the areas of employment, federal social insurance and tax laws, and federal and state labor laws with regard to hours, wages, and night work. In addition the commission concerned itself with differences in legal treatment of men and women, services provided for women in education, counseling, job training, and day care centers. This report led to the passage of the Equal Pay Act in 1963 and the following year Title VII of the Civil Rights Act of 1964 which prohibited employment discrimination by the federal government.

While the expansion of women's role in the economy and the entrance of increasing numbers of women into the professions represent the extension of nineteenth century trends, the changes in social life and behavior—the "revolution in manners and morals"—constitute a basic shift in the history of women in American life. By the 1920s the alteration in sexual norms was clearly apparent. The decade witnessed not only a new emphasis upon sexuality which permeated the culture, but also the emergence of women's demands for equality of sexual pleasure. In "The American Woman's Pre-World War I Freedom in Manners and Morals" James R. McGovern discusses the nature of these changes and shows clear evidence that a radical shift in sexual behavior and attitudes appeared among the upper classes of the cities in the decade before 1920. He associates these shifts with the effects of economic change and urbanization upon American women.

The family also reflected the effects of these alterations in American life. Stripped of its traditional functions, the family became primarily concerned with serving the personalities of its members. Its main function came to be psychological. "Marriage was in a sense displacing the family itself; a husband and wife now referred colloquially to their 'marriage,' implying not so much a fixed social institution as a special arrangement between two people who had 'fallen in love.' "[4] Held together solely by the tenuous bonds of personal relationships, marriages dissolved with increasing rapidity. Divorces which had reached 100,000 per year in 1914 passed the

200,000 mark by 1929.[5] With some degree of economic independence many women were unwilling to tolerate unhappy marriages. At the same time the decline in the birthrate represented the deliberate choice of couples to limit their families in order to maintain their standard of living after children became an economic liability rather than an economic asset.

The hard times of the Depression dampened the divorce rate as couples chose security above personal happiness.[6] At the same time the emphasis on personal fulfillment which emerged in the 1920s altered the ideals and aspirations of American women. In the decade after World War II prosperity made large families possible, and women accepted the cult of domesticity—"the feminine mystique"—which idealized the affluent suburban housewife devoted to home and family. The emphasis on home economics and the "scientific" home rationalized domestic drudgery; The Ideal Marriage, which appeared in the United States in 1931, charted the course to sexual bliss. However, by the 1960s these trends reversed themselves as birthrates fell and increasing numbers of women sought their own careers.

The decade also witnessed a new permissiveness in sexual behavior and a rebirth of feminism. Erwin O. Smeigal and Rita Seiden assay the changes in contemporary sexual behavior in "The Decline and Fall of the Double Standard." Surprisingly, they show that changes of actual sexual behavior have not been as great as they were in the 1920s. "If there has been a sexual revolution . . . it is in terms of frankness about sex and the freedom to discuss it." This has meant for women a greater control over their lives and a tendency toward a single standard of sexual behavior rooted in shared affection. However, Smeigal and Seiden are quick to add that the double standard has declined but not fallen.

Since 1920 American feminism has been a fragmented movement which seemed to collapse following its greatest legislative successes. Not until the appearance of the Women's Liberation movement in the 1960s did feminism regain popularity.[7] Carl Degler connects the decline of feminism to the emancipating effects of social changes unrelated to feminism and the general American hostility to ideology.[8] In "Feminism as a Radical Ideology," William L. O'Neill presents a contrasting argument in which he makes conceptual distinctions between "the woman movement," "social feminism," and "hard core" or "extreme feminism." Using these distinctions he traces the contradictions within the movement from the nineteenth century in order to account for its collapse after 1920 and to lay the historical groundwork for "a genuine feminist renaissance."

The feminist movement split asunder on the rock of racial prejudice in the early part of this century, and the relation of black women to the contemporary movement remains a problem. To a large degree black women have thus far remained outside, a fact which Pauli Murray, one of the founders of the National Organization of Women (NOW), deplores. Murray contends that the issue is one of human rights—women must "transcend the racial barrier" and form an alliance beginning with educated, middle class women of both races.

Presently, according to Jean E. Friedman's analysis of the movement in "Contemporary Feminism: Theories and Practices," there are three major groups of contemporary feminists: privatists, hoping to achieve personal solutions within the context of their marriages; moderates, actively working toward political and legal changes; and radicals, who have reintroduced consideration of basic questions concerning sex and the social order.[9] This latter group has been heavily influenced by Marxist writings, and seems to Friedman to be moving toward a truly feminist ideology. However, today Friedman believes that the most pressing need for women is to understand the nature of their traditional roles and the ways in which those roles have hindered self-realization. American women must comprehend the paradoxical nature of their existence in a society in which equality remains an illusion.

NOTES

1. Max Lerner, *America as a Civilization* (New York: Simon and Schuster, 1957), 604.
2. U.S. Department of Labor, "Employment of Women in the Early Postwar Period," *Bulletin of the Women's Bureau,* no. 211 (Washington, D.C.: Government Printing Office, 1947), 5.
3. Carl Degler, "Revolution Without Ideology: The Changing Place of Women in America," *Daedalus,* (Spring, 1964), 662.
4. Rowland Berthoff, *An Unsettled People: Social Order and Disorder in American History* (New York: Harper and Row, 1971), 403. See also: William Ogburn and Clark Tibbitts, "The Family and Its Functions,"

Recent Social Trends in the United States (New York: McGraw-Hill, 1933), I, 661-679; John Sirjamaki, *The American Family in the Twentieth Century* (Cambridge, Mass.: Harvard University Press, 1953).

5. William E. Leuchtenburg, *The Perils of Prosperity, 1914-32* (Chicago: University of Chicago Press, 1958), 162.

6. For an interesting discussion of women in the Depression see Caroline Bird, *The Invisible Scar* (New York: David McKay, 1966), *passim.*

7. Gerda Lerner, "The Feminists: A Second Look," *Columbia Forum*, XIII (Fall, 1970); Judith Hole and Ellen Levine, *Rebirth of Feminism* (New York: Quadrangle Books, 1971).

8. Carl Degler, "Revolution Without Ideology . . ." 653-670. For a different view see: Christopher Lasch, *The Agony of the American Left* (New York: Alfred A. Knopf, 1969), 23-27.

9. A useful anthology sampling mainly radical feminist views is Robin Morgan, ed., *Sisterhood Is Powerful* (New York: Vintage Books, 1970).

Article 1

The American Woman's Pre-World War I Freedom in Manners and Morals

James R. McGovern

The Twenties have been alternately praised or blamed for almost everything and its opposite,[1] but most historians hold, whether to praise or to condemn, that this decade launched the revolution in manners and morals through which we are still moving today. This judgment seems to be part of an even more inclusive one in American historiography to exceptionalize the Twenties. No other decade has invited such titles of historical caricature as *The Jazz Age, This Was Normalcy, Fantastic Interim*, or *The Perils of Prosperity*. Richard Hofstadter's classic, *The Age of Reform*, subtly reinforces this view by seeing the Twenties as "Entr'acte," an interim between two periods of reform, the Progressive era and the New Deal, which themselves display discontinuity.[2]

Revisionism, in the form of a developmental interpretation of the relationship between the Progressive era and the Twenties, has been gaining strong support in recent years. De-emphasizing the disruptive impact of World War I, Henry F. May asked whether the 1920s could be understood fully "without giving more attention to the old regime."[3] He declared that "Immediately prewar America must be newly explored," especially "its inarticulate assumptions— assumptions in such areas as morality, politics, class and race relations, popular art and literature, and family life."[4] May pursued his inquiry in *The End of American Innocence* and showed that for the purposes of intellectual history, at least, the Twenties were not as significant as the preceding decade.[5] Political historians have been reassessing the relationship of the Progressive era to the Twenties as well. Arthur Link has demonstrated that progressivism survived

From the *Journal of American History*, LV (September, 1968), 315-333. Reprinted by permission.

World War I,[6] and J. Joseph Huthmacher has established continuity between progressivism and the New Deal in the immigrant's steadfast devotion to the ameliorative powers of the government.[7] Together with May's analysis, their writings suggest that the 1920s are much more the result of earlier intrinsic social changes than either the sudden, supposedly traumatic experiences of the war or unique developments in the Twenties. Since this assertion is certain to encounter the formidable claims that the 1920s, at least in manners and morals, amounted to a revolution, its viability can be tested by questioning if the American woman's "emancipation" in manners and morals occurred even earlier than World War I.

Even a casual exploration of the popular literature of the Progressive era reveals that Americans then described and understood themselves to be undergoing significant changes in morals. "Sex o'clock in America" struck in 1913,[8] about the same time as "The Repeal of Reticence."[9] One contemporary writer saw Americans as liberated from the strictures of "Victorianism," now an epithet deserving criticism, and exulted, "Heaven defend us from a return to the prudery of the Victorian regime!"[10] Conditions were such that another commentator asked self-consciously, "Are We Immoral?"[11] And still another feared that the present "vice not often matched since [the time of] the Protestant Reformation" might invite a return to Puritanism.[12] Yet, historians have not carefully investigated the possibility that the true beginnings of America's "New Freedom" in morals occurred prior to 1920.[13] The most extensive, analytical writing on the subject of changing manners and morals is found in Frederick L. Allen's *Only Yesterday* (1931), William Leuchtenburg's *The Perils of Prosperity* (1958), May's *The End of American Innocence* (1959), and George Mowry's *The Urban Nation* (1965).

Allen and Leuchtenburg apply almost identical sharp-break interpretations, respectively entitling chapters "The Revolution in Manners and Morals" and "The Revolution in Morals."[14] Both catalogue the same types of criteria for judgment. The flapper, as the "new woman" was called, was a creature of the 1920s. She smoked, drank, worked, and played side by side with men. She became preoccupied with sex—shocking and simultaneously unshockable. She danced close, became freer with her favors, kept her own latchkey, wore scantier attire which emphasized her boyish, athletic form, just as she used makeup and bobbed and dyed her hair. She and her comradely beau tried to abolish time and succeeded, at least to the extent that the elders asked to join the revelry. Although there were occasional "advance signals" of "rebellion" before the war, it was not until the 1920s that the code of woman's innocence and ignorance crumbled.

May, who comes closest to an understanding of the moral permissiveness before the 1920s, describes in general terms such phenomena of the Progressive era as the "Dance Craze," birth control, the impact of the movies, and the "white-slave panic."[15] He focuses on the intellectuals, however, and therefore overlooks the depth of these and similar social movements. This causes him to view them as mere "Cracks in the Surface" of an essentially conservative society. He quotes approvingly of the distinction made by the *Nation* "between the fluttering tastes of the half-baked intellec uals, attracted by all these things, and the surviving soundness of the great majority."[16] His treatment also ignores one of the most significant areas of changing manners and morals as they affected the American woman: the decided shift in her sex role and identification in the direction of more masculine norms. Again, *The End of American Innocence* does not convincingly relate these changes to the growth of the cities. Perhaps these limitations explain Mowry's preference for a "sharp-break" interpretation, although he wrote seven years after May.

Mowry, who acknowledges especial indebtedness to Leuchtenburg,[17] is emphatic about the "startling" changes in manners and morals in the 1920s.[18] He highlights "the new woman of the twenties"[19] whose "modern feminine morality and attitudes toward the institution of marriage date from the twenties."[20] Mowry concedes to the libidos of progressives only the exceptional goings-on in Greenwich Village society.

These hypotheses, excluding May's, hold that the flapper appeared in the postwar period mainly because American women en masse then first enjoyed considerable social and economic freedom. They also emphasize the effect of World War I on morals.[21] By inference, of course, the Progressive era did not provide a suitable matrix. But an investigation of this period establishes that women had become sufficiently active and socially independent to prefigure the "emancipation" of the 1920s.

A significant deterioration of external controls over morality had occurred before 1920. One of the consequences of working and living conditions in the cities, especially as these affected women, was that Americans of the period 1900–1920 had experienced a vast dissolution of moral authority, which formerly had centered in the family and the small community. The traditional "straight and narrow" could not serve the choices and opportunities of city life.[22] As against primary controls and contacts based on face-to-face association where the norms of family, church, and small community, usually reinforcing each other, could be internalized, the city made for a type of "individualization" through its distant, casual, specialized, and transient clusters of secondary associations.[23] The individual came to determine his own behavioral norms.

The "home is in peril" became a fact of sociological literature as early as 1904.[24] One of the most serious signs of its peril was the increasing inability of parents to influence their children in the delicate areas of propriety and morals.[25] The car, already numerous enough to affect dating and premarital patterns,[26] the phone coming to be used for purposes of romantic accommodation,[27] and the variety of partners at the office or the factory,[28] all together assured unparalleled privacy and permissiveness between the sexes.

Individualization of members served to disrupt confidence between generations of the family, if not to threaten parents with the role of anachronistic irrelevance. Dorothy Dix observed in 1913 that there had been "so many changes in the conditions of life and point of view in the last twenty years that the parent of today is absolutely unfitted to decide the problems of life for the young man and woman of today. This is particularly the case with women because the whole economic and social position of women has been revolutionized since mother was a girl."[29] Magazine articles lamented "The Passing of the Home Daughter" who preferred the blessed anonymity of the city to "dying of asphyxiation at home!"[30] The same phenomenon helps to explain the popularity in this period of such standardized mothers as Dorothy Dix, Beatrice Fairfax, and Emily Post, each of whom was besieged with queries on the respective rights of mothers and daughters.

Woman's individualization resulted mainly because, whether single or married, gainfully employed or not, she spent more time outside her home. Evidence demonstrates that the so-called job and kitchen revolutions were already in advanced stages by 1910. The great leap forward in women's participation in economic life came between 1900 and 1910; the percentage of women who were employed changed only slightly from 1910 to 1930. A comparison of the percentages of gainfully employed women aged 16 to 44 between 1890 and 1930 shows that they comprised 21.7 percent of Americans employed in 1890, 23.5 percent in 1900, 28.1 percent in 1910, 28.3

percent in 1920, and 29.7 percent in 1930.[31] While occupational activity for women appears to stagnate from 1910 to 1920, in reality a considerable restructuring occurred with women leaving roles as domestics and assuming positions affording more personal independence as clerks and stenographers.[32]

Married women, especially those in the upper and middle classes, enjoyed commensurate opportunities. Experts in household management advised women to rid themselves of the maid and turn to appliances as the "maid of all service."[33] Statistics on money expended on those industries which reduced home labor for the wife suggest that women in middle-income families gained considerable leisure after 1914.[34] This idea is also corroborated from other sources,[35] especially from the tone and content of advertising in popular magazines when they are compared with advertising at the turn of the century. Generally speaking, women depicted in advertising in or about 1900 are well rounded, have gentle, motherly expressions, soft billowy hair, and delicate hands. They are either sitting down or standing motionless; their facial expressions are immobile as are their corseted figures.[36] After 1910, they are depicted as more active figures with more of their activity taking place outside their homes.[37] One woman tells another over the phone: "Yes[,] drive over right away—I'll be ready. My housework! Oh that's all done. How do I do it? I just let electricity do my work nowadays."[38] Vacuum cleaners permitted the housewife to "Push the Button—and Enjoy the Springtime!"[39] Van Camp's "Pork and Beans" promised to save her "100 hours yearly,"[40] and Campbell's soups encouraged, "Get some fun out of life," since it was unnecessary to let the "three-meals-a-day problem tie you down to constant drudgery."[41] Wizard Polish, Minute Tapioca, and Minute Gelatine also offered the same promise. The advertising image of women became more natural, even nonchalant. A lady entertaining a friend remarks: "I don't have to hurry nowadays. I have a Florence Automatic Oil Stove in my kitchen."[42] It had become "so *very* easy" to wax the floors that well-dressed women could manage them.[43] And they enjoyed a round of social activities driving the family car.[44]

It was in this setting that the flapper appeared along with her older married sister who sought to imitate her. No one at the office or in the next block cared much about their morals as long as the one was efficient and the other paid her bills on time. And given the fact that both these women had more leisure and wished "to participate in what men call 'the game of life' " rather than accept "the mere humdrum of household duties,"[45] it is little wonder that contemporaries rightly assessed the danger of the situation for traditional morals by 1910.

The ensuing decade was marked by the development of a revolution in manners and morals; its chief embodiment was the flapper who was urban based and came primarily from the middle and upper classes. Young—whether in fact or fancy—assertive, and independent, she experimented with intimate dancing, permissive favors, and casual courtships or affairs. She joined men as comrades, and the differences in behavior of the sexes were narrowed. She became in fact in some degree desexualized. She might ask herself, "Am I Not a Boy? Yes, I Am—Not."[46] Her speech, her interest in thrills and excitement, her dress and hair, her more aggressive sexuality, even perhaps her elaborate beautification, which was a statement of intentions, all point to this. Women, whether single or married, became at once more attractive and freer in their morals and paradoxically less feminine. Indeed, the term sexual revolution as applied to the Progressive era means reversal in the traditional role of women just as it describes a pronounced familiarity of the sexes.

The unmarried woman after 1910 was living in the "Day of the Girl."[47] Dorothy Dix described "the type of girl that the modern young man falls for" in 1915 as a "husky young woman who can play golf all day and dance all night, and drive a motor car, and give first aid to the injured if anybody gets hurt, and who is in no more danger of swooning than he is."[48] Little wonder she was celebrated in song as "A Dangerous Girl"; the lyrics of one of the popular songs for 1916 read, "You dare me, you scare me, and still I like you more each day. But you're the kind that will charm; and then do harm; you've got a dangerous way."[49] The "most popular art print . . . ever issued" by Puck depicts a made-up young lady puckering her lips and saying "Take It From Me!"[50] The American girl of 1900 was not described in similar terms. The lovely and gracious Gibson Girl was too idealized to be real.[51] And when young lovers trysted in advertising, they met at Horlick's Malted Milk Bar; he with his guitar, and she with her parasol.[52] Beatrice Fairfax could still reply archaically about the need for "maidenly reserve" to such queries as those on the proprieties of men staring at women on the streets.[53] And the Wellesley College News in 1902 reported that students were not permitted to have a Junior Prom because it would be an occasion for meeting "promiscuous men," although the college sanctioned "girl dances."[54]

The girls, however, dispensed with "maidenly reserve." In 1910, Margaret Deland, the novelist, could announce a "Change in the Feminine Ideal."

> This young person ... with surprisingly bad manners—has gone to college, and when she graduates she is going to earn her own living ... she won't go to church; she has views upon marriage and the birth-rate, and she utters them calmly, while her mother blushes with embarrassment; she occupies herself, passionately, with everything except the things that used to occupy the minds of girls.[55]

Many young women carried their own latchkeys.[56] Meanwhile, as Dorothy Dix noted, it had become "literally true that the average father does not know, by name or sight, the young man who visits his daughter and who takes her out to places of amusement."[57] She was distressed over the widespread use by young people of the car which she called the "devil's wagon."[58] Another writer asked: "Where Is Your Daughter This Afternoon?" "Are you sure that she is not being drawn into the whirling vortex of afternoon 'trots' . . . ?"[59] Polly, Cliff Sterrett's remarkable comic-strip, modern girl from *Polly and Her Pals,* washed dishes under the shower and dried them with an electric fan; and while her mother tried hard to domesticate her, Polly wondered, "Gee Whiz! I wish I knew what made my nose shine!"[60]

Since young women were working side by side with men and recreating more freely and intimately with them, it was inevitable that they behave like men. Older people sometimes carped that growing familiarity meant that romance was dead[61] or that "nowadays brides hardly blush, much less faint."[62] And Beatrice Fairfax asked, "Has Sweet Sixteen Vanished?"[63] But some observers were encouraged to note that as girls' ways approximated men's, the sexes were, at least, more comradely.[64] The modern unmarried woman had become a "Diana, Hunting in the Open."[65] Dorothy Dix reported that "nice girls, good girls, girls in good positions in society—frankly take the initiative in furthering an acquaintance with any man who happens to strike their fancy." The new ideal in feminine figure, dress, and hair styles was all semi-masculine. The "1914 Girl" with her "slim hips and boy-carriage" was a "slim, boylike creature."[66] The "new figure is Amazonian, rather than Miloan. It is boyish rather than womanly. It is strong rather than soft."[67] Her dress styles, meanwhile, de-emphasized both hips and bust while they permitted the large waist. The boyish coiffure began in 1912 when young women began to tuck-under their hair with a ribbon;[68] and by 1913-1914, Newport ladies, actresses like Pauline Frederick, then said to be the prettiest girl in America, and the willowy, popular dancer Irene Castle were wearing short hair.[69] By 1915, the *Ladies Home Journal* featured women with short hair on its covers, and even the pure type of woman who advertised Ivory Soap appeared to be shorn.[70]

The unmarried flapper was a determined pleasure-seeker whom novelist Owen Johnson described collectively as "determined to liberate their lives and claim the same rights of judgment as their brothers."[71] The product of a "feminine revolution startling in the shock of its abruptness," she was living in the city independently of her family. Johnson noted: "She is sure of one life only and that one she passionately desires. She wants to live that life to its fullest. . . . She wants adventure. She wants excitement and mystery. She wants to see, to know, to experience. . . ." She expressed both a "passionate revolt against the commonplace" and a "scorn of conventions." Johnson's heroine in *The Salamander*, Doré Baxter, embodied his views. Her carefree motto is reminiscent of Fitzgerald's flappers of the Twenties: " 'How do I know what I'll do to-morrow?' "[72] Her nightly prayer, the modest " O Lord! give me everything I want!' "[73] Love was her "supreme law of conduct,"[74] and she, like the literary flappers of the Twenties, feared "thirty as a sort of sepulcher, and end of all things!"[75] Johnson believed that all young women in all sections of the country had "a little touch of the Salamander," each alike being impelled by "an impetuous frenzy . . . to sample each new excitement," both the "safe and the dangerous."[76] Girls "seemed determined to have their fling like men," the novelist Gertrude Atherton noted in *Current Opinion*, "and some of the stories [about them] made even my sophisticated hair crackle at the roots. . . ."[77] Beatrice Fairfax deplored the trends, especially the fact that "Making love lightly, boldly and promiscuously seems to be part of our social structure."[78] Young men and women kissed though they did not intend to marry.[79] And kissing was shading into spooning (" 'To Spoon' or 'Not to Spoon' Seems to Be the Burning Question with Modern Young America")[80] and even "petting," which was modish among the collegiate set.[81] In fact, excerpts from the diary of a co-ed written before World War I suggest that experimentation was virtually complete within her peer group. She discussed her "adventures" with other college girls. "We were healthy animals and we were demanding our rights to spring's awakening." As for men, she wrote, "I played square with the men. I always told them I was not out to pin them down to marriage, but that this intimacy was pleasant and I wanted it as much as they did. We indulged in sex talk, birth control. . . . We thought too much about it."[82]

One of the most interesting developments in changing sexual behavior which characterized these years was the blurring of age lines between young and middle-aged women in silhouette, dress, and cosmetics.[83] A fashion commentator warned matrons, "This is the day of the figure. . . . The face alone, no matter how pretty, counts for nothing unless the body is as straight and yielding as every young girl's."[84] With only slight variations, the optimum style for women's dress between 1908 and 1918 was a modified sheath, straight up and down and clinging.[85] How different from the styles of the high-busted, broad-hipped mother of the race of 1904 for whom Ella Wheeler Wilcox, the journalist and poet, advised the use of veils because "the slightest approach to masculinity in woman's attire is always unlovely and disappointing."[86]

The sloughing off of numerous undergarments and loosening of others underscored women's quickening activity and increasingly self-reliant morals. Clinging dresses and their "accompanying lack of undergarments" eliminated, according to the president of the New York Cotton Exchange, "at least twelve yards of finished goods for each adult female inhabitant."[87] Corset makers were forced to make adjustments too and use more supple materials.[88] Nevertheless, their sales declined.[89]

The American woman of 1910, in contrast with her sister of 1900, avidly cultivated beauty of face and form. In fact, the first American woman whose photographs and advertising image we can clearly recognize as belonging to our times lived between 1910 and 1920. "Nowadays," the speaker for a woman's club declared in 1916, "only the very poor or the extremely careless are old or ugly. You can go to a beauty shop and choose the kind of beauty you will have."[90] Beautification included the use of powder, rouge, lipstick, eyelash and eyebrow stain. Advertising was now manipulating such images for face powder as "Mother tried it and decided to keep it for herself,"[91] or "You can have beautiful Eyebrows and Eyelashes. . . . Society women and actresses get them by using Lash-Brow-Line."[92] Nearly every one of the numerous advertisements for cosmetics promised some variation of "How to Become Beautiful, Fascinating, Attractive."[93]

In her dress as well as her use of cosmetics, the American woman gave evidence that she had abandoned passivity. An unprecedented public display of the female figure characterized the period.[94] Limbs now became legs and more of them showed after 1910, although they were less revealing than the promising hosiery advertisements. Rolled down hose first appeared in 1917.[95] Dresses for opera and restaurant were deeply cut in front and back, and not even the rumor that Mrs. John Jacob Astor had suffered a chest cold as a result of wearing deep decolleté[96] deterred their wearers. As for gowns, "Fashion says—Evening gowns must be sleeveless. . . . afternoon gowns are made with semi-transparent yokes and sleeves."[97] Undoubtedly, this vogue for transparent blouses and dresses[98] caused the editor of the *Unpopular Review* to declare: "At no time and place under Christianity, except the most corrupt periods in France. . . . certainly never before in America, has woman's form been so freely displayed in society and on the street."[99]

In addition to following the example of young women in dress and beautification, middle-aged women, especially those from the middle and upper classes, were espousing their permissive manners and morals.[100] Smoking and, to a lesser extent, drinking in public were becoming fashionable for married women of the upper class and were making headway at other class levels.[101] As early as 1910, a prominent clubwoman stated: "It has become a well-established habit for women to drink cocktails. It is thought the smart thing to do."[102] Even before Gertrude Atherton described in the novel *Black Oxen* the phenomenon of the middle-aged women who sought to be attractive to younger men, supposedly typifying the 1920s,[103] it was evident in the play "Years of Discretion." Written by Frederic Hatton and Fanny Locke Hatton, and staged by Belasco, the play was "welcomed cordially both in New York and Chicago" in 1912. It featured a widowed mother forty-eight years of age, who announces, "I intend to look under forty—lots under. I have never attracted men, but I know I can."[104] Again, "I mean to have a wonderful time. To have all sorts and kinds of experience. I intend to love and be loved, to lie and cheat."[105] Dorothy Dix was dismayed over "the interest that women . . . have in what we are pleased to euphoniously term the 'erotic.'" She continued, "I'll bet there are not ten thousand women in the whole United States who couldn't get one hundred in an examination of the life and habits of Evelyn Nesbitt and Harry Thaw. . . ."[106] Married women among the fashionable set held the great parties, at times scandalous ones which made the 1920s seem staid by comparison.[107] They hired the Negro orchestras at Newport and performed and sometimes invented the daring dances.[108] They conscientiously practiced birth control, as did women of other classes.[109] And they initiated divorce proceedings, secure in the knowledge that many of their best friends had done the same thing.

Perhaps the best insights on the mores and morals of this group are to be found in the writings of the contemporary, realistic novelist, Robert Herrick.[110] Herrick derived his heroines from "the higher income groups, the wealthy, upper middle, and professional classes among which he preferred to move."[111] His heroines resemble literary flappers of the 1920s in their repudiation of childbearing. "It takes a year out of a woman's life, of course, no matter how she is situated," they say, or, "Cows do that."[112] Since their lives were seldom more than a meaningless round of social experiences, relieved principally by romantic literature, many of them either contemplated or consented to infidelity. Thus Margaret Pole confesses to her friend, Conny Woodyard, " 'I'd like to lie out on the beach and forget children and servants and husbands, and stop wondering what life is. Yes, I'd like a vacation—in the Windward Islands, with somebody who understood.' 'To wit, a man!' added Conny. 'Yes, a man! But only for the trip.' "[113] They came finally to live for love in a manner that is startlingly reminiscent of some of the famous literary women of the Twenties.[114]

Insights regarding the attitudes of married women from the urban lower middle class can be found in the diary of Ruth Vail Randall, who lived in Chicago from 1911 to the date of her suicide, March 6, 1920.[115] A document of urban sociology, the diary transcends mere personal experience and becomes a commentary on group behavior of the times. Mrs. Randall was reared in a family that owned a grocery store, was graduated from high school in Chicago, and was married at twenty to Norman B. Randall, then twenty-one. She worked after marriage in a department store and later for a brief period as a model. She looked to marriage, especially its romance, as the supreme fulfillment of her life and was bitterly disappointed with her husband. She began to turn to other men whom she met at work or places of recreation, and her husband left her. Fearing that her lover would leave her eventually as well, she killed him and herself.

The diary focuses on those conditions which made the revolution in morals a reality. The young couple lived anonymously in a highly mobile neighborhood where their morals were of their own making. Mrs. Randall did not want children; she aborted their only child.[116] She was also averse to the reserved "womanly" role, which her husband insisted that she assume.[117] She complained, "Why cannot a woman do all man does?"[118] She wished that men and women were more alike in their social roles.[119] She repudiated involvement in her home, resolved to exploit equally every privilege which her husband assumed, drank, flirted, and lived promiscuously. Telephones and cars made her extramarital liaisons possible. Even before her divorce, she found another companion; flouting convention, she wrote, "He and I have entered a marriage pact according to our own ideas."[120] Throughout her diary she entertained enormous, almost magical, expectations of love. She complained that her lovers no more than her husband provided what she craved—tenderness and companionship. Disillusionment with one of them caused her to cry out, "I am miserable. I have the utmost contempt for myself. But the lake is near and soon it will be warm. Oh, God to rest in your arms. To rest—and to have peace."[121]

That America was experiencing a major upheaval in morals during the Progressive era is nowhere better ascertained than in the comprehensive efforts by civic officials and censorial citizens to control them. Disapproval extended not only to such well-known staples as alcohol, divorce, and prostitution, but also to dancing, woman's dress, cabarets, theaters and movies, and birth control. "Mrs. Warren's Profession" was withdrawn from the New York stage in 1905 after a one night performance, the manager of the theater later being charged with offending public decency.[122] When a grand jury in New York condemned the "turkey trot and kindred dances" as "indecent," the judge who accepted the presentment noted that "Rome's downfall was due to the degenerate nature of its dancers, and I only hope that we will not suffer the same result."[123] Public dancing was henceforth to be licensed. Mayor John Fitzgerald personally assisted the morals campaign in Boston by ordering the removal from a store of an objectionable picture which portrayed a "show-girl" with her legs crossed.[124] Meanwhile, the "X Ray Skirt" was outlawed in Portland, Oregon, and Los Angeles;[125] and the police chief of Louisville, Kentucky, ordered the arrest of a number of women appearing on the streets with slit skirts.[126] Witnessing to a general fear that the spreading knowledge of contraception might bring on sexual license, the federal and several state governments enacted sumptuary legislation.[127] And in two celebrated incidents, the offenders, Van K. Allison (1916) in Boston and Margaret Sanger (1917) in New York, were prosecuted and sent to jail.[128]

Public officials were apprehensive about the sweeping influence of the movies on the masses, "at once their book, their drama, their art. To some it has become society, school, and even church."[129] They proceeded to set up boards of censorship with powers to review and condemn movies in four states: Pennsylvania (1911), Ohio (1913), Maryland (1916), and Kansas (1917), and in numerous cities beginning with Chicago in 1907.[130] The Pennsylvania board, for example, prohibited pictures which displayed nudity, prolonged passion, women drinking and smoking, and infidelity. It protected Pennsylvanians from such films produced between 1915 and 1918 as "What Every Girl Should Know," "A Factory Magdalene," and "Damaged Goodness."[131]

Such determination proved unavailing, however, even as the regulatory strictures were being applied. According to one critic the "sex drama" using "plain, blunt language" had become "a commonplace" of the theater after 1910 and gave the "tender passion rather the worst for it in recent years."[132] Vice films packed them in every night, especially after the smashing success of "Traffic in Souls," which reportedly grossed $450,000.[133] In Boston the anti-vice campaign itself languished because there was no means of controlling "the kitchenette-apartment section." "In these apartment houses, there are hundreds of women who live as they please and who entertain as they will."[134] Mayor Fitzgerald's "show-girl," evicted from her saucy perch, gained more notoriety when she appeared in a Boston newspaper the following day.[135] Even Anthony Comstock, that indefatigable guardian of public morals, had probably come to look a bit like a comic character living beyond his times.[136]

When Mrs. Sanger was arrested for propagating birth control information in 1917, she confidently stated, "I have nothing to fear ... Regardless of the outcome I shall continue my work, supported by thousands of men and women throughout the country."[137] Her assurance was well founded. Three years earlier her supporters had founded a National Birth Control League; and in 1919, this organization opened its first public clinic.[138] But most encouraging for Mrs. Sanger was the impressive testimony that many Americans were now practicing or interested in birth control.[139] When Paul B. Blanchard, pastor of the Maverick Congregational Church in East

Boston, protested the arrest of Van K. Allison, he charged, "If the truth were made public and the laws which prevent the spreading of even oral information about birth control were strictly enforced how very few of the married society leaders, judges, doctors, ministers, and businessmen would be outside the prison dock!"[140]

The foregoing demonstrates that a major shift in American manners and morals occurred in the Progressive era, especially after 1910. Changes at this time, though developing out of still earlier conditions, represented such visible departures from the past and were so commonly practiced as to warrant calling them revolutionary. Too often scholars have emphasized the Twenties as the period of significant transition and World War I as a major cause of the phenomenon. Americans of the 1920s, fresh from the innovative wartime atmosphere, undoubtedly quickened and deepened the revolution. Women from smaller cities and towns contested what was familiar terrain to an already seasoned cadre of urban women and a formidable group of defectors. Both in their rhetoric and their practices, apparent even before the war, the earlier group had provided the shibboleths for the 1920s; they first asked, "What are Patterns for?" The revolution in manners and morals was, of course, but an integral part of numerous, contemporary, political and social movements to free the individual by reordering society. Obviously, the Progressive era, more than the 1920s, represents the substantial beginnings of contemporary American civilization.

The revolution in manners and morals, particularly as it affected women, took the twofold form of more permissive sexuality and diminished feminity. Women from the upper classes participated earlier, as is evidenced by their introductory exhibition of fashions, hair styles, dances, cosmetics, smoking, and drinking. Realistic novels concerned with marriage suggest that they entertained ideas of promiscuity and even infidelity before women of the lower classes. Yet the cardinal condition of change was not sophistication but urban living and the freedom it conferred. As technology and economic progress narrowed the gap between the classes, middle-class women and even those below were free to do many of the same things almost at the same time. Above all, the revolution in manners and morals after 1910 demonstrates that sexual freedom and the twentieth-century American city go together.

NOTES

1. Henry F. May, "Shifting Perspectives on the 1920's," *Mississippi Valley Historical Review,* XLIII (Dec. 1956), 405-27.
2. Richard Hofstadter, *The Age of Reform: From Bryan to F. D. R.* (New York, 1955), 282-301.
3. May, "Shifting Perspectives on the 1920's," 426. See also Henry F. May, "The Rebellion of the Intellectuals, 1912-1917," *American Quarterly,* VIII (Summer 1956), 115, wherein May describes 1912-1917 as a "pre-revolutionary or early revolutionary period."
4. May, "Shifting Perspectives on the 1920's," 427.
5. Henry F. May, *The End of American Innocence: A Study of the First Years of Our Own Time, 1912-1917* (New York, 1959).
6. Arthur S. Link, "What Happened to the Progressive Movement in the 1920's?" *American Historical Review,* LXIV (July 1959), 833-51.
7. J. Joseph Huthmacher, "Urban Liberalism and the Age of Reform," *Mississippi Valley Historical Review,* XLIX (Sept. 1962), 231-41. Other political and economic historians concur on a developmental interpretation. Gerald D. Nash, *State Government and Economic Development: A History of Administrative Policies in California, 1849-1933* (Berkeley, 1964), 250, 291, 326, views the period 1900-1933 as a unit because it was characterized by notable coordination and centralization of authority by agencies of state government in California. Donald C. Swain, *Federal Conservation Policy, 1921-1933* (Berkeley, 1963), 6, sees the national conservation program making continuous advances through the 1920s based upon beginnings in the Progressive period.
8. "Sex O'clock in America," *Current Opinion,* LV (Aug. 1913), 113-14. The anonymous author borrowed the phrase from William M. Reedy, editor of the St. Louis *Mirror.*
9. Agnes Repplier, "The Repeal of Reticence," *Atlantic Monthly,* CXIII (March 1914), 297-304, objected to the "obsession of sex which has set us all a-babbling about matters once excluded from the amenities of conversation" (p. 298). Articles on birth control, prostitution, divorce, and sexual morals between 1910 and 1914 were cumulatively more numerous per thousand among articles indexed in the *Reader's Guide to Periodical Literature* than for either 1919 to 1924 or 1925 to 1928. Hornell Hart, "Changing Social Attitudes and Interests," *Recent Social Trends in the United States: Report of the President's Research Committee on Social Trends* (2 vols., New York, 1933), I, 414.
10. H. W. Boynton, "Ideas, Sex, and the Novel," *Dial,* LX (April 13, 1916), 361. In Robert W. Chambers, *The Restless Sex* (New York, 1918), 143, the heroine remarks, "What was all wrong in our Victorian mothers' days is all right now."

11. Arthur Pollock, "Are We Immoral?" *Forum,* LI (Jan. 1914), 52. Pollock remarks that "in our literature and in our life to-day sex is paramount."

12. "Will Puritanism Return?" *Independent,* 77 (March 23, 1914), 397.

13. Mark Sullivan, *Our Times: The War Begins* (New York, 1932), 165-93, states in colorful and impressionistic terms that significant changes in moral attitudes had taken place in the Progressive era. He attributes much of this to the influence of Freud, Shaw, and Omar Khayyám. Preston William Slosson, *The Great Crusade and After: 1914-1928* (New York, 1930), describes the period 1914-1928 as a unit, but his material dealing with morals centers on the 1920s. For example, there are only five footnotes based on materials written between 1914 and 1919 in his chapter, "The American Woman Wins Equality," 130-61. Samuel Eliot Morison makes brief mention of a "revolution in sexual morals" before 1920 in *The Oxford History of the American People* (New York, 1965), 906-08.

14. Frederick Lewis Allen, *Only Yesterday: An Informal History of the Nineteen-Twenties* (New York, 1931), 88-122; William E. Leuchtenburg, *The Perils of Prosperity: 1914-32* (Chicago, 1958), 158-77.

15. May, *The End of American Innocence,* 334-47, is lightly documented; there are only twelve footnotes to support his discussion of these and similar developments.

16. *Ibid.,* 347. May's view of women's changing attitudes is contradicted by Margaret Deland: "Of course there were women a generation ago, as in all generations, who asserted themselves; but they were practically 'sports.' Now, the simple, honest woman ... the good wife, the good mother—is evolving ideals which are changing her life, and the lives of those people about her." Margaret Deland, "The Change in the Feminine Ideal," *Atlantic Monthly,* CV (March 1910), 291.

17. George E. Mowry, *The Urban Nation: 1920-1960* (New York, 1965), 250.

18. *Ibid.,* 23.

19. *Ibid.*

20. *Ibid.,* 24.

21. "By 1930 more than ten million women held jobs. Nothing did more to emancipate them." Leuchtenburg, *Perils of Prosperity,* 160. See also Allen, *Only Yesterday,* 95-98. For estimates of the effects of World War I on morals, see Leuchtenburg, *Perils of Prosperity,* 172-73; Allen, *Only Yesterday,* 94; Mowry, *Urban Nation,* 24.

22. Population in urban territory comprised only about 28 percent of the total American population in 1880; but by 1920, approximately 52 percent were living there. Department of Commerce, Bureau of the Census, *Historical Statistics of the United States, Colonial Times to 1957* (Washington, 1960), 14.

23. Scott Nearing and Nellie M. S. Nearing, *Woman and Social Progress*

(New York, 1912), 137-41. The Nearings wrote: "The freedom which American Women have gained through recent social changes and the significance of their consequent choice, constitutes one of the profoundest and at the same time one of the most inscrutable problems in American life" (p. 138). William I. Thomas, *The Unadjusted Girl: With Cases and Standpoint for Behavior Analysis* (Boston, 1923), 86. Ernest R. Mowrer, *Family Disorganization* (Chicago, 1927), 6-8. Mowrer attributes "Family Disorganization" to the "conditions of city life" which resulted in a "rebellion against the old ideals of family life. . . ."

24. George Elliott Howard, "Social Control and the Functions of the Family," Howard J. Rogers, ed. *Congress of Arts and Sciences: Universal Exposition, St. Louis, 1904* (8 vols., Boston, 1906), VII, 702.

25. Louise Collier Willcox, "Our Supervised Morals," *North American Review*, CXCVIII (Nov. 1913), 708, observes: "The time is past when parents supervised the morals of their children. . . ."

26. There was a surprisingly large number of cars sold and used in America between 1910 and 1920. Approximately 40 percent as many cars were produced each year between 1915 and 1917 as were manufactured between 1925 and 1927. *Facts and Figures of the Automobile Industry* (New York, 1929), 6, 22. There were approximately 7,500,000 cars registered in 1919. "Existing Surfaced Mileage Total" on a scale of 1,000 miles was 204 in 1910, 332 in 1918, 521 in 1925, and 694 in 1930. *Historical Statistics of the United States,* 458. Newspapers reported the impact of the automobile on dating and elopements. For a moralistic reaction to the phenomenon, see Dorothy Dix, Boston *American,* Sept. 5, 1912. For an enthusiast of "mobile privacy" in this period, see F. Scott Fitzgerald, "Echoes of the Jazz Age," *Scribner's Magazine,* XC (Nov. 1931), 460. Fitzgerald wrote: "As far back as 1915 the unchaperoned young people of the smaller cities had discovered the mobile privacy of that automobile given to young Bill at sixteen to make him 'self-reliant.' "

27. Dorothy Dix, "A Modern Diana," Boston *American,* April 7, 1910.

28. Beatrice Fairfax, *ibid.,* May 28, 1908; Dorothy Dix, *ibid.,* Sept. 9, 1912.

29. *Ibid.,* Aug. 21, 1913.

30. Marion Harland, "The Passing of the Home Daughter," *Independent,* LXXI (July 13, 1911), 90.

31. Sophonisba P. Breckinridge, *Women in the Twentieth Century: A Study of Their Political, Social and Economic Activities* (New York, 1933), 112. Overall percentages of women gainfully employed rose from 19 percent of the total work force in 1890 to 20.6 percent in 1900, 24.3 percent in 1910, 24 percent in 1920, and 25.3 percent in 1930. *Ibid.,* 108.

32. While the number of women who worked as domestics declined after

1910, large numbers of women were employed for the first time as clerks and stenographers. In fact, more women were employed in both these occupations between 1910 and 1920 than between 1920 and 1930. *Ibid.*, 129, 177.

33. Martha Bensley Bruere and Robert W. Bruere, *Increasing Home Efficiency* (New York, 1914), 236–41.

34.

Item	Total Amount Expended in Millions of Dollars				
	1909	1914	1919	1923	1929
(a) canned fruits and vegetables	162	254	575	625	930
(b) cleaning and polishing preparations	6	9	27	35	46
(c) electricity in household operation	83	132	265	389	615.5
(d) mechanical appliances (refrigerators, sewing machines, washers, cooking)	152	175	419	535	804.1
Percentage of expenditures on household equipment to total expenditures	9.9%	9.2%	10.3%	11.6%	13.2%

(a-b) is found in William H. Lough, *High-Level Consumption: Its Behavior; Its Consequences* (New York, 1935), 236, 241. These figures are tabulated in millions of dollars for 1935. Items (c-d) and the percentage of expenditure on household equipment to total expenditures were taken from James Dewhurst, *America's Needs and Resources: A New Survey* (New York, 1955), 702, 704, 180.

35. Realistic novelists note the leisure of the middle-class women. David Graham Phillips, *The Hungry Heart* (New York, 1909) and *Old Wives for New* (New York, 1908); Robert Herrick, *Together* (New York, 1908), especially 515–17.

36. For example, see *Cosmopolitan*, XXXV (May-Oct. 1903); *Ladies Home Journal*, XXI (Dec. 1903-May 1904). A notable exception showing a woman riding a bicycle may be found in *ibid.* (April 1904), 39.

37. *Ladies Home Journal*, XXXIV (May 1917), for example, shows a woman entertaining stylish women friends (34, 89, 92), driving the car or on an automobile trip (36–37, 74), economizing on time spent in housework (42), the object of "outdoor girl" ads (78), beautifying at a social affair or appearing very chic (102, 106). Perhaps the best illustration for woman's activity in advertisements was employed in *Ladies Home Journal* by Williams Talc Powder. It read, "After the game, the ride, the swim, the brisk walk, or a day at the sea-shore, turn for comfort to Williams Talc Powder." *Ibid.*, XXXIV (July 1917), 74.

38. *Collier's*, 56 (Nov. 27, 1915), 4.

39. *Cosmopolitan,* LIX (June 1915), advertising section, 50.
40. *Collier's,* 56 (Sept. 25, 1915), 22.
41. *Ibid.* (Nov. 27, 1915), 25.
42. *Ladies Home Journal,* XXXV (April 1918), 58.
43. *Ibid.,* 57.
44. *Ibid.,* XXXIII (Jan. 1916), 46-47. Women drove their friends and families about in their cars. *Ibid.,* XXXII (July 1915), 34-35; (Aug. 1915), 38-39; (Oct. 1915), 86; XXXIII (Nov. 1916), 71.
45. Susanne Wilcox, "The Unrest of Modern Women," *Independent,* LXVII (July 8, 1909), 63.
46. Nell Brinkley, a nationally syndicated cartoonist and commentator on women's activities, asked this question of one of her young women. Boston *American,* July 14, 1913.
47. Nell Brinkley coined the phrase. *Ibid.,* Nov. 14, 1916.
48. *Ibid.,* May 4, 1915. See also *Ladies Home Journal,* XXXII (July 1915), which depicts a young woman driving a speedboat while her boyfriend sits next to her.
49. Boston *American,* Oct. 1, 1916.
50. *Collier's,* 56 (March 4, 1916), 38.
51. Emma B. Kaufman, "The Education of a Debutante," *Cosmopolitan,* XXXV (Sept. 1903), 499-508.
52. *Cosmopolitan,* XXXIX (Oct. 1905).
53. "Girls, Don't Allow Men to be Familiar," Boston *American,* June 17, 1904; *ibid.,* July 15, 1905.
54. *Wellesley College News,* Feb. 20, 1902. Wellesley relented on "men dances" in 1913.
55. Deland, "The Change in the Feminine Ideal," 291.
56. *Ibid.,* 289.
57. Boston *American,* May 6, 1910.
58. *Ibid.,* Sept. 5, 1912.
59. Ethel Watts Mumford, "Where Is Your Daughter This Afternoon?" *Harper's Weekly,* LVIII (Jan. 17, 1914), 28.
60. Boston *American,* Sept. 5, 1916; *ibid.,* Jan. 4, 1914.
61. Alice Duer Miller. "The New Dances and the Younger Generation," *Harper's Bazaar,* XLVI (May 1912), 250.
62. Deland, "Change in the Feminine Ideal," 293.
63. Boston *American,* March 24, 1916. In a letter to the editor of the New York *Times,* one critic of the "women of New York" complained that they seemed to be part of a "new race" or even a "super-sex." He waxed poetic: "Sweet seventeen is rouge-pot mad, And hobbles to her tasks blase, . . . Where are the girls of yesterday?" New York *Times,* July 20, 1914.
64. Miller, "New Dances and the Younger Generation," 250. According to Helen Rowland, the woman was "no longer Man's plaything, but his

playmate. . . ." Helen Rowland, "The Emancipation of 'the Rib,' *Delineator*, LXXVII (March 1911), 233.

65. Boston *American*, April 7, 1910.
66. *Ibid.*, March 20, 1914.
67. *Ibid.*, June 11, 1916.
68. *Ibid.*, Nov. 27, Dec. 8, 1912.
69. On Newport and Boston society women see *ibid.*, July 6, 27, Aug. 10, 24, 1913. Pauline Frederick's picture may be found in *ibid.*, Aug. 2, 1913. For Irene Castle, see Mr. and Mrs. Vernon Castle, *Modern Dancing* (New York, 1914), 98, 105.
70. *Ladies Home Journal*, XXXII (July and Sept. 1915); *ibid.* (Nov. 1915), 8.
71. Owen Johnson, *The Salamander* (Indianapolis, 1914), Foreword, n.p.
72. *Ibid.*, 9.
73. *Ibid.*, 129.
74. *Ibid.*, 66.
75. *Ibid.*, 61.
76. *Ibid.*, Foreword, n.p. Chamber's young heroine Stephanie Cleland in *The Restless Sex*, 191, practiced trial marriage in order to learn by experience. See also Phillips, *Hungry Heart*, 166-80; Terry Ramsaye, *A Million And One Nights: A History of the Motion Picture* (2 vols., New York, 1926), II, 702-04.
77. "Mrs. Atherton Tells of Her 'Perch of the Devil,' " *Current Opinion*, LVII (Nov. 1914), 349.
78. Boston *American*, Feb. 8, 1917.
79. The "kiss of friendship" criticized by Fairfax had become a major issue of her mail by 1913. See, for example, *ibid.*, July 5, 1913. Girls shocked her with inquiries as to whether it was permissible to "soul kiss' on a first date. *Ibid.*, Feb. 13, 1914. An engaged girl asked whether it would be all right to kiss men other than her fiance. *Ibid.*, May 2, 1916.
80. *Ibid.*, Feb. 8, 1917.
81. Fitzgerald, "Echoes of the Jazz Age," 460.
82. Thomas, *Unadjusted Girl*, 95.
83. "Today in the world of fashion, all women are young, and they grow more so all the time." Doeuilet, "When All The World Looks Young," *Delineator*, LXXXIII (Aug. 1913), 20. Advertisements used flattery or played up the value of youth for women and warned that they might age unless certain products were used. *Cosmopolitan*, LIX (Nov. 1915), 112; *ibid.* (July 1915), 81; *Ladies Home Journal*, XXXII (Nov. 1915), 65; *Cosmopolitan*, LIX (Oct. 1915), 57.
84. Eleanor Chalmers, "Facts and Figures," *Delineator*, LXXXIV (April 1914), 38.
85. Boston *American*, March 20, 1910; *Delineator*, LXXXIX (Oct. 1916), 66.

86. Boston *American,* March 28, 1904.
87. New York *Tribune,* April 4, 1912; Eleanor Chalmers, "You and Your Sewing," *Delineator,* LXXXIII (Aug. 1913), 33.
88. Eleanor Chalmers, *Delineator,* LXXXIV (April 1914), 38. The sense of relief these changes brought is amusingly described in Dorothy A. Plum, comp., *The Magnificent Enterprise: A Chronicle of Vassar College* (Poughkeepsie, 1961), 43–44.
89. Percival White, "Figuring Us Out," *North American Review,* CCXXVII (Jan. 1929), 69.
90. Boston *American,* Dec. 10, 1916.
91. *Delineator,* LXXXV (July 1914), 55.
92. Boston *American,* Sept. 3, 1916.
93. *Cosmopolitan,* LIX (July 1915).
94. An editorial declared that women's dresses in 1913 had approached "the danger line of indecency about as closely as they could." New York *Times,* July 6, 1914.
95. *Ladies Home Journal,* XXXIV (Oct. 1917), 98.
96. Boston *American,* June 8, 1907. "The conventions of evening dress have changed radically in the last four or five years. Not so very long ago a high-necked gown was considered *au fait* for all evening functions except formal dinners and the opera. Nowadays, well-dressed women wear decolleté dresses even for home dinners, and semi-decolleté gowns for restaurants and theaters." *Delineator,* LXXV (Jan. 1910), 60.
97. *Cosmopolitan,* LIX (July 1915).
98. *Ladies Home Journal,* XXXII (Oct. 1915), 108; *ibid.,* XXXIII (Oct. 1916), 82; *ibid.,* XXXIII (Nov. 1916), 78–79; *ibid.,* XXXIV (Jan. 1917), 53.
99. "The Cult of St. Vitus," *Unpopular Review,* III (Jan.-March 1915), 94.
100. Boston *American,* July 6, 1912. Dix noted "flirtatious" middle-aged women were "aping the airs and graces of the debutante" and "trying to act kittenish" with men.
101. *Ibid.,* Dec. 6, 10, 1912. Anita Stewart, a movie star who wrote "Talks to Girls," though personally opposed to smoking, admitted that "lots of my friends smoke" and "they are nice girls too." *Ibid.,* Dec. 14, 1915. In 1916, the Boston *American* titled a column on a page devoted to women's interests "To Smoke or Not to Smoke." *Ibid.,* April 12, 1916. The *Harvard Lampoon,* LXXI (June 20, 1916), 376, spoofed women smoking: it carried a heading "Roman Society Women Agree to Give Up Smoking" and a commentary below, "Oh, Nero, how times have changed!"
102. Boston *American,* March 7, 1910.
103. Leuchtenburg, *Perils of Prosperity,* 174–75.

104. " 'Years of Discretion'—A Play of Cupid at Fifty," *Current Opinion*, LIV (Feb. 1913), 116.
105. *Ibid.*, 117.
106. Boston *American*, April 10, 1908. Evelyn Nesbitt, the wife of Harry Thaw, was romantically involved with architect Stanford White, whom Thaw shot to death.
107. *Ibid.*, Aug. 25, Sept. 1, 1912.
108. Most of the dances which became very popular after 1910, such as the Turkey Trot, the Bunny Hug, and the Grizzly Bear, afforded a maximum of motion in a minimum of space. The Chicken Flip was invented by a Boston society woman. *Ibid.*, Nov. 11, 1912. See also "New Reflections on The Dancing Mania," *Current Opinion*, LV (Oct. 1913), 262.
109. Louis I. Dublin, "Birth Control," *Social Hygiene*, VI (Jan. 1920), 6.
110. Alfred Kazin, "Three Pioneer Realists," *Saturday Review of Literature*, XX (July 8, 1939), 15. Herrick's biographer, Blake Nevius, declares, "It can be argued that Herrick is the most comprehensive and reliable social historian in American fiction to appear in the interregnum between Howells and the writers of the Twenties. . . ." Blake Nevius, *Robert Herrick: The Development of a Novelist* (Berkeley, 1962), Preface.
111. Nevius, *Robert Herrick*, 177.
112. Herrick, *Together*, 91, 392.
113. *Ibid.*, 263, 250-51, 320-24.
114. Herrick describes the temperament of the modern woman as one of "mistress rather than the wife. . . . 'I shall be a person with a soul of my own. To have me man must win me not once, but daily.' " *Ibid.*, 516. The last sentence above nearly duplicates Rosalind's statement to her beau in *This Side of Paradise*, "I have to be won all over again every time you see me." F. Scott Fitzgerald, *This Side of Paradise* (New York, 1920), 194.
115. Chicago *Herald and Examiner*, March 10-17, 1920.
116. *Ibid.*, March 10, 1920.
117. *Ibid.*, March 11, 1920.
118. *Ibid.*
119. *Ibid.*, March 11, 12, 1920.
120. *Ibid.*, March 13, 14, 1920.
121. *Ibid.*, March 15, 1920.
122. New York *Tribune*, Nov. 1, 1905.
123. New York *Times*, May 28, 1913.
124. *Ibid.*, Dec. 20, 1912.
125. *Ibid.*, Aug. 20, 23, 1913.
126. *Ibid.*, June 29, 1913.
127. Carol Flora Brooks, "The Early History of the Anti-Contraceptive Laws in Massachusetts and Connecticut," *American Quarterly*, XVIII

(Spring 1966), 3-23; George E. Worthington, "Statutory Restrictions on Birth Control," *Journal of Social Hygiene,* IX (Nov. 1923), 458-65.

128. Boston *American,* July 14, 21, 1916; New York *Times,* Feb. 6, 1917.

129. *Report of the Pennsylvania Board of Censors,* June 1, 1915 to Dec. 1, 1915 (Harrisburg, 1916), 6.

130. Ellis Paxson Oberholtzer, *The Morals of the Movie* (Philadelphia, 1922), 115-23.

131. *Report of the Pennsylvania State Board of Censors,* 1915, pp. 14-15; *ibid.,* 1916, pp. 24-25; *ibid.,* 1917, pp. 8-9.

132. Boston *American,* Aug. 10, 1913.

133. Ramsaye, *A Million and One Nights,* II, 617.

134. Boston *American,* July 7, 1917.

135. *Ibid.,* Dec. 20, 1912.

136. Heywood Broun, *Anthony Comstock: Roundsman of the Lord* (New York, 1927); Mary Alden Hopkins, "Birth Control and Public Morals: An Interview with Anthony Comstock," *Harper's Weekly,* LX (May 22, 1915), 489-90.

137. Boston *American,* Jan. 4, 1917.

138. Norman E. Himes, "Birth Control in Historical and Clinical Perspective," *Annals of the American Academy of Political and Social Sciences,* 160 (March 1932), 53.

139. Dublin, "Birth Control," 6.

140. Boston *American,* July 16, 1916. According to International News Service, "Mrs. Rose Pastor Stokes was literally mobbed by an eager crowd in Carnegie Hall when she offered, in defiance of the police, to distribute printed slips bearing a formula for birth control." *Ibid.,* May 6, 1916.

Article 2

The Campaign for Women's Rights in the 1920's

Clarke A. Chambers

The children of the nation were always the special concern of humanitarian reformers in the 1920's. Especially were the children of the poor the object of programs aimed at liberation from premature and excessive labor, at the enlargement of opportunity through educational, recreational, and welfare measures. If efforts had often been thwarted, the results of reform activity were nevertheless substantial. If the decade had proved uncongenial to statutory regulation, at least the advances in other areas gave cause for authentic satisfaction.

The hope that another disadvantaged group in the population—working women—could win the protection of the state against unreasonable exploitation proved less valid. Two lines of ameliorative action had taken form during the Progressive Era. One pointed toward the organization of women workers into labor unions in order that they might gain, through union, the strength to bargain collectively with employers. It was for this end that the Women's Trade Union League, with the nominal and rhetorical support of the AFL, strove with zeal if not with very large success. The second path led toward legislation, particularly at the state level of government, which would set standards of maximum hours, minimum wages, and decent conditions for women employees. Here notable advances had been won during the culminating years of the Progressive Era just before the nation's entrance into the Great War.

The regulation of hours and conditions had come first, the Supreme Court in the classic *Muller v. Oregon* case in 1908 upholding such legislation as an entirely reasonable exercise of the state's police power to promote the health, morality, and welfare of the

From *Seedtime of Reform: American Social Service and Social Action 1918-1933* (Minneapolis: University of Minnesota Press, 1963), 61–83. Copyright © 1963, University of Minnesota. Reprinted by permission.

community. Minimum-wage legislation came a bit later, but in the five years before America went to war, eleven states invoked the power to set a floor under wages earned by women. The argument that women, as mothers of the race, required the special protection of the community acting through government presumably applied as logically to the one area, minimum wages, as to the other, maximum hours. The Supreme Court did not see the parallel quite as clearly as the reformers did, but in 1917—as noted earlier—it had sustained by a tie vote an affirmative ruling of the Oregon Supreme Court. Following this *Stettler v. O'Hara* decision, three other states, Puerto Rico, and the federal Congress acting for the District of Columbia had established special commissions with the power to set minimum-wage levels in accordance with subjective criteria of health and morality.

Wartime demands had brought tens of thousands of women into the labor force, where they enjoyed relatively high wages and augmented opportunity, if never equal pay for equal work with men, or equal opportunity to enter certain crafts and trades, restricted to men as often by custom and prejudice as by physical requirements. The Woman in Industry Service had proved competent, however, in winning for women special positions of economic influence not previously enjoyed. Women continued, in the postwar decade, to join the labor force, often to supplement the husband's income when it was insufficient to support the family at a decent level, until by 1929 over ten million women were gainfully employed where but eight million so labored at the end of the war. The ratio of working women to all women of working age in the nation remained roughly constant—approximately one to five.

With a total labor force pushing fifty million by the end of the decade, women constituted approximately one-fifth of all those employed. Millions of girls and married women worked in the service trades, of course, as waitresses or hotel domestics or telephone operators, as stenographers and as retail clerks; millions more were employed in textile mills, in the garment trades, and on the assembly lines of light industries, many of them, like the household appliance industries, new in the 1920's. The proportion of women working in a particular area of the economy changed but slightly within the decade: about a third of all working women were employed in domestic or personal service, a quarter in manufacturing, a fifth in agriculture, and a tenth in trade and transportation.

Motives for entering the labor force remained much as they had been before the war—to earn at least partial financial independence, to escape from household drudgery, to save up a little extra money before marriage, to find companionship and a more satisfying career than housewifery or spinsterhood offered, and above all necessity. Careful studies of the female working force made during the 1920's indicated that most women sought gainful employment outside the home because they had no alternative—they had to find a job or be thrown onto charity. Many working women were widows or victims of desertion; others were wives of chronically sick or unemployed husbands, or were married to men who could not command wages sufficiently high to supply the family's basic needs. The old notion that women worked for "pin money" was dispelled by studies that proved that most working women earned "the whole or a necessary part of the family income." In any case there was no wage differential between those who worked for the "extras" of life and those who drudged from sheer necessity. A very substantial number were not only wives but mothers of young children as well, driven out of the home into the labor market by the pressures of existence. One analysis, made in mid-decade at the very peak of prosperity, concluded that "the mother works because she has to work, and unless some other method of raising the family income is devised she is in industry to stay."[1] Another study of 728 working mothers in Philadelphia, made by Gwendolyn S. Hughes under the auspices of the Seybert Institution and the graduate department of Bryn Mawr College, indicated that 89 per cent worked from economic necessity—some to meet emergencies, sickness, or unemployment; more to meet regular household expenses.[2]

Although the Women's Trade Union League continued to seek better conditions for women workers through unionization and stepped up these organizational efforts toward the end of the decade, many reformers drew the lesson from long and often humiliating experience that only the rigid enforcement of regulative legislation could be counted on to alleviate the grievances which sprang from the excessive exploitation of the labor of women. Women workers for the most part were lacking in skill; they had few resources to fall back upon other than their availability for cheap labor; the organization of women into trade unions was "a slow and arduous process requiring long periods of time."[3] Frances Perkins added the salient observation, derived from hard factual analysis of female labor in the state of New York, that nearly three-quarters of all women factory workers were employed in plants with fewer than fifty workers; in these small plants the unionization of employees, never easy, was particularly difficult; and management in these small factories could rarely afford the luxury of enlightened or "scientific" policies.[4]

Some studies stressed the objective causes of exploitation and proposed specific remedies; other surveys stressed the subjective costs paid by working women and ultimately by society itself. Those who strained, day after day, month after month, on the assembly line or in sweated industries, before the loom or the sewing machine, could best testify as to what the pace of machine labor involved. Asked by the instructor of a course in remedial English, established by the Women's Trade Union League for immigrant working girls, to write compositions on their factory experience, the class responded with essays later compiled and edited for publication. Complaining of constant fatigue and depression, the girls noted that even the machines on which they toiled were rested and oiled; why, then, could not the same concern be shown for the health and vigor of the workers, whose energies were sapped often beyond repair. From experience they had learned the costs in health and character that excessive hours of labor under conditions of the stretchout and speedup exacted. From their evening classes, apparently, they had picked up a bit of basic economics as well. Maximum-hour legislation, they argued, would spread employment; minimum-wage legislation would increase purchasing power; enlarged leisure and purchasing power would promote sound prosperity throughout the entire economy. Rarely was the pragmatic argument for maximum hours, minimum wages, and full employment put more cogently in that decade.[5]

Confident that their cause was just and that their arguments were irrefutable, encouraged by the sense of organic community which the war had fostered, the reformers set out to consolidate their gains and advance into new frontiers of social action. The immediate goals were the achievement for women workers of an eight-hour day and a forty-eight-hour week, one day of rest in seven, and a prohibition on night work in every state in the Union. Massachusetts led the way with the passage of a forty-eight-hour bill in April 1919. Exemptions there were—of chambermaids, stenographers, and domestic servants—but the Consumers' League and the Women's Trade Union League were generally pleased. Their pleasure was short-lived. The pattern in New York soon proved different.

In New York, the Women's Joint Legislative Conference was able to win a nine-hour day and a fifty-four-hour week for a limited number of women workers in 1919, but subsequent attempts to broaden the coverage and to reduce the maxima were blocked by the Republican-dominated State Assembly. Probably in no other state was there quite such a vigorous proponent of protective labor legislation as Governor Alfred E. Smith, but neither his endorsement nor favorable action by the State Senate was ever sufficient to override the negative of the lower house. Up to Albany from New York City the women went to lobby, only to be rebuffed by arguments of the conservative speaker of the Assembly, Thaddeus Sweet, and others that labor legislation would increase costs and drive industry from the state. Florence Kelley might argue that the "orderly processes of the law" were to be preferred to "clumsy, costly, painful" strikes, but few seemed to fear that the alternative of direct action would be resorted to. "More leisure and more money women must have unless the public health and morals are to suffer irreparably," she protested; but the times seemed prosperous, and to the comfortable and complacent an enlargement of government power appeared not only inappropriate, but downright wicked.[6] Moreover, was not the liberty of employer and employee to bargain and make contracts a sacred freedom? Far from winning new gains, the reform groups had to throw all their resources into a struggle to block repeal of the prohibition on night work in some industries. Distraught and giddy from months of frustrating toil, the WTUL solemnly recorded in the minutes of the executive board, toward the end of the session in 1921, a bit of doggerel which labeled their foes as "tools" and "fools," as "bad" and "mad":

> They're overfed,
> And anti-red,
> And rave around like loons.
> They wave the flag,
> And chew the rag,
> But all of them are prunes,
> Prunes, prunes!
> Yes, all of them are prunes![7]

In 1924, Molly Dewson, formerly of the Consumers' League but now civic secretary of the Women's City Club of New York (whose vice president was Eleanor Roosevelt), carried through a survey of women workers to test their attitudes toward maximum-hour regulations. She reported her findings to bureaus of the state government and to the legislature—a substantial majority of working women desired a forty-eight-hour week, even if a cut in weekly income were involved. A bill put forward in 1926 was set aside and a study of the issue proposed in its place. When the special Industrial Survey Commission reported back, its recommendations included not only a forty-eight-hour week, but minimum wages and equal pay for equal work as well. With these recommendations before it, the state legislature reduced the maximum from fifty-four hours to fifty-one and adjourned.[8]

New York, not Massachusetts, set the pace for the nation. Here and there, partial gains were achieved. As often as not the gains were illusory or temporary as in Minnesota, for example, where a fifty-four-hour law was set aside by the State Supreme Court on a technicality; efforts to amend the bill to make it constitutional were unavailing. Over and over legislative committees and governors, ladies' clubs and associations of social workers were told that "Physical debility follows fatigue. Laxity of moral fibre follows physical debility."[9] But the nation's attention was focused on other issues; the nation's energies were consumed by other affairs. From the end of the war to the election of 1932, only two states added maximum-hour legislation where none existed before; substantial improvements of the regulations were won in twelve of the forty states which had statutes on the books by 1918.

At mid-decade, a special subcommittee of the WTUL, charged with re-evaluating the league's entire legislative program, acknowledged broad and increasing "dissatisfaction with legislation for women as a means to the end for which the Women's Trade Union League" was organized. Political action had become a "slow and painful process" of achieving reform. Perhaps it was time to consolidate forces and place emphasis again on the league's alternative line of action—the organization of women into unions. The board, after prolonged and bitter debate, finally accepted the recommendation to close its Chicago office and invest legislative moneys in one central office in the nation's capital, and acted at the same time to reopen the unionization campaign.[10] . . .

If the women's reform associations had been able to hold the line on maximum-hour legislation and win a few slight gains from time to time, no such good fortune attended the parallel movement for minimum-wage statutes. The Consumers' League, the Trade Union League, and the American Association for Labor Legislation had seized the initiative during the years preceding America's entrance in World War I in coordinating the drive for state minimum-wage legislation. They had joined to persuade Massachusetts, in 1912, and eight more states the following year to establish minimum-wage commissions, with permissive rather than mandatory authority. By 1918, eleven states plus the District of Columbia and by 1923 fifteen states in all had regulations of some sort. There the matter rested. That moderate but nonetheless significant benefits had derived from this body of legislation the reform groups knew. The procedures of enforcement were often clumsy and rested as frequently upon the sanction of good will and enlightened public opinion as upon the coercive power of the state; but levels of wages for women had generally been raised, and the minima had not become maxima as some trade union spokesmen had feared. Ten years of experience, it was believed, gave ample evidence that higher wages had a clear bearing on health, moral decency, and industrial efficiency. Furthermore, it was argued, the extension of the principle was justified on the premise that employers properly should bear the costs that society otherwise had to assume in the form of charitable relief to those who broke down from ill health, fatigue, and insufficient income. The minimum wage was a means to prevent the delinquency and disease which, if unprevented, society would have to cure. To the employers it was said that regulations lessened labor turnover, increased worker morale and efficiency; no one, save the marginal, unscrupulous, and unfair producer, had anything to lose.

There was, of course, overt opposition to the extension of minimum-wage regulations. A move in Ohio by the Council of Women and Children in Industry (composed of representatives of the Consumers' League, the Women's Trade Union League, the Urban League, the YWCA, and the WCTU) was successfully blocked by the Ohio Manufacturers' Association. More often, however, the drive for minimum wages was diverted or stopped by apathy and unconcern, and by a widespread feeling that such legislation was of doubtful constitutionality. The Supreme Court of the state of Oregon had upheld minimum-wage legislation in two parallel cases, back in 1914, on the ground that the wages of women workers were a legitimate concern of the state in seeking to improve the health, morals, and general welfare of the community. But the tie vote by which the United States Supreme Court in 1917 sustained the *Oregon* decision certainly was no ringing mandate to encourage other states to act.

Then, in 1921, the constitutionality of the District of Columbia's minimum-wage act was challenged. The Consumers' League rushed to the defense. Molly Dewson was retained to prepare the factual material for the case, while Felix Frankfurter volunteered his services as counsel. Florence Kelley sensed at once that the crucial battle was at hand. Dropping everything else for the moment, she threw herself into the task of finding the money to underwrite the legal and research costs and to publicize the cause. There is "Merry Hell in general," wrote Mrs. Kelley to Adolf Berle, Jr., describing the office of the Consumers' League as the brief was finally being assembled. "Even Felix up in Cambridge is jumping high jumps twice daily," she added in a postscript.[11] In November 1922 the District Court of Appeals, by a vote of two to one, found the law null and void. The *Adkins* case was taken on appeal at once to the Supreme Court. But Florence Kelley was not hopeful. "There is no short road to Justice and Mercy in this Republic," she wrote dejectedly to an old friend.[12]

Mrs. Kelley's forebodings proved accurate. By five to three (Justice Brandeis again abstaining), the highest tribunal knocked down the District's act, sounding the "death knell" (as Felix Frankfurter said later in life) for all kinds of social legislation and inhibiting the launching of new welfare experiments.[13] Frankfurter had argued that the statute Congress had passed, sitting as the "state legislature" for the District of Columbia, fell well within the boundary of what was reasonable; it was not "arbitrary, wanton, or spoilative." That wages for women workers were considered to have a clear bearing upon health and morality was evidenced by many regulations of several states and by the action of nearly every industrial nation.

To George Sutherland, who had been recently added to the Supreme Court by President Harding, it was not all that clear. Drawing upon the ancient and honorable tenets of nineteenth-century individualism, Sutherland announced for the majority its conviction that minimum-wage legislation constituted arbitrary interference of the state in the private affairs of citizens competent to use their inviolable liberties in such ways as to promote the well-being and progress of society. The freedom of employers and employees to make a contract clearly was covered by the due process clause of the Fifth Amendment. As for the unanimous decision of the court in the *Oregon* case, the premises on which it rested no longer applied, for women, he argued, had gained a kind of equality with men that rendered special legislative protection for women obsolete. He cited the Nineteenth Amendment as proof that differences in civil status between men and women had reached the "vanishing point." The law was, in light of these historic changes, "a naked, arbitrary exercise of power."

To William Howard Taft, new chief justice, Sutherland's logic was deficient. "The Nineteenth Amendment did not change the physical strength or limitations of women upon which the decision in *Muller v. Oregon* rests," he wrote in dissent. Oliver Wendell Holmes, Jr., made a more elaborate attack upon the majority decision. "Freedom of contract" was nowhere to be found in the Constitution. The state had for generations legitimately restricted individual freedom; if legislatures deemed it essential that the government set minimum wages as well as maximum hours, the courts were obliged to accept their judgment as reasonable unless there were overwhelming evidence to the contrary. "It will need more than the Nineteenth Amendment to convince me that there are no differences between men and women or that legislation cannot take those differences into account." Irony and indignation availeth not; Sutherland spoke for the majority of five, and that was that.[14] Mary Dewson, who had labored for months on the case, recalled later in life the bitter conclusion of her legal comrade, Felix Frankfurter: "Molly, you must learn that if the U.S. Supreme Court says a red rose is green, it is green. That's final."[15]

John Kirby, in a cartoon for the *New York World,* depicted a gracious Justice Sutherland handing a scroll to a shabbily-dressed and dejected woman worker and saying: "This decision affirms your constitutional right to starve." Other comments were no more subtle. Even the usually mild-mannered and courtly Mr. Gompers announced that the court had "usurped" authority nowhere granted to it in the Constitution, and concluded that the "brutality of the majority decision can beget nothing but wrath." A more careful critic, Henry R. Seager, noted that five men had overridden three other justices, majorities of two houses of Congress and thirteen state legislatures, thirteen governors, the President of the United States, and many previous courts. It was left to the good gray feminist, Florence Kelley, to comment that not a single woman had participated in the judicial process at any point. Francis Bowes Sayre concluded that the traditional judicial practice of finding in favor of a law in the absence of substantial legal doubt had been violated by the majority. The decision, he said, indicated that the

Supreme Court was arrogating to itself a veto power not unlike that exercised by a House of Lords. Governor Louis F. Hart of the state of Washington labeled the decision as infamous as the *Dred Scott* ruling and stated categorically that any business that could not pay a decent wage was not a desirable business. Governor Walter M. Pierce from Oregon (home of so many pioneer measures of social legislation) was more temperate, but perhaps more to the point: "It is neither humane nor wise socially to allow the untrained to become public charges or worse through lack of a living wage. It is detrimental to the future of individuals as well as the nation to permit child labor under improper conditions. Since the untrained and young cannot hope to stand up under the competition and demands of industry, only government had so far been able to afford them protection." Father John A. Ryan, one of the very first propagandists for the living wage principle, particularly in its application to women workers, blamed the court's ruling upon the persistence of nineteenth-century utilitarianism with its extravagant insistence upon the individual's freedom to do what he wished as long as the freedom of other autonomous individuals was not thereby limited; that such a philosophy was irrelevant in an industrial era, that its capricious application led to inhumane practices, was clear to him as to many others.[16]

Florence Kelley had been through enough battles to know that verbal protest alone was never sufficient to carry the day: the heavier artillery of action would have to be unloosed. Invitations were sent to reform association leaders and to state officials to confer jointly on how best to meet the emergency. On 20 April 1923—Felix Frankfurter and Florence Kelley taking the lead—the delegates gathered in New York City to deliberate upon strategy. Jesse C. Adkins, chairman of the District of Columbia Minimum Wage Board, was there; so were representatives of law-enforcement agencies in this area of social legislation from Wisconsin, Washington, North Dakota, Minnesota, Massachusetts, and New York. Representatives were sent by all the major reform associations—the Consumers' League, of course, the Women's Trade Union League, the League of Women Voters, the National Catholic Welfare Association and the National Council of Catholic Women, the Child Labor Committee, the American Association for Labor Legislation, and the WCTU. The chief of the Women's Bureau, Mary Anderson, arrived; so too did Mary Van Kleeck, now with the Russell Sage Foundation; and Paul Kellogg of the *Survey*.

Felix Frankfurter led the discussion. There was little hope that the court would reverse itself in the near future, he observed. Justice Brandeis' vote could be counted on, of course, in cases on which he would not feel obliged to abstain; but otherwise the lines were drawn rather sharply for the moment. Sutherland was clearly hopeless; and as for Justice Butler, "He is a farmer, and spent from twenty to thirty years of his life in working up a practice [in law]. This is very confining and limited." His major recommendation, therefore, was to revise state minimum-wage legislation along the permissive lines of Massachusetts' law rather than try to incorporate mandatory provisions. In the meantime, he reminded the conference, the court had acted on the District of Columbia statute and nothing else. The "continued aggressive enforcement" of all state laws was absolutely essential. The court had always recognized local differences and until it specifically rejected state laws, the presumption that they were constitutional stood. The analysis and the conclusions were generally shared by the other delegates. F. A. Duxbury, chairman of Minnesota's Industrial Commission, resented, however, what seemed to him slurs on the integrity of Sutherland and Butler; respect for the law and for the courts was called for, even by those who could not agree with the decision. Father Ryan, who had joined Frankfurter in chiding Sutherland and Butler, replied that he had intended no disrespect, that he had merely wished to point out that the five justices were living in the eighteenth century. If any feelings were hurt, he was sorry but he felt it was hardly appropriate for him, above all others, to concur in any notion of judicial infallibility.

Out of the conference came no formal resolution, but only a general agreement. State laws should be enforced with vigor, as always. The suggestion that New York press for a permissive law, on the Massachusetts model, was endorsed. Further study of the economic and legal aspects of the decision would be made, and at once.[17]

Not satisfied with the inconclusive results of the April meeting, the WTUL called one of its own in mid-May, on the eve of the annual Conference of Social Work. Many of the groups represented at the April gathering sent delegates to this one as well. Mary Anderson set a tone of objective analysis, presenting evidence of the disparity in bargaining power that women workers suffered under, of the sub-standard wages that existed in states and in industries not covered by wage minima, and of the obvious relation between decent wages and community health. The presentation was forceful, if objective, but added little to the conclusions stated so cogently, although with so little practical effect, by Frankfurter and Dewson in the *Adkins* case. Dean Acheson was present to offer advice similar to Frankfurter's several weeks earlier—the states should continue to enforce their own minimum-wage laws; all interested groups should work unceasingly for a redefinition of due process of law along lines that would permit and encourage a reasonable extension of the state's police power. Other delegates were less patient. To wait for the Supreme Court to change its mind on what constituted reasonable regulations and proper procedures was to postpone indefinitely the enforcement of sound measures. Why not amend the Constitution, asked Molly Dewson, to authorize federal regulation of women's wages? Why so delimited a proposal, replied Maud Swartz for the Trade Union League? Why not work for an amendment which would grant broad powers to regulate conditions of labor, of men workers as of women? Elisabeth Christman and Rose Schneiderman, on the other hand, despairing of both judicial self-reform and the amendment procedure, demanded an energetic campaign to organize women into unions as the only valid course. Still others suggested that perhaps the time had come to limit the powers of the high tribunal to review both state and federal legislation.[18]

Divided counsel merely deepened the sense of demoralization. More than two decades of crusading had taught the reformers how to lobby, how to get around recalcitrant employers, how to by-pass stubborn legislative committees, how to stir up public support, how to argue the rule of reason before reasonable courts. It had not taught them how to react to hostile court decisions from which there was no appeal. For the moment they had lost both momentum and equilibrium. John R. Commons, accepting election as president of the Consumers' League in the autumn of 1923, summed it up exactly: "You find yourselves baffled and your work, at least an essential part of it, brought to a standstill by the recent adverse decisions of the Supreme Court" bearing upon child-labor and minimum-wage legislation.[19] Florence Kelley put it more picturesquely: "Truly we are like a semi-paralyzed centipede with its legs all moving at different rates of speed, if at all, and how few legs moving!"[20] In the middle years of the decade, she fell into the closing salutation when writing to intimate friends "Yours, *still* hopefully." But throughout 1923 and 1924, and on into 1925 when the child-labor amendment failed to win ratification, there was little cause for hopefulness.

Reporting to the Board of Directors of the Consumers' League in October 1923, Jeanette Rankin, field secretary for the league in Illinois, reported that the "total legislative harvest" for that year was "a law adopting a state flower!"[21] And two years later, with reform still in eclipse, a Seattle lawyer confessed his discouragement to Mrs. Kelley: "the tide is running out now and all we can do is hold fast to our moorings until the tide turns."[22]

Mrs. Kelley was not about to accept the Supreme Court's negative actions as final and irrevocable. Other obstacles had yielded; the court could be circumvented or brought to its senses. The task was clear—to modernize the eighteenth-century Constitution in such ways as to make it possible to meet the new industrial demands of an urban civilization. Until the Constitution was transformed, and until the "court that interprets the Constitution" was modernized, it was "purely academic" to discuss industrial legislation.[23] The goal was clear enough, but not the means. Some advised an amendment authorizing Congress to reenact by a two-thirds majority any federal statute found to be unconstitutional by the court. Others would require a two-thirds majority of the court to rule a state or federal legislative enactment null and void. (At various times the ante was raised to seven and eight judges, until finally a unanimous court was suggested.) A more widely favored proposal was to grant to Congress, by the amendment procedure, broad authority to act in the large arena of social legislation. The legalists tended to prefer persuading the courts, by trying one case after another, to adopt a more permissive attitude toward legislative experiments; judicial self-restraint, not coercive action against the court, was the more efficacious path, they insisted. A few hardy souls suggested enlarging the court to fifteen members, or eighteen; but with Harding and then Coolidge in the White House, what a later generation would know as "packing" the court did not win wide support among reformers who were disrespectful enough of the court as then constituted but were not foolhardy. Whatever means were explored, even Florence Kelley knew they were "far easier to name than to draft."[24]

For a while Mrs. Kelley leaned toward an amendment requiring a seven to two majority to find state and federal legislation unconstitutional, but her closest legal adviser, Felix Frankfurter, would have none of it. "The 7 to 2 proposal will not come off," he advised, "and at the rate at which the Sutherlands and the Butlers are being appointed to the Court, it wouldn't do any good if it did."[25] This proposal might have the backing of Senator Borah and Father Ryan, but it was "utterly hopeless" to expect that either a bill or an amendment so providing could ever be passed. It was unwise, in any case, to seek such a deceptively simple "mechanical remedy" for a complex legal dilemma. The point rather, Frankfurter continued, was to improve the quality of the court itself.[26] Roscoe Pound concurred. The amendment procedure was clumsy; "legislative revision of judicial action" was inadvisable. Ultimately the only proper means of securing the court's approval for social and industrial legislation, without jeopardizing other rights, was to persuade the justices to make a broader and more flexible interpretation of the due process of law provision and the police power. He recommended popular agitation for court reform, however, as one way to bring about "a better judicial frame of mind."[27] Zechariah Chafee added one final caveat—reformers should not forget, in their desire to limit property rights, that legislative bodies often limit personal rights; if a seven to two majority were required to set aside a law, a minority of three could block the unconstitutionality of laws subversive of civil rights.[28]

Agreement upon a single viable course of action was not to be had. The inadvisability of restricting the court's powers came to be abundantly evident. To wait for the court to change its mind seemed futile. In the meantime, as Florence Kelley noted, women and children remained exposed to exploitative actions of unscrupulous employers.[29] A move to win agreement on a strategy of assault upon the court, in July 1924, was abortive.[30] Reformers by that time were focusing their energies upon the child-labor amendment and upon La Follette's crusade for the presidency. The court issue was relevant enough, there was just no way to bring the court to its senses without jeopardizing the equilibrium of government and the security of individual rights. Another battle had been lost, but not before the need for judicial self-restraint had been recognized by this handful of rebels. Almost every legal and political argument of the great court fight in 1937 was anticipated back in 1923 and 1924. Ultimately the issue was resolved as Frankfurter, Pound, Chafee, Freund, and Acheson had recommended—not by statute, not by amendment, but by the addition of new personnel to the court dedicated to a broader interpretation of social welfare and willing to accept legislative action as legitimate unless obviously unconstitutional beyond all reasonable doubt. The frontal assault upon the wisdom—and even, at times, the integrity—of the court may have helped to clarify the issues and thus served to prepare the way for the constitutional revolution that began in 1937.

As for practical and immediate achievements, there were few. The court continued on its path, undeflected by the feeble efforts of the critics. "Don't hurry away from the scene of battle," pleaded Florence Kelley to Molly Dewson in 1924. "So long as there is a *glimmering* chance of usefulness, that's the place to be."[31] Three years later, Mrs. Kelley confided to John R. Commons that their function should be study, research, publicity until the times should change: "Keeping the light on is probably the best contribution that we can make where there is now Stygian darkness."[32]

The candle was kept lit, and was set upon a hill. It was no floodlight or searchlight as long as the mood of normalcy prevailed, but it burned persistently. The motto of the Consumers' League continued to be implemented—"Investigate, Record, Agitate." Throughout the remainder of the decade, the league regularly remained in touch with state officials desirous of enforcing industrial minima. Effective regulation, however, all but collapsed. The voluntary, permissive arrangement in Massachusetts won partial advances for limited numbers of women workers but never more than that. And, at that, Massachusetts led the nation. Arizona's law was struck down by the Supreme Court in 1925, Arkansas' in 1927; local courts followed suit in Kansas and Puerto Rico; in Texas and Nebraska the laws were repealed; in Minnesota the attorney general ruled that its law was no longer enforceable. As late as June 1936, the United States Supreme Court in *Morehead v. Tipaldo* ruled that the *Adkins* decision was still controlling, this in negation of a 1933 New York State fair-wage law. Not until 1937 was the *Adkins* rule explicitly overridden.

Just as the Children's Bureau under Julia Lathrop and Grace Abbott was the coordinating agency of federal government in the field of child welfare, so the Women's Bureau under Mary Anderson played a similar role in parallel fields. Its central commitment was to the national community's obligation through government to protect the women of the land for the general good of society. With no regulatory laws to administer, it relied entirely upon "fact finding and fact furnishing" to achieve its ends. "Every movement making for reform needs a reservoir of reliable data upon which to draw and by which to be guided," an official publication of the Women's Bureau declared.[33] Through research and publication, speeches and reports, and sponsorship of conferences, and through cooperation with state labor bureaus and with voluntary associations, its influence was extended to every section of the nation. When the occasion demanded, it could call out a host of allies: the Women's Trade Union League, the Consumers' League, the League of Women Voters, the WCTU, the YWCA, the PTA, the General Federation of Women's Clubs, the American Association of University Women, church and labor union groups. These associations had been formed into a loose alliance in the Women's Joint Congressional Committee, the clearinghouse and coordinating federation which crusaded for maternal and infant health programs, the regulation of child labor, adequate appropriations for the Children's and Women's bureaus, welfare legislation for the District of Columbia, social hygiene, and public health. Mrs. Maud Wood Park, president of the League of Women Voters from 1920 to 1924 and Belle Sherwin, its president from 1924 to 1934, were among the committee's most effective and loyal leaders, but every other member group could also be counted upon to work with Grace Abbott and Mary Anderson within government for common objectives.

Of the making of committees, of course, there was no end; and committee meetings and resolutions can never be taken for effective action. With the best of intentions, women reformers often assembled determined to strike a blow for welfare only to play out a ritualistic role of protest. One woman reformer, long active in the WTUL, once wrote to a friend about the quality of committee work and rhetoric: "I was trying to *show* a dear old Boston lady how a rich man's *do-nothing* son was a worse tramp than the *other* tramps—'Oh Mrs. Faxon, I don't believe you mean that.'—'Yes, I do.'—'O,' she says, 'I've heard people talk on committees like that!'—Now my family says whenever I *get to* talking—'Now don't talk like a committee!' "[34]

There was a good deal of committee talk in the 1920's, particularly when the National Woman's party, a stridently feminist group that had fought for the Nineteenth Amendment, proposed still another amendment to the federal Constitution designed to remove all legal discriminations relating to sex. The proposed amendment took several forms during the decade, but the intent of its original phrasing persisted: "Men and women shall have equal rights throughout the United States and every place subject to its jurisdiction." Put forward by ladies drawn primarily from the wealthy and professional classes, the proposed amendment was viewed at once by a vast majority of women reformers as a measure subversive of all protective and welfare legislation. Florence Kelley, herself a suffragette and feminist, would have nothing to do with a measure that proposed to establish complete "legal equality of the sexes," when it was clear, on the face of it, that because of the special sexual functions of women they could not be afforded absolute equality of treatment without placing in jeopardy their hard-won legal right to special protection.[35] It would be "insanity," she wrote to Newton Baker, to follow the lead of Alice Paul and the Woman's party down a path that would utterly destroy maximum hours and minimum wages, mothers' pensions, and maternity insurance.[36] The proposal, moreover, was legally ambiguous: no one was really against "equal rights," Mary Anderson later recalled of the struggle, but what did "equal" mean and what really constituted "rights"?[37] For a generation women had benefited from legislation designed to protect them from "untrammeled exploitation," wrote Dean Acheson to Ethel Smith. "All this, to my mind, is now threatened by this sweeping prohibition of unnamed inequalities and disabilities." The courts were likely to rule, he warned, "that this new-won equality guarantees to women all the intolerable and anti-social conditions which their brothers in industry now enjoy."[38] What of the status of laws of desertion and nonsupport, queried Florence Kelley? What of the rules of illegitimacy, seduction, and rape? What of conscription in time of war? "Will husbands need to continue to support their wives?"[39] A special conference of women's groups, in early December 1921, arranged by Florence Kelley, concluded with Alice Paul's announcement that despite the fears of the reformers that, even if the amendment did not pass Congress, its agitation would imperil the whole movement for social legislation, the Woman's party was determined to press for its enactment and ratification.

From this point forward the dispute became increasingly embittered. Alice Hamilton set down her indignation in a draft letter to one of the "equal rights" proponents: "I could not help comparing you as you sat there, sheltered, safe, beautifully guarded against even the ugliness of life, with the women for whom you demand 'freedom of contract.' " Laundry workers, textile workers, "the great army of waitresses and hotel chambermaids, unorganized, utterly ignorant of ways of making their grievances known, working long hours and living wretchedly" would be left unprotected if the amendment carried. A sweeping amendment was not the proper means for removing the discriminations and legal disabilities of sex.[40]

The main business of the Women's Industrial Conference, called by the Women's Bureau in January 1923, was interrupted by altercations over the amendment; the conference in January of 1926 was all but broken up by this hotly disputed issue. Sarah Conboy of the AFL fired a parting shot by publicly expressing her wish that the Woman's party ladies might be afforded the opportunity of working in mine and factory so they could learn first hand the problems of working women. Mabel Leslie reported to the Trade Union League that the Woman's party members were "merely theoretical ultra-feminists who [did] not have to work for a living."[41]

The squabble was of no particular significance—the proposed amendment never had a chance of serious consideration—except that it illustrates the kind of irrelevant wrangle which so often engaged the social reformers during the twenties. Their energies were often dissipated in countering charges of radicalism and subversion, and in this instance charges of antifeminism. The thousands of reform-hours consumed in fruitless and rancorous debate with the Woman's party represented time the reformers would have preferred to invest in other pursuits. Year after year, Mary Anderson recorded bitterly in her reminiscences, reform associations "had to lay aside the work they were doing to improve conditions for women and spend their time combating the equal rights amendment."[42]

Less spectacular but of surpassing significance was the workers' educational movement which was so often linked to the reform activities of women's associations in these years. The WTUL had pioneered during the years before the war in training potential trade union leaders in a program that Margaret Dreier Robins inaugurated in Chicago. Arrangements had been made for young working women to enroll as special students at Northwestern University and in the Chicago School of Civics and Philanthropy. Of the forty working girls from seventeen different trades who enjoyed formal course work from 1913 until the program was discontinued in 1926, nearly three-quarters remained active in trade union leadership, a record which the league took as justification of the time and money it had invested in the enterprise. The difficulty of integrating young working women, who were so often of recent immigrant origin and who so rarely had formal educational training, into university classes (even when conducted by such sympathetic professors as Paul Douglas) tended to vitiate the experiment, however, and this particular form of workers' education was never widely adopted.

Established in April of 1921, the Workers' Educational Bureau set out to stimulate and coordinate educational efforts of all sorts. Chaired by James H. Maurer, a functionary of the Socialist party and president of the Pennsylvania Federation of Labor, the bureau drew as well upon the diverse talents of such typical reform leaders as Fannia M. Cohn, of the International Ladies' Garment Workers' Union and the Trade Union League; John Brophy of the United Mine Workers and Abraham Epstein, then secretary of the labor education committee of the Pennsylvania Federation of Labor. Through the Workers' Educational Bureau and through the Brookwood Labor College which it helped to sponsor, the promotion of the ideas of industrial unionism and of political action by labor was achieved. Generally "leftist" in its leanings, the Brookwood Labor College, directed by A. J. Muste, trained a number of young trade union officials who would later contribute substantially to the formation of the CIO.

The major effort for the education of women workers came at the Bryn Mawr summer school, opened first in 1921 on the instigation of Mary Anderson, Hilda Smith, and Dr. M. Carey Thomas, president of the college. Hilda Smith, who later headed up workers' education in the WPA, was named the summer school's director. Raised in a devout Episcopalian household, Hilda Smith turned very early in her life to a career of social service. A graduate of Bryn Mawr in 1910, she had worked summers in settlement camps and had gone on to do casework with the Girls' Friendly Society and to take courses at the New York School of Philanthropy before returning to her alma mater as dean of the college in 1919. Under Miss Smith's direction from 1921 to 1934, the Bryn Mawr School for Working Women drew its students from the trade union movement, from local units of the WTUL and, in the South where trade unionism was unknown, from the YWCA. Here the students received courses in economics, government, the history of the labor movement, remedial social legislation, the causes and cures of unemployment, trade union procedures, public speaking, and composition. That the sessions offered a lively opportunity for curious young women is attested to by the mixture of ethnic and religious groups that composed the student body and by the excellence of its faculty which included outstanding experts like Paul Douglas, Alice Henry, Broadus Mitchell, Carter Goodrich, Colston Warne, Mark Starr, and Stephen Raushenbush. Dedicated to such objectives as widening the influence of the trade union movement, training the students in "clear thinking," stimulating in them "an active and continued interest in the problems of [the] economic order," and promoting "the coming social reconstruction," the Bryn Mawr school made a major contribution to the elaboration of concepts and leadership in the social reform movement.[43] The school had immediate practical consequences as was evidenced by the successful move on the part of the students to organize college employees and to win for them an eight-hour day not only during the summer session but during the regular academic year as well.[44]

The significance of the Bryn Mawr School for Working Women and similar programs conducted at Barnard (1927-1934), the Vineyard Shore School for Women Workers in Industry (1929-1934), and the Brookwood Labor College is difficult to measure. It is fair to suggest, however, that they kept alive a commitment to trade union activity; they trained many young men and women who were to become union and political leaders of some note during the depression decade; they kindled the aspirations of many young people in times of moral slump; they kept open the path of purposeful social change. Eleanor Roosevelt summed it up at a banquet honoring Dr. M. Carey Thomas, whose initiative had been crucial in the establishment of the Bryn Mawr school: If the New Deal were to win through to higher levels of life, the people must participate intelligently and constructively in social affairs. It was to this end that worker education had been directed, she said, toward giving "people the tools so that they [could] work out their own salvation wisely and well."[45] In so doing the workers' education movement contributed to the larger movement for reform.

Together, proponents of industrial minima, particularly for women and children, enlarged the rationale for legislative action, until by the end of the decade the philosophy of New Deal action in this arena had been elaborated in nearly every detail. Research notes of John R. Commons, made sometime in the mid-1920's, included an observation of Lord Northington's: "Necessitous men are not, truly speaking, free men, but, to answer to present exigency, will submit to any terms that the crafty may impose upon them."[46] The idea could hardly claim originality, but in the United States it did not, until the interwar era, receive much notice or elaboration. It came to be basic to every consideration by liberals whose central commitment was still to the enlargement of individual opportunity and freedom. Necessitous men, insecure men, men made anxious by low wages, uncertain employment, long hours at labor, and arbitrary industrial discipline were truly not free men. The establishment of industrial minima, of measures of social security broadly conceived, it followed, was essential to human liberty.

On the heels of this simple conclusion came another axiom— society, through government, had an obligation to force industry to bear its just burden of responsibility for community welfare. If industry paid sub-standard wages, argued Ethel M. Johnson in 1927, society would somehow in some way have to make up the difference. It might be through "hospitals and dispensaries to care for women who are broken down in health because they did not earn enough to permit them sufficient wholesome food and suitable living arrangements." Or it might be through charitable relief. A minimum wage assessed the burden upon industry where it belonged.[47] If floors under wages could be set by law or administrative ruling as a proper charge against industry, then it could be left to collective bargaining by unions to win living wages above that level.[48] Unless workers, particularly women workers, enjoyed these minimum guarantees, they could not build up reserves for sickness or unemployment. A woman employed at "oppressive" levels, below the minimum, thereby became a "liability rather than an asset to the community," and a burden upon society.[49]

Over and over the point was hammered home—industrial minima were required not alone as humanitarian considerations or as charity but as measures essential to the over-all long-run efficiency of industry, to community health and welfare, and to social stability and orderly progress. The New York Consumers' League offered as its slogan for 1927 "Social Justice Is the Best Safeguard against Social Disorder"; while Florence Kelley, commenting on the violent textile strikes of 1929, insisted that the only alternative to industrial disorder and social strife was "peaceful progress" through legislation.[50]

It was perhaps Newton Baker who best summarized the need for social action to remedy the grievances associated with intense industrialization. Given the growing impersonality of all society, the sanctions of civilization were not as easily applied as once they were. The role of voluntary associations, such as the Consumers' League, was to "investigate, record, agitate" in order that men of good will might act with the knowledge of the consequences of their behavior, while the law coerced the "recalcitrants." The league and its allies could show the way for society to accomplish "on a large and collective scale, in a collective way, that which we so delighted to do as individuals under simpler conditions."[51]

The New Deal drew heavily and specifically upon these concepts, which had grown out of progressivism and had been tempered in the 1920's. The depression afforded the occasion for their implementation, because economic crisis overrode most other considerations in 1933. The National Recovery Administration prohibited child labor, and encouraged codes of labor standards governing hours, wages, and conditions for both women and men workers. When the NRA was broken, the industrial minima were rewritten in the Fair Labor Standards Act of 1938; and this time the Supreme Court concurred. The contribution of liberal reform in the 1920's had been to keep alive the progressive objectives, and then to modify them, extend them, and elaborate a rationale which, under the pressure of emergency, was incorporated as part of the New Deal consensus and program.

NOTES

1. Helen Glenn Tyson, "Mothers Who Earn," *Survey*, 67:5 (1 December 1926), pp. 275-279.
2. Nelle Swartz, review of *Mothers in Industry*, in *Survey*, 67:6 (15 December 1926), pp. 400-401.
3. Resolution in *Proceedings* (1924), pp. 336-337, WTUL, Box 15.
4. Frances Perkins, "Do Women in Industry Need Special Protection? Yes," *Survey*, 55:10 (15 February 1926), pp. 529-531.
5. Monthly Labor Bulletin of Massachusetts WTUL (January 1928), in WTUL Local Bulletins (Radcliffe), Box 1. Box 3, in same collection, contains comments of factory girls to an investigator of the Connecticut Consumers' League.
6. Florence Kelley, "The Inescapable Dilemma," *Survey*, 41:25 (22 March 1919), p. 885.
7. Executive Board of the New York WTUL, Minutes (6 June 1921), in WTUL (Radcliffe), Box 2.
8. The stories in Massachusetts and New York may be traced in WTUL, Box 15; NCL, Box 20; Dewson Papers (F. D. R. Library), Box 17.
9. Dr. George W. Webster quoted in "The Woman's Work Day," *Survey*, 46:4 (23 April 1921), p. 121.
10. Report of Rose Schneiderman, Julia S. O'Connor, and Matilda Lindsay (8 November 1925), WTUL, Box 3.

11. Florence Kelley to Adolf A. Berle, Jr. (31 January 1923), NCL, Box 8.
12. Florence Kelley to Mildred Chadsey (8 March 1923), NCL, Box 11.
13. Felix Frankfurter, *Felix Frankfurter Reminisces* (New York: Reynal, 1960), pp. 101-104.
14. Felix Frankfurter and Mary R. Dewson, *District of Columbia Minimum Wage Cases* (New York: Steinberg, 1923); *Adkins v. Children's Hospital,* 261 U.S. 525 (1923).
15. Mary R. Dewson to Isador Lubin (April 1957), Dewson Papers (F. D. R. Library), General Correspondence, Box 18.
16. "The Minimum Wage—What Next?" *Survey,* 50:4 (15 May 1923), pp. 215-222, 256-258, 263; Francis B. Sayres, "The Minimum Wage Decision," *Survey,* 50:3 (1 May 1923), pp. 150-151, 164, 172; Florence Kelley to Mrs. John Blair (1 May 1923), NCL, Box 10.
17. Typescript of Stenographic Report of Minimum Wage Conference (20 April 1923), NCL, Box 10.
18. Mimeographed Report on Conference in Tilton Papers, Box 3; Press Releases, WTUL, Box 25; Correspondence, WTUL, Box 2; Florence Kelley to Edward P. Costigan (31 May 1923), NCL, Box 10.
19. John R. Commons, Notes for Speech (9 November 1923), NCL, Box 8.
20. Florence Kelley to Amy G. Maher (17 March 1923), NCL, Box 11.
21. Jeanette Rankin, Report to Executive Board (25 October 1923), NCL, Box 8.
22. James A. Haight to Florence Kelley (19 December 1925), NCL, Box 11.
23. "Highlights of a Speech Made by Florence Kelley in 1923," in Massachusetts Consumers' League (Radcliffe), Drawer 1.
24. Florence Kelley to Board of Directors (12 June 1923), NCL, Box 11.
25. Felix Frankfurter to Florence Kelley (19 October 1923), NCL, Box 10.
26. Felix Frankfurter to Florence Kelley (25 October 1925), NCL, Box 10.
27. Roscoe Pound to Florence Kelley (22 October 1923), NCL, Box 10.
28. Zechariah Chafee to John R. Commons (1 April 1924), NCL, Box 11. See also Florence Kelley's correspondence, 1923-1924, with Charles Beard, Ernst Freund, Charles Warren, Ethel Smith, Newton D. Baker, Edward P. Costigan, NCL, Boxes 10 and 11.
29. Florence Kelley to Felix Frankfurter (25 June 1924), NCL, Box 11.
30. Correspondence in regard to conference (1 July 1924) that broke up with no agreement having been reached, NCL, Box 11.
31. Florence Kelley to "Dear Sister Dewson" (8 April 1924), NCL, Box 8.
32. Florence Kelley to John R. Commons (13 April 1927), NCL, Box 8.
33. Women's Bureau, *Fact Finding with the Women's Bureau* (Bulletin 84, 1931).
34. Mrs. Peake Faxon[?] to Leonora O'Reilly (no date, c. 1919), O'Reilly Papers (Radcliffe), Box 7.
35. Florence Kelley, "The New Woman's Party," *Survey,* 45:23 (5 March 1921), pp. 827-828.
36. Florence Kelley to Newton D. Baker (3 June 1921), NCL, Box 13.

37. Mary Anderson, *Woman at Work: The Autobiography of Mary Anderson as Told to Mary N. Winslow* (Minneapolis: University of Minnesota Press, 1951), Chapter 16.
38. A carbon copy of Dean Acheson's letter to Ethel M. Smith (8 September 1921) found its way into the files of the NCL, Box 13.
39. Florence Kelley to Mrs. C. J. Evans (16 December 1921), NCL, Box 13.
40. Alice Hamilton, draft of letter to Mrs. Hooker (16 January 1922), Hamilton Papers, Box 1. There is no evidence that the letter was ever sent, but it reflects the feelings of the amendment's opponents.
41. Mabel Leslie to Maud Swartz (4 May 1926), WTUL, Box 3.
42. Mary Anderson, *Woman at Work,* pp. 171-172.
43. Quotation from official statement of the Bryn Mawr School for Working Women (1921 and 1923), in Hilda Smith, *Women Workers at the Bryn Mawr Summer School* (New York: American Association for Adult Education, 1927), p. 7. Papers, bulletins, reports, memoranda of the school, 1921-1933, may be found in Smith Papers, Boxes 2, 3, and 16.
44. Mary Anderson, *Woman at Work,* Chapter 25.
45. Eleanor Roosevelt, Address (24 October 1933), quoted in Hilda Smith, "Autobiography," Smith Papers, Box 16.
46. Research folder on Minimum-Wage Legislation, Commons Papers, Box 9.
47. Ethel M. Johnson, "Fourteen Years of Minimum Wage in Massachusetts" (Typescript, 1927), WTUL (Radcliffe), Box 3.
48. Elizabeth Brandeis to Florence Kelley (20 June 1929), NCL, Box 10.
49. "What Girls Live On and How," *Survey,* 64:6 (15 June 1930), p. 277.
50. Leaflet of New York Consumers' League (1927) in Dewson Papers (Radcliffe), Box 2; Florence Kelley, Report to Board of Directors (27 September 1929), NCL, Box 8.
51. Newton D. Baker, Preface to Maud Nathan, *Story of an Epoch-Making Movement* (Garden City, N.Y.: Doubleday, 1926), pp. xii-xiv.

Article 3

The Decline and Fall of the Double Standard

Edwin O. Smigel
Rita Seiden

To find meaningful correlations,[1] especially in a pluralistic society, between the multitude of social forces and sexual behavior is difficult; to determine these correlations accurately, when appropriate data on sexual behavior are not available, is impossible. Nonetheless, it is our assignment to examine these social forces in order to see what effect they have had on sexual behavior and attitudes—specifically on sexual behavior and attitudes of unmarried heterosexuals of college age and younger in the United States.

Most recent examinations of sexual behavior still cite Kinsey's data[2] (1938–1949) and/or Terman's[3] (1934–1935). No one has published a Kinsey-type study for the United States in the 1960's. However, a few limited studies[4] on premarital sexual behavior have been completed since Kinsey published *The Human Male* in 1948. The various studies of college students show percentages of premarital coitus for males and females which range from 54.35 in 1929;[5] 51:25 in 1938;[6] to 56:25 in 1951;[7] and, in 1953, 68:47, 41:9, or 63:14, depending on whose figures are accepted.[8] The most recent examination of sexual behavior puts the rate of college female premarital experience at 22 per cent.[9] This is consistent with Kinsey's findings that 20 per cent of all college women had had premarital intercourse.[10]

Most of the studies of sex completed after Kinsey's main works appeared have been limited to collecting statistics on attitudes. The most extensive of these studies, for which data was collected through 1963, was conducted by Ira Reiss, on sexual permissiveness.[11] Reiss's

From "Sex and the Contemporary American Scene," *The Annals* of the American Academy of Political and Social Science, CCCLXXVI (March, 1968), 7–17. Reprinted by permission of the authors and The American Academy of Political and Social Science.

findings point to a coming together of sexual practices, and, for the young at least, of attitudes about sex. He found definite movement away from the orthodox double standard toward a standard of permissiveness with affection (shorthand for "premarital sex is acceptable when there is mutual affection between the partners").

The earlier statistics of Kinsey and Terman point up important differences in sexual behavior between the generation of women born before 1900 and the generation born in the following decade. Kinsey found that 73.4 per cent of women born before 1900 had had no premarital intercourse, but among those born between 1900 and 1909, only 48.7 per cent had been virgins at marriage. The figures for those born in the 1920-1929 generation are the same—48.8 per cent.[12] Terman's findings are essentially in agreement. The statistics for both the Kinsey and Terman studies referred to here are for women of all ages, and not just for college women.[13] Terman found that 74 per cent of the females born between 1890 and 1899 had had no premarital intercourse, whereas among those born between 1900 and 1909, the percentage of virgin brides had dropped to 51.2. His figures reveal that this trend also held for men: of those interviewees born between 1890 and 1899, 41.9 per cent had had no premarital coitus, whereas of the interviewees born in the next generation, 32.6 per cent had had no such premarital experience.[14] Clearly, the major change in sex practices occurred in the generation born in the decade 1900-1909, which came to sexual age during or immediately after World War I, a period characterized by marked social change and innovation.

It may well be true that changes in sexual behavior and attitudes are related to the social changes which began in the late nineteenth century and accelerated rapidly over the past 67 years. It is not as clear, except perhaps for the post-World War I years, exactly what the effects of these social changes have been on sexual behavior. Reiss argues that, despite popular belief to the contrary, "the sexual revolution [is] a myth and the only basic change [is] a trend toward more equality between the sexes. . . . There has been less change than [is] popularly believed between modern American males and their Victorian grandfathers."[15]

It is generally thought, however, that the late-nineteenth-century break with Victorian morality was a tangential result of the Industrial Revolution, urban migration, war, the feminist movement, and the scientific study of once-taboo topics. Wilbert Moore, a leading authority on social change, credited industrialization with certain effects on the social structure;[16] and it is our opinion that industrialization affected sex attitudes and behavior as well. He specified increased social and geographic mobility; growth of industrial centers with concomitant concentration of population in urban areas; empahsis on rationality as a necessary part of an industrialized society (for example, a lessening of the influence of religion); transition from extended (rurally located) families to nuclear (urban) families; emphasis on individualism resulting from the breakdown[17] of the extended kinship system; decreased family size accompanied by a decline in the economic significance of the family unit as the unit of survival; and, finally, increased education.

Each of these general effects of social change can be shown, at least theoretically, to have potential impact on sexual behavior and attitudes. As the population moves from small towns and intimate personal relationships to urban centers, old forms of social control break down. This disintegration and the accompanying anonymity is speeded by new and faster forms of transportation which further increase the possibilities of anonymity and independence. A rational society affects the individual's world view, and he tends to see his own life in terms of more rational standards. As the extended kinship system dissolves or loses its importance, mate-selection processes become a more personal responsibility, and increase the importance of peer group norms, which take precedence over family norms. In the evolving industrial society, women take a new and larger part in the working world, thereby securing greater independence for themselves and increased equality in male-female relationships. The general increase in education has made possible widespread dissemination of sex information to the public.

In sum, the family has declined in importance as the unit upon which or around which society is organized, and individualism, in relationship to the family, is in the ascendency. As individualism has grown, sexual behavior has become more a personal matter and is less exclusively influenced by family and procreational considerations.

The complex social changes discussed have been gradual, but the impact of war can be immediate and abrupt. This is clearly indicated in the data on sexual behavior during and immediately after World War I. In any war, the mores governing family life tend to decay. Removed from some of the responsibilities, restrictions, and supports of the family, removed from the all-seeing eye of the small town or the neighborhood, soldiers are suddenly subject only to the mostly approving observations of their fellow soldiers. In the face of death or the possibility of being severely wounded, hedonism becomes the prevailing attitude. This attitude appears to be contagious and spreads to the civilian population. In World War I, it particularly affected the young women who were working in factories, taking on roles and responsibilities that had once belonged exclusively to men, often for the first time living alone in relative anonymity, and in many instances emotionally involved with men who were scheduled to be sent overseas. (This same hedonistic philosophy may be held by contemporary young people who are faced with the dangers of limited wars and the always present possibility of extinction by nuclear explosion.)

Many soldiers had contact with prostitutes and contracted venereal diseases. The United States Interdepartmental Social Hygiene Board reports: "Between September, 1917, and February 14, 1919, there were over 222,000 cases of veneral disease in the army and there were over 60,000 in the navy.[18] Venereal disease and the prostitute taught the soldier more about sex in his relatively short career in the armed services than he might normally have learned. The incidence of venereal disease was so high that it became a matter of both private and official army talk. The consequence was that most soldiers left the service knowing not only the protective effects but also the birth control uses of prophylactic sheaths. This kind of sex education became a standard part of the army curriculum.

The soldier who went abroad had new sexual experiences and came in contact with women whose behavior derived from different and more permissive sex norms; the returned veteran brought back with him sexual attitudes shaped by these new norms. Although they were not consciously intended for his mother, sister, wife, or wife-to-be, they tended to affect them as well.

War also tends to spread industrialization and to extend the need for women in industry, and, in turn, to increase their economic independence. The war and wartime experiences intensified the gradual way in which industrialization was changing the social structure.

War, industrialization, and an increase in political democracy seem to have led to the struggle for equal rights for women. The nineteenth-century feminists, who fought for finanical and social rights and by 1920 had been enfranchised, were now also demanding more sexual freedom. Margaret Sanger, an American housewife, was a leader in this war. She waged a courageous battle for the control of pregnancy, and she was brought to trial for making birth control information available to interested persons. It was the trial, the wide publicity she received, and her persistence which helped to acquaint the public with the possibilities of birth control. She and other fighters for female sexual freedom were supported by a backdrop of the new norms of the returning soldiers, the effects of economic gains for women, and an increase in the scientific study of sex.

Although Krafft-Ebing,[19] Havelock Ellis,[20] and others were writing about sex pathology and sexuality, Freud's writings about the unconscious and the effect of sex on personality had the most influence upon American behavior and attitudes. Although *Studies in Hysteria,* written by Freud and Breuer, which made these ideas available to the public, was published in 1895, "it was not until after the war that the Freudian gospel began to circulate to a marked extent among the American reading public."[21] No one can estimate what popularization of psychoanalytic theory has done to free individuals—particularly women—from the puritan anxieties about sex. The fact of its influence, however, cannot be doubted. These studies by the sexologists and those by the sociologists, anthropologists, and psychologists studying and writing in the late 1920's and early 1930's provided the setting for the public acceptance of Kinsey's impressive work—which may in turn have had great influence on a society already impatient with Victorian sex mores. In any event, studies of sex were being undertaken, and they provided information about taboo topics which helped to free the average individual from the restraint against serious discussion of sexual behavior. Each generation of sex researchers has extended the study and broadened the understanding of sex, from Kinsey's counting of sexual outlets in the 1940's to Masters and Johnson's detailed study of human sexual response[22] in the early 1960's.

In addition to those factors already described, which have affected so many aspects of the social structure, other elements, although less powerful forces for general change, have also contributed to the alteration of sexual mores in a more immediate sense. Cultural interchange resulting from wartime contact since World War I and from the great increase in travel has led to a broadened participation with other societies. Furthermore, the disappearance of the chaperon undoubtedly created opportunities for sexual freedom which are not subject to the social sanctions of one's own society. The availability of the automobile, the affluent society which permits young people to live apart from their parents, and the growth of community size made privacy much more accessible. There has been a virtual removal of "fear-evoking" deterrents with the development of effective contraceptive devices.

All of these factors seem to be related to the change in sexual practices and to the apparent liberalization of sexual standards reflected in Reiss's data.[23] Since these social forces are still operating in the same direction, we should also expect to see changes in the direction of permissive sexual attitudes and behavior to continue.

The data we have on sexual behavior are limited; but more data are available on attitudes.

The research statistics are analyzed in Tables 1, 2, 3, and 4.[24]

Reiss's later data, collected in 1959 and 1963,[25] confirm the trends evidenced in the findings of the earlier studies (see Table 2).

We can probably safely conclude from these data:

(1) Abstinence and permissiveness with affection are the favored standards for both males and females.

(2) There has been a rise in female approval of permissiveness with affection and a decline in approval of the abstinence standard.

(3) Permissiveness without affection, if we consider it comparable to a blanket endorsement of casual sex relations for both, is apparently on the decline—even more sharply for men than for women.

(4) The orthodox double standard is also on the decline if we compare the Table 1 data (sex relations for men only) with the Table 2 data (orthodox double standard).

(5) The percentage of men who favor permissiveness with affection has increased markedly while the female endorsement remains about the same. The redistribution of women's attitudes seems to be away from abstinence and the orthodox double standard toward greater endorsement of the transitional double standard— coitus is all right for men under any condition, but is acceptable for women only if they are in love. Therefore, while women still endorse abstinence more highly than other standards, they are coming to favor sexual relations in the context of affection. Reiss's 1963 data support the 1959 evidence which indicates an increasingly favorable attitude on the part of females[26] toward sex with affection. Eighteen per cent favor permissiveness with affection; one per cent endorse permissiveness without affection; 56 per cent support abstinence. The percentage endorsing the transitional double standard was not given.[27]

Table 1   Attitudes toward Premarital Intercourse (in Percentages)

Approve of	1940 Cornell[a]			1947 Michigan State University[b]			1952–1955 11 Colleges[b]			1958 University of Florida[c]		
	M	F	Total	M	F	Total	M	F	Total	M	F	Total
1. Sex relations for both	15	6	9	16	2		20	5		42	7	25
2. Abstinence	49	76	65	59	76		52	65		20	86	52
3. Sex relations for men only	23	11	16	10	15		12	23		33	0	17
4. Sex relations for engaged/ in love	11	6	8	15	7		16	7		5	7	6
(N)	(73)	(100)	(173)		(2000)			(3000)		(45)	(42)	(87)

[a] Percentages are based on N of 173, but 3 per cent (1 per cent male, 2 per cent female) did not answer the question. The total per cent appearing in Reiss is 101; therefore, ours totals 98.

[b] Separate N's for the male and female samples were not given; therefore, it was not possible to compute total percentage advocating each standard.

[c] Total percentages were not shown by Reiss and were computed by the authors of this article.

(6) Succinctly: The percentage of both men and women who accept increased permissiveness with affection as their standard has increased (see Table 3).

Since the 1947, 1952–1955, and 1959 studies used the largest number of subjects and employed somewhat more rigorous sampling techniques, they are probably more reliable indicators of the trend in these attitudes. They strongly support the assumption that there has been an important change in attitudes toward sex in the direction of permissiveness.

In explaining the differences between statistics on sexual behavior and statistics on attitudes (namely, that behavior seems to have changed little since the 1920's, but attitudes have become more liberal), Reiss suggests that we are seeing a "consolidation process" taking place, that is, "a change in attitudes to match the change in behavior" is occurring.[28] Nelson Foote cites a variety of evidence

Table 2   Percentage[a] Accepting Each Standard

| | 1959[c] | | |
Standard	Male	Female	Total
Permissiveness with affection	24	15	19
Permissiveness without affection	13	2	7
Abstinence	28	55	42
Orthodox double standard	9	13	11
Transitional double standard[b]	18	10	14
N =	(386)	(435)	(821)

[a] Percentages of adherents to the reversed double standard have been omitted. Therefore, totals do not equal 100 per cent.

[b] Transitional double standard means that sex relations are considered all right for men under any condition, but are acceptable for women only if they are in love.

[c] The 1959 sample was drawn from the student populations of five schools: two Virginia colleges (one Negro, one white); two Virginia high schools (one Negro, one white); and one New York college.

which, he claims, indicates the decline of the double standard: decline in prostitution, increasingly equal sexual opportunities and experiences for women, increase in orgasm in marital sex relations, "the steady approach to equivalence of male and female premarital petting and marital sex play techniques," the increase of extramarital coitus, decreasing insistence on virginity in females at marriage, and "some decline in frequency of marital coitus implying more mutual consent and less unilateral demand."[29]

Finally, in line with both Reiss's and Foote's arguments that there is a trend toward a new single standard of permissiveness with affection, Robert Bell suggests that for young adults, sex becomes acceptable today when the couple feels they are in love. Peer group members accept and approve of sex without marriage, but not of sex without love.[30]

For the unmarried, there is an increasing tendency to reject marriage as the arbitrary dividing line between "socially approved and socially disapproved sexual intimacy."[31] And in the same way that male and female roles have become more equal in other areas of life, greater equality has come to the area of sexual relations: "fair play has been replacing chastity as the badge of honor in the interpersonal relations of the sexes."[32]

The results of the various studies of attitudes show two particularly interesting and possibly related findings:

First, there has been an increase in permissive attitudes toward

Table 3   Percentage Accepting the Standard

	1940		1947		1952–1955	1958		1959[a]		1963[a]	
Sex relations for engaged/ in love	M	F	M	F	M	F	M	F	M	F	M	F
	11	6	15	7	16	7	5	7	24	15	[b]	18

[a] We are considering Reiss's "permissiveness with affection" as equivalent to "sex relations for engaged/in love."

[b] Figure for men has been omitted as total number of male interviews is a small proportion of the total sample.

sex since the 1940's. This may be due to the accumulating reforming influence of those social factors which was operating in the twentieth century. Certainly, the changed attitude shows itself sharply in the increase in sexual content of movies, the candid use of sexual lures in advertising, an increasing social sanctioning (if not precisely approval) of sexual material in popular literature, and a generally freer atmosphere which permits open talk about sex. But the new standard for coital involvement insists on permissiveness with affection.

Second, the parent generation (sampled in 1963 by Reiss) is far more conservative than the younger generation—and is apparently more conservative than it was when it was the younger generation. In Reiss's 1963 adult sample, only 17 per cent endorsed permissiveness with affection for males and only 5 per cent endorsed this standard for females.[33]

Apparently, the conservative parent generation refuses to endorse for their children standards of behavior in which members of their generation, and perhaps they themselves, engaged. What appears to be a "generation gap," however, is probably a manifestation of a change in role.[34] Reiss's data on his adult sample give a concise picture of the relationship between role position and attitudes.

Permissiveness evidently reaches its highest point on one curve (for the college student) while it reaches its lowest point on another curve (for the parents of the college student). What the data describe, then, are changes which occur as individuals come to occupy parental role positions, and they are not descriptive of differences between individuals of the post-World War II generation and their parents' generation.

In part, this information suggests that parents try to modify behavior in their children in which they themselves participated as young adults. This reaction may portend how the current young

Table 4   *"Marital and Family Status and Permissiveness in the Adult Sample"*[a]

Marital and Family Status	Per Cent Permissive	N
Single	44	(108)
Married		
No Children	23	(124)
All Preteen	22	(384)
Preteen and Older	17	(218)
All Teen and Older	13	(376)

[a] Reiss, *The Social Context of Premarital Sexual Permissiveness,* p. 142, Table 9.2 (some data omitted).

adult generation will feel when they are parents themselves. However, the qualification to be noted here is that the generation which came to maturity in the 1920's broke with previous generations in terms of behavior. The following generations continued in the same kind of practices but gradually came to express more liberal attitudes. The new liberalism of the younger generation may very well contribute to a shift in expressed adult values for the parent generations of the late 1960's and 1970's.

We know that several attitudes have changed and that sexual standards appear to be in a period of transition. "What was done by a female in 1925 acting as a rebel and a deviant can be done by a female in 1965 as a conformist."[35]

Data based on a large sample are available on sex behavior up to 1949 and on attitudes up to 1963. We do not know what has happened during the last five years or what is happening now. The general public impression is that there has been a very recent sexual revolution and that it is still going on. Most researchers do not believe that this is the case. The authors of this article, as social observers and recent reviewers of the literature on sexual behavior and attitudes toward sex, will attempt to "crystal ball" what has occurred during the last five years and what is occurring now. What follows, then, is not fact, but guess.

Past trends in social change, in behavior, and in attitudes toward sex are continuing. What seems to be taking place (except for pockets of our society) is a growing tendency toward more sexual permissiveness among the young unmarried. Sex with affection appears to be increasingly accepted. More and more this norm is based on personal choice, and it manifests itself for middle-class college

293

youth in the form of trial marriage, for the girl, and for the boy at least as a stable, monogamous relationship, to the point of setting up housekeeping. Increasingly, this happens with parental knowledge though not necessarily with parental approval. If Kinsey repeated his study today, he would probably find premarital virginity slightly lower and figures for those who have had premarital intercourse only with their spouse, a circumstance which was already on the increase in 1947 (born before 1900, 10.4 per cent; born 1920–1929, 27.3 per cent),[36] somewhat higher.

Promiscuity, a word objected to by many young people, probably has lessened. Certainly the use of prostitutes has diminished. If we are correct in believing that more young people are living monogamously together, and if marriage for both men and women (the figures are: median age of first marriages in 1890 for brides was 22.0 and for grooms was 26.1;[37] for 1966, the median age for brides was 20.5 and for grooms 22.8[38]) is occurring at earlier ages, then the statistical probabilities of premarital promiscuity have lessened, except when it is a reflection of mental illness. Today, except for the "hippies," who, according to the press, indulge in group sex, promiscuity as a form of rebellion is significantly on the decline.

We are living in a much more permissive society, and we are much more vocal about sex. As Walter Lippman put it, even as early as 1929: "It was impossible to know whether increased openness about sex reflected more promiscuity or less hypocrisy."[39] While we do not have much new evidence concerning sexual behavior, we do have nonsystematic overt indications about attitudes. It is seen in advertisements which are much more suggestive than they used to be. At one time, an advertiser would indicate to a male reader that, if he used a certain product, a pretty girl would kiss him. Now the ads suggest that she will have intercourse with him: "When an Avis girl winks at you she means business," and as Chateau Martin asks, leering only slightly, "Had any lately?" Movies have become less suggestive and more obvious; nudity as well as intercourse have become not uncommon sights. The Scandinavian picture, *I, A Woman*, for example, consists of a number of seductions with a number of different men. Perhaps what is more significant is that censorship boards, the courts, and power groups in this country have sharply amended their definitions of obscenity. The theater has, for some time, been more open about sex and its various ramifications, and four-letter words are becoming a theatrical cliché.

Another indicator of this generation's expressed attitudes toward sex are the omnipresent buttons, which express not only political, but also sexual opinions. The buttons are designed for fun and shock, and for public declaration for sexual freedom. Sold in large cities all over this country, they range from simple position-statements such as "Make Love Not War," "I'm for Sexual Freedom," or "Equality for Homosexuals," to invitations which read "Roommate Wanted," "Join the Sexual Revolution—Come Home With Me Tonight," to such shock jokes as "Phallic Symbols Arise," "Stand Up for S-X," and "Come Together."

More sophisticated young people feel that the dirty-word movements or the shock words no longer have any impact. In the October 26, 1967, *Washington Square Journal,* a New York University publication, the student reviewer of an off-Broadway production, *The Beard,* which freely uses four-letter words and ends with an act of cunnilingus on stage, says: "Unfortunately the force of the play rests on the anticipated violation of social taboo, and violating social taboos just isn't what it used to be."

Except for the rediscovered poor, the United States is a society of unprecedented abundance. Upper- and middle-class white Americans pamper their children, give them cars and money, send them to college and abroad, and set them up in their own apartments while they are going to school. These young people have leisure and the wherewithal to use it in amusing themselves—only the war is real, which gives a special significance to college as a way of avoiding the war. This abundance means that college-age men and women can travel together, live together, and have a sex life encouraged by their peers, whose opinions they have now come to value more than those of their elders.

Abundance for the young unmarrieds in the city has made it possible to meet other young unmarrieds in new ways. Apartment houses are being built for them; clubs are formed for them, but perhaps the most significant of all the developments is the use of bars, now often called pubs, which serve as meeting places where singles can meet without prejudice. A girl who visits the pub is under no obligation to "go to bed" with the man whom she meets and with whom she may leave. These pubs (and they begin to specialize in different kinds of singles), in a sense, institutionalize a system of bringing together like-minded people; they speed the dating and the trial-and-error process, for they offer this particular group of affluent young people a wide variety of partners to choose from, and they can choose quickly, independently, and frequently.[40]

Many observers of the current scene consider the "pill" the most significant single force for increased sexual freedom. A count of the articles listed in the *Reader's Guide to Periodical Literature* reveals that more articles were published about birth control in the period March 1965 to February 1966 than were listed in a ten-year sampling starting with 1925 and ending with 1957. The sampling yielded 89 titles. But we doubt that the pill has added materially to the increase in the numbers of young adults or adolescents who have had premarital sex. Effective techniques of birth control existed, and were used, before the pill. True, the pill makes birth control easier to manage (except for the memory requirement), but romantic love is still important; it makes taking the pill, when no definite partner is available, undesirable. What the pill does is to give sexual freedom to those who are having steady sexual relationships, for then the use of the pill adds to romantic love by making elaborate preparations unnecessary.

According to our crystal ball, which, of course, may be clouded, we have not had a recent or current sexual revolution in terms of behavior. However, there probably has been some increase in the proportion of women who have had premarital intercourse. It is our guess that the increase has occurred largely among women who have had premarital sex only with their spouses-to-be. If there has been a sexual revolution (similar to the 1920's but ideologically different[1]), it is in terms of frankness about sex and the freedom to discuss it. Women have demanded and have achieved more education, more independence, and more social rights; one of these is the right to choose a partner for sex. Men are accepting many of these changes in the status of women and are tempering their insistence on what have generally been considered male prerogatives, for example, the right to demand that a bride be a virgin. Young men today are probably less promiscuous and more monogamous, and their relationships tend to be more stable. Both sexes are approaching a single standard based on sex with affection. We are still in a stage of transition. Despite the title of this article, the only indisputable conclusion which we can draw from the current scene is that we are witnessing the decline, but not yet the fall, of the double standard.

NOTES

1. It is understood that even if it were possible to determine these correlations accurately, we would not have an explanation of causation.

2. Alfred C. Kinsey, Wardell B. Pomeroy, Clyde E. Martin, Paul Gebhard *et al., Sexual Behavior in the Human Female* (Philadelphia: W. B. Saunders, 1953). The data on the female subjects were collected from 1938 through 1949. Alfred C. Kinsey, Wardell B. Pomeroy, and Clyde E. Martin, *Sexual Behavior in the Human Male* (Philadelphia: W. B. Saunders, 1948). Data on the male subjects were collected from 1938 to 1947.

3. Lewis M. Terman *et al., Psychological Factors in Marital Happiness* (New York: McGraw-Hill, 1938).

4. Gilbert Youth Research, "How Wild Are College Students?," *Pageant*, Vol. 7 (1951), pp. 10-21, Ernest W. Burgess and Paul Wallin, *Engagement and Marriage* (Chicago: J. P. Lippincott, 1953); Judson T. Landis and Mary Landis, *Building a Successful Marriage* (3rd ed. rev.; Englewood Cliffs, N.J.: Prentice-Hall, 1957); Winston Ehrmann, *Premarital Dating Behavior* (New York: Henry Holt, 1959); Mervin B. Freedman, "The Sexual Behavior of American College Women: An Empirical Study and an Historical Study," *Merrill-Palmer Quarterly*, Vol. 2 (1965), pp. 33-48; Ira L. Reiss, *The Social Context of Premarital Sexual Permissiveness* (New York: Holt, Rinehart and Winston, 1967), chap. vii. Reiss's primary purpose was not to examine behavior (at least not in this latest presentation); he was interested in attitudes. He asked 268 students (42 of them males) in an Iowa college about their behavior. What he did was to correlate expressed feelings of guilt with behavior, and found relationships with age and behavior and relationships between expressed standards and behavior. The Institute for Sex Research at Indiana University conducted a 1967 study of sex behavior among college students, but the final results have not as yet been published.

5. Gilbert V. Hamilton, *A Research in Marriage* (1st ed., New York: Albert and Charles Boni, 1929; 2nd ed., New York: Lear, 1948), p. 348.

6. D. D. Bromley and F. H. Britten, *Youth and Sex* (New York: Harper, 1938), p. 36.

7. Gilbert Youth Research, *op. cit.*, p. 15.

8. Burgess and Wallin, *op. cit.*, p. 330; Landis and Landis, *op. cit.*, pp. 216 and 212; Ehrmann, *op. cit.*, pp. 33-34 and p. 46.

9. Freedman, *op. cit.*, p. 47.

10. Kinsey, *The Human Female*, p. 288.

11. Reiss, *op. cit.*

12. Ira L. Reiss, "Standards of Sexual Behavior," in Albert Ellis and Albert Abarbanel (eds.), *Encyclopedia of Sex* (New York: Hawthorne Books, 1961), p. 999. "These data were based on Kinsey (1953), but were especially prepared for [Reiss's] paper ... [by] Drs. Gebhard and Martin of the Institute of Sex Research. These were based on 2,479 women who either were or had been married by the time of the interview."

13. Confirming this change are data reported by K. B. Davis, *Factors in the Sex Life of Twenty-two Hundred Women* (New York: Harper, 1929), p. 232. Of those women who attended college in the early 1900's (that is, were born before 1900), only 7 per cent had premarital intercourse. According to Bromley and Britten, *loc. cit.,* 25 per cent of the college women of the 1930's had premarital intercourse. And according to Freedman, *op. cit.,* p. 45: "The rate of premarital nonvirginity tripled from 1900 to 1930."

14. Terman, *op. cit.,* p. 321; Kinsey, *The Human Male,* p. 395. Kinsey noted generational differences within his male sample; but the "generations" were formed by dividing his subjects into "younger" (under 33 years of age at the time of the interview) and "older" (over 33 years of age at the time interviewed) groups. He did not compare them by decade of birth as he did the women. The median age of the younger group was 21.2 years, that is, born approximately between 1917 and 1926. The median age of the older group was 43.1 years, that is, born approximately between 1895 and 1904 (Kinsey, *The Human Female,* chap. vii). Information is provided here that premarital petting had increased with each generation since 1920 even though incidence or premarital coitus had not. One of the possible explanations for the continued relatively high number of virgins is that heavy petting is now very common, so that there are a large number of "technical" virgins who engage in almost everything except coitus.

15. "Iowa Sociologist Calls Sex Revolution A Myth," *New York Times,* October 22, 1967, Section I, p. 80.

16. Wilbert E. Moore, *Social Change* (Englewood Cliffs, N.J.: Prentice-Hall, 1963), pp. 100-103.

17. In a recent article, Thomas K. Burch casts doubt on whether there has indeed been a breakdown of the extended family or a decline in the size of the family because of urbanization. See Thomas K. Burch, "The Size and Structure of Families: A Comparative Analysis of Census Data," *American Sociological Review,* Vol. 32 (1967), pp. 347-363. We feel, however, that there can be little doubt about the relation between urbanization and changes in function and meaning of the family.

18. T. A. Storey, "The Work of the United States Interdepartmental Social Hygiene Board" (New York: United States Interdepartmental Social Hygiene Board, 1920), p. 6.

19. *Psychopathia Sexualis,* the best known work of Krafft-Ebing, was originally published in German in 1886. The first English translation was published shortly thereafter.

20. *The Psychology of Sex,* which represents Ellis' main body of work, was published in English in six separate volumes from 1900 to 1910 by F. A. Davis, Philadelphia. Volumes I and II had appeared in French (1897) before they appeared in English.

21. Frederick Lewis Allen, *Only Yesterday: An Informal History of the Nineteen-Twenties* (New York: Blue Ribbon Books, 1932), p. 98.
22. William H. Masters and Virginia E. Johnson, *Human Sexual Response* (Boston: Little, Brown, 1966).
23. Ira L. Reiss, *Premarital Sexual Standards in America* (New York: Free Press of Glencoe, 1960), pp. 219-221.
24. These tables are rearranged in chronological order and condensed for our purposes from the ones appearing in Reiss, *The Social Context of Premarital Sexual Permissiveness,* pp. 16-18. The categories used by L. Rockwood and M. Ford in their (1940) study of Cornell students, *Youth, Marriage, and Parenthood* (New York: John Wiley and Sons, 1945), p. 40, were used for classifying the data of the other studies. The 1947 and 1952-1955 studies were made by J. T. Landis and M. Landis and reported in *Building a Successful Marriage,* p. 215. Their categories were: "Sexual Relations: For both, None for either, For men only, Between engaged only." The 1958 study by Ehrmann, *op. cit.,* p. 189, used the standards: "Double (comparable to Sex Relations for men only), Conservative single (Abstinence), General liberal single (Sex Relations for both), and Lover liberal single (Sex Relations for those engaged or in love)" as categories.
25. Reiss, *The Social Context of Premarital Sexual Permissiveness,* pp. 25-27, Tables 2.5, 2.6, and 2.7. The reverse double standard category has been omitted, for Reiss says that this "response is almost certainly an error." For his discussion of this point, see *ibid.,* p. 24. Reverse double standard adherents are understood to believe that women should have greater sexual freedom than men. Percentage accepting this standard were: 1959—9 per cent male, 6 per cent female, 7 per cent total; 1963—0 per cent male, 5 per cent female, 4 per cent total.
26. *Ibid.,* p. 128. The data for males have not been utilized because the men represent only a small percentage of the total number of cases in the sample.
27. Reiss reported 20 per cent of the females endorsing the double standard, but did not break down the figure to show the percentage accepting the orthodox standard nor the percentage accepting the traditional standard.
28. Reiss, *Premarital Sexual Permissiveness in America,* p. 233.
29. Nelson N. Foote, "Sex As Play," *Social Problems,* Vol. 1 (1964), p. 161.
30. Robert Bell, "Parent-Child Conflict in Sexual Values," *Journal of Social Issues,* Vol. 22 (1966), pp. 38-39.
31. *Ibid.,* p. 43.
32. Foote, *op. cit.,* p. 161.
33. Reiss, *The Social Context of Premarital Sexual Permissiveness,* p. 142. From Table 2.7.
34. *Ibid.,* pp. 140-143, and Bell, *op. cit.,* pp. 38-39.

35. Reiss, "The Sexual Renaissance: A Summary and Analysis," *Journal of Social Issues,* Vol. 22 (1966), p. 126.
36. Reiss, "Standards of Sexual Behavior," *loc. cit.*
37. U.S., Department of Health, Education, and Welfare, *Vital Statistics: National Summaries,* Vol. 50, 28 (November 1959). Source: U.S., Department of Commerce, Bureau of the Census, "Population Characteristics," *Current Population Reports,* Series P-20, 105-3.
38. U.S., Bureau of the Census, *Statistical Abstracts of the United States,* 1967 (88th ed.; Washington, D.C.: U.S. Government Printing Office, 1967), Table 75: "Median Age at First Marriage, by Sex: 1920-1966." Source: U.S., Department of Commerce, Bureau of the Census, *Current Population Reports,* Series P-20, No. 159.
39. Walter Lippman, *A Preface to Morals* (New York: The Macmillan Company, 1939; originally published in 1929; Beacon edition, 1960), p. 228.
40. For an interesting comment on this phenomenon see "The Pleasures and Pain of the Single Life," *Time,* September 15, 1967, pp. 26-27.
41. See Bennett M. Berger, "The New Morality," Unpublished paper, read at the Plenary Session of the Society for the Study of Social Problems, August 27, 1967.

Article 4

Feminism as a Radical Ideology

William L. O'Neill

Several years ago, in his cogent and provocative essay on the changing place of women in American life, Carl Degler argued that feminism failed because it was unable to construct a viable ideology.[1] Feminism, however, produced an immense literature, and much of it was ideological in that it attempted to frame the "woman question" in such a way as to force solutions.[2] Instead of writing off this material as inadequate—although it was—I think something is to be gained from tracing the principal lines of thought that feminism developed in order to pinpoint the weaknesses that permitted it to collapse once equal suffrage had been secured.

Because feminism was such a widespread, indistinct, poorly defined phenomenon, feminists never developed a precise vocabulary. Indeed, the vagueness of their language reflected larger confusions of thought and perception that kept them from building a successful ideology. No historian, to my knowledge, has found it necessary to remedy this defect, but, because I intend to show that there were several kinds of feminism, a word about terms is necessary.

The phrase most commonly used by women in the nineteenth and early twentieth centuries to describe their expanding activities was "the woman movement." This movement included not only those things pertaining to women's rights but almost any act or event that enlarged woman's sphere, increased her opportunities, or broadened her outlook. It covered everything from woman suffrage and social reform down to the individual accomplishments of gifted, ambitious women. "Feminism," a more limited word, related specifically to the advancement of women's legal and political rights. The feminist movement, in turn, was broadly divided into two wings,

From Alfred F. Young, ed., *Dissent: Explorations in the History of American Radicalism* (DeKalb: Northern Illinois University Press, 1968), 275–300. Copyright © 1968 by Northern Illinois University Press. Reprinted by permission of the publisher.

but, because feminists themselves did not recognize this until the very end of the period, i.e. in the 1920's, I have coined the phrases *"social feminism"* to describe that part of the movement that put social reform ahead of women's rights and "hard-core" or "extreme feminists" to describe those who put women's rights before all else. A "suffragist" was simply one who worked for equal suffrage, irrespective of her views on other questions.[3]

During much of its history feminism was considered extremely radical; indeed, suffragists did not triumph until after they had persuaded the public that they constituted a "bourgeois, middle-class, . . . middle-of-the-road movement."[4] Although equal suffrage was an absurdly controversial issue, and there was little basis for the repeated charge that it was revolutionary, for a long time there was good reason to think that the feminist program—of which suffrage was only a part—had revolutionary implications. This was so because, by the Victorian era, women were locked into such a tight domestic system—their role so narrowly defined—that granting them real equality was impossible without overhauling the entire social structure. Full equality required drastic readjustments on two levels. If women were to have an equal chance with men to develop themselves, not only would they need equal educational and vocational opportunities but they would somehow have to be relieved of the domestic obligations that bound most of them to the home. And, because every system encourages the attitudes that are appropriate to it, the whole complex of ideas and assumptions that "justified" women's inferior status would have to be changed.

At the beginning of the nineteenth century the only acceptable roles for women were domestic; there was virtually nothing for them to do except stay at home or hire out as maids, governesses and, before long, teachers. A handful made other places for themselves, but until the middle of the century they were too few to affect the system. The cultural rationale that kept women in the home, however, was more complex and demands further attention. The Victorian woman was part of a network of ideas, prejudices, and religious emotionalism that simultaneously degraded and elevated her. "The cult of true womanhood" (as one historian calls it) emphasized women's piety, purity, submissiveness, and domesticity. Religious work was almost the only form of outside activity permitted women because it did not take them away from their "true sphere." "From her home woman performed her great task of bringing men back to God."[5] Woman, it was believed, was morally and spiritually superior to man because of her highly developed intuition, refined sensibilities, and especially because of those life-giving maternal powers that defied man's comprehension. But woman was physically weaker than man, inferior to him in cognitive ability, and wholly unsuited to the rough world outside the home. This was just as well, however, because women were largely responsible for "The Family," the chief adornment of Christian society and the foundation of civilized life.[6]

Although the concept of women as wan, ethereal, spiritualized creatures bore little relation to reality by mid-century, when women operated machines, worked in the fields, hand-washed clothing, and toiled over kitchen ranges, it was endorsed by science and by religion. A vast and constantly growing body of polemical literature was churned out by physicians, clergymen, and journalists in support of this thesis. Even fashion conspired to the same end; the bustles and hoops and the corsets and trailing skirts in which women were encased throughout much of the century seemed designed to hobble them and prevent all but the most desperate from leaving their homes for long. (The weight of metal, cloth, and bone that women were expected to bear should itself have disproved the notion that they were peculiarly delicate creatures, but of course it did not). Feminine "delicacy" was considered the visible evidence of their superior sensibilities, the "finer clay" of which they were made. Women who were not delicate by nature became so by design. In the end, the fashion was self-defeating for it aroused fears that women would become so ornamental as to be incapable of discharging their essential functions. The Civil War helped wake middle-class women from "their dream of a lady-like uselessness," and in 1861, when Vassar College was founded, its trustees put physical education at the head of their list of objectives.[7]

The Victorian idealization of women was self-defeating in another and more important way. The Victorians attempted to compensate women for their domestic and pedagogic responsibilities by enveloping them in a mystique that asserted their higher status while at the same time guaranteeing their inferiority; hence the endless polemics on the moral purity and spiritual genius of woman that found its highest expression in the home and that had to be safeguarded at all costs from the hopelessly corrupting effects of the man-made society without. But, as William R. Taylor and Christopher Lasch have suggested, the cult of women and the home contained contradictions that tended to undermine the very things they were supposed to safeguard. Implicit in the myth was a repudiation not only of heterosexuality but of domesticity itself. It was her purity, contrasted with the coarseness of men, that made woman the head of the home (though not of the family) and the guardian of public morality. But the same purity made intercourse between men and women at last almost literally impossible and drove women to retreat almost exclusively into the society of their own sex, to abandon the very home which it was their appointed mission to preserve.[8]

Thus the "woman movement" had its origins in the sexual segregation that Victorians considered essential for an ideal domestic system. Beginning with church societies and a few women's clubs, associationism grew and grew, until by the end of the century millions of women were caught up in it, and their old isolation was broken.

As we noted earlier, the woman movement was not the same thing as feminism. Women who worked for their church or met in literary societies were, however, indirectly helping themselves by developing aspirations that promoted the larger growth to come. They began to press for more education and to manifest intellectual and literary interests. The acute Englishwoman, Harriet Martineau, noted that "in my progress through the country I met with a greater variety and extent of female pedantry than the experience of a lifetime in Europe would afford." This pedantry, she hastened to add, "was not to be despised in an oppressed class as it indicates the first struggle of intellect with its restraints; and it is therefore a hopeful symptom."[9]

Even more hopeful, of course, was the next step that these developments made possible: the formulation of a distinct women's rights movement. In the 1830's women were stirred by the currents of reform that were sweeping the country, and those who were moved to action discovered that their status as women told against their ambitions as abolitionists, temperance workers, or whatever. Sarah M. Grimké was inspired to write the first American feminist tract of consequence[10] because some clergymen objected to her antislavery work. Elizabeth Cady Stanton was started on her career as a women's rights leader after she was denied a seat, by reason of her sex, at a World Anti-Slavery Convention in London. Susan B. Anthony became a feminist after she was discriminated against by her male colleagues in the temperance movement.

In 1848 these separate streams of dissent came together at the first Woman's Rights Convention in Seneca Falls, New York. The "Declaration of Sentiments" that was adopted by the meeting indicated another element that infused the early feminist movement: the libertarianism of the age of reform. Modeled in part on the Declaration of Independence, this manifesto declared that "the history of mankind is a history of repeated injuries and usurpations on the part of man toward woman, having in direct object the establishment of an absolute tyranny over her."[11] It was, in fact, a decidedly radical document—not that it called for an end to private property, or anticipated a good society along socialist lines, but in storming against every iniquity from votelessness to the double standard of morals it made demands that could not be satisfied without profound changes in the social order. The most sophisticated feminists appreciated, in some measure at least, that they were not merely asking for their rights as citizens, that what they wanted called for new institutions as well as new ways of thinking. They seem to have been feeling their way toward a new domestic order. Mrs. Stanton, who denounced marriage as "opposed to all God's laws," wanted to begin its reformation by liberalizing divorce.[12] The magazine she and Susan B. Anthony ran after the Civil War, *Revolution,* was full of references to the "marriage question" at a time when no orthodox person was willing to admit that there was a marriage question.

Logic alone had forced extreme feminists to sail these dangerous waters because even then it was clear that if women were fully emancipated by law, their domestic obligations would nevertheless prevent them from competing with men on an equal basis. There were only two (by no means mutually exclusive) ways of dealing with this problem: Either women must be supported by the kind of welfare measures (guaranteed maternity leaves with pay, family allowances, and the like) that the advanced social democracies have devised, or marriage and the family must be more flexibly defined.

Because the first alternative did not exist in the mid-nineteenth century, far-sighted women had to consider how the essential domestic institutions could be revised to free women from the tyranny of home and family; they had some precedents to guide them. For their own reasons the Mormons practiced polygamy, while the Shaker communities went to the opposite extreme by abolishing not only marriage but sexual relations as well. A number of perfectionist groups explored the varieties of free love, such as John Humphrey Noyes, who (at Oneida, New York) combined the equality of the sexes, perfectionism, socialism, and "complex marriage" (the sharing of spouses) in a bizarre but strikingly successful way. In such an atmosphere it was natural for the boldest feminists to flirt with radical approaches to the domestic problem. It is impossible to tell where these speculations would have led Mrs. Stanton and her followers, but the Victoria Woodhull affair suggests a likely possibility.

Victoria Woodhull and her equally vivid sister, Tennessee Celeste Claflin, burst upon the New York scene in 1868. Although nominally lady stockbrokers, they were agitators and evangelists by persuasion, and enthusiasts for everything radical, or just plain wild—socialism, spiritualism or women's rights. Their magazine, *Woodhull and Claflin's Weekly,* promoted such causes, as well as the peculiar interests of their mentor, Stephen Pearl Andrews, a self-proclaimed universal philosopher and linguist. The surprising thing about the raffish sisters is that they rapidly became celebrated champions of the cause of women, admired by such shrewd and experienced figures as Elizabeth Cady Stanton and Susan B. Anthony. In 1871, for example, Victoria Woodhull persuaded a congressional subcommittee to hold hearings on woman suffrage, and she testified before it with great effect.

Their *Weekly* was interested in marriage from the beginning. Stephen Pearl Andrews believed in free love in the usual Victorian sense (that is, in extramarital sexual relationships contracted as a matter of principle), and the Claflin sisters had practiced free love long before they understood its theoretical possibilities. Having thrown out a good many hints, Mrs. Woodhull finally called a mass meeting and on the stage of Steinway Hall declared herself a free lover. She seems to have been genuinely astonished at the ferocious reaction to this public confession; newspapers hounded her, cautious feminists snubbed her, and the sisters fell on hard times, financially and emotionally. Victoria struck back by disclosing that Henry Ward Beecher, the most famous preacher of the day and a good friend of woman suffrage, had been having an affair with the wife of Theodore Tilton, Mrs. Woodhull's friend, her biographer, and perhaps her lover. The ensuing scandal destroyed the Claflins and the Tiltons; but Beecher survived it, thanks to his great reputation, considerable courage, and influential friends.[13]

The effect of this debacle on the suffrage movement's fortunes is hard to determine because the cause was already in bad shape when the Claflins took it in hand. Suffragists had been disappointed at the end of the Civil War when they were asked to sacrifice votes for women to secure votes for Negro men. Some of them refused to admit that the freedman's need was greater than theirs and, because of this and other frictions, the suffrage movement had divided into two organizations: the staid, Boston-based American Woman's Suffrage Association and the more aggressive National Woman's Suffrage Association, led by Miss Anthony and Mrs. Stanton. Both groups were tarnished by the Beecher-Tilton affair, but the AWSA suffered less because it had always been anti-Claflin. The NWSA came in for a larger measure of abuse because of its closer association with the sisters, but the unquestionable virtue and integrity of its leaders saved it from total eclipse. It used to be thought that the affair had set back equal suffrage for decades; today, however, the movement's temporary decline seems to have been only one feature of the conservative backlash of the Gilded Age. Suffragists had expected too big a reward for their services during the Civil War as nurses, propagandists and sanitary commission volunteers. The country was grateful to them, but not all that grateful—as the defeat of woman suffrage in the hotly contested Kansas referendum of 1866 demonstrated. In freeing and enfranchising the Negro, America, it seemed, had exhausted its supply of liberalism.

The Woodhull affair had one lasting effect, however: it reaffirmed the general conviction that suffrage politics and radical speculations, particularly those affecting marriage and the family, did not mix. In consequence the movement, although it never disowned the social goals that women's votes were presumably to implement, emphasized the most conservative aspects of the suffrage question. The vote was shown to be compatible with the existing domestic economy, and—at best—with those reforms that would elevate and refine domesticity to the level of perfection for which society yearned. Suffragists thereafter, vigorously resisting the temptation to think seriously about the domestic institutions that ruled their lives, made sexual orthodoxy their ruling principle.

In the long run these shocks had two important consequences: feminism rapidly became more conservative and more altruistic. Its conservatism—not the doing of Victoria Woodhull—stemmed from the tightening up of morals and manners that occurred in the high Victorian era. Bills like the Comstock Act (1873) made it impossible for John Humphrey Noyes and other sexual radicals to use the mails, choking off the lively debate that had flourished earlier. The porous or open quality that had characterized American life in the age of refom gave way to the censorious prudery we associate with Victorianism. It is very likely that the extreme feminists would have had to abandon their tentative explorations, if only because of social purity. Earlier there had been sporadic attempts by organized women to eliminate the double standard of morals by holding men to a higher level of conduct. The radical feminists who toyed with free love approached the same goal from an opposite direction, by proposing a sort of convergence in which men and women would occupy a middle ground between the old extremes of absolute license and complete chastity. After the war, however, all doubts as to which line feminists would follow were relieved by the social purity movement, which enlisted the energies of public-spirited women all over the country in a crusade to abolish prostitution and infidelity.[14] Mrs. Stanton continued to advocate free divorce, to the great embarrassment of her younger followers, but she was very much the exception.

At the same time that feminists abandoned their more advanced positions they took on a great range of activities that often had little to do with women's rights. Extreme feminists, for example, displayed a keen sense of self-interest in the struggle over Negro suffrage after the Civil War. The Stantonites as a rule were more radical and more sensitive to the needs of others than the Boston faction, but when they were forced to choose between the Negroes' interests and their own they unflinchingly went down the line for feminist objectives.

The feminism of later years, however, was much more generous and diffuse. A hardy band of suffragists fought the good fight for the vote while most feminists devoted themselves to charities, philanthropies, and reforms. As social workers, settlement house residents, members of women's clubs, advocates of the reform of child labor and women's working conditions, of municipal government, public health, education and housing, and as temperance workers and conservationists they submerged their interests as women in a sea of worthy enterprises. These social justice activities became the principal justification for feminism, and are what historians most admire about the movement, but feminists paid a high price for their good deeds in two important ways. First, these activities drained off personnel from the women's rights movement and protracted the suffrage struggle. Second, they led to ideological confusions that played a large role in the collapse of feminism once the vote was won.

Social feminism also perpetuated the confusion between class and sex, that false sense of solidarity that characterized the entire woman movement. In a way this was natural, because all women suffered from disabilities that were imposed upon men only discriminatingly. It was not possible to have a "man movement" because most men enjoyed all the rights and opportunities that God and nature presumably intended them to have. Equal rights for women, however, did not mean the same thing to a factory girl that it meant to a college graduate, and feminists invariably refused to admit that differences in station among women were of any importance. In the beginning this hardly mattered, because the early feminists were mainly bourgeois intellectuals who were struggling to improve their own immediate circumstances. As the woman movement matured, however, its sociological evasions and self-deceptions attained critical proportions.

This analytic failure, which was characteristic of a movement that (with the notable exceptions of Elizabeth Cady Stanton and Charlotte Perkins Gilman) produced few intellects of the first rank, was compounded by an insistence that women were united in a selfless sisterhood by their maternal capacities, real or potential. "Women," it was declared over and over again, "stand relatively for the same thing everywhere and their first care is naturally and inevitably for the child."[15] Maternity was not only a unifying force but the enabling principle that made the entrance of women into public life imperative. As another suffragist put it in 1878, "the new truth, electrifying, glorifying American womanhood today, is the discovery that the State is but the larger family, the nation the old homestead, and that in this national home there is a room and a corner and a duty for mother."[16] Not only was the nation a larger home in need of mothering, but, by impinging upon the domestic circle, it made motherhood a public role.

As Jane Addams saw it, "many women today are failing properly to discharge their duties to their own families and household simply because they fail to see that as society grows more complicated it is necessary that woman shall extend her sense of responsibility to many things outside of her own home, if only in order to preserve the home in entirety."[17] Thus the effort to escape domesticity was accompanied by an invocation of the domestic ideal: women's freedom road led in a circle, back to the home from which feminism was supposed to liberate them. Feminism was made respectable by accommodating it to the Victorian ethos that had forced it into being.

Given the plausibility and flexibility of this contention, women were (perhaps inevitably) lured into using it to secure their immediate aims; but in retrospect it does not seem to have been an unqualifiedly successful ploy. The Women's Christian Temperance Union is a case in point. Although one historian recently hailed Frances Willard's "supreme cleverness" in using "this conservative organization to advocate woman suffrage and child labor laws and other progressive legislation always in the name of purity and the home."[18] the history of the WCTU illustrates the weakness of an argument that begins by accepting the opposition's premise. In conceding that better homes were of equal importance to feminists and anti-feminists alike, these women reduced their case from one of principle to a mere quarrel over tactics. All the opposition had to do to redeem itself was prove that its tactics were superior. This apparently is what happened to the WCTU after the death of Frances Willard (which coincided with a significant change in its social composition), when new leaders came to believe that temperance was more crucial to the home than suffrage, child welfare, and other progressive causes. Perhaps this new orientation would have come about in any event, but surely such WCTU suffragists as Frances Willard made it much easier by their willingness to utilize the cult of domesticity in pursuit of quite separate and distinctively feminist objectives.

The truth was that while these feminists resented the demands made upon them in their roles as wives and mothers, they were insufficiently alert to the danger presented by even a partial accommodation to the maternal mystique. Gravely underestimating the tremendous force generated by the sentimental veneration of motherhood, they assumed they could manipulate the emotions responsible for the condition of women without challenging the principles on which these feelings rested. Moreover, while denying that under the present circumstances mothers could be held accountable for the failings of their children, they implied that, once emancipated, women could legitimately be indicted for their progenies' shortcomings. In 1901 Susan B. Anthony declared that "before mothers can rightfully be held responsible for the vices and crimes, for the general demoralization of society, they must possess all possible rights and powers to control the conditions and circumstances of their own and their children's lives."[19] Her remark would seem to mean that, once granted political equality, mothers would have to answer for all the ills of society. This was a great weight to lay on female posterity, and such statements contributed to the unhealthy and unrealizable expectations that feminism encouraged.

A further hazard of the feminist emphasis on motherhood was the support it lent the notion that women were not only different from men, but superior to men. Julia Ward Howe, a moderate and greatly admired feminist, persistently implied that emancipation was intended to make women better mothers as well as freer persons.

> Woman is the mother of the race, the guardian of its helpless infancy, its earliest teacher, its most zealous champion. Woman is also the home-maker, upon her devolve the details which bless and beautify family life. In all true civilization she wins man out of his natural savagery to share with her the love of offspring, the enjoyment of true and loyal companion-ship.[20]

Definitions like this left men with few virtues anyone was bound to admire, and inspired women to think of themselves as a kind of super-race that had been condemned by historical accident and otiose convention to serve its natural inferiors.

Such indeed was the case with women who, encouraged by the new social sciences (especially anthropology, which demonstrated that matriarchies had existed and may once have been common, if not universal), took themselves with a new seriousness that few men could share. Elizabeth Cady Stanton argued that prehistoric women had been superior to men, or at least equal to them, but that Christianity, and especially Protestantism, had driven the feminine element out of religion and had subordinated women to the rule of men. Society thereby had lost the beneficent moral and conservative forces of the female intellect and the mother instinct.[21]

With this line of argument Walter Rauschenbush, no enemy of women's rights, was compelled to take issue. Alarmed by what he regarded as the feminists' moral pretensions, he wrote: "Many men feel that women are morally better than men. Perhaps it is right that men should instinctively feel so. But it is a different matter when women think so too. They are not better. They are only good in different ways than men."[22] Rauschenbush believed in the emancipa-tion of women, but he reminded his readers that the feminine virtues could easily be exaggerated, and that in recent times both Christian Science and theosophy had demonstrated a particular appeal to women even though both stressed authority and unexamined belief.

311

As Rauschenbush's observation suggests, the attempt to demonstrate women's superior nature led nowhere. In essence it was just one more variation of the Victorian mystique, another way of exploiting the belief that woman's unique power was rooted in the mystery of her life-giving capacities. Taken one way, it led back to a preoccupation with motherhood. Read differently, it supported so complete a rejection of men that women could retain their integrity and spirituality only in spinsterhood. Or—by subscribing to the principles of Ellen Key, who elevated motherhood even above marriage and made the right to have illegitimate children the central aspect of feminism—women could have their cake and eat it too.[23] They could realize their generative and instinctual potential without an unseemly dependence on the contaminating male. Deliberately having an illegitimate child necessitated an act of masculine cooperation, and in a delicious reversal of ancient custom man became an instrument of woman's purpose and his ungoverned passion the means to her full emancipation. This was radicalism with a vengeance, but a radicalism that had curiously little to do with the normal objects of revolutionary ardor.

Most organized women, however, were neither radical nor especially feministic. The woman movement as a whole, and most social feminists in particular, were satisfied with the comparatively modest programs of the WCTU and the General Federation of Women's Clubs. These programs, despite the fears of conservatives, were no threat to what Mrs. Gilman scornfully called the domestic mythology; in fact, they rested largely on the domestic and maternal mystique that was characteristic of the Victorian era. Not only did organized women continuously invoke "home and mother," for the most part their serious enterprises dealt with such related social matters as pure foods and drugs, child welfare, and working mothers. Whenever suffragists were able to tie in the ballot with a specific problem of special interest to women, they gained adherents. Through most of the nineteenth century suffragists maintained that women were entitled to vote as a matter of right and that they needed the vote to protect themselves and to advance the causes that were important to them. Neither argument was very persuasive in the age of Victoria, and always the suffragists' greatest obstacle was the indifference of their own sex.

As late as 1908 Theodore Roosevelt could comfortably, and quite rightly, say that "when women as a whole take any special interest in the matter they will have suffrage if they desire it."[24] But only a few years later the picture had changed entirely. In 1914 the General Federation of Women's Clubs endorsed woman suffrage in the name of its two million members; in 1917 membership in the NWSA soared to something like two million; and in that same year 500,000 women in New York City alone put their signatures to a suffrage petition. By 1917 it was obvious that women wanted the vote, and by 1920 they had it.

Few feminists seemed to realize that although winning the vote had been a feminist victory, it had not been won for feminist reasons. Suffragists had merely persuaded the organized middle-class women, who had become a potent force for reform in the Progressive era, that they needed the vote in order to secure the healthier and broader domestic life that was their main objective; feminists had not, however, convinced bourgeois women that they were greatly deprived and oppressed and that they had vast unrealized capabilities. From a strictly feminist point of view, the vote had been wrongly obtained. It neither reflected nor inspired a new vision of themselves on the part of most American women. Moreover, the suffrage could not but demoralize feminists who had worked so hard for so long, only to find that success had little effect upon the feminine condition.

The immediate consequence of feminine emancipation, then, was the fading away of the woman movement as it became apparent that the great organizations had less in common than they supposed. Moreover, the organizations themselves were changing in character. The WCTU was obsessed with prohibition (although it did not entirely lose interest in other social problems during the 1920's). The NWSA was transformed into the League of Women Voters; and although the league struggled valiantly to advance the old causes beloved of women reformers, it lacked the drive, funds, and numerical membership of its predecessor. The General Federation suffered least, because it had always been less committed to major reforms than its sister groups, and if its member clubs slackened their efforts, the national leadership continued to support the federation's traditional interests. The best evidence of the movement's decline was the fate of the Women's Joint Congressional Committee, which had been formed in 1920 to lobby for bills in which organized women took a special interest. Although it enjoyed some success (it helped keep Muscle Shoals out of private hands and it preserved a measure of federal support for mothers' pensions and other welfare programs), it lost more battles than it won, especially in the crucial struggle to ratify the Child Labor Amendment.

In the 1920's the split between social feminism and hard-core feminism emerged as a fundamental distinction. During the voteless years a common interest in women's suffrage and a general if vague commitment to women's and children's welfare had saved feminists from having to chose between equal rights and social reform. Then, in the twenties, a sharp cleavage opened between feminists in the League of Women Voters and the Joint Committee—which labored mainly for civic-virtue and welfare measures—and the militant Woman's Party, which singlemindedly pursued a narrow program that was signified by the title of its periodical *Equal Rights*. The most divisive feature of the Woman's Party program was its espousal of an equal rights amendment to the Constitution. Social feminists were alarmed by the Lucretia Mott Amendment (as the Woman's Party called it) because of the possibility that the courts would define equal rights as equal treatment. If this happened, the entire array of protective legislation that had been enacted for the benefit of working women during the Progressive era would be swept away. Inasmuch as the courts had already interpreted the Clayton Act to the disadvantage of working men, had twice declared congressional child labor bills unconstitutional, and had struck down minimum wage laws for women, this was not an unreasonable fear. The Woman's Party insisted that equal rights and equal treatment would not be confused, or, if they were confused, so much the better: protective laws discriminated against working women by denying them the competitive advantages of men, who could work whatever jobs and hours they pleased. In reality the competition issue was relevant mainly to business and professional women who had to function in the job market as individuals. It hardly applied to wage-earning women, who could not bargain individually over wages, hours, or working conditions. Thus, feminists of every kind discovered that women did not constitute a real social class but were subject to the same distinctions that obtained among men.

Throughout the decade, and indeed long afterward, an unseemly struggle was waged over equal rights and protective legislation, but this quarrel was only symptomatic of the deeper confusions into which the entire movement had fallen as a result of the Nineteenth Amendment. It was not merely a question of whether complete equality was more risky than advantageous, nor even where, having won the vote, feminism ought to go, but what being a woman

314

in America really meant. In short, feminists had traveled a long, circuitous, ascending path—to find themselves in 1920 about where they had been in 1830. They had not failed to better their condition along the way, but in avoiding fundamental questions for the sake of immediate advantages they had merely postponed the inevitable confrontation with themselves. Now the day of reckoning was at hand.

In the 1920's, then, it became clear that the anti-suffragists had been right all along in saying that the vote would neither change the lives of women as individuals nor greatly aid the causes in which organized women were most interested. Most women soon lost interest in overthrowing such remaining barriers to full emancipation as the WP urgently, and the LWV rather perfunctorily, called to their attention. The surviving hard-core feminists abandoned the fight for social justice (except for themselves), while the social feminists devoted themselves to such causes as peace, poverty, and prohibition, which had little to do with the status of women.

Under these circumstances it was no longer possible to speak with accuracy of a "woman movement," and the term fell into disuse, although such organizations as the International Woman's Suffrage Alliance and the International Council of Women perpetuated the cosmopolitan and cooperative spirit that had been such a striking and useful feature of the old movement. Hard-core feminism, on the other hand, contracted in size and spirit, so that it came to resemble its own mid-Victorian predecessor.

In the 1920's the movement's focus of interest shifted from organized to unorganized women, from the sober clubwoman and earnest social worker to the flapper. This in turn signaled a rebirth of the old popular sociology that considered women only as individual members of an undifferentiated mass. Although the greatest achievement of the woman movement had been to expand the definition of woman, the movement had only modified, not rejected, the biological imperatives of the Victorian ethos; and when the movement began to subside it left the contradiction between woman's sexual identity and her unique persona to be resolved, if possible, in a wholly new context. This new environment was created partly by feminism's successes, partly by its failures, and to a large extent by things over which it had no control. The movement admired daring and independence, to a degree, but it associated these qualities with large and generous purposes. The "new woman" of the twenties was indeed bold and venturesome—but in pursuit of what the older generation considered trivial if not ignoble objectives. The woman movement wanted to eliminate the double standard in morals by making men practice the sexual ethics they preached. The flapper also endorsed a single standard of morality, but she wanted sexual ethics to conform to reality rather than the reverse. Most of all, of course, young women in the postwar era were molded by the characteristic novelties of the period: the ebbing of reform, the demoralizing aftermath of the "war to end war," the emergence of mass society and mass culture, the new technology, and the higher standard of living that permitted the merchandising of pleasure on an immense scale.

The change in feminine sexual behavior was not only the most sensational aspect of these changes but a striking evidence of the shift in women's lives from organization to individuality. Woman suffrage had been a public question that enlisted collective energies; sexuality was a private concern that women had, perforce, to cope with as individuals. Our own atmosphere is so sexually charged and we hear so much about the "sexual revolution" that it is easy to forget the significant changes that took place more than a generation ago. Not only was sex discussed publicly and with a previously forbidden candor in the twenties, there is good reason to think that people, especially women, experienced sex in a different manner. At the end of the decade a gynecologist remarked that in 1885 his typical patient was "the woman 'who would rather die than be examined.' In the early nineties the patient instantly covered the least bare spot with the sheet, but in 1920 full exposure is taken for granted by the young."[25] In another of those remarkable studies that preceded the Kinsey reports a psychiatrist discovered that the sexual experiences of one hundred women correlated with their year of birth. In his admittedly small and arbitrary example, of fifty women who had been born before 1890 only seventeen had engaged in either pre- or extramarital intercourse, compared with thirty of the fifty women who were born after 1890. It seemed to him that the sexual behavior of men and women was converging.[26]

These few bits of evidence lend substance to the feeling of most contemporary observers that important changes in the sexual patterns of the young were taking place during the 1920's. But the new sexuality was accompanied by new attitudes of even greater importance. A juvenile court referee wrote that the younger generation did not admire its parents. The old maxim that age and experience command respect no longer carried weight. Girls and young women were much more aggressive in finding husbands than their mothers were. They expected to work after they were married, mostly for the added income, but they were vague about what they would work at and reluctant to train for particular occupations. A girl "intends to marry at a more specific date if she can bring it about, have a definite number of children at desirable intervals, and earn a definite sum toward the upkeep when she needs to." Most disturbing of all, the younger generation had rejected the idealism of the previous generation. "So for lack of other vision they believe in themselves."[27]

Over and over again the same refrain was heard. Even when girls expressed more or less traditional sentiments, they did so for sensible reasons, which were very different from the principled stands of their mothers. Thus a study of 252 middle-class girls disclosed that although they thought chastity good and promiscuity undesirable, they generally advanced practical rather than moral arguments for this position. Only one girl in three said that in every case she would disapprove of a friend's affair.[28]

A thoughtful ex-suffragist writer for the League of Women Voters (which was distressed by its difficulties in recruiting young members) pointed out that "the feministic movement isn't at all smart among the juniors. But it is interesting to observe that such rights as the old feministic movement has already won for the females of the species, the young accept as a matter of course. Especially when these rights mean personal and individual privileges."[29] Her informants used the First World War, much as a later generation would use The Bomb, to deflate what they regarded as the moral pretensions of their elders and expose the uselessness of their advice.

At least one young woman struck closer to home when she bluntly observed that the previous generation always put off its own ambitions until after some job of reform had been done. "They were all going to return to their personal knitting after they had tidied up the world. Well look at the world! See how they tidied it up! Do you wonder that our generation says it will do its personal knitting first?" Indeed, this girl expressed a high degree of moral fervor in proclaiming her amoral credo:

> But we're not out to benefit society, to remold existence, to make industry safe for anyone except ourselves, to give any small peoples except ourselves their rights. We're not out for submerged tenths, we're not going to suffer over how the other half lives. We're out for Mary's job and Luella's

art, and Barbara's independence and the rest of our individual careers and desires.[30]

In one sense this outburst suggests that there was a feminist equivalent of Dada: an insistence that the private vision takes precedence over the social will, that art exists for its own sake and woman for her own sake, a repudiation of the grand causes and glorious rhetoric that had moved the older generation. It was also a logical conclusion to the feminist hardline.

We have seen how dismaying this attitude was to the social feminists who had viewed women's rights as only one aspect of the good society that women could bring into being if given the chance, but it was almost as disconcerting to those who saw feminism as an end in itself. A collective impulse is not the same thing as a social movement, and to the privatized young women of the twenties, luxuriating in their emancipation, the demand of the Woman's Party that they rise up and strike another blow for freedom seemed ludicrous and anachronistic. They had all the freedom they could use; the problem was what to do with it. Having rejected both the woman movement's thesis that the purpose of emancipation was service and the feminists' call to compete fiercely with men at every occupational level, what else remained?

What remained, as events would soon demonstrate, was the "feminine mystique." The feminine mystique, as Betty Friedan recently defined it in her lively polemic, is not much different from the nineteenth century's cult of domesticity. It too glorifies the role of woman as wife and mother, finds domestic impulses at the heart of woman's nature, and warns against the dangers of feminine competitiveness. It updates the old familial ideology, however, in several ways. Feminine emancipation brought with it a better-educated womanhood, with higher cultural and aesthetic expectations. Because the home could no longer be defended with religious sentimentalities, moral authorities joined with the mass media to depict the home (in the words of an advertising man) as "the expression of her creativeness. We help her think of the modern home as the artist's studio, the scientist's laboratory."[31] Women were encouraged to regard child-rearing and home economics as complicated, lofty enterprises that demanded a skillful mixture of exact science and aesthetic inspiration. This development, already well under way in the Progressive era, required almost no effort to convince bewil-

dered young women in the post-suffrage area that the home—
cleansed of its imperfections by modern science, capitalism, and
enlightened thought—was a fit object for their attention and a
worthy challenge to their sharpened talents.

The task of pouring old wine into new bottles was made easier
by psychoanalysis, which offered a popular solution to the problem
of reconciling sexual freedom with the necessary limitations of domestic life. The woman movement had drawn a line between eroticism and sex. It accepted, with qualifications, the role of women as
fundamentally determined by sex, but it vigorously rejected any
suggestion that sexuality was a human right. As it turned out, however, motherhood and sensuality were largely compatible with one
another. Pre-marital intercourse could be and was justified as preparation for that perfect physical union that modern science insisted
was a necessary ingredient of married bliss. Freud seemed not only
to rationalize a sexuality that society would in any case have to live
with, he did this in the context of a remarkably conventional view of
feminine nature. Freud, after all, was a Victorian, and his American
popularizers translated his concept of women as inherently passive,
dependent, and childlike creatures as meaning that women were
most in harmony with their true natures when they functioned as
sexually fulfilled housewives.[32]

Thus the popular science of the twentieth century recapitulated
the popular science of the nineteenth century in discovering that the
laws of nature decreed woman's sphere to be the home. The revolution in morals was, then, no revolution at all. Without for a moment
denying the importance of that measure of erotic libertarianism that
was gained in the 1920's, and admitting that the emancipation of
women really broadened their opportunities (although most of the
broadening took place before 1920), woman in the twentieth century
looks surprisingly like woman in the nineteenth century.[33]

With the emergence of the feminine mystique we can see more
clearly the ideological failure that kept feminists from preventing the
collapse of their movement. This failure consisted largely of an
inability to determine where their interests lay. Because they could
not clearly define their problem, they could not devise a successful
strategy for solving it. The most perceptive of the first-generation
feminists understood that overcoming the prohibitions that confined
them to the home made it necessary for them to challenge the
polarized definitions of male and female nature upon which the
prohibitions rested. This meant, in practice, denying that there were

any important differences between the sexes, apart from the inescapable fact that only women bear children. So direct a challenge, of course, provoked extreme responses, which frightened all but the bravest women, but led the more far-sighted among them to consider what would happen if the formal barriers were removed. Obviously, women would still be at a disadvantage because of their maternal obligations, and in the first half of the nineteenth century there was only one way this handicap could be minimized: marriage and the family would have to be reorganized. Because the Woodhull affair had vividly demonstrated the risks inherent in this line of thought, feminists withdrew to a more defensible position, which enabled them (so they believed) to exploit the successes of the woman movement. The movement, and especially its social feminist divisions, employed a sort of moral judo against the masculine establishment by relating its goals to the Victorian stereotype. Woman, the argument ran, needed to be free in order to fulfill her larger destiny as mother of the nation.

This strategy, however, was fatal to the feminists' long-range objectives. Although social feminism promoted many desirable reforms, few of them did much for women's rights, and when social feminism secured a notable feminist objective (such as equal suffrage), it did so in ways that undermined the movement's larger program. Moreover, this alliance with the woman movement led to such confusions and evasions among feminists that it prevented them from formulating an ideology that was adequate to the complex circumstances in which they found themselves. From the outset, feminists had defined their position negatively; they were against a host of specific disabilities—unequal laws, closed professions, votelessness—and their concentration on these barriers made them vulnerable to the opportunism that characterizes political movements, which puts action ahead of theory. Their need for allies, as well as their intellectual failures, made it even harder for them to resist the blandishments of the woman movement. It is a historiographical cliché that in America such opportunism is normal, even desirable, but pragmatism (as political expediency is always called) has the defects of its virtues. If ideological formlessness promotes flexibility, moderation, and useful alliances, it also blurs the vision and encourages what can be a fatal confusion between ends and means.

After women's suffrage was won, feminists discovered that it cost more than anyone a generation earlier could have foreseen. Social feminism was discredited when the vote failed materially to assist organized women in getting what they wanted. Hard-core feminism suffered for lack of an issue that could rouse women as equal suffrage had—and also because, in calling upon women to consider their own interests first, it went against the whole tradition of selfless altruism that had become firmly associated with organized womanhood. Valuable and ennobling as this tradition was, it prevented women from addressing their problems as women, from coming to terms with their disadvantaged status, and from organizing effectively to deal with it. The decline of the woman movement after 1920 further discredited organization along sex lines as an approach to public questions. Thus the post-suffrage era was characterized by the view that women were so different from men that real integration was out of the question, by the failure of organization as a distinctively feminine tactic, and by a general refusal to recognize that women constituted a disadvantaged group that was entitled to pursue its interests in the way that minority groups have historically done in America.

Since 1930 American women have lost ground in relation to their peers in other industrial societies and in relation to their position in the twenties. Not only Russia and Scandinavia but most of western Europe have a higher percentage of women who are physicians than does the United States. There are more women in Parliament than in Congress. The number of women pharmacists and dentists is negligible here but noteworthy in Sweden and France. The percentage of A.B. and Ph.D. degrees awarded to women in America has declined since 1920. Today the percentage of women who work is larger than ever before, but their occupational segregation is as great as it was in 1900, and the dollar gap between the incomes of working men and women has been rising steadily since World War II. Measured by almost any index, the position of American women, almost half a century after their formal emancipation, is neither enviable nor admirable. Countless articles and books, most notably Betty Friedan's, have in recent years documented these points and made us aware that feminism has failed and that the conditions it struggled against remain.[34]

If my analysis is correct, modern women will have to do two things to secure equality of opportunity and treatment. They must organize in a serious, deliberate, and self-interested fashion, which would seem obvious were it not for the fact that women's right to function as a pressure group is generally denied. Most Americans will admit that individual Negroes and workers may improve their circumstances without affecting the overall position of Negroes and workers in the slightest, but this principle is rarely applied to women, who are expected to deal with their problems by going to college, taking a job, undergoing psychotherapy, or by finding another personal solution.

The reason for this analytical myopia seems to be related to the same anxieties that kept Victorian society from penetrating to the heart of the woman question. The woman movement allayed the nineteenth century's worst fears by showing that formal emancipation and a high degree of organization were largely compatible with the existing social order. Unfortunately this development, tactically sound though it was, disregarded what was most fundamental and important about feminism as a response to modern conditions. It now appears that the unrest of women is directly related to those fundamental institutions, monogamy and the conjugal family, that the Victorian world was so determined to preserve. In theory women today are free to do as they please; in practice, their heavy obligations as wives and mothers prevent them from exercising the rights they nominally enjoy.

This brings me to the second task that confronts a new feminist movement, should one emerge from the present unrest. Before women can organize effectively they must clearly understand what it is they mean to effect. They must construct an ideology that will be superior to anything that has been seen in America; but those who now are engaged in the field of women's rights seem to me insufficiently aware of this need. Such organizations as the President's Commission on the Status of Women and its counterparts on the state level, the National Woman's Party (which still is working to secure equality of women by constitutional amendment), and Mrs. Friedan's National Organization for Women operate too much as their predecessors did. They see the problem in negative terms and they appear to take it for granted that the basic questions have been answered—that we know who women are, what they can do, and what they need.

More than anything else, women must understand the Victorian roots of their situation. The social feminist route (marvelous as it was from a humanitarian point of view) led to a dead end. The radical feminist solution was aborted before it had a real chance to work, but it may well be the key to a genuine feminist renaissance. Radical feminism was suppressed because it threatened to revolutionize the domestic structure, as it still does. I think, however, that the whole of the American experience shows that nothing less profound will give women the freedom in fact that we concede them only in theory.

It may be that little can be done along these lines, that woman's dilemma is one of those facts of life that simply have to be endured. But if a social revolution is wanted, and a drastic change in the position of American women would amount to just that (however unrelated it may seem to the economic problems that are the usual objects of radical concern), it must be preceded by deep and serious thought which up to this point has been conspicuously absent. To put it another way, feminism must have its Marx before it can expect a Lenin.

NOTES

1. See Carl N. Degler, "Revolution without Ideology: The Changing Place of Women in America," in *The Woman in America* (Boston, 1965), pp. 193-210. The best guide to the history of women's rights is Eleanor Flexner, *Century of Struggle* (Cambridge, Mass., 1959). A good analysis of the movement's thought in its salad days is Aileen S. Kraditor's *The Ideas of the Woman Suffrage Movement* (New York, 1965).
2. See, for example, Professor Degler's evaluation of the movement's best ideologue, "Charlotte Perkins Gilman on the Theory and Practice of Feminism," *American Quarterly*, 8 (Spring, 1956): 21-39.
3. "Suffragette" was the English equivalent of "suffragist." The former term was used in America mainly as a derisive term by critics of woman suffrage.
4. "A Bourgeois Movement," *The Woman Citizen,* July 7, 1917, p. 99.
5. Barbara Welter, "The Cult of True Womanhood: 1820-1860," *American Quarterly*, 18 (Summer, 1966): 162.
6. For a more complete description of this idea, see my *Divorce in the Progressive Era* (New Haven, 1967), pp. 58-61.
7. Amy Louise Reed, "Female Delicacy in the Sixties," *Century*, 68 (October, 1915): 258-70.
8. "Two 'Kindred Spirits': Sorority and Family in New England, 1839-1846," *New England Quarterly*, 36 (March, 1963): 35.
9. In *Society in America*, 3 vols. (London, 1837), 3: 107.
10. *The Equality of the Sexes and the Condition of Women* (Boston, 1838).
11. *History of Woman Suffrage*, 1: 70. This immense documentary history of the suffrage movement from 1848 to 1920 ran to six fat volumes and

was published between 1881 and 1922. The first three volumes (1881, 1882, 1887) were edited by Elizabeth Cady Stanton, Susan B. Anthony, and Matilda Joslyn Gage. Volume 4 (1902) was edited by Susan B. Anthony and Ida Husted Harper, and volume 5 and 6 (1922, 1922) by Miss Harper.

12. A letter to Lucy Stone, November 24, 1856, in *History of Woman Suffrage*, 1: 860.

13. For a compact description of these events, see Robert E. Riegel, *American Feminists* (Lawrence, Kan., 1963), pp. 144-50. A recent biography of Victoria Woodhull is Johanna Johnston's *Mrs. Satan: The Incredible Saga of Victoria C. Woodhull* (New York, 1967). The best single source on these events is the *Weekly* itself, a fascinating publication that deserves more attention than most historians have given it.

14. For this important but little-studied reform, see David Jay Pivar's "The New Abolitionism: The Quest for Social Purity, 1876-1900," (Ph.D. diss., University of Pennsylvania, 1965).

15. Mrs. Ellis Meredith at the 1904 NWSA convention, in *History of Woman Suffrage*, 5: 101.

16. Elizabeth Boynton Harbert, *ibid.*, 3: 78-79.

17. "Woman's Conscience and Social Amelioration," in Charles Stelzle, ed., *Social Applications of Religion* (Cincinnati, 1908), p. 41.

18. Andrew Sinclair, *The Better Half* (New York, 1965), p. 223.

19. In *History of Woman Suffrage*, 5: 5-6.

20. Florence Howe Hall, ed., *Julia Ward Howe and the Woman Suffrage Movement* (Boston, 1913), p. 158.

21. See her paper, "The Matriarchate, or Mother-Age," in Rachel Foster Avery, ed., *Transactions of the National Council of Women of the United States* (Philadelphia, 1891), pp. 218-27.

22. "Moral Aspects of the Woman Movement," *Biblical World,* 42 (October, 1913): 197.

23. See esp. Key's *Love and Marriage* (New York, 1911).

24. In a letter to Lyman Abbott, dated November 10, 1908, published in "An Anti-Suffrage Meeting in New York," *Remonstrance,* (January, 1909), p. 3.

25. Robert Latou Dickinson and Lura Beam, *A Thousand Marriages* (Baltimore, 1931), pp. 12-13.

26. See Gilbert V. Hamilton, *A Research in Marriage* (New York, 1929). Although Hamilton's sample was a small one, his findings "parallel those of Kinsey for the same grouping of subjects 20 years later" (in Aron Krich, ed., *The Sexual Revolution* [New York, 1965], p. xii).

27. Eleanor R. Wembridge, "The Girl Tribe—An Anthropological Study," *Survey* (May 1, 1928), p. 198.

28. See Phyllis Blanchard and Carlyn Manasses, *New Girls for Old* (New York, 1937), chap. 5. (This book was completed in 1930 but was not published until 1937.)

29. Anne O'Hagan, "The Serious-minded Young—If Any," *Woman's Journal* 13 (April, 1928): 7.

30. *Ibid.*, p. 39.

31. In Betty Friedan, *The Feminine Mystique* (New York, W. W. Norton, 1963), p. 217.

32. For an exceptionally astute critique of Freud's views on women, see Ronald V. Sampson, *The Psychology of Power* (New York, 1966).

33. Physically (or outwardly), of course, modern women look very different from their Victorian predecessors, thanks especially to the revolution in women's dress that was completed in the twenties. The early feminists placed great emphasis on dress reform, but they gave this up after the "Bloomer fiasco," even though such men as Gerrit Smith thought it was the most desperately needed reform of all. Certainly few other changes that were desired by women have benefited so many people for so long a time. Ironically—as was so often the case—women were liberated from the crippling burdens of their dress by accident rather than by intent; fashion, not reason, called the turn.

34. For the declining position of women, see also Degler's essay cited in n. 1. Mabel Newcomer, *A Century of Higher Education for American Women* (New York, 1959), also is illuminating. For the position of women workers, Mary Keyserling's "Facing the Facts about Women's Lives Today" (*New Approaches to Counseling Girls in the 1960's* [Washington, D.C., 1966], pp. 2-10), is compelling. Sex discrimination is accurately demonstrated in Edward Gross, *"Plus ça change . . .* The Sexual Structure of Occupations over Time," a paper Gross delivered to the 1967 meeting of the American Sociological Association in San Francisco, Calif.

Article 5

The Liberation of Black Women

Pauli Murray

Black women, historically, have been doubly victimized by the twin immoralities of Jim Crow and Jane Crow. Jane Crow refers to the entire range of assumptions, attitudes, stereotypes, customs, and arrangements which have robbed women of a positive self-concept and prevented them from participating fully in society as equals with men. Traditionally, racism and sexism in the United States have shared some common origins, displayed similar manifestations, reinforced one another, and are so deeply intertwined in the country's institutions that the successful outcome of the struggle against racism will depend in large part upon the simultaneous elimination of all discrimination based upon sex. Black women, faced with these dual barriers, have often found that sex bias is more formidable than racial bias. If anyone should ask a Negro woman in America what has been her greatest achievement, her honest answer would be, "I survived!"

Negro women have endured their double burden with remarkable strength and fortitude. With dignity they have shared with black men a partnership as members of an embattled group excluded from the normal protections of the society and engaged in a struggle for survival during nearly four centuries of a barbarous slave trade, two centuries of chattel slavery, and a century or more of illusive citizenship. Throughout this struggle, into which has been poured most of the resources and much of the genius of successive generations of American Negroes, these women have often carried a disproportionate share of responsibility for the black family as they strove to keep its integrity intact against a host of indignities to which it has been subjected. Black women have not only stood shoulder to shoulder with black men in every phase of the struggle, but they have often continued to stand firmly when their men were

From Mary Lou Thompson, ed., *Voices of the New Feminism* (Boston: Beacon Press, 1970), 88–102. Reprinted by permission.

destroyed by it. Few blacks are unfamiliar with that heroic, if formidable, figure exhorting her children and grandchildren to overcome every obstacle and humiliation and to "Be somebody!"

In the battle for survival, Negro women developed a tradition of independence and self-reliance, characteristics which according to the late Dr. E. Franklin Frazier, Negro sociologist, have "provided generally a pattern of equalitarian relationship between men and women in America." The historical factors which have fostered the black women's feeling of independence have been the economic necessity to earn a living to help support their families—if indeed they were not the sole breadwinners—and the need for the black community to draw heavily upon the resources of all of its members in order to survive.

Yet these survival values have often been distorted, and the qualities of strength and independence observable in many Negro women have been stereotyped as "female dominance" attributed to the "matriarchal" character of the Negro family developed during slavery and its aftermath. The popular conception is that because society has emasculated the black male, he has been unable to assume his economic role as head of the household and the black woman's earning power has placed her in a dominant position. The black militant's cry for the retrieval of black manhood suggests an acceptance of this stereotype, an association of masculinity with male dominance and a tendency to treat the values of self-reliance and independence as purely masculine traits. Thus, while Blacks generally have recognized the fusion of white supremacy and male dominance (note the popular expressions "The Man" and "Mr. Charlie"), male spokesmen for Negro rights have sometimes pandered to sexism in their fight against racism. When nationally known civil rights leader James Farmer ran for Congress against Mrs. Shirley Chisholm in 1968, his campaign literature stressed the need for a "strong male image" and a "man's voice" in Washington.

If idealized values of masculinity and feminity are used as criteria, it would be hard to say whether the experience of slavery subjected the black male to any greater loss of his manhood than the black female of her womanhood. The chasm between the slave woman and her white counterpart (whose own enslavement was masked by her position as a symbol of high virtue and an object of chivalry) was as impassable as the gulf between the male slave and his arrogant white master. If black males suffered from real and psychological castration, black females bore the burden of real or psychological rape. Both situations involved the negation of the individual's personal integrity and attacked the foundations of one's sense of personal worth.

The history of slavery suggests that black men and women shared a rough equality of hardship and degradation. While the black woman's position as sex object and breeder may have given her temporarily greater leverage in dealing with her white master than the black male enjoyed, in the long run it denied her a positive image of herself. On the other hand, the very nature of slavery foreclosed certain conditions experienced by white women. The black woman had few expectations of economic dependence upon the male or of derivative status through marriage. She emerged from slavery without the illusions of a specially protected position as a woman or the possibilities of a parasitic existence as a woman. As Dr. Frazier observed, "Neither economic necessity nor tradition has instilled in her the spirit of subordination to masculine authority. Emancipation only tended to confirm in many cases the spirit of self-sufficiency which slavery had taught."

Throughout the history of Black America, its women have been in the forefront of the struggle for human rights. A century ago Harriet Tubman and Sojourner Truth were titans of the Abolitionist movement. In the 1890's Ida B. Wells-Barnett carried on a one-woman crusade against lynching. Mary McLeod Bethune and Mary Church Terrell symbolize the stalwart woman leaders of the first half of the twentieth century. At the age of ninety, Mrs. Terrell successfully challenged segregation in public places in the nation's capital through a Supreme Court decision in 1953.

In contemporary times we have Rosa Parks setting off the mass struggle for civil rights in the South by refusing to move to the back of the bus in Montgomery in 1955; Daisy Bates guiding the Little Rock Nine through a series of school desegregation crises in 1957-59; Gloria Richardson facing down the National Guard in Cambridge, Maryland, in the early sixties; or Coretta Scott King picking up the fallen standard of her slain husband to continue the fight. Not only these and many other women whose names are well known have given this great human effort its peculiar vitality, but also women in many communities whose names will never be known have revealed the courage and strength of the black woman in America. They are the mothers who stood in schoolyards of the South with their children, many times alone. One cannot help asking: "Would the black struggle have come this far without the indomitable determination of its women?"

Now that some attention is finally being given to the place of the Negro in American history, how much do we hear of the role of the Negro woman? Of the many books published on the Negro experience and the Black Revolution in recent times, to date not one has concerned itself with the struggles of black women and their contributions to history. Of approximately 800 full-length articles published in the *Journal of Negro History* since its inception in 1916, only six have dealt directly with the Negro woman. Only two have considered Negro women as a group: Carter G. Woodson's "The Negro Washerwoman: A Vanishing Figure" (14 *JNH*, 1930) and Jessie W. Pankhurst's "The Role of the Black Mammy in the Plantation Household" (28 *JNH*, 1938).

This historical neglect continues into the present. A significant feature of the civil rights revolution of the 1950's and 1960's was its inclusiveness born of the broad participation of men, women, and children without regard to age and sex. As indicated, school children often led by their mothers in the 1950's won world-wide acclaim for their courage in desegregating the schools. A black child can have no finer heritage to give a sense of "somebodiness" than the knowledge of having personally been part of the great sweep of history. (An older generation, for example, takes pride in the use of the term "Negro," having been part of a seventy-five-year effort to dignify the term by capitalizing it. Now some black militants with a woeful lack of historical perspective have allied themselves symbolically with white racists by downgrading the term to lower case again.) Yet, despite the crucial role which Negro women have played in the struggle, in the great mass of magazine and newspaper print expended on the racial crisis, the aspirations of the black community have been articulated almost exclusively by black males. There has been very little public discussion of the problems, objectives, or concerns of black women.

Reading through much of the current literature on the Black Revolution, one is left with the impression that for all the rhetoric about self-determination, the main thrust of black militancy is a bid of black males to share power with white males in a continuing patriarchal society in which both black and white females are relegated to a secondary status. For example, *Ebony* magazine published a special issue on the Negro woman in 1966. Some of the articles attempted to delineate the contributions of Negro women as heroines in the civil rights battle in Dixie, in the building of the New South, in the arts and professions, and as intellectuals. The editors, however, felt it necessary to include a full-page editorial to counter the possible effect of the articles by women contributors. After paying tribute to the Negro woman's contributions in the past, the editorial reminded *Ebony*'s readers that "the past is behind us," that "the immediate goal of the Negro woman today should be the establishment of a strong family unit in which the father is the dominant person," and that the Negro woman would do well to follow the example of the Jewish mother "who pushed her husband to success, educated her male children first and engineered good marriages for her daughters." The editors also declared that the career woman "should be willing to postpone her aspirations until her children, too, are old enough to be on their own," and, as if the point had not been made clear enough, suggested that if "the woman should, by any chance, make more money than her husband, the marriage could be in real trouble."

While not as blatantly Victorian as *Ebony*, other writers on black militancy have shown only slightly less myopia. In *Black Power and Urban Crisis,* Dr. Nathan Wright, Chairman of the 1967 National Black Power Conference, made only three brief references to women: "the employment of female skills," "the beauty of black women," and housewives. His constant reference to Black Power was in terms of black males and black manhood. He appeared to be wholly unaware of the parallel struggles of women and youth for inclusion in decision-making, for when he dealt with the reallocation of power, he noted that "the churches and housewives of America" are the most readily influential groups which can aid in this process.

In *Black Rage,* psychiatrists Greer and Cobbs devote a chapter to achieving womanhood. While they sympathetically describe the traumatic experience of self-depreciation which a black woman undergoes in a society in which the dominant standard of beauty is "the blond, blue-eyed, white-skinned girl with regular features," and make a telling point about the burden of the stereotype that Negro women are available to white men, they do not get beyond a frame-work in which the Negro woman is seen as a sex object. Emphasiz-ing her concern with "feminine narcissism" and the need to be "lovable" and "attractive," they conclude: "Under the sign of dis-couragement and rejection which governs so much of her physical operation, she is inclined to organize her personal ambitions in terms of her achievements serving to compensate for other losses and hurts." Nowhere do the authors suggest that Negro women, like women generally, might be motivated to achieve as *persons.* Implied throughout the discussion is the sexuality of Negro females.

The ultimate expression of this bias is the statement attributed to a black militant male leader: "The position of the black woman should be prone." Thus, there appears to be a distinctly conservative and backward-looking view in much of what black males write today about black women, and many black women have been led to believe that the restoration of the black male to his lost manhood must take precedence over the claims of black women to equalitarian status. Consequently, there has been a tendency to acquiesce without vigorous protest to policies which emphasize the "underemployment" of the black male in relation to the black female and which encourage the upgrading and education of black male youth while all but ignoring the educational and training needs of black female youth, although the highest rates of unemployment today are among black female teenagers. A parallel tendency to concentrate on career and training opportunities primarily for black males is evident in government and industry.

As this article goes to press, further confirmation of a patriarchal view on the part of organizations dominated by black males is found in the BLACK DECLARATION OF INDEPENDENCE published as a full-page advertisement in *The New York Times* on July 3, 1970. Signed by members of the National Committee of Black Churchmen and presuming to speak "By Order and on Behalf of Black People," this document ignores both the personhood and the contributions of black women to the cause of human rights. The drafters show a shocking insensitivity to the revitalized women's rights/women's liberation movement which is beginning to capture the front pages of national newspapers and the mass media. It evidences a parochialism which has hardly moved beyond the eighteenth century in its thinking about women. Not only does it paraphrase the 1776 Declaration about the equality of "all Men" with a noticeable lack of imagination, but it also declares itself "in the Name of our good People and our own Black Heroes." Then follows a list of black males prominent in the historic struggle for liberation. The names of Harriet Tubman, Sojourner Truth, Mary McLeod Bethune, or Daisy Bates, or any other black women are conspicuous by their absence. If black male leaders of the Christian faith—who concededly have suffered much through denigration of their personhood and who are committed to the equality of all in the eyes of God—are callous to the indivisibility of human rights, who is to remember?

In the larger society, of course, black and white women share the common burden of discrimination based upon sex. The parallels between racism and sexism have been distinctive features of American society, and the movements to eliminate these two evils have often been allied and sometimes had interchangeable leadership. The beginnings of a women's rights movement in this country is linked with the Abolitionist movement. In 1840, William Lloyd Garrison and Charles Remond, the latter a Negro, refused to be seated as delegates to the World Anti-Slavery Convention in London when they learned that women members of the American delegation had been excluded because of their sex and could sit only in the balcony and observe the proceedings. The seed of the Seneca Falls Convention of 1848, which marked the formal beginning of the women's rights struggle in the United States, was planted at that London conference. Frederick Douglass attended the Seneca Falls Convention and rigorously supported Elizabeth Cady Stanton's daring resolution on woman's suffrage. Except for a temporary defection during the controversy over adding "sex" to the fifteenth Amendment, Douglass remained a staunch advocate of women's rights until his death in 1895. Sojourner Truth and other black women were also active in the movement for women's rights, as indicated earlier.

Despite the common interests of black and white women, however, the dichotomy of a racially segregated society which has become increasingly polarized has prevented them from cementing a natural alliance. Communication and cooperation have been hesitant, limited, and formal. In the past Negro women have tended to identify discrimination against them as primarily racial and have accorded high priority to the struggle for Negro rights. They have had little time or energy for consideration of women's rights. And, until recent years, their egalitarian position in the struggle seemed to justify such preoccupation.

As the drive for black empowerment continues, however, black women are becoming increasingly aware of a new development which creates for them a dilemma of competing identities and priorities. On the one hand, as Dr. Jeanne Noble has observed, "establishing 'black manhood' became a prime goal of black revolution," and black women began to realize "that black men wanted to determine the policy and progress of black people without female participation in decision-making and leadership positions." On the other hand, a rising movement for women's liberation is challenging the concept of male dominance which the Black Revolution appears to have embraced. Confronted with the multiple barriers of poverty, race, and sex, the quandary of black women is how best to distribute their energies among these issues and what strategies to pursue which will minimize conflicting interests and objectives.

Cognizant of the similarities between paternalism and racial arrogance, black women are nevertheless handicapped by the continuing stereotype of the black "matriarchy" and the demand that black women now step back and push black men into positions of leadership. They are made to feel disloyal to racial interests if they insist upon women's rights. Moreover, to the extent that racial polarization often accompanies the thrust for Black Power, black women find it increasingly difficult to make common cause with white women. These developments raise several questions. Are black women gaining or losing in the drive toward human rights? As the movement for women's liberation becomes increasingly a force to be reckoned with, are black women to take a backward step and sacrifice their egalitarian tradition? What are the alternatives to matriarchal dominance on the one hand or male supremacy on the other?

¬Much has been written in the past about the matriarchal character of Negro family life, the relatively favored position of Negro women, and the tensions and difficulties growing out of the assumptions that they are better educated and more able to obtain employment than Negro males. These assumptions require closer examination. It is true that according to reports of the Bureau of the Census, in March 1968 an estimated 278,000 nonwhite women had completed four or more years of college—86,000 more than male college graduates in the nonwhite population (Negro women constitute 93 per cent of all nonwhite women), and that in March 1966 the median years of school completed by Negro females (10.1) was slightly higher than that for Negro males (9.4). It should be borne in mind that this is not unique to the black community. In the white population as well, females exceed males in median years of school completed (12.2 to 12.0) and do not begin to lag behind males until the college years. The significant fact is that the percentage of both sexes in the Negro population eighteen years of age and over in 1966 who had completed four years of college was roughly equivalent (males: 2.2 per cent; females: 2.3 per cent). When graduate training is taken into account, the proportion of Negro males with five or more years of college training (3.3 per cent) moved ahead of the Negro females (3.2 per cent). Moreover, 1966 figures show that a larger proportion of Negro males (63 per cent) than Negro females (57 per cent) was enrolled in school and that this superiority continued into college enrollments (males: 5 per cent; females 4 per cent). These 1966 figures reflect a concerted effort to broaden educational opportunities for Negro males manifested in recruitment policies and scholarship programs made available primarily to Negro male students. Though later statistics are not now available, this trend appears to have accelerated each year.

The assumption that Negro women have more education than Negro men also overlooks the possibility that the greater number of college-trained Negro women may correspond to the larger number of Negro women in the population. Of enormous importance to a consideration of Negro family life and the relation between the sexes is the startling fact of the excess of females over males. The Bureau of the Census estimated that in July 1968 there were 688,000 more Negro females than Negro males. Although census officials attribute this disparity to errors in counting a "floating" Negro male population, this excess has appeared in steadily increasing numbers in every census since 1860, but has received little analysis beyond periodic comment. Over the past century the reported ratio of black males to black females has decreased. In 1966, there were less than 94 black males to every 100 females.

The numerical imbalance between the sexes in the black population is more dramatic than in any other group in the United States. Within the white population the excess of women shows up in the middle or later years. In the black population, however, the sex imbalance is present in every age group over fourteen and is greatest during the age when most marriages occur. In the twenty-five to forty-four age group, the percentage of males within the black population drops to 86.9 as compared to 96.9 for white males.

It is now generally known that females tend to be constitutionally stronger than males, that male babies are more fragile than female babies, that boys are harder to rear than girls, that the male death rate is slightly higher and life expectancy for males is shorter than that of females. Add to these general factors the special hardships to which the Negro minority is exposed—poverty, crowded living conditions, poor health, marginal jobs, and minimum protection against hazards of accident and illness—and it becomes apparent that there is much in the American environment that is particularly hostile to the survival of the black male. But even if we discount these factors and accept the theory that the sex ratio is the result of errors in census counting, it is difficult to avoid the conclusion that a large number of black males have so few stable ties that they are not included as functioning units of the society. In either case formidable pressures are created for black women.

The explosive social implications of an excess of more than half a million black girls and women over fourteen years of age are obvious in a society in which the mass media intensify notions of glamour and expectations of romantic love and marriage, while at the same time there are many barriers against interracial marriages. When such marriages do take place they are more likely to involve black males and white females, which tends to aggravate the issue. (No value judgment about interracial marriages is implied here. I am merely trying to describe a social dilemma.) The problem of an excess female population is a familiar one in countries which have experienced heavy male casualties during wars, but an excess female ethnic minority as an enclave within a larger population raises important social issues. To what extent are the tensions and conflicts traditionally associated with the matriarchal framework of Negro family life in reality due to this imbalance and the pressures it generates? Does this excess explain the active competition between Negro professional men and women seeking employment in markets which have limited or excluded Negroes? And does this competition intensify the stereotype of the matriarchal society and female dominance? What relationship is there between the high rate of illegitimacy among black women and the population figures we have described?

These figures suggest that the Negro woman's fate in the United States, while inextricably bound with that of the Negro male in one sense, transcends the issue of Negro rights. Equal opportunity for her must mean equal opportunity to compete for jobs and to find a mate in the total society. For as long as she is confined to an area in which she must compete fiercely for a mate, she will remain the object of sexual exploitation and the victim of all the social evils which such exploitation involves.

When we compare the position of the black woman to that of the white woman, we find that she remains single more often, bears more children, is in the labor market longer and in greater proportion, has less education, earns less, is widowed earlier, and carries a relatively heavier economic responsibility as family head than her white counterpart.

In 1966, black women represented one of every seven women workers, although Negroes generally constitute only 11 per cent of the total population in the United States. Of the 3,105,000 black women eighteen years of age and over who were in the labor force, however, nearly half (48.2 per cent) were either single, widowed, divorced, separated from their husbands, or their husbands were absent for other reasons, as compared with 31.8 per cent of white women in similar circumstances. Moreover, six of every ten black women were in household employment or other service jobs. Conversely, while 58.8 per cent of all women workers held white collar positions, only 23.2 per cent of black women held such jobs.

As working wives, black women contribute a higher proportion to family income than do white women. Among nonwhite wives in 1965, 58 per cent contributed 20 per cent or more of the total family income, 43 per cent contributed 30 per cent or more and 27 per cent contributed 40 per cent or more. The comparable percentages for white wives were 56 per cent, 40 per cent, and 24 per cent respectively.

Black working mothers are more heavily represented in the labor force than white mothers. In March 1966, nonwhite working mothers with children under eighteen years of age represented 48 per cent of all nonwhite mothers with children this age as compared with 35 per cent of white working mothers. Nonwhite working mothers also represented four of every ten of all nonwhite mothers of children under six years of age. Of the 12,300,000 children under fourteen years of age in February 1965 whose mothers worked, only 2 per cent were provided group care in day-care centers. Adequate child care is an urgent need for working mothers generally, but it has particular significance for the high proportion of black working mothers of young children.

Black women also carry heavy responsibilities as family heads. In 1966, one-fourth of all black families were headed by a woman as compared with less than one-tenth of all white families. The economic disabilities of women generally are aggravated in the case of black women. Moreover, while all families headed by women are more vulnerable to poverty than husband-wife families, the black woman family head is doubly victimized. For example, the median wage or salary income of all women workers who were employed full time the year round in 1967 was only 58 per cent of that of all male workers, and the median earnings of white females was less than that of black males. The median wage of nonwhite women workers, however, was $3,268, or only 71 per cent of the median income of white women workers. In 1965, one-third of all families headed by women lived in poverty, but 62 per cent of the 1,132,000 nonwhite families with a female head were poor.

A significant factor in the low economic and social status of black women is their concentration at the bottom rung of the employment ladder. More than one-third of all nonwhite working women are employed as private household workers. The median wages of women private household workers who were employed full time the year round in 1968 was only $1,701. Furthermore, these workers are not covered by the Federal minimum wage and hours law and are generally excluded from state wage and hours laws, unemployment compensation, and workmen's compensation.

The black woman is triply handicapped. She is heavily represented in nonunion employment and thus has few of the benefits to be derived from labor organization or social legislation. She is further victimized by discrimination because of race and sex. Although she has made great strides in recent decades in closing the educational gap, she still suffers from inadequate education and training. In 1966, only 71.1 per cent of all Negro women had completed eight grades of elementary school compared to 88 per cent of all white women. Only one-third (33.2 per cent) of all Negro women had completed high school as compared with more than one-half of all white women (56.3). More than twice as many white women, proportionally, have completed college (7.2 per cent) as black women (3.2 per cent).

The notion of the favored economic position of the black female in relation to the black male is a myth. The 1966, median earnings of full-time year-round nonwhite female workers was only 65 per cent of that of nonwhite males. The unemployment rate for adult nonwhite women (6.6) was higher than for their male counterparts (4.9). Among nonwhite teenagers, the unemployment rate for girls was 31.1 as compared with 21.2 for boys.

In the face of their multiple disadvantages, it seems clear that black women can neither postpone nor subordinate the fight against sex discrimination to the Black Revolution. Many of them must expect to be self-supporting and perhaps to support others for a considerable period or for life. In these circumstances, while efforts to raise educational and employment levels for black males will ease some of the economic and social burdens now carried by many black women, for a large and apparently growing minority these burdens will continue. As a matter of sheer survival black women have no alternative but to insist upon equal opportunities without regard to sex in training, education, and employment. Given their heavy family responsibilities, the outlook for their children will be bleak indeed unless they are encouraged in every way to develop their potential skills and earning power.

Because black women have an equal stake in women's liberation and black liberation, they are key figures at the juncture of these two movements. White women feminists are their natural allies in both causes. Their own liberation is linked with the issues which are stirring women today: adequate income maintenance and the elimination of poverty, repeal or reform of abortion laws, a national system of child-care centers, extension of labor standards to workers now excluded, cash maternity benefits as part of a system of social insurance, and the removal of all sex barriers to educational and employment opportunities at all levels. Black women have a special stake in the revolt against the treatment of women primarily as sex objects, for their own history has left them with the scars of the most brutal and degrading aspects of sexual exploitation.

The middle-class Negro woman is strategically placed by virtue of her tradition of independence and her long experience in civil rights and can play a creative role in strengthening the alliance between the Black Revolution and Women's Liberation. Her advantages of training and her values make it possible for her to communicate with her white counterparts, interpret the deepest feelings within the black community, and cooperate with white women on the basis of mutual concerns as women. The possibility of productive interchange between black and white women is greatly facilitated by the absence of power relationships which separate black and white males as antagonists. By asserting a leadership role in the growing feminist movement, the black woman can help to keep it allied to the objectives of black liberation while simultaneously advancing the interests of all women.

The lesson of history that all human rights are indivisible and that the failure to adhere to this principle jeopardizes the rights of all is particularly applicable here. A built-in hazard of an agressive ethnocentric movement which disregards the interests of other disadvantaged groups is that it will become parochial and ultimately self-defeating in the face of hostile reactions, dwindling allies, and mounting frustrations. As Dr. Caroline F. Ware has pointed out, perhaps the most essential instrument for combating the divisive effect of a black-only movement is the voice of black women insisting upon the unity of civil rights of women and Negroes as well as other minorities and excluded groups. Only a broad movement for human rights can prevent the Black Revolution from becoming isolated and can insure its ultimate success.

Beyond all the present conflict lies the important task of reconciliation of the races in America on the basis of genuine equality and human dignity. A powerful force in bringing about this result can be generated through the process of black and white women working together to achieve their common humanity.

Article 6

Contemporary Feminism: Theories and Practice

Jean E. Friedman

The 1960s witnessed a revival of feminism with the Women's Liberation movement. Cynics considered the movement a creation of the media, because the women's early protests, "bra-burning"[1] and the crowning of a sheep at Atlantic City's Miss America Pageant, had all the elements of theater. Too much emphasis has been placed on the sensational and peripheral aspects of the women's movement. As a result, ridicule detracted from the most substantial issue of the movement—the question of women's identity.

The concept of identity has such broad and indeterminate meaning in both popular and scientific usage that perhaps we can speak only of a few of its "dimensions" as they relate to women.[2] Simone De Beauvoir in *The Second Sex*[3] wrote that throughout history the clearest identity has been male. Women as a sex never claimed an historic role; civilization as we know it is man-made. Even the universal term for all human beings is *man*. Why? Because, De Beauvoir says, men defined themselves as Self, the Absolute, and relegated women to the status of "Other" or Object, a referent incidental to the Self. Similarly, Vivian Gornick, a freelance writer and frequent contributer to the *Village Voice* considers woman an "outsider," an object onto whom man projects his fears and fantasies. Woman as seducer and goddess is, "steeped in sex, drugged on sex, defined by sex, *but never actually realized through sex.*"[4] It is evident that Gornick touched upon the primal antagonism to the Women's Liberation movement—the deep-seated fear that women's fully developed identity would unleash the supposed, terribly destructive forces of her sexuality.[5] To men who reason this way, Gornick passionately argues, women could not be real; only the "idea" of woman is real to them. Gornick, like De Beauvoir, suggests that women have been defined by others and concludes that the psychic effect of this lack of self-definition is that today women

340

cannot take themselves seriously. The solution as Gornick sees it lies in "responsibility." Like the blacks, barred from assuming the responsibility of "serious" work (problem solving), and thus deprived of a sense of self, women through their relegation to the routine and monotonous household tasks, have been cut off from both "serious" work and the realization of their own womanhood.[6] De Beauvoir and Gornick typify the general focus of contemporary feminist thought.

The three main groups within the movement—privatists, reformers and radicals—respond to the problem of identity with differing programmatic alternatives. Privatists probably make up the bulk of the movement but generally are not members of any organized group. They prefer to operate within the confines of their families and concentrate upon a highly individual development of their own identity. The reformers are the white middle class and professional women who responded to Betty Friedan's *The Feminine Mystique,* a study which examined the restlessness of educated suburban wives whose only measure of personal fulfillment was through their children and husbands. It was from this group that Friedan recruited a base for NOW (National Organization for Women). Founded in 1966, NOW has worked for equal opportunity in business and professional jobs and in education. NOW women tend to emphasize the social aspect of identity. The individual woman identifies with the organization, its principles and her work for NOW. Radical women, angry when they were treated as second class citizens in the New Left movement, became more militant. By encouraging women to talk to each other radical groups hope to build some thoughtful awareness of what sexual roles are and how they affect women's lives. Radicals view revolutionary change as the only recourse. The emphasis upon individual identity more often than not leads to a social or revolutionary purpose in radical groups.

The theories of each feminist group become clearer upon closer examination. For Jane Gallion privatism has meaning in that each woman must face herself and have the courage to grow up. Gallion claims liberation of oppressed womankind is valueless unless directed to the fulfillment of individual needs and potential. In her witty and insightful book, *The Woman as Nigger,* Gallion contends women have been sold an adulterated product—themselves. To understand themselves women must cut through artificial media and advertising images. The lie is that women are liberated; the truth is women dare not ask for freedom. So women live the lie exchanging overt for covert bondage. In an ironic and biting play on women's submission Gallion thanked society for her privileges:

> Thank you for giving me a cigarette of my own. Thank you for giving me a thousand red buttons to push. Thank you for giving me Section IV of the newspaper. Thank you, thank you, thank you. . . .
>
> Thank you for giving me money instead of love. Thank you for telling me that when I am good. . . . I am masculine, that I think like a man.
>
> Thank you for making my greatest expectation my subjugation, body and soul and spirit, to any man alive, if he will only notice me.
>
> Thank you for allowing me to serve you.[7]

In the battle of the sexes Gallion encourages women to take the first step and try to understand male fears. She views women's subjugation as a projection of male insecurities—fears of sexual inadequacy, of growing old, of losing power. Understand these anxieties, she urges, and then like Nora in Ibsen's *A Doll's House,* say no to being used. Gallion's is a personal solution. Liberation begins, she says, when the men in your life know that you are no longer a servant.

Caroline Hennessey, a more militant privatist, believes in the efficacy of individual guerilla action that would break patterns of docility and submission; individual employees can sabotage business by causing slowdowns, cutting efficiency, misfiling documents. Personal commitment will then lead to broader involvement—groups of women banded together to pressure schools, universities, or businesses that discriminate, but Hennessey's alternative rests basically upon her faith in individual action or commitment.[8]

Privatism is characteristic of some movement organizations as well. Suburban women, who meet in various Women's Liberation groups, have a tendency to concentrate on problems of their individual identities and needs. Painful transitions to personal autonomy challenge traditional sex roles, but discussion rarely goes beyond informal, unstructured rap sessions. For many privatists the group sessions provide an escape from anomie. For others, invigorated marital relations have allowed them to adapt to their lives.[9]

Much of the initial political drive of the women's movement was supplied by *The Feminine Mystique,* the publication of which raised feminist expectations. Betty Friedan cut through the accepted notion that women had a certain "nature" which predetermined their role. The argument is a variation on the conservative theme that "whatever is, is natural," a proposition designed to set limits on highly variable human personality. The feminine mystique defined feminity solely in terms of the housewife-mother role, "the mistake, says the mystique, the root of women's troubles in the past is that· women envied men . . . instead of accepting their own nature, which can find fulfillment only in sexual passivity, male domination and nurturing maternal love."[10] Denied access to personal satisfaction in careers outside the home women found they had "no image of themselves" and were vulnerable, Friedan says, to "public images" manipulated by Madison Avenue, "Freudian" psychologists, "functional" behavioral scientists, and "sex-directed" educators.

Freud's tentative theories about women supported much of the feminine myth. Friedan challenged Freudian assumptions of women's biological inferiority and attacked his concept of "penis envy" which she described as particularly degrading to women. The motivation which Freud claimed led, "in normal femininity, to the wish for the penis of her husband, a wish that is never really fulfilled until she possesses a penis through giving birth to a son,"[11] Friedan explained, is understood by some modern behavioral analysts as simply a manifestation in the human personality of the need to grow and develop an ego. Freud's theory was culturally determined according to Friedan; he had simply rationalized Victorian ethos which glorified women's servility. He directed his efforts toward maintaining the status quo, helping men and women adjust to their roles in society.

For Friedan, Margaret Mead represented the prime "functionalist," another progenitor of the feminine mystique. In her early study, *Sex and Temperament in the South Seas,* Friedan noted that Mead found variety as characteristic of sexual patterns, reasoning from this that masculinity or femininity cannot be regarded as derived from sex. But as her work progressed she considered differentiation as universal and interference in the cultural definition disastrous. Therefore, she supported the traditional sexual roles of wife and mother so prevalent in Western society. Friedan wryly noted Mead's personal life-pattern deviated from the norm, and that she created a significant body of work in a man's world.

Finally, college and university educators, who have viewed women as totally sexual beings and taught them to adjust to motherhood as their sole function, have been equally important in prepetuating the feminine mystique. Friedan maintained greater concern was given to women's biological functioning than to cultivating their creative abilities. The mystique was further reinforced by advertisers in the media who exploited housewives in order to guarantee the most lucrative market-products for home. Producers and advertisers displaced women's feeling of "emptiness" by crowding the home with the latest household gimmicks.

In the years following the publication of *The Feminine Mystique* important issues of concern to women were being debated in Congress and the courts. An amendment to the Civil Rights Act of 1964 prohibiting employment discrimination on the basis of sex was proposed jokingly by southern congressman Howard W. Smith in order to defeat the bill. When the act passed, there was a question whether Title VII which banned sex discrimination would ever be enforced. It became evident to Betty Friedan and others concerned that without pressure from organized women's groups attempts to counter discrimination would be largely ineffectual. It was this realization that prompted the founding of NOW in 1966.[12]

NOW is in the women's rights tradition by virtue of its leadership principles, organization, and its political-legal reform strategy. The businesslike structure of NOW attempts to obtain for women "a truly equal partnership with men." A social consciousness very much in the Liberal-Progressive tradition, NOW believes its legal and political reforms will find a response in the government. NOW has claimed some victories, such as an amendment of the president's executive order to prohibit job discrimination by the government and its contractors and subcontractors. In addition, the Equal Employment Opportunity Commission ruled sex-segregated "help-wanted-male" and "help-wanted-female" advertisements violated Title VII. Currently, NOW is campaigning for the repeal of abortion laws in line with its belief in the right of women to control their own bodies. NOW has also been active in the campaign for passage of the Equal Rights Amendment, first proposed by Alice Paul in 1923. It provides that "equality of rights under the law shall not be denied or abridged by the United States or by any state on account of sex.' The amendment will affect marriage and employment laws in some forty states. Directly related to the ERA is the campaign to establish child care centers by law "on the same basis as parks, libraries and public schools."[13]

NOW insists that it is "'an action organization" and holds to the belief that feminism cannot be defined until it has been realized through action. NOW seeks to multiply the options for women by securing greater opportunity in "church, state, college, or office" and providing upward mobility for women who although they are 40 per cent or more of the labor force, occupy routine or undesirable positions. Work is institutionalized according to sex roles with women occupying the supportive positions. Women are nurses rather than doctors, and secretaries not executives. Paralleling the division in work is the differentiation in salaries. The reasoning behind these discrepancies is that it is assumed a woman's salary is supplementary; furthermore, she is not expected to remain permanently on the job. A study made in 1967 revealed the contrary. Over 60 per cent of women worked because of economic necessity, either they or their husbands earned less than $5,000 a year. Women's full-time employment contributed 35 per cent to 40 per cent of the family income while part-time employment allowed for 15 per cent to 20 per cent of the combined income. With regard to turnover and absenteeism, Caroline Bird argued that that is related to job and not sex.[14] "Equal pay for equal work" is one of NOW's primary demands.

Friedan insists her views and those of NOW are realistic; that revolutionaries talk in terms of visionary abstractions. Retaining a liberal's optimism, Friedan believes institutions will change and that decisions concerning sex and children will be much more responsible and rational, because they will be controlled by both men and women. Manless revolution is nonsense, a "cop-out" when a majority of women want children. However, Friedan does argue that "revolutionary" concepts in education are needed to develop women's potential. Sweden is her idea of utopia. The government subsidizes equality of the sexes; boys and girls take cooking and shop; in the universities dormitories are integrated sexually. Swedish husbands and wives adjust their work schedules to share household duties; the adjustment is temporary pending the establishment of government supported day care centers.[15] Friedan supports evolutionary change that would benefit, rather than disrupt, the system.

Reform is unacceptable to radical women for whom the only alternative is a fundamentally altered society. Sexual roles institutionalized in family, state, and church can be transformed only by overthrowing present institutions. The radicals object to the idea of an "equal partnership with men," because it implies partnership in a system in which social institutions have been constructed by the traditionally dominant groups.[16]

The problem of instituting a new society has created something of an ideological crisis in radical feminist ranks. New Left experience found Marxism useful only in a limited sense. Radical women activists are struggling to construct an ideology capable of competing with established political systems. In classical Marxism the modes of production determine social, cultural, and intellectual structures. History is a struggle between economic classes—those who own the means of production and those who do not, bourgeoise and proletariat, master and slave, exploiter and exploited. Engels theorized women were the first exploited class; "within the family ... [the husband] is the bourgeoise and the wife ... the proletariat."[17] To feminists the problem with Marx and Engels is that they discuss women primarily in relation to questions of family and private property; in fact, they define the patriarchial family as a means of controlling property. Juliett Mitchell, a Marxist, has observed, "The liberation of women remains a normative ideal, an adjunct to socialist theory, not structurally integrated into it."[18]

Lenin regarded "the emancipation of women" as a bourgeoise ruse. The woman question was part of the social working class question, the proletarian class struggle, and above all, the revolution. The great revolutionary chided Clara Zetkin, leader of the international women's communist movement, because she allowed sex and marriage problems to be discussed in meetings of women workers. He argued that such questions were not private matters since marriages involved children and the future of the community. Lenin's myopia can be attributed to his assumption that full equality was a working principle within the party even though he recognized that there were "philistines" indifferent to their wives double burden of housework and "productive labor." Liberation in socialist terms has meant simply full participation in production.[19]

Influenced by the New Left, most radical feminists have ceased to accept orthodox Marxism. They no longer believe that economic determinism is the most significant factor of women's oppression. Celestine Ware notes that the difficulty of socialist theory is that it "would emancipate women in order to acquire a larger work force and not aid in their self-actualization."[20] The development of the radical idea of self-actualization as a revolutionary principle grew directly out of women's experience in the New Left. Radical women, activists in the Civil Rights movement, SNCC, and SDS resented being relegated to the routine jobs while the men assumed decision-making positions inside and outside the organization. Most striking to activist women was the elitism displayed by radical men. Bullying tactics, the "I am more revolutionary than you" ploy, accusations of "sloppy thinking" effectively stymied women "socialized to fear aggression [and] who tend[ed] to lack experience in articulating abstract concepts."[21] Radical men pontificating the orthodox line insisted that the woman question was part of the "social, working class question." As far as radical women were concerned the movement had left them; the "philistines" were not to be persuaded. Some women did remain in the New Left movement. Radical feminists refer to them as "politicos," those who tend to see "feminism as only tangent to 'real' radical politics instead of directly radical in itself."[22]

The radical women who split from the New Left were forced to reevaluate Marx in feminist terms. Roxanne Dunbar in her essay, "Female Liberation as the Basis for Social Revolution," argued that the women's movement contains revolutionary potential because women developed as a separate caste. She claims that although women have shared in the predominate male culture, they have had a separate experience. Woman's special capacity for reproduction forced her into a sedentary life where she developed a community based upon cooperation. With the overthrow of woman's primitive communist society, women were subjugated in a lower caste. Caste is assigned from birth by physical characteristics and unlike economic class a woman cannot escape from it. "It means," Dunbar explains, "that whatever traits [are] associated with the lower caste will be devalued in the society or will be mystified in some way."[23] The caste system rooted in the patriarchal family will be destroyed, Dunbar explains, only when a cooperative society is created.

For Dunbar, women must lead the revolution and use feminist principles to reorganize society. She never identifies the feminist principles that will replace established ones. Marx identified women's oppression as part of proletarian class oppression. Dunbar claims that because women have had a separate experience they exist as a caste apart from the proletariat. To exploit the revolutionary potential of class and caste radicals must relate to both working class and women's experience. Dunbar believes that the woman revolution will precede social revolution.

A similar but less orthodox position is taken by Ti-Grace Atkinson.[24] She argues that biological and sociological functions of child bearing and child rearing determined women's class status. This role reduced women to the "functional" rather than human level. Atkinson, however, is best known as a proponent of the "new politics" of egalitarianism within the movement. As president of the New York chapter of NOW in 1968, Atkinson and the by-laws committee proposed executive rotation to facilitate a more equitable power distribution and counteract government by a few. This issue split the movement. Betty Friedan, then national president of the organization earnestly promoted her case, "I want to get women into positions of power." Friedan's statement provoked Atkinson to reply, "We want to destroy the positions of power . . . not get into those positions."[25]

Atkinson's group (later called the Feminists) broke from NOW to initiate a more radical feminism dedicated to the "annihilation of sex roles" and the elimination of the politics of domination. The Feminists instituted the lot method of leadership. The principle justification for the measure is that "all women are capable . . . of leadership"; Feminists refused to duplicate the male power hierarchy which implies domination of those below them in the structure.[26]

The egalitarian principle is exemplified by the way Atkinson and the Feminists use consciousness-raising. Women meet in small unstructured groups and examine the lives of group members. The object of these sessions is to relate individual problems to the pattern of discrimination which society perpetuates. In the process women attempt to construct political issues from the problems discussed, and promote self-awareness and a sense of solidarity.[27] Through consciousness-raising, radical groups such as the Redstockings, WITCH, and the New York Radical Feminists offer critiques of sexist society and, in the case of the NYRF, have begun to construct an ideology that deals with the reconstruction of women's roles.

The Redstockings, an offshoot of New York Radical Women, abandoned New Left activism for consciousness-raising. The Redstockings reject all ideologies as male rationales, and insist that only out of their own experience can they reveal sexism in our society. The group supports any action for liberation regardless of its sponsor. Similarly, WITCH (Women's International Terrorist Conspiracy from Hell), engages in consciousness-raising and in a bizarre guerilla theater type of action. WITCH organized the famous protest against the Miss America Pageant indicting society's commercialization of feminine beauty.[28]

The New York Radical Feminists is an amalgam of former members of the Feminists and Redstockings. The NYRF responds to political issues connected with the family, motherhood, marriage, sexual intercourse, and love. On the subject of love NYRF declared, "in the context of an oppressive male-female relationship, [love] becomes an *emotional* cement to justify the dominant-submissive relationship." From this perspective the aim of the NYRF is to break the pattern of the sexual role system and "develop a new dialectic of sex class."[29] Shulamith Firestone, one of the founders of the NYRF, elaborated the ideology of the group in *The Dialectic of Sex: The Case for Feminist Revolution*.[30]

Firestone, a utopian feminist, adapted Marx to her own radical analysis. *The Dialectic of Sex* is a theory of class conflict which Firestone traces to the differing biological functions of the sexes and the domination of one sex by the other. A caste system of discrimination she argues became institutionalized in the family by the division of labor. Women's oppression in the family can then be traced to her childbearing capacity, economic dependence, the segregation of the sexes within the family, and sexual repression.

To eliminate this class oppression, Firestone says women must revolt and seize both the means of production and the means of artificial reproduction in order to restore the ownership of their own bodies. The goal of Firestone's feminist revolution is abolition of not only male class privileges, but sexual distinction itself and its mythic embodiment in the incest taboo. The consequence of this would be a reversion to a more "natural" state of polymorphous perversity in which sexual relations between all persons regardless of age, sex, or familial relationship would be legitimatized. Firestone is convinced that sexual repression learned in the family is the basis of all "political, ideological, and economic" oppression. With artificial reproduction children would be born independently of the sexes and reared communally in licenced households; the family system would cease to exist. In this utopia of "cybernetic socialism," machines would eliminate the wage system, the foundation for class oppression.

Love and motherhood have different connotations for Firestone than for the more moderate members of the movement. Romantic love, according to her, is the "pivot of woman's oppression" because the woman is trapped in a one-sided political situation in which the male absorbs her "emotional strength" with no return commitment. The "sexual revolution" to Firestone is nothing but a complete capitulation to the male will. In reconsidering the hallowed institution of motherhood, the author insists that since "pregnancy is barbaric" and "childbirth hurts," there should be no conflict in introducing artificial reproduction, especially if the system is administered humanely without sinister motives of racial or intellectual control.

Firestone's utopian scheme is, at best, an optimistic statement that envisions a time when relationships between the sexes cease to be political and equality is substituted for domination. In contrast, Valerie Solanas' *SCUM* (Society for Cutting Up Men) *Manifesto,* which circulated underground in women's liberation circles for several years, is a dark vision of a society without men. Her piercing manifesto expresses neurotic hostility against the male domination of society. Just hours before Robert Kennedy's assassination, Valerie shot artist Andy Warhol because, she said, "he had too much control over my life."[31] Her acute sensibility to women's role as sexual object has led her to resist male domination and submission to the traditional female role through asexuality. "You've got to go through a lot of sex to get to anti-sex"[32] says Solanas, insisting that "sex is the refuge of the mindless"[33]—the refuge of those who indulge in the male "culture." In Solanas' revolution women will refuse to act out their customary role, remaining cool, cerebral, and asexual. Solanas presents the eternal female dilemma: defined in unrealistic sexual terms, the woman becomes obsessed by sex and must either transcend it or cease to live.[34] In SCUM's mirror view of male-female relationships the images are reversed:

> The male is psychically passive. He hates his passivity so he projects it onto women ... Being an incomplete female, the male spends his life attempting to complete himself to become female. He attempts to do this ... by claiming as his own all female characteristics—emotional strength and independence, forcefulness, dynamism, decisiveness, coolness, objectivity, assertiveness, courage ... and projecting onto women all male traits—vanity, frivolity, triviality, weakness, etc. It should be said, though, that the male has one glaring area of superiority over the female—public relations. (He has done a brilliant job of convincing millions of women that men are women and women are men.)[35]

It is intriguing to observe that in the *SCUM Manifesto,* the most radical and extreme statement in the woman's movement, the concepts of male and female follow traditional stereotypes. The "psychic" division between the sexes remains passive-aggressive, passive tendencies are regarded as inferior. To refute the proposition that women are inferior because they are passive, Solanas simply reverses the usual sexual attributes. In a sense her dilemma is an historic feminist one.

Much of the confusion that plagues feminist thought can be attributed to what historian David Potter termed the "dualism" with regard to women's roles. Accepting the traditional role of wife and mother, women allowed for the corollary assumption that they were best suited for that role by their "natural" traits of docility and maternity. Feminists are then trapped in reconciling "a new condition with an old one, to hold in balance the principle of equality, which denies a difference [between the sexes,] and the practice of wifehood which recognizes a difference in the roles of men and women."[36] Both moderates and radicals within the movement have given attention to the problem of the family as a barrier to liberation. Their proposed solutions reveal the main reason why the two strands of feminism are antagonistic. The reformers are reluctant to tamper with the nuclear family. Child care centers and repeal of abortion laws are their methods for relieving the strains upon the women within the family. Radicals prefer to consider basic structural changes in the social order that would eliminate the family, claiming that its power structure serves as the basis of all hierarchies of dominance.

It is true that the family pattern has changed. In our agrarian past the family was a coordinated economic unit which provided an array of functions from education to recreation. The urban nuclear family, however, is chiefly an agent of socialization. It is not inconceivable, therefore, that day care centers and nurseries will cooperate in performing residual family duties just as schools have shared in socialization. In addition, communal living and collective child rearing are providing possible alternatives to the nuclear family pattern. However, indications are that mixed communes do not in themselves liberate either sex from their customary roles.[37] What is evident in the evolution of the family is that changes have been made in response to economic and social conditions rather than to the demands of any group. This may account for the movement's lack of success in instituting either reforms or radical change in the family structure.

In attempting to understand contemporary feminism one might conclude that there is no movement. Confusion on this point is understandable in light of the multiplicity of groups and conflicts among self-proclaimed feminists. More to the point, however, most observers do not grasp the multifarious nature of feminist activism.

Most social movements have used political means to change the
order of things. The main goal of nineteenth century feminism was
the suffrage. Today the women's movement continues to be political.
Disparate groups such as the American Home Economics Association joined with radical feminists, NOW, and the National Women's
Political Caucus in carrying the Equal Rights Amendment through
the House and Senate. State ratification is now in order. With 8
states left to vote on the amendment it is likely that cooperation on
the local level among the various groups will continue. The NWPC,
which has channeled considerable energy in traditional political
avenues, is not an independent "women's party" but a bi-partisan
pressure group designed to support women candidates. Recently,
they have organized state and regional caucuses to encourage
women to stand as delegates to the Democratic and Republican
National Conventions. In addition, the Caucus campaigned for national day care legislation which President Nixon ultimately vetoed.[38]

While certain women's groups today are involved in traditional
political ventures, an important element of the Women's Liberation
movement has always emphasized consciousness-raising as prelimi-
nary to social action. At this level the direction of the movement is
inward, toward self-actualization. Until a majority of women develop a critical attitude toward the society which discriminates
against them, political success will be elusive. Whether the movement's political caucus is successful or not, the problem of reaching
the vast woman population remains. There's always that "doubt,"
the nameless fear that keeps women from approaching a solution.
M. Carey Thomas talked about that private anguish in 1908, "The
passionate desire of women of my generation for higher education
was accompanied throughout its course by the awful doubt, felt by
women themselves as well as by men, as to whether women as a sex
were physically and mentally fit for it."[39] That sense of inferiority
socialized deep in the female psyche prevents all kinds of action,
collective and private. Miriam Allen de Ford in a searching article,
"Women Against Themselves," noted that women obligingly assume
secondary roles, preferring to deal with men "by indirection, eva-
sion, subterfuge, by the 'power behind the throne syndrome,' " but
by so doing De Ford contends women exhibit "the classical symptom of self-hatred."[40] It is these self-destructive tendencies which
divide women among themselves and form the main resistance to
the woman's movement. The political success of the movement is

wholly dependent upon the individual woman's attitude and her refusal to play her traditional role.

NOTES

1. A municipal fire ordinance prevented any burning demonstration by the women. "Bra-burning" never took place at Atlantic City.
2. Erik H. Erikson, *Identity, Youth and Crisis* (New York: W. W. Norton, 1968), 19-22.
3. New York: Alfred A. Knopf, 1953.
4. "Woman as Outsider," in Vivian Gornick and Barbara K. Moran, eds., *Woman in Sexist Society* (New York: Basic Books, 1971).
5. For a discussion of the range of male fears see "Are American Men Afraid of Women?" *Sexual Behavior,* I (May, 1971), 34-36.
6. "Women's Liberation, The Next Great Movement in History Is Theirs," *The Village Voice,* November 27, 1969. Reprints available from KNOW, Inc., Pittsburgh, Pennsylvania.
7. *The Woman as Nigger* (Canoga Park, California: Weiss, Day & Lord, 1970), 78-79.
8. *The Strategy of Sexual Struggle* (New York: Lancer Books, 1971).
9. *The New York Times,* April 7, 1971, p. c-28.
10. New York: W. W. Norton, copyright © 1963 by Betty Friedan.
11. *Ibid.,* 106.
12. Julie Ellis, *Revolt of the Second Sex* (New York: Lancer Books, 1970), 22.
13. Gornick, "Women's Liberation. . . ."
14. Caroline Bird with Sara Welles Briller, *Born Female: The High Cost of Keeping Women Down* (New York: David McKay, 1968), 81-84; Marlene Dixon, "Why Women's Liberation," in Thomas R. Frazier, ed., *Underside of American History* (New York: Harcourt Brace Jovanovich, 1971), 326.
15. "Our Revolution Is Unique," in Mary Lou Thompson, ed., *Voices of the New Feminism* (Boston: Beacon Press, 1970), 37-42.
16. Alice S. Rossi, "The Beginnings of Ideology," in Thompson, *Voices of the New Feminism,* 72.
17. *The Origin of the Family, Private Property and the State* (New York: International Publishers, 1942), 65-66.
18. "Women, the Longest Revolution," *New Left Review* (November/December 1966). Reprint available from the New England Free Press, Boston, Massachusetts. See quote p. 5.
19. Clara Zetkin, "My Recollections of Lenin," in *The Emancipation of Women* (New York: International Publishers, 1934), 97-123. See also

Juliet Mitchell, "Women, the Longest Revolution," *New Left Review* (November/December 1966), *passim*.

20. *Woman Power: The Movement for Women's Liberation* (New York: Tower Publications, 1970), 101.

21. Kathy McAfee and Myrna Wood, "Bread and Roses," in Leslie B. Tanner, ed., *Voices from Women's Liberation* (New York: New American Library, 1971), 425; see also Marge Piercy, "The Grand Coolie Damn" in Robin Morgan, ed., *Sisterhood Is Powerful* (New York: Random House, 1970), 421–438.

22. Shulamith Firestone, *The Dialectic of Sex: The Case for Feminist Revolution* (New York: Bantam Books, 1970), 33.

23. In *Sisterhood . . .*, 482.

24. "Radical Feminism," in Shulamith Firestone and Anne Koedt, eds., *Notes from the Second Year: Women's Liberation* (New York, 1970), 32–37.

25. Ware, *Woman Power . . .*, 25.

26. Unfortunately, the Feminists rigidified their system and imposed penalties on those who missed meetings or opposed the will of the group. One-third of the membership was limited to married women or women living with men. Heterosexual relations were considered exploitative. The authoritarianism and separatism of Atkinson and her supporters destroyed the Feminists. See Ware, *Woman Power . . .*, 27–32.

27. Ware, *Woman Power . . .*, 109–110.

28. Gornick, "Woman's Liberation. . . ."

29. Ware, *Woman Power . . .*, 60, 61.

30. New York: William Morrow, 1970.

31. Ellis, *Revolt . . .*, 138.

32. New York: Olympia Press, 1967, 32.

33. *Ibid.*, 30.

34. Gornick, "Woman as Outsider," 68.

35. Solanas, *SCUM*, 5–6.

36. David Potter, "American Women and the American Character," in John A. Hague, ed., *American Character and Culture* (DeLand, Fla.: Everett Edwards Press, 1964), 82.

37. See Joseph J. Downing, "The Tribal Family and the Society of Awakening," in Herbert A. Otto, ed., *The Family in Search of a Future* (New York: Appleton-Century-Crofts, 1970), 123; Herbert A. Otto, "Communes: The Alternative Life-Style," *Saturday Review* (April 24, 1971), 20.

38. Gloria Steinem, "What Nixon Doesn't Know About Women," *New York*, IV (July 26, 1971), 8–9.

39. "Present Tendencies in Women's College and University Education," quotation reprinted by permission of Quadrangle Books from *Up From the Pedestal*, edited by Aileen S. Kraditor, copyright © 1968 by Aileen S. Kraditor.

40. In *The Humanist*, XXXI (January/February 1971), 8–9.